Horrible Shipwreck!

ANDREW C. A. JAMPOLER

Horrible Shipwreck!

A full, true and particular account of the melancholy loss of the

British convict ship *Amphitrite*,

the 31st August 1833, off Boulogne,

When 108 female convicts, 12 children, and 13 seamen

Met with a watery grave, in sight of thousands,

None being saved out of 136 souls but three!

ANDREW C. A. JAMPOLER

NAVAL INSTITUTE PRESS
Annapolis, Maryland

Naval Institute Press
291 Wood Road
Annapolis, MD 21402

Library of Congress Cataloging-in-Publication Data

Jampoler, Andrew C. A.

  Horrible shipwreck! : a full, true and particular account of the melancholy
loss of the British convict ship Amphitrite, the 31st August 1833, off Boulogne, when 108 female convicts, 12 children, and 13 seamen met with a
watery grave, in sight of thousands, none being saved out of 136 souls but
three! / Andrew C.A. Jampoler.

    p. cm.

  Includes bibliographical references and index.

  ISBN 978-1-59114-411-3 (hardcover : alk. paper) 1. Shipwrecks—
France—Boulogne. 2. Penal transportation—New South Wales—History.
3. Women prisoners—Transportation—England. 4. Australia—History—1788–1851. I. Title.

  G530.A2363J36 2010

  910.9163'38—dc22

                           2010037981

Printed in the United States of America on acid-free paper

14 13 12 11 10   9 8 7 6 5 4 3 2
First printing

Book layout and composition: Alcorn Publication Design

To Suzy, after forty-five years,
with my promise that the best is yet to be.

CONTENTS

ILLUSTRATIONS

MAPS

CHARTS

"THE FEMALE CONVICT SHIP"

Thomas Haynes Bayly, 1833

The tide is in, the breeze is fair,
The vessel under weigh;
The gallant prow glides swiftly on.
And throws aside the spray:
The tranquil ocean, mirror-like
Reflects the deep blue skies;
And, pointing to the destin'd course,
The straighten'd pennon flies.

Oh! None of those heart-cradled prayers
That ever reach the lip,
No benedictions wait upon
That fast-receding ship:
No tearful eyes are strain'd to watch,
Its progress from the land,
And there are none to wave the scarf,
And none to kiss the hand.

Yet women throng that vessel's deck—
The haggard and the fair,
The young in guilt, and the depraved
Are intermingled there!
The girl, who from her mother's arms
Was easily lured away;
The hardened hag, whose trade hath been
To lead the pure astray.

A young and sickly mother kneels
Apart from all the rest;
And with a song of home she lulls
The babe upon her breast.
She falters—for her tears *must* flow—
She cannot end the verse;
And nought is heard among the crowd
But laughter, shout, or curse!

'Tis sunset. Hark! The signal gun;
All from the deck are sent—
The young, the old, the best, the worst,
In one dark dungeon pent!
Their wailings, and their horrid mirth,
Alike are hush'd in sleep:
And now the female convict-ship
In silence plows the deep.

But long the lurid tempest-cloud
Hath brooded o'er the waves;
And suddenly the winds are roused,
And leave their secret caves;
And up aloft the ship is borne,
And down again as fast;
And every mighty billow seems
More dreadful than the last.

Oh! Who that loves the pleasure-barque,
By summer breezes fann'd,
Shall dare to paint the ocean-storm,
Terrifically grand?
When helplessly the vessel drifts,
Each torn sail closely furl'd;
When not a man of all the crew
Knows wither she'll be hurled!

And who shall tell the agony
Of those confined beneath,
Who in the darkness dread to die—
How unprepared for death!
Who, loathing, to each other cling,
When every hope has ceased,
And beat against their prison door,
And shriek to be released.

Three times the ship hath struck. Again!
She never more will float.
Oh! Wait not for the rising tide;
Be steady—man the boat.
And see, assembled on the shore,

The merciful, the brave; —
Quick, set the female convicts free,
There still is time to save.

It is in vain! What demon blinds
The captain and the crew?
The rapid rising of the tide
With mad delight they view.
They hope the coming waves will waft
The convict ship away!
The foaming monster hurries on,
Impatient for his prey.

And he is come! The rushing flood
In thunder sweeps the deck;
The groaning timbers fly apart.
The vessel is a wreck!
One moment from the female crowd
There comes a fearful cry;
The next, they're hurl'd into the deep,
To struggle, and to die!

Their corpses strew a foreign shore,
Left by the ebbing tide;
And sixty in a ghastly row
Lie number'd side by side!
The lifeless mother's bleeding form
Comes floating from the wreck;
And lifeless is the babe she bound
So fondly round her neck!

Tis morn; —the anxious eye can trace
No vessel on the deep;
But gathered timber on the shore
Lies in a gloomy heap:
In winter time those brands will blaze
Our tranquil homes to warm,
Though torn from that poor convict ship
That perished in the storm!

Thomas Haynes Bayly was a popular and fecund poet, balladeer, and play-wright who worked in Dublin and London in the 1820s and 1830s. His writing style, of which "The Female Convict Ship" is a fair example, fit the liter-ary taste of the times, although it sounds maudlin today. Bayly's pieces also appeared in periodicals. This poem about the wreck of *Amphitrite* comes from a late 1833 issue of the *New Monthly Magazine and Literary Journal.*

Bayly was born into the family of a successful solicitor. He bypassed careers in the law and the church to write. A contemporary biographer described the young Bayly as "a gentleman, of handsome person and distinguished man-ners." Poor investment of his wife's dowry in the turbulent market of the 1820s forced the Baylys to live on his income as an author after 1830. The resulting austerity and his declining health ("an attack of brain-fever . . . dropsy suc-ceeded [by] confirmed jaundice") shaped the last decade of his short life. He died in 1839 at age forty-two.

Bayly's widow, Helena, had "The Female Convict Ship" reprinted in *Songs, Ballads, and Other Poems, by the Late Thomas Haynes Bayly,* 2 vols. (London: R. Bentley, 1844).

Horrible Shipwreck!

ANDREW C. A. JAMPOLER

GIVE EAR, YOU FEELING CHRISTIANS, THAT DWELL UPON THE SHORE;

A tale so sad and yet so true; You seldom heard before:

The *Amphitrite*, a Convict Ship, from Woolwich sailed away,

On the twenty-fifth of August, she was bound for Botany Bay.

CHAPTER I

Fire at Sea

I

In late 2007 the National Gallery of Art, in Washington, D.C., proudly hosted a large exhibition of the oil and watercolor paintings of J. M. W. Turner (1775–1851), England's finest landscape painter and arguably its premier artist. From Washington the exhibition was scheduled to travel to Dallas, New York, Moscow, and Beijing before returning home to the Tate Britain and to other lenders in mid-2009.

Among the paintings on exhibition in these five cities were several dozen of Turner's seascapes, pictures with maritime or, more specifically, naval themes. Their subject matter was an obvious choice for a landscape artist looking to expand his market and increase sales, whose island home was the heart of a globe-girdling empire built on the command of the seas. The first of Turner's major "sea pieces" in oil paint, *Dutch Boats in a Gale*, commissioned for £250 by the last Duke of Bridgewater, was finished in 1801 when the artist was twenty-six. The central vessels in the large painting, a trio of pudgy, single-masted Dutch galliots, vie for attention against brilliantly realized white-capped rollers beneath a dramatic sky.

Oddly, what was perhaps Turner's best representation of British naval power in the age of fighting sail came in the peaceful image of *A First-Rate*

Fig. 1

A First-Rate Taking in Stores. J. M. W. Turner, pencil and watercolor, 1818. More than half of the crew of a Royal Navy line-of-battle ship served its great guns, the largest of which were each more than ten feet long and weighed about three tons. A first rate at sea, manned by a thousand sailors and marines (many, in Brian Lavery's phrase, "disaffected, unwilling, illiterate, or stupid"), was the most complex human organization of the early nineteenth century. Reportedly, Turner completed this painting in a single morning in November, in response to a request from his patron, Sir Walter Fawkes.

Taking in Stores. In this small 1818 watercolor (done soon after the triumphant end of the Napoleonic Wars), three 110-gun line-of-battle ships lie quietly at anchor in light, choppy seas off the Dutch coast. The three are being resupplied from "hoys," small, single-masted and gaff-rigged provisioning boats. One of the trio, a huge man of war, rises in the right foreground like a wooden fortress, gunports open and cast-iron guns run out on all three decks, dwarfing everything else in the scene and suggesting the potential for death and destruction explicit in Turner's two well-known oil paintings of the Battle of Trafalgar.

The most numerous of the broadside guns (all seemingly enlarged slightly by Turner to maximize the effect) jutting from the open ports of this nameless battleship were each at high elevation, capable of hurling 32-pound, 6-inch, solid-iron shot more than a nautical mile. Inside of several hundred yards, the usual engagement range, a round propelled by a full charge (twelve pounds of black powder) and moving at 1,600 feet per second on a flat trajectory could have punched through three to five *feet* of seasoned hardwood and still had sufficient energy to do terrible damage. A first rate's broadside, almost fifty 32-, 24-, and 12-pound guns firing nearly at once, threw more than half a ton of iron at its target, the firepower equivalent of all the field artillery attached to an army of the day in a single ship. Well-trained Royal Navy gun crews could have launched one such devastating barrage every four to five minutes early in a battle, until slowed by exhaustion or return fire.

A *First-Rate* shows Turner's draftsmanship and mastery of perspective at their best. The big three-decker is drawn starboard side-to in wonderful detail, angled just so across the painting to expose both the curve of her bow and the bulge of her stern galleries, and the elegant, decorative carvings that adorned both places. (This is the last era during which fighting ships called "beautiful" really were beautiful.) Just enough of the ship's colors shows to make clear the nationality of these leviathans at rest.

That precise draftsmanship is nowhere evident in one of Turner's later and larger nautical paintings also exhibited in Washington in 2007, this one an oil started in the mid-1830s. Perhaps it would have been had Turner finished it. As we have the incomplete painting today (reproduced on the cover), a ship in extremis is suggested by a few bare poles and a cluster of bodies—some living, some seemingly already dead, all sketched rather than drawn—awash on the deck or afloat nearby. In Martin Butlin and Evelyn Joll's definitive *catalogue raisonné* of Turner's work, this painting, number 461, was described as possibly reflecting Turner's renewed interest in painting fire after the blaze at the Houses of Parliament.[1] That notion stood unchallenged for a decade after their revised edition was published, but it's wrong. Turner's subject was a shipwreck, not a fire.

The work's name for many years, *Fire at Sea*, was not Turner's but that of an unknown curator. It must have been suggested by what could have been seen as smoke billowing from the ship, and by the palette of hot yellow colors—a Turner trademark later in life—that dominates the painting. A *First-Rate* is a portrait of potential energy, serene despite its busy sea and sky. In contrast, *Fire at Sea* is kinetic: a great boiling mass of whitecaps, spindrift, and shredded clouds punctuated by indistinct, suffering forms atop the suggestion of a ship. In October 2003 a *New York Times* art critic writing about the painting on exhibition then called it "frothy," an apt description.

Notwithstanding the suggestion in the Washington exhibition catalogue, Turner probably did not get the idea to do a shipwreck painting by recollecting Théodore Géricault's stunning and huge oil, *The Raft of the Medusa*. Completed just a few years after the French frigate *Medusa* blundered in July 1816 onto the Arguin Bank, a shoal off Senegal, West Africa, Géricault's canvas recalled the agony of 147 men and women from among the *Medusa*'s complement of 400 settlers and sailors, who after their ship ran aground were quickly abandoned on an improvised raft while the others rowed off to the distant shore in *Medusa*'s boats. All had been on the way to reestablish a French colony in West Africa.

Only fifteen on the raft survived the nearly two weeks afloat until rescue, the intervening desperate days while their raft drifted aimlessly marked by riot, suicide, murder, and cannibalism. As Jonathan Miles explained in his *Wreck of the Medusa* (2007), Géricault's painting was simultaneously a genre painting, an antiroyalist propaganda piece, and an exercise in catharsis for the deeply troubled and fatally ill artist. (Géricault died of tuberculosis in January 1824, at age thirty-two.) Withal, *The Raft of the Medusa* was a mixed success at the Paris salon of 1819, and only marginally better received when exhibited in London in 1820. It hangs in the Louvre's Room 77 today.

Others have made this connection, too, noting that Turner's and Géricault's paintings share a pyramidal structure, but they share nothing else. Large, intertwined, and carefully molded figures dominate *The Raft of the Medusa*, and their obvious suffering is entirely manmade. By contrast, the people in all of Turner's shipwreck paintings are tiny, trapped in a cauldron of wind and water that emphasizes nature's violence and the helplessness of men—and women—in tempests at sea.

Turner did not need to be prompted by Géricault to take up the subject of disaster at sea; he'd done it at least twice before, once in 1805 with *The Shipwreck* and again five years later with *The Wreck of a Transport Ship*. For a time, *Wreck of a Transport* was associated with the loss of HMS *Minotaur*, a 74-gun third rate that in December 1810 ran aground on the Haak Sands off the mouth of the Texel in Holland, capsized, and broke up, drowning hundreds of her crew. Turner had begun the painting several years before that calamity so the connection was spurious, but *Minotaur*'s agony would have resembled his painting: a dismasted ship aground on her port side, some of the crew afloat in a trough between great waves, several apparently in the uniform of the Royal Marines.[2]

Instead, the inspiration for this new sea piece was probably a stream of outraged newspaper and monthly journal articles that appeared in London and elsewhere in Great Britain through late summer and autumn of 1833 reporting on the wreck of the female convict transport *Amphitrite* near Boulogne-sur-Mer, a French port on the English Channel Turner knew well. These stories contained the germ of an image he began to paint the following year, one that he didn't finish and that was never exhibited while he was alive.

Standing before an empty, primed white canvas in his studio on London's Harley Street, Turner, then in his late fifties, might have been drawn to paint

Amphitrite's fate by its irresistible combination of powerful narrative and stunning imagery, the common elements of his best early work. By 1835, however, Turner was already painting at the edge of impressionism (a style that clearly discomforted the author of his generally admiring obituary in *The Times* of London, published December 19, 1851). The wreck of *Amphitrite* and the deaths of almost all on board her would have been difficult to depict that way. Perhaps, midway through the painting, Turner simply didn't like what he had done; perhaps he decided there was no way to get from this brightly colored image to the dark essence of despair and suffering in the event he was describing. Turner's sketchbook during this period (one of three hundred such books of his, this one also called *Fire at Sea*) contains several relevant color sketches and a few on other subjects, but is otherwise almost entirely blank.

Why Turner never finished *Fire at Sea* is unknowable. The mid-1830s were a busy period of work and foreign travel for this astonishingly productive artist. (His life's work encompassed hundreds of oils and thousands of watercolors and drawings, an inventory that explains, in part, why he died a wealthy man.) It might be that the catastrophic fire in the Houses of Parliament on October 16, 1834, was a more compelling subject, or the eleven new, large oils he painted for exhibition in 1834–35 at the Royal Academy and the British Institute consumed his attention. It is also possible that Turner intended to finish this painting swiftly while it hung in an exhibition hall during the few "varnishing days" prior to public display, a showy demonstration of his mastery performed several other times. He never explained the lapse. For whatever reason, the painting once begun never managed to return to the front of the queue in his imagination.

If Turner didn't like *Fire at Sea*, others do. In September 2007 art historian Simon Schama called it "a painting of timeless tragic power: the 'Guernica' of nineteenth-century British art. The bodies are a curling ribbon of writhing, pathetic, naked women, arms flung out to the babes who slip from them into the sea. . . . Turner's bodies are already bobbing flotsam. They are helpless, ugly, manic, and they tear us apart. . . . The pity of the thing is relentless, because of the phenomenal coherence of Turner's draftsmanship, the violence of the storm, and the desperation of the victims—who should be flying away, centrifugally, but instead are sucked into the whorl of merciless elements."[3] "The 'Guernica' of nineteenth-century British art"—high praise to compare an unfinished Turner to Picasso's iconic, enormous antiwar mural, if a little bit strained.

Although Turner put *Fire at Sea* aside undone, the painting reemerged some twenty-five years later in finished form by John Cousen (1804–1880), an English landscape engraver who often worked with the artist.

Fig. 2

Fire at Sea. John Cousen, steel engraving, 1859–61. It is unlikely that Turner would
have finished his painting exactly as Cousen did this engraving, with spectral figures
clustered atop the wreck's flooded deck, dark eye sockets bored into skeletal heads that
resemble skulls as much as the faces of living people. Turner, a printmaker himself,
usually participated extensively (almost obsessively) in the translation of his paintings from one medium to the other. This engraving was done years after the artist's
death and so it is Cousen's work alone. Cousen (1804–1880) and his younger brother,
Charles, were popular engravers in Victorian England. The senior Cousen's plates illustrated many books. Several of his engravings were exhibited at the Royal Academy in
the early 1860s.

Tate Collection TO6369, Rawlinson number 750A., © 2009 Tate, London.

Evidently ignorant of the historical context of Turner's painting, the
National Gallery's 1889 catalogue described the scene in Cousen's engraving
in generic terms, hinting at a connection to Géricault and otherwise imagina-
tively misconstruing the subject: "To the right is seen the flaming fire, reaching to the water; on the left the boisterous sea; in the centre is a vast raft
crowded with human beings, men, women, and children, while others are
already washed by the waves from their precarious refuge; all are threatened
by both the fire and the storm, alternately drenched by the one and scorched
by the other; fire rains upon them from above, and the waves are yawning to
engulf them from below."[4]

Fire at Sea has, since March 1993, been agreed to be a misnomer. That's
when Cecilia Powell, art historian and *Turner Society News* editor, first noted

that almost all the bodies visible seemed to be women and small children and decided that this was no generic catastrophe. Instead, she concluded, Turner had illustrated a specific event: the loss of *Amphitrite*, destroyed by a murderous storm the last day of August 1833, just one week out of port, and the subject of great contemporary interest in England. "But in *Fire at Sea*," Powell wrote in issue number 63 of the *Turner Society News*,

> every single drowning figure is either a woman or an infant. Everywhere you look, softly rounded limbs reach out for others equally soft and rounded but much tinier. Only two males are present in this terrible scene, clinging to the mast to the right of centre. What event can Turner possibly be evoking or depicting? A variety of scholars— all male—have related this painting to Turner's rekindled interest in fire-subjects following the burning of the Houses of Parliament in 1834 and have assigned it to a date c. 1835. But this does nothing to solve the central mystery of the painting.
>
> Only one type of vessel would have confined its passenger list to women in Turner's day: and that was a female convict ship. And it just so happens that a female convict ship was destroyed in a violent storm in the English Channel in the autumn of 1833 in circumstances so dramatic that it filled newspaper columns day after day. ... Turner's painting is about the women and children who were deliberately sacrificed to the waves when they could have been rescued.[5]

Even a casual glance at Cousen's version of Turner's painting confirms that Powell's identification is correct. In the engraving the mass of women and children huddled on the flooded deck (not a raft at all), the sea furiously swirling about them, removes any possible ambiguity about what the artist was painting. The mystery is not what Turner's subject was, but rather how in the decades between 1860 and 1990 that subject could have been forgotten.

Both the Turner painting and Cousen's engraved translation of it are misleading as illustrations of history. In them *Amphitrite* appears to be on blue water, in the open ocean. There is no hint that this wreck, with its soon-to-be-dead tenants clustered on the deck, is ashore in the surf. What's clear in Turner's *Wreck of a Transport Ship*, that the ship is aground, is not evident here, and by setting the scene as he did Turner glossed over the central element of the tragedy. Had the artist's point of view been rotated—turned 180 degrees from looking west to looking east—the port city and the bluffs above the shore would have appeared in the background, showing that refuge and succor were only a few hundred yards away, that the loss of young lives ought not to have happened at all. Géricault deliberately politicized his wreck painting, but Turner,

FIGS. 3 AND 4

Details from Cousen's *A Fire at Sea*. The survivors of the shipwreck reported that there were twelve children aboard *Amphitrite* when she sailed, that the eldest was fourteen, and that the others were between five weeks and nine years old. At least eight small children can be discerned in Cousen's engraving among the figures about to drown.
© 2009 TATE, LONDON.

who knew well from newspaper reporting the many controversies complicating the *Amphitrite* story, equally deliberately depoliticized his.

2

Amphitrite was a small vessel: 92 feet long and a little over two hundred tons burden; her usual crew of fourteen would have been just large enough to work a single 32-pound great gun on a warship. She was not only the first transport with female convicts and children embarked to be lost at sea but also the first lost in more than forty years, since the very beginning of transportation in 1787–88 to the British convict colony at Botany Bay, soon relocated to Port Jackson.[6] Even so, had *Amphitrite* sunk somewhere on her track across the open ocean or near her distant destination, like the female transport *Neva* did in May 1835 during her second convict voyage, drowning 159 women and their 55 children, the wreck would likely not have been the great sensation that it swiftly became.

But *Amphitrite*'s agony played out in public. The ship was aground through a long, stormy afternoon on a sandbar off Boulogne-sur-Mer before she broke up completely in the evening, finally killing the last of her victims. Two brave

French rescue attempts failed. During the dreadful hours the waves attacked and then disassembled her hull, Amphitrite was in sight of the shore and seen by countless local citizens and many English expatriates living in and near the small port city, every one of whom became a reporter of the event. Witnesses and victims were so near to one another that people moving about the ship's deck were clearly visible to watchers ashore, watchers who soon would be collecting bodies thrown up by the sea.

Inflamed by newspaper accounts and broadsheet doggerel, British reaction across the Channel to Amphitrite's destruction and the deaths at Boulogne quickly flared into an outburst of indignant outrage mingled with ghoulish fascination, reflashing each time additional details were exposed in the press or in government reports. That uproar must have suggested the subject to Turner.

In the nineteenth century well-documented or even mysterious losses of ships at sea were commonplace. Amphitrite was one of hundreds of merchant ships of British registry that sank in 1833, an average of six every week of the year. Practically one a day, a letter writer reminded the editor of Edinburgh's Scotsman two years later, apparently neglecting to count more than one hundred miscellaneous other vessels that also went down the same weekend that Amphitrite was lost. (One informal count had the annual number as high as eight hundred.) In every other year literally hundreds of British ships sank and hundreds on board them drowned. Parliamentary committees met regularly to identify, study, and then denounce the reasons for this dreadful attrition.

Storms, fire, ice and other floating hazards to navigation; mischarted waters; and seamanship errors were all accepted and understood risks of ocean commerce. There was nothing new in this: More than two centuries before Amphitrite and Turner, Shakespeare had written about shipwreck in The Tempest and The Merchant of Venice, and his were not by many centuries the first familiar accounts of peril at sea. For that you'd have to go back at least to Homer's Odyssey. Reflecting this long history, in 2001 UNESCO's Convention on the Protection of the Underwater Heritage estimated that the earth's sea floor is spangled with the remains of fully three million sunken ships.

What made Amphitrite's wreck unique and sensational was the public's suspicion that callous poop deck leadership and inept seamanship, coupled to contracting corruption and a civil servant's disinterest, had produced the tragedy—a suspicion illustrated by mental images of dozens of dead, "perfectly formed women," some with their clothes stripped from their bodies (or, less probably, removed before a last, fatal dive into the sea), strewn along a foreign beach. Questions about the seaworthiness of the ship and the rumored inhumanity of French government officials—always easy targets for English contempt—at the peak of the crisis sharpened the general outrage at this horrible shipwreck.

THE CONVICTS ALL WERE FEMALES, ONE HUNDRED AND EIGHT,

And crew sixteen in number, How dreadful to relate;

With 12 sweet innocent babies, From Woolwich sailed away,

One hundred and thirty-six, were bound for Botany Bay.

CHAPTER 2

Crime and Punishment

3

In mid-October 1781 Lieutenant General Charles, Earl Cornwallis, who had led an army of British and German regulars through the Carolinas during the year just past with mixed results, suddenly ran out of momentum and tactical options at the same time. Cornwallis—then forty-three, but always wealthy, urbane, and well connected—would later have an incandescent military career, rising in 1786 to become the able first governor general of India (only to die in 1805 near Varanasi on the Ganges River during his second posting to the subcontinent), but this autumn was a dark detour on his path to that distinction. Cornwallis and his roughly eight thousand men now found themselves confined under artillery bombardment in Yorktown, Virginia, behind defensive works, surrounded on their three landward sides by French and American infantry and artillery and hemmed in on the fourth by a French fleet, whose many sails had filled the York River estuary and the lower Chesapeake Bay uncontested since early September.

On October 18 Cornwallis, his army outnumbered nearly three to one and exhausted from three weeks under siege, surrendered to General George Washington and his French ally, Lieutenant General Jean-Baptiste Donatien de Vimeur, comte de Rochambeau. Admiral François-Joseph-Paul, comte de Grasse (who, on September 5, had commanded the French fleet at the Battle of the Chesapeake Capes that made this victory on land possible) didn't go ashore for the ceremony. When Cornwallis gave up, a Royal Navy relief squadron was still a day away from leaving the port of New York to deliver reinforcements and supplies to his beleaguered outpost. (The humiliating defeat prompted an extended exchange of dueling pamphlets by the two British generals responsible, in which each tried to defend his reputation. Sir Henry Clinton, the commander in chief in North America and first into print, charged his deputy with insubordination and other failings. In response, Cornwallis, who ultimately won the debate, accused his superior of a lack of zeal. The same kind of name calling also went on between Admirals Sir Thomas Graves and Sir Samuel Hood of the Royal Navy, each trying to escape blame for the precursor naval defeat at the hands of de Grasse.)

Once General Cornwallis concluded it was all over, negotiating the fourteen Articles of Capitulation took the sides only one day. As agreed, Article III provided in part that the garrison of York, surrendering one of the redoubts on the British left flank, was to march out from its position at two in the afternoon with "shouldered arms, colors cased, and drums beating a British or German march" to give up its weapons. An hour later the defeated cavalry was to join the parade of the losers by emerging from behind the battered fortifications "with swords drawn and trumpets sounding." From this thin stuff, "drums beating . . . and trumpets sounding," and from suspect descriptions of the carefully scripted ceremony written long after the fact, a story emerged after 1828 that British regimental field music had played a popular ballad, "The World Turned Upside Down," while their comrades in arms formally gave up the fight and stacked their firearms. (Some of the same Brown Bess flintlock muskets later turned up as trade goods in distant places of the world.)

It's a great story because the title of the tune, and at least one version of its lyrics, are perfect descriptions of the general sense of upset and vertigo that must have marked the end to the fighting:

> If Buttercups buzz'd after the bee,
> If boats were on land, churches on sea,
> If ponies rode men and grass ate the cows,
> And cats should be chased into holes by the mouse,
> If the mamas sold their babies to the Gypsies for half a crown,
> If summer were spring and the other way around,
> Then all the world would be upside down.[1]

The stunning reversal—European regulars bested decisively by rude backwoodsmen—astonished everyone in Europe and North America, observers who had long since absorbed General John Burgoyne's defeat by the rebels at Saratoga in October 1777 and the capture of his 5,900-man army. Most then had continued confidently to believe (or to fear) that the mighty British Empire would in the end trounce the rustics fighting for independence and force them back into the imperial fold battered and humbled. (Everyone but the French, who after Saratoga saw the glimmer of an opportunity to remedy the unsatisfactory outcome of the French and Indian War.) An American victory did indeed "turn the world upside down."

A great story, but almost certainly apocryphal. The fifes and drums of the British most likely played traditional marches—short tunes with much less ironic titles, rhythms meant to set a marching cadence rather than to provide a soundtrack to wry commentary on the odds of successful colonial revolution in the eighteenth century.

Washington was elated by the victory, or as near to elation as the famously stone-faced general would permit himself to be. "I have the honor to inform Congress," he began his report to the Continental Congress on the day of the triumph, "that a Reduction of the British Army under the Command of Lord Cornwallis, is most happily effected. The unremitting Ardor which actuated every Officer and Soldier in the combined Army on this Occasion has principally led to this important Event, at an earlier period than my most sanguine Hopes had induced me to expect." Ten paragraphs of welcome details followed. Congress received the news from a courier on October 24, whose best efforts took him five days of around-the-clock travel to move between the Virginia Capes and Philadelphia, where the legislature was sitting.

Near-contemporary paintings of the surrender at Yorktown, notably oils by Colonel John Trumbell (he served with Washington; the later of his two is exhibited in the Capitol Rotunda in Washington, D.C.) and a gouache by Louis-Nicholas van Blarenberghe that hangs in Versailles (one of four paintings he did of the scene), like the legend of the music, reach for the drama of the event but are not scrupulous depictions of history. Each painting is not much more, in fact, than a cluster of staged, flattering portraits of the assembled principals, fleshed out with remembered or imagined details to fix a time and place.[2]

After Yorktown skirmishing continued fitfully in the South for nearly another year, but Cornwallis' surrender on the banks of the York River marked the real end of the war. Some think his defeat signaled much more than that. Piers Brendon, author of a wise and witty history, *The Decline and Fall of the British Empire, 1781–1997* (2007), starts his description of the humbug at the heart of empire at the moment of the surrender at Yorktown, describing the progress of sullen British soldiers on the way to surrender their weapons through ranks of bedraggled and shoeless, but triumphant, rebels and their handsomely attired French allies. The dispirited parade of losers moved forward, Brendon writes, preserving imagery too good to give up, with their field music earnestly playing "The World Turned Upside Down."

It was British logisticians in London rather than British strategists in the field whose efforts permitted the American war to go on as long as it did, argued the late Professor David Syrett in his 1966 Ph.D. thesis, and in the book that emerged from it a few years later. A global shortage of transport vessels probably would have forced an end to expeditionary warfare in the revolting colonies sometime in 1782 or not long after, even if Cornwallis had not been humiliated at Yorktown in 1781. The same shortage of transatlantic shipping that paced the return deployment, Syrett suggested, would have soon strangled the army overseas had fighting continued.

For whichever reason, lack of shipping or lack of enthusiasm, the British took until November 1783 to withdraw fully from their former American colonies. While their troops proceeded slowly home, British diplomats in Europe negotiated, equally slowly, an end to hostilities with France, Spain, the Netherlands, and the new United States.[3]

The defeat in North America caused the collapse of Lord North's government, in power in London at the time and throughout the past eleven years. It also very nearly triggered the abdication of King George III—then in the twenty-first year of his reign and for a while longer still quite sane—one year later.[4] Postwar distress at the top of British society, however, was no greater than it was at the bottom. Down there, among the unemployed and impoverished, the suffering was economic, not political.

Once back in Great Britain and demobilized, the tens of thousands of former soldiers looking for sustenance further strained a domestic economy already under great stress, one that offered no employment to absorb them and no safety net beside the crabbed mercies of the Poor Law. The arrival of these defeated veterans of the American Revolution—young, hardened, dispossessed men, a classic criminal demographic even now—swiftly heightened the trials of the urban poor in England and Wales, Scotland, and Ireland, while it multiplied their numbers. Crime, most commonly minor thievery, rose in a tide that those with titles believed threatened to flood the home islands' institutions of social control. (Such bursts of criminality were familiar features of previous and future postwar periods. One followed the end of the War of Spanish Succession in 1713; another came after the Napoleonic Wars a century later.)[5]

Real and imagined crime was, in any case, the great boogeyman of Georgian England. During these many decades under the House of Hanover, while Great Britain industrialized and parlayed new manufacturing technology and a chesty blue water navy into a global empire, Britain's elite feared assaults against their persons and property by a huge, permanent, and professional

criminal underclass at least as much—or even more—than they did the evil
designs and global ambitions of the French.[6] "The chief towns of Great Britain
were haunted by innumerable thieves"—this description of that fear by the
Tasmanian historian (and Congregationalist minister) John West in 1852—
"who were organized for purposes of robbery. In London armed men assailed
passengers by night and by day. . . . A vast multitude of persons had degen-
erated into a robber caste. They lodged under the arches of bridges, or nestled into nooks and corners, wherever they could burrow. The districts of the
city occupied by the better class of society, seemed but a small portion of the
metropolis—like islands in a sea of vice and destitution. There were numerous
places of savage amusement."[7]

<h1 style="text-align:center">4</h1>

Nothing in the ten articles of the Definitive Treaty of Peace Between the
United States of America and His Britannic Majesty, the treaty signed in Paris
September 3, 1783, that ended the American Revolution, addressed the subject, but one result of the British defeat was that Great Britain no longer had
any American colonies to serve as a place of exile for convicted felons shipped
abroad as a condition of pardon.[8]

"Transportation," a euphemism for the banishment of convicted criminals from Great Britain under Privy Council or trial court order, already had
a long history by the late eighteenth century, dating back to Elizabeth I in
1597 and "An Acte for the Punyshment of Rogues, Vagabonds, and Sturdy
Beggars."[9] "Dangerous rogues, and such as will not be reformed of their roguish
course of life," that act provided, "may lawfully by the justices in their quarter sessions be banished out of the realm and all the dominions thereof, and
to such parts beyond the seas as shall for that purpose be assigned by the privy
council." White prisoners transported to the new colonies for indentured service in Virginia predated the arrival there, on a Dutch ship, of the first twenty
black slaves from Africa in 1619.[10] When the American Revolution began,
banishing convicts to "beyond the seas" had been practiced on an increasingly
large scale ever since the reign of Charles II (1660–85).

Banishment was simultaneously a near-perfect government policy and
an inspired punishment for "bad subjects" of many stripes. On one hand it
was cheap. It cost practically nothing and, at least initially, required little
infrastructure beyond a fleet of privately owned transport vessels and a system of government contracting for ship charters that was perfected during the
American Revolution. On the other, transportation seemingly served simultaneously as punishment for crimes committed and as deterrent for those contemplated but not yet perpetrated.

Moreover, in the face of a criminal code that mandated execution for literally hundreds of offenses, transportation provided an out: a way for the sovereign to appear merciful while preserving order. In one scholar's words, "[Transportation] nestled tidily in between a cruel legal code that prescribed the death sentence for dozens of infractions (some quite trivial) which, if observed, to the horror of good citizens would have filled the big trees of England with hanged men, and a native unwillingness to build sufficient prisons and to fill them with felons at hard labor. Consequently, transportation was the preferred sentence for all but the most dreadful crimes." *The Hanging Tree*, a 1994 study of execution in England from 1770 to 1830, found that only 20 percent of those convicted and condemned to death during those sixty years actually went to the gallows.[11] Many among the remaining 80 percent were banished.

A decision to construct prisons for the purpose of long-term confinement was announced in "An Act to explain and amend the Laws relating to the Transportation, Imprisonment, and other Punishment, of Certain Offenders" (19 Geo. III cap. 74, enacted in the nineteenth year of King George III's reign) but never implemented. Such jails ("gaols") as there were in Great Britain housed debtors or detained criminal suspects pre-trial and held convicts post-trial until either transportation or the execution of their sentences—often, literally, execution, but occasionally corporal punishment such as whipping or branding. Accordingly, confinement itself wasn't the punishment and would not be until later in the next century, when Great Britain finally began the construction of a national prison infrastructure in parallel with the slow rise of professional police officers and corrections officials.

Not surprisingly, while banishment might have been welcome as an alternative to execution for a capital offense (not always a welcome exchange, curiously enough; some fatalists preferred the gallows), those who had committed larceny and lesser crimes often were desperate to avoid being shipped to a distant, isolated place where they could expect years of exploitation and abuse followed by a life apart from everything familiar.[12] For their part, successive kings and ministries supported transportation because it was a permanent solution, every banishment reducing forever the feared burgeoning criminal class of the islands by one and by that one's possible progeny.

Under the Stuart monarchs through the seventeenth century and until Parliament passed the Transportation Act of 1718 (5 Geo. IV cap. 74), British convicts sailed to the American colonies as a condition of pardon rather than as a punishment, or at least that was the legal fiction.[13] Accordingly, they arrived at their destination (usually Virginia or Maryland) not under criminal sentence but as free citizens encumbered only by a financial obligation to the quasi-benefactor who had funded their passage to the New World and who meant to recover his investment and realize a profit by the long-term lease of their services at auction. Once ashore and under contract to an employer in the colonies, new arrivals began a period of indentured servitude that, in theory, at least, ended after seven years with receipt of their "freedom dues" (a quantity of food and money and, for men, a firearm) meant to ease the former servant into society in the New World.[14] While under contract, such servants were a bargain. Their labor typically sold at auction for half to a third the price of a healthy male slave, granting that the first transaction was a lease while the second was an outright purchase.

At the outset, at least until slaves arrived in the colonies in significant numbers, many planters welcomed British convicts, thinking that their "labour was more beneficial than their vices pernicious." Transplanted felons were a valuable labor resource for the colonies, especially in the plantations of Maryland and Virginia, where tobacco and grain cultivation absorbed large numbers of unskilled workers, but their presence was not an unalloyed benefit. Provoked by a change in the legal status of the new arrivals after 1718 and as the century wore on, the shipment of British felons to the mid-Atlantic colonies became increasingly offensive to their law-abiding citizens. Transports were widely feared for their presumed ineradicable criminal tendencies; they were feared also as carriers of "gaol fever" (typhus) and the other lethal diseases they brought with them, and for their potential leadership of slaves and home-grown malefactors in riot and revolt. As Jamaica's provincial council had it in 1731, "[If] it be prudence in England to banish Rogues; it must certainly be prudence here to endeavour to keep them out." London, meaning the king, cabinet, and Parliament, rejected or ignored repeated colonial efforts through exclusionary laws or import duties to do just that.

The "abominable cargoes" of convicts infuriated Benjamin Franklin, whose home colony of Pennsylvania was third in popularity as a convict destination behind Virginia and Maryland. In an April 1751 issue of the *Pennsylvania Gazette* he pungently likened the stream of unwelcome arrivals to imports of excrement. "In what can *Britain* show a more Sovereign Contempt for us," Franklin asked rhetorically, "than by emptying their *Jails* into our Settlements; unless they would likewise empty their *Jakes* [chamber pots] on our Tables?" (The same imagery had occurred to others, minus the alliteration. Jeremy Bentham, the English jurist and philosopher famous for his liberal social stance, once described London's criminals as "a sort of *excrementitious mass*.")

A month later, and still hyperventilating, Franklin wrote another letter "to the Printers of the *Pennsylvania Gazette*" about convict transportation, scattering capital letters and italics about like an apprentice typesetter. His second piece, signed "Americus," proposed, perhaps half-seriously, delivering

American rattlesnakes to the gardens of the British ruling class in a one-for-one trade for convicts crossing the Atlantic in the other direction.[15] "Inconveniences have been objected to that good and wise Act of Parliament by virtue of which all the *Newgates* and *Dungeons* of *Britain* are emptied into the Colonies," Franklin fulminated, and then he continued:

> I understand that the Government at home [London] will not suffer our mistaken Assemblies to make any Law for preventing or discouraging the Importation of Convicts from Great Britain, for this kind Reason, *"That such Laws are against the Publick Utility, as they tend to prevent the* IMPROVEMENT *and* WELL PEOPLING *of the Colonies.'*
>
> Such a tender *parental* Concern in our *Mother Country* for the *Welfare* of her Children, calls aloud for the highest *Returns* of Gratitude and Duty. . . .
>
> Some Thousands [of rattlesnakes] might be collected annually, and *transported* to Britain. There I would propose to have them carefully distributed in *St James's Park*, in the Spring-Gardens and other Places of Pleasure about London; in the Gardens of all the Nobility and Gentry throughout the Nation; but particularly in the Gardens of the *Prime Ministers*, the *Lords of Trade* and *Members of Parliament*; for to them we are *most particularly* obliged. . . .
>
> *Rattle-Snakes* seem the most *suitable Returns* for the *Human Serpents* sent by our Mother Country. In this, however, as in every other branch of trade, she will have the Advantage of us. . . . For the Rattle-Snake gives Warning before he attempts his mischief, which the Convict does not.

From research done in the 1980s, Virginia Polytechnic Institute historian Roger Ekirch, the chief scholar of British convict transportation to the American colonies, estimated that some 50,000 to 60,000 English, Irish, and Scottish prisoners were shipped from London and Bristol to American ports for sale into servitude between 1718 and 1775.[16] Perhaps four or five thousand had come to the colonies before passage of the Transportation Act. That total represents fully one-quarter of all immigration to the English colonies in that span of time (and approaches 40 percent of the number that were to be transported to prisons in Australia during the next century, where they became the root stock for a new nation).

The business of transporting felons to the American colonies was so profitable for the contractors and ship masters who actually hauled this miserable human freight westward (often in chains and otherwise under shipboard conditions reminiscent of the African slave trade) that there was great reluctance to give it up, even after the open door to transports seemingly slammed shut for good when the fighting started in 1775. George III's government, without a profit motive but with no alternative to exporting its problem, was also loathe to stop. Conveniently, the Treaty of Paris said nothing about the one-way commerce in convicts, leaving open at least the possibility that it could be resumed at war's end, a back door to North America.

Attempts to restart convict transports to the former colonies were made surreptitiously in mid-1783 and again the following year.[17] That first August 143 unfortunates were loaded on board *George* in the port of London for passage to Maryland. The expressed plan was that the vessel, rechristened *Swift*, would get underway for Halifax, but proceed to Baltimore instead. The ship finally arrived in Maryland in late December, after a revolt on board allowed some forty to escape, to discover that her merchants' and master's subterfuge had been exposed. Even so, over the winter months the entrepreneurs managed to move most of their stock, but at a substantial loss. A second attempt at convict smuggling to the United States in 1784 ended not in the former American colonies but in British Honduras.[18]

In 1788 the Continental Congress urged the states to pass legislation prohibiting the transportation of "convicted malefactors from foreign countries" into the United States. Several states were quick to do so. With that the back door, left ajar in 1783, closed for good.

5

During the run-up to the Revolutionary War and then after the fighting began, no one in London focused on the fact that Great Britain was at risk of losing permanently its principal nonlethal deterrent to and punishment for crime or planned for the possibility that an alternative might become necessary. Accordingly, the immediate government response to the disappearance of the American colonies as a dump site for felons after 1776 was the conversion of several dismasted ships, "hulks," moored in the Thames River just below London at Woolwich, into dormitories for male convicts sentenced to hard labor on public works. Parliament hastily passed the enabling legislation as 16 George III, cap. 43 in the same year.[19] Optimistically foreseeing that the requirement would be temporary, that act ran for only two years.

From loading convicts into ships for transportation to loading them awaiting transportation onto ships permanently at anchor was a short step.[20] A short step, but not an improvisation. Prison ships had been perfected during the wars of the eighteenth century, through which Great Britain continued her steady climb to global power. A fleet of such hulks, some twenty-two by name in Edwin Burrows' splendid *Forgotten Patriots* (2008), including the notorious former HMS *Jersey* (anchored with others on the mud flats of Wallabout Bay off Brooklyn), held thousands of prisoners of war during the American Revolution. Burrows estimates that some 30,000 colonials were confined afloat and ashore by the British. Perhaps 18,000, 60 percent, of these unfortunates did not survive their captivity, some among them described as "dying like rotten sheep."[21] If his estimate is accurate, the death rate among these prisoners of war was much higher than that suffered by either side in the most lethal camps of the American Civil War.

In 1783, coincident with the final victory of the revolutionaries in the American colonies, Parliament passed 24 George III sess. 1, cap. 12, "An Act to Authorize the Removal of Prisoners in certain cases; and to amend the Laws respecting the Transportation of Offenders." This act converted the hulks from prisons into places of temporary confinement for convicts awaiting transportation. Subsequent legislation put the hulks under contractor management, from which many, but not all, of the ensuing abuses flowed. Investigations soon reported maltreatment of convicts, on the one hand, and their depravity on the other. The hulks, a committee of the House of Commons concluded in 1785, "had singularly contributed to improve the practice of villainy; that the convicts had formed distinct societies for the more complete instruction of all new-comers, who after the expiration of their sentences, returned into the mass of the community, not reformed in their principles, but confirmed in every vicious habit."

The first four hulks were the *Tayloe*, *Censor*, *Reception*, and *Justitia*, all put into service in 1777. They differed from their military counterparts then at anchor off the American coast principally because of the expectation that civil prisoners would labor at public works and so had to be sustained at some minimum level of vitality; rebel prisoners of war did not.

The *Justitia*, a retired East Indiaman of some five hundred tons burden was the first flagship of this morose squadron. She had for seven years before the war (1765–72) moved convicts from England to the American colonies. Two later hulks were also named *Justitia*, like the first after the Roman goddess of justice. No other ship's name appeared more than once in the hulk fleet. To be used again and again, "Justitia" must have been especially appealing because of its righteous ring and classical reference. It put a nice gloss of legitimacy on the whole nasty business. *Reception*'s name might have been unintentionally ironic; the *Captivity* and *Retribution*, and perhaps *Hardy* and *Fortitude*, had more forthright names. Candor, however, lacked the power that "Justitia" had to elevate foul, floating prisons onto a plinth next to a blindfolded, bare-breasted goddess holding a sword and scales.

By mid-July 1788, about the time the Continental Congress asked states to plug the opening that could let "foreign malefactors" leak into the United

FIG. 5

The Prison Hulk Discovery *at Deptford in 1828.* Edward William Cooke, etching, 1828.
Discovery, shown here when she was nearly forty years old, was a typical convict hulk.
Some two hundred men were confined on board when not laboring on shore. In better
days *Discovery* was the flagship of Captain George Vancouver's 1791–95 Pacific expedition. She was dismasted and converted into a prison in 1808 and broken up in 1834.
This is one of Cooke's famous etchings of "shipping and craft," published in eleven
or twelve lots of several plates at a time beginning in 1828, when the artist was eighteen. His identification of this hulk, aground at low tide, as the support ship of the
same name that sailed with Captain Cook's last voyage in 1776–79 was an error. That
Discovery was broken up in 1797 at Chatham. Cooke (1811–1880) was a polymath.
Elected to the Royal Academy on the strength of his marine engravings and paintings
in 1864, he was also a member of several learned scientific societies.
© 2010 NATIONAL MARITIME MUSEUM, GREENWICH, LONDON, PU 6034.

States, there were already more than 1,900 convicts afloat in English waters—
nearly 1,200 at Plymouth, Gosport, and Portsmouth, and more than 700 at
Woolwich on the Thames. All awaiting transportation to somewhere "beyond
the seas."

Between 1777 and 1848 forty other ships, formerly merchants or surplus
Royal Navy combatants, were pressed into this service, sprinkled about eleven
different anchorages, including Bermuda (after 1824) and Gibraltar (after
1842), near places where public works needed to be done.[22]

At the peak, during the late 1820s and early 1830s, more than four thousand men and boys were locked up every night in these floating hovels, some

convicts held by chains stapled to the deck and all under wary guard. *Anson* was the only hulk with female convicts aboard. Decommissioned and converted to a convict transport in 1844, the former Royal Navy frigate was more than thirty years old when she delivered nearly 500 male convicts to Van Diemen's Land (after 1856 Tasmania).[23] Once there *Anson* spent the next seven years—she was finally broken up in 1851—moored off Hobart with as many as 350 women berthed on her two lowest decks.

What began in the summer of 1776 as a two-year-long expedient became, inevitably, a semipermanent solution. The last convicts assigned to hulks would not emerge for the last time from the fetid holds of the last hulks until 1854, almost seventy-five years after the first men had been sent below to start their sentences confined behind rotting English oak. In time and in warm weather, the foul odors seeping from a line of such immobile hulks would be sensible downwind at a range of many miles. In twilight or at night, in haze or through a light fog, the hulks could be smelled much farther than they could be seen.

In an era when steam power was in its infancy and when men and animals still provided much of the energy to make and move things, "hard labor"— such as dredging sand and gravel from the bottom of the Thames, and building dockyard facilities from stone—was truly hard. The hours of daylight labor in leg irons were exhausting; the intervening hours in the hulks were almost unimaginably horrid. The hulks were, in one description, a scene of "Blasphemy, Imprecation, and Woe," and in another of "vice and profligacy too shocking to relate." All that and pestilential besides. Although fatality rates (measured in percentage as deaths per 100 per year) dropped off from roughly 21 percent in 1776–79 to less than 4 percent per year through the first half of the nineteenth century, malnutrition was ever-present, and debilitating if not necessarily deadly disease was common.

Among the dreadful burdens that life in the hulks inflicted, the worst must have been the horrors of long nights spent aboard. Until 1812, when the Royal Navy came up with a below-decks design for communal cells to either side of a central passageway that provided for safe warder supervision, the entire interior prison space in a hulk had been a single locked enclosure. Most convicts could move freely at night inside this hold, entirely unobserved and unrestrained by guards—a sort of overnight mosh pit operating under the law of the jungle. Only imagination could limn the scope of criminal and depraved acts that must have been regularly committed in these places before they were subdivided, before the rudiments of a convict classification system were put in place (1819), and before boys (some as young as ten) were removed to a children's hulk (1824), where at least they were free from abuse by adults if not by one another.

In August 1833, when *Amphitrite* sailed for New South Wales, there were thirteen operational convict hulks in the fleet, nine in home waters and another four in Bermuda. Some 1,100 convicts were laboring in the summer heat on this tiny island group (scraps of a long-gone volcano's caldera), most in the quarries and on the docks at the western end of the archipelago and the remainder in St. George, the colony's principal town at its eastern end. These unfortunates were, literally, at the end of the line. Bermuda's Ireland Island and St. George were transportation end points. The convicts there had arrived at their place of exile.

At the same time, 3,600 other convicts worked ashore near the familiar anchorages in England, the homeports of this immobile fleet for decades, or bent over work benches in the shops of *Euryalus*. Unless a pardon intervened, these men and boys were awaiting transportation to New South Wales or Van Diemen's Land.

6

Crowding in the hulks afloat and in holding cells ashore, an inability to get more hulls and an unwillingness to spend more on jails, and general revulsion at what the hulks had inevitably become eventually forced the government into an urgent search for alternatives. Restarting transportation and shipping convicted felons out of sight and mind forever was everyone's preferred solution, triggering a worldwide hunt for a suitably distant and unpleasant substitute for North America. Between the end of the American Revolution and August 1786, when a decision favoring Botany Bay on the east coast of New South Wales was finally reached, London considered and rejected one after the other half a dozen alternatives, some very reluctantly. These included exile to places in the Caribbean, Asia, or Africa and, briefly, the enlistment of convicts in special military units, a type of foreign legion reserved for service in the empire's hellish places.

This last initiative failed dismally. Two convict companies "recruited" directly from prison hulks and deployed to Ghana's Gold Coast in 1782 arrived there practically without kit and proved, as they died off, that this had been a crackpot idea. The underlying concept, an imaginative extension of the enduring notion that army service was a reasonable alternative to time in jail, was not tried again in this form.

Nova Scotia and British Honduras were the first sites considered for exile, and even though in Honduras at least the local officials seemed willing enough at the beginning, residents of these colonies were no more interested in hosting convicts than Ben Franklin had been. As Hondurans' reaction made clear in 1784, when *Mercury* materialized in port with her cargo of 183 convicts, no British colony would willingly accept an *"excrementitious mass"* from the mother country. Having, perhaps, learned a lesson from their recent experience with Americans, the cabinet was already looking at places where pesky colonials couldn't stymie Crown policy even before *Fair American* and her load of twenty-nine convicts was chased away from the same place two years later.

The next idea was to send convicts to Lemain Island in the Gambia River, about 175 miles inland from the Atlantic Ocean and less than eight miles square, to fend for themselves or die. The impression is that either outcome was acceptable so long as nobody left the island, an objective to be guaranteed by the presence of a Royal Navy picket ship downriver. Conveniently, the Gambia was navigable by oceangoing vessels to well upstream of the island.

Great Britain would learn more about lethal African fevers and the continent's inhospitality to white men during the next century, thanks to quixotic expeditions launched by Sir John Barrow at the Admiralty, to the campaigns for empire, and later to Henry Morton Stanley's celebrated treks, but the certain result of a scheme to abandon shoplifters from London on a swampy West African island cannot have been unforeseen. What was being contemplated was a tropical version of a medieval dungeon *oubliette*, a concealed pit in which to cast prisoners and forget them while they died. When the scheme was finally presented to a select committee of the House of Commons in the spring of 1785, it collapsed under the weight of testimony that suggested the plan was "likely to start a war with the natives, lead to escapes and cause many deaths from sickness and starvation."[24]

Through the nineteenth century malaria and yellow fever exacted a horrific price from Europeans in tropical West Africa, death rates right at the edge and beyond of sustainable, eventually forcing at some garrisons the replacement of European troops by West Indian regulars originally from Africa. One analysis concluded that in some places annual death rates, largely from these same two diseases, were from two to ten times as high as comparable rates in Europe. The worst was Sierra Leone, commonly known as "the white man's grave." "The annual mortality rate for Europeans stationed there was 483 per thousand, more than thirty times that of England," wrote Alan Bewell in his *Romanticism and Colonial Disease* (1999). "Every year, in other words, *almost half* of the soldiers stationed there died."[25] Prison colonies would have collapsed into extermination camps in the face of that kind of pressure, which could not be relieved until quinine, pure water in camp and in the bush, and mosquito controls became generally available decades later.

Next, the search for a solution drifted even further into the unknown, down the West African coast to Das Voltas Bay, almost nine hundred miles south of the Gambia on the shore of what is Namibia today. Preparations were soon underway to ship 850 male and 150 female convicts there.

A hasty, precautionary survey by HMS *Nautilus* of the place, discovered by Portuguese explorer Bartolomeo Dias in 1487, returned in mid-1786 to report a barren desert where some had imagined "wood, water, antelopes and wild fowls." After sailing past more than a thousand miles of coast line, the *Nautilus* reported seeing neither a tree nor a drop of fresh water. And that ended that, but establishment of prison colonies in littoral West Africa had been a very near thing.

7

Eventually the prison hulks became intolerable, even for civil servants comfortably situated ashore, and when prison sites in Africa proved impossible, the pressure was on to find a suitable place on another continent. By a historic coincidence, one had been found nearly twenty years earlier, but not visited since.

The solution to the problem would be a prison colony in New South Wales, first suggested for this purpose by Joseph Banks, the amateur botanist in Captain James Cook's bark HMS *Endeavour*, who had spent weeks ashore there in 1770 during Cook's first around the world cruise. ("Captain" because Cook commanded one of His Majesty's ships. He was a lieutenant in the Royal Navy at the time.)[26]

It was Banks who named Botany Bay—Cook had wanted to call it "Skate Bay"—and it was Banks' descriptions of the area in April 1779 to a parliamentary committee enquiring into possible transportation destinations that, wrongly, made the scrub and stands of eucalyptus sound like an Eden crying out for human settlement. "Human" in this instance meaning "British." In the eighteenth century the continent's resident aborigines, estimated at perhaps half a million, were not considered as holding a prior claim to the place. Seven and a half years later, with every other possible destination for convicts rejected for one good reason or another, Botany Bay came up again, this time for keeps. Banks' long-ago endorsement, seconded by another of Cook's officers, James Mario Matra, was finally decisive, proving that nothing so clears the mind as an absence of alternatives.

The testimony of the two men was allowed to substitute for a site survey, which would have delayed progress for more than a year. And so, suddenly, with no one who either participated in the decision or would execute it having ever been there before or thought much about it, by Orders in Council His Majesty's government committed itself in December 1786 to establishing a prison colony on the far side of the planet. It was a little bit like launching the first mission to the moon: The destination was certainly there, and the necessary technology was available if one accepted some risk in transit, but no one knew enough about conditions on the ground to be certain of the result. Fortunately, when the First Fleet sailed the transports carried two years of supplies and victuals, not the single year supply that Banks had said would be ample. One year of stocks would have condemned them all to death by starvation.

The most outspoken opposition to the new initiative ("intemperate" may be more apt than "outspoken") came from Alexander Dalrymple, a feisty Scot who, in 1786, while serving as the Honorable East India Company's hydrographer, published in London *A Serious Admonition to the Public on the Intended Thief-Colony at Botany Bay*. Others criticized transportation on the basis of practical, humanitarian, or moral grounds, but it was Dalrymple's insight to see transportation as a clever scheme to circumvent the company's monopoly on trade with the Orient.

Glancing back at the economics of transportation, beginning in the 1950s some scholars argued that broad strategic objectives must have underlain the decision in London to ship convicts halfway around the world. The cost of transporting them and maintaining prison colonies abroad was simply too great, they thought, for the initiative to have made sense exclusively as a solution to a problem in criminal justice. Perhaps, they posited, the real purpose of this distant presence was to support the global reach of the Royal Navy, or the vessels of the East India Company and the British Pacific whaling fleet, or to obtain naval stores from the pine forests and flax fields of Norfolk Island. There's something to this idea that Australia was more than a distant substitute for the American colonies. The British presence there filled this square on the great global game board, and by blocking the French from the best position in the region, it powerfully strengthened British commercial interests every place washed by the Indian Ocean.

While such broad concerns might well have played a role in the decision to colonize, the driving impetus behind it was not global strategy but domestic tranquility. An economic analysis by Professor Frank Lewis (now of Queens University, Ontario) indicated that beginning in 1801 the net cost of a convict in Australia was lower than that of a convict in a prison hulk, and across the fourteen years of the period he studied (1796–1810), the government had benefited to the extent of more than £1 million.[27] The benefit was progressively greater in later years.

The original plan was that convict transports would sail twice each year, in May and September, if not in convoy with an armed Royal Navy escort as the First and Second Fleets were to do in 1787 and 1789, then at least in loose company for mutual support like the sailing of the Third Fleet in 1791. This timing had transports that departed in the spring at sea during the best weather possible for the long Atlantic Ocean transit, but it exposed those sailing later to the bad weather typical of year's end, and both to the still-mysterious perils of the Atlantic hurricane season. In all cases the long voyages would end in good weather, spring and summer in the Southern Hemisphere.

That was the plan, but there was no Fourth Fleet, and even before the Third left port, other transports sailed independently when jails and the hulks reached saturation and as soon thereafter as a shipload of felons could be chivvied out of confinement and delivered aboard. Lady Juliana, the first female convict transport and the first to New South Wales sailing under private contract, left alone from Plymouth at the end of July 1789, some six months ahead of the rest of the Second Fleet's departure. Her cruise was memorably long, 309 days with four stops on the way, and memorable, too, for the lusty whoring at all four ports of call en route. That excitement aside—and glossing over a dozen pregnancies, some babies born at sea, an outbreak of scurvy, a fire underway, and five deaths—her interminable voyage seems to have been relatively smooth, although one convict's unruly behavior managed to provoke time wearing a flour barrel first and later a flogging, a punishment very rarely inflicted on women.

In 1959 Charles Bateson called this vessel "nothing more than a floating brothel," from where Siân Rees might have gotten the title of her book in 2002. Lady Juliana arrived in New South Wales early June 1790, just a few weeks ahead of the Second Fleet. (The previous Christmas Eve, HMS Guardian, also nominally a part of the fleet and then two weeks out of Cape Town in the empty spaces of the southern Indian Ocean, hit an iceberg. A few of her crew, passengers, and convicts managed—incredibly—to survive the catastrophe that followed, but the loss of a thousand tons of stores nearly condemned the new colony to death by starvation. Lady Juliana's extra mouths could not have been welcome.)

Nothing that happened on board Lady Juliana in transit could have been a surprise to any veteran sailor. Randy behavior erupted in ships every time there was an opportunity, meaning almost any time women were on board. In 1836 "Jack Nastyface" saw his short tale of life between decks in the Royal Navy, Nautical Economy; or Forecastle Recollections of Events during the last War published.[28] Jack Nastyface was a pseudonym for William Robinson, who in between volunteering for the Royal Navy in 1805 and deserting from it in 1811 served six years in the HMS Revenge. In January 1811 he was de-rated from purser's steward to landsman for some unknown infraction, which probably prompted him to jump ship and take his "leave from the naval service."

Revenge, Robinson wrote, moored at Spithead and was instantly surrounded by a great many boom boats "freighted with cargoes of ladies, a sight that was truly gratifying and a great treat; for our crew, consisting of six hundred and upwards, nearly all young men had seen but one woman on board for all of eighteen months":

So soon as these boats were allowed to come alongside, the seamen flocked down pretty quick, one after the other, and brought their choice up, so that, in the course of the afternoon we had about four hundred and fifty on board.

Of all the human race, these poor young creatures are the most pitiable; the ill-usage and degradation they are driven to submit to are indescribable; but from habit they become callous, indifferent as to delicacy of speech and behavior, and so totally lost to all sense of shame that they seem to retain no quality which properly belongs to woman but the shape and name. . . . It may seem strange to many persons that seamen before the mast should be allowed to have these ladies on board, while the officers must not, on pain of being tried by a court-martial for disobedience of orders, the Admiralty having made a regulation to that effect. The reason of this is, that the seamen are not allowed to go ashore, but the officers are.[29]

The ensuing scene of frantic, indiscriminate fornication on an industrial scale is difficult to square with the usual image of the Royal Navy of this era as a superbly disciplined fighting force. The HMS *Revenge*, a large 74-gun frigate ("large" meaning her upper deck guns were 24-pounders rather than the usual 18-pounders), like all Royal Navy ships was built to optimize her performance in combat. She had no enclosed crew messing or berthing spaces and few concealed or cozy nooks that offered privacy, just open decks. Even the captain's cabin aft was designed for easy conversion into a semicircular extension of the gun deck. At anchor with prostitutes on board after months at sea, *Revenge* would have resembled not a warship in port but a fraternity party in hell. The occasional scrums in *Lady Juliana*, although much smaller, could not have been very different.

8

Convict transports were not the only vessels heading out or preparing to get underway for the distant Australian colony in late summer and early autumn 1833. The emigrant transport *Layton*, out of London for Port Jackson, was already two weeks down track toward Australia when *Amphitrite* left Woolwich. A former convict transport (later she would carry male convicts several more times), *Layton* also had women on board. All of them, however, were voluntary emigrants sailing to Sydney on government subsidized fares and looking to start life anew.

The East Indiaman *Resource*, the "well known, fast sailing, British built, armed ship" *Planter*, and a third, but unnamed, "fine ship of 400 tons burden" were all advertised in August on the first page of *The Times* as preparing to sail for Australia and taking reservations for passengers and cargo. Their advertisements, hinting vaguely at imminent departures, ran day after day in the newspaper alongside much more numerous ads offering accommodations for passengers and cargo to the Americas and Asia.

Notices of ship sailings were among the many advertisements that appeared on the paper's front page. In one issue, in the next column over from an announcement of regular cross-Channel service to Boulogne from Dover on Tuesdays, Fridays, and Saturdays in the steam packets *Royal George* and *Sovereign*, was an ad selling tickets to see (and hear) Mr. Kelyser's euterpeon (a type of orchestrion). It was "a grand, self-acting military band, with twelve cylinders, two acting at one time," two key frames for fingers, and a row of pedals for the feet, named—probably libelously—for Euterpe, the Greek muse of lyric poetry and music. The whole unlikely device, a mechanical barrel organ, was allegedly capable of playing the works of Haydn and Mozart, among others. "This instrument utilizes the full effect of a first-rate military band," Kelyser assured his readers, "with the appropriate modulations, pauses, cadences, in the most splendid style; the solos and accompaniments being as separately, distinctly, and accurately performed, as though played by artists of the first ability. . . . By the musical and mechanical world, this instrument is allowed to be the finest specimen of art ever produced, either for its beautiful and musical expression, or its ingenious and highly finished mechanism." Tickets one shilling. "N.B.," note well, Maestro Kelyser added hopefully, "the Euterpeon is for sale."

Layton, owned by London's biggest ship broker, Joseph Somes, was the first of the vessels chartered to take destitute women volunteers to the colony by the new Committee for Promoting the Emigration of Single Women to Australia.[30] She arrived in Sydney Harbour on Tuesday, December 17, 1833, after eighteen weeks at sea "in beautiful weather," very near the date that *Amphitrite* should have finished her voyage. The *Layton's* crossing appears to have been a by-then typically healthy one, marked only by two women's deaths, both from tuberculosis, and by four live births. It was in all other respects, however, a famously wretched voyage.

For months after she made port *The Times* ran articles detailing the horrors of life in *Layton* at sea by quoting from her passenger's letters about "four in every birth [berth]," "infamous treatment," "vile society," "green biscuit," "lean beef as hard as wood," and the topper, hunger that "sent nine quite mad. They declared when they got better, that it was nothing but starvation that made them insane." Depending on who you were, either the captain or the superintendent was an ogre, too.

Apparently her passengers also fell well short of the mark. If some critics are to be believed, on arrival *Layton's* emigrants spilled out of her hold and into grim temporary accommodations ashore that Tuesday like the poisonous contents of Pandora's Box. The chief critic was the superintendent on board, Doctor Beilby, who evidently had passed the last four and a half months at sea impotently observing debauchery and dissipation writhing around him. A curious pamphlet he published anonymously in Sydney nearly three years after *Layton* arrived (*A Few Copies of Letters and Some Remarks Upon Sundry Documents on the Subject of Female Emigration*) was intended to defend his reputation and to substantiate his charges that corruption and vice were the common features of every aspect of the voyage: The charter and loading of the vessel, the selection of her female passengers, the behavior of all on board during the crossing, their impact upon arrival on the community ashore, and that the committee and its shipping agent, John Marshall, not he, were responsible for the debacle. *Layton* was *Lady Juliana* redux. The next two emigrant transports launched by the committee, *Bussorah Merchant* and *David Scott*, sadly got no better reviews. (*Bussorah Merchant*, like *Layton*, sailed in convict transport service before and after carrying emigrants. She was one of the few transports that had smallpox on board.)

From the outset Australia was meant to be a self-sustaining, self-funding colony of the empire. Those goals took a long time to achieve, but that was not due to any doubt about their desirability as objectives. Almost 25,000 convict women were transported to Australia between May 1787 and April 1853, to join the roughly 132,000 men also banished to penal servitude in what were then called New South Wales and (for a few years longer) Van Diemen's Land. For decades the presence of women in the prison colony had as much of animal husbandry about it as of jurisprudence, a dimension unapologetically acknowledged fifty years later by the name of the sixteen-member, all-male Committee for Promoting the Emigration of Single Women to Australia. For this reason, it was rare that convicts long past child-bearing age, such as Elizabeth Glen, a well-known thief and drunkard in Glasgow but nearing sixty during her trial there in 1833, were sentenced to transportation. She was, however, and she likely became the oldest of the Scottish women on board *Amphitrite*.

Recruiting immigrants to Australia was not an easy sell during the first half of the nineteenth century. Through New South Wales' first forty-five years, until 1833, fewer than 2,500 free adult women immigrated to the colony; nearly four times that number were transported there under confinement. Young women (and men) looking for a fresh start had ports in Canada and the United States to consider first, a much shorter voyage to well-known places not bearing names saddled with off-putting adjectives such as "penal" and "convict." Moreover, emigrant fares to North America typically were one-quarter, or less, of the eighteen- to twenty-pound fare to Australia. Before the midcentury gold rush, not until the early 1830s, when government fare subsidies funded by land sales in Australia brought down the price of a passage there to roughly what a North Atlantic crossing cost, was voluntary emigration viable at a significant level. Beginning in that decade and powered by those subsidized fares, thousands of women eventually immigrated more or less freely to Australia, encouraged on this bold adventure by broadsheets that held out the promise of a fresh start in life.

A typical sheet in May 1834 was addressed to "single women and widows of good character, from 15 to 30 years of age, desirous of bettering their Condition by Emigrating to that healthy and highly prosperous Colony, where the number of Females compared with the entire Population is greatly deficient." Upon payment of five pounds or a promise to pay and the display of a certificate of good character, a young woman could sail to Sydney that year in "the splendid teak-built ship 'David Scott'" in company with "an experienced surgeon and a respectable Person and his Wife as Superintendents to secure the Comfort and Protection of the Emigrants during the voyage." Upon arrival in Sydney, she could select freely from among a list of "Female Employments" at, so the broadsheet promised, the high wages typical of a tight labor market.

If a medical man, a respectable couple to superintend the crossing, and a subsidized fare were not inducements enough to board *David Scott*, there was also, allegedly, the encouraging experience of the 217 women immigrants who had gone to Australia in the former convict transport *Bussorah Merchant* the year before. One hundred eighty found "good situations within three Days of their Landing." The remaining thirty-seven, the broadsheet claimed, had been "well-placed within a few days." The 650-ton *Bussorah Merchant* could have packed another sixty to eighty passengers below decks, but evidently no more volunteers could be found for this subsidized voyage to Australia.

Reality fell short of expectations. *David Scott* entered Sydney Harbor in early November 1834 after the usual four months at sea. If the Reverend John Dunmore Lang, a pioneer minister of the Church of Scotland in Australia, is to be believed, the ship's arrival in port brought with it amphibious vice and dissipation, the same charge that had attended *Layton's* arrival.[31] "Sixty of the females who formed part of her cargo were common prostitutes," Lang wrote,

> forty of whom were so thoroughly vile, that my informant, a respectable free emigrant, who arrived in the colony as a cabin passenger by that vessel, assured me "he did not believe they could be matched in England." The captain's authority was accordingly set at defiance by the crew, and the vessel converted into a scene of the most abandoned

licentiousness during the whole voyage . . . although a considerable number of respectable females emigrated by both vessels [the reference is to *Layton*] many were ruined forever from the vile society into which they were thus thrown.

Ruined in transit or not, what had been a trickle of a few thousand free migrants annually in the 1830s later grew into a freshet, with the peak years early in the 1840s (before the gold rush) and again in the 1850s, seeing about twenty thousand arriving per year. Together these women, young petty thieves for the most part leavened by equally young but hopeful immigrants, became, literally, the mothers of a new nation. This book is not about them. It is about the hundred or so others like them who, on August 25, 1833, left Woolwich, England, in the *Amphitrite* to join their sisters far away but never arrived.

On the 30th day of August, A dreadful storm did arise,

The roaring waves ran mountains high, Dark and dismal was the skies;

To the Captain on their bended knees, They did for mercy crave,

But he unto those weeping souls, Would no compassion have.

CHAPTER 3

◇◇

His Majesty's Hired Transport
Amphitrite

9

Moving dozens of disoriented and miserable women with their possessions, some of them with small children, to the Thames embankment and then into and out of the wherries that ferried them from shore to ship took time. Days, in fact, while first one then another lot of convicts arrived in London, or emerged from Newgate Prison, where they had been held in the group cells on the second story of the women's wing, and was delivered to the ship, anchored in the stream at Woolwich, some nine miles downriver from London Bridge. The historic practice had been to move convicts in chains between prison and their transport, not only to deter escape attempts but also as an object lesson to watching would-be offenders, a sort of perp ride in open wagons, but by 1833 women had been transported to the riverfront in closed carriages for years. The first lot of convicts went on board *Amphitrite* several weeks before sailing. By the time the anchor was weighed, the cannier among these early arrivals already knew their way around the ship and her crew.

At least some of the women were lifted onto *Amphitrite*'s deck more or less willingly, viewing transportation not so much as exile to a dreadful unknown place but as relief from certain, familiar misery. Maria Hoskins, twenty-eight, was one such woman. William, her husband, had abandoned Maria and their four year old to the grudging care of their parish, St. Martin-in-the-Fields, in September 1832. Later she was quoted as saying at trial that "if she was not transported for this [stealing a watch] she would commit something more heinous that would send her out of the country." Australia could have represented a fresh start for her and their child. As a petition Maria sent to "the Hon[orable] Sheriffs of the City of London" quoted in several newspapers suggests, she intended that to be so. "We, the unfortunate convicts in Newgate," she wrote (or someone wrote for her), "humbly solicit a continuance of the sheriff's favor, that they will supply those who stand in need with clothing, as they have done for other convicts. Some of us are entirely destitute; some are more fortunate in being assisted by their friends. We are anxious to alter our way of living, and, by a strict adherence to the rules laid down for our future conduct, are in hopes partly to retrieve our reputations, which we have unfortunately forfeited."

After mother and child were reported lost off Boulogne, parish officers reluctantly forgave William—now a widower, unemployed and indigent but still showing "the remains of former respectability"—the £31 4s. 3d. they had sued to collect from him for the "maintenance and support" of the two. That proceeding identified one of the dozen or so children drowned in the wreck.

Six others also have a last name. On September 16 Edinburgh's *Caledonian Mercury* reported that Mary Thornton, from Dundee and sentenced to seven years transportation, left England for New South Wales with two children, and that Janet Crerar, from Perth, had with her a daughter about twelve years old when she left to serve her seven-year exile. To those three can be added an equal number of young Turners, the least of which was an infant. Mothers with babies not yet weaned were supposed to be held ashore, so presumably the youngest Turner was around two years of age or older, but perhaps not.

The remaining five children in *Amphitrite* died anonymously. According to John Owen, one of the surviving crewmembers, two of the women were pregnant and expected to deliver during the voyage. "Enceinte" is the delicate way this fact was presented to readers of *The Times*, the use of French for some reason deemed superior in this instance to English. The number is much smaller than one would expect given the average age of the convicts and their apparently active sex lives.

Jane Becket, twenty-one, was another willing deportee. She explained in court that she was "induced to commit these thefts in order that she might be sent out of the country because she had lost her character and was ashamed to show her face." Becket, it was revealed, had delivered a stillborn baby, the child of a man she was to marry but for some unexplained reason had not.

Wronged woman in tragic circumstances, maybe; there were many such. But then in March 1833 Becket ran off with her live-in boy friend's wages after stealing from their landlady and burglarizing two houses in Glasgow.

For many on both sides of the law, however, transportation was a dreadful prospect if not necessarily the perfect deterrent to crime. Mary Ann Bland, convicted July 3 in Northumberland of the theft of one pair of "drab trowsers" and sentenced to seven years, was the subject of an eloquent, albeit fruitless, petition for commutation. "Previous to her unfortunate marriage and the committing of the offence," six petitioners wrote on her behalf,

> [she] ever conducted herself in a moral upright just and proper manner, was by all who knew her deemed highly respectable in the Circle of Life in which she moved discharging as well as the duties of an affectionate daughter as an industrious member of society. . . . If the sentence so passed were mitigated to Imprisonment, the said Mary Ann Bland might for many years afterwards be a useful Member of Society, while such Confinement by cherishing the hope of being restored to her friends would save her from that fatal despondency which is too often the extinction of all virtuous habits.

Her petition was denied. Malcolm and Mary Ann Williams, the parents of sixteen-year-old Margaret, sentenced in Lancaster on July 8 to seven years for stealing a shawl, presented a similar argument. They told the court their daughter was of "a weak and delicate condition and we fear much she will not be able to bear the terms of her transportation." They begged that sentence might be altered to "serving her time in a penitentiary in London." It was not.

10

For the few eager to leave the British Isles, their enthusiasm for escape might have been heightened by the special danger being left behind in *Amphitrite*'s wake: 1832–33 were cholera epidemic years in the British Isles, the first time in history this fearsome disease invaded western Europe from deep in the Indian subcontinent.

In earlier centuries European explorers had unknowingly loosed their lethal diseases onto native peoples unprotected by natural immunity. (Africa, defended by its own terrible fevers south of the Sahara, for a short while managed to hold off white men and their appetite for empire.) The ensuing population crash made possible the easy conquest of continents by a relative handful of adventurers riding horses and carrying firearms, an outcome that encouraged Europeans to confuse their own ambitions with the will of God. Cholera presented the opposite scenario. Like bubonic plague and yellow fever, but like no other malady European medical men of the early nineteenth century had knowledge of, it emerged from a foreign reservoir and moved to infect its European victims where they lived.

"Cholera is a horrific illness," Steven Shapin wrote in a *New Yorker* magazine book review in November 2006, describing its symptoms and course:

> The first sign you have it is a sudden and explosive watery diarrhea, classically described as "rice water stool," resembling the water in which rice has been rinsed and sometimes having a fishy smell. White specks floating in the stool are bits of lining from the small intestine. As the result of water loss—vomiting often accompanies diarrhea, and as much as a litre of water may be lost per hour—your eyes become sunken; your body is racked with agonizing cramps; the skin becomes leathery; lips and face turn blue; blood pressure drops; heartbeat becomes irregular; the amount of oxygen reaching your cells diminishes. . . . Through it all and until the very last stages, is the added horror of full consciousness. You are aware of what's happening: "the mind within remains untouched and clear,—shining strangely through the glazed eyes . . . a spirit looking out in terror from a corpse."[1]

The disease had been recognized in South Asia for some two thousand years, where it dehydrated and then killed as many as half all those afflicted in the short time cholera usually took to run its course. In the early nineteenth century, provoked by a still-unknown impetus, cholera spread from Bengal into Asia, Europe, and the wider world and transformed itself from the curse of the rural poor in India to one of the urban poor elsewhere. The first pandemic began in India in 1816 and moved through Asia toward Europe before mysteriously withdrawing in 1826. The second reached Russia in 1829–30 and then accelerated. It appeared in England in 1831, in western Europe, Scandinavia, and North America in 1832, and in southern Europe and Central and South America in 1833.

Beginning with the first, cholera's several marches westward were followed with anxiety by European doctors, many of whom believed the disease to be caused by a mysterious poisoned agent in the air, a "miasma" that somehow infected the damp ground below. British physicians fearfully watched cholera advance for years before it finally appeared in the home islands on the way to encompassing the globe. In November 1831 cholera reached the northeast

Fig. 6

The Miasma Thought to Cause Cholera was Linked to the Squalor of the Poor. Joost Swarte, pen and colored inks, 2006. Through several visitations of the disease beginning in the early 1830s, Great Britain's upper classes smugly believed that the vile practices of their social inferiors predisposed them to cholera, and that they largely escaped the disease's horrors through superior virtue and not, as it developed from the pioneering research of Dr. John Snow in midcentury, thanks to a relatively less contaminated water supply. Swarte is a prominent Dutch graphic artist with a studio in Haarlem, The Netherlands. This illustration was originally published in the *New Yorker*, November 5, 2006.

CourtESY ATELIER SWARTE.

coast of England at Sunderland, apparently by ship from Riga (then Russian). The next month the disease appeared in Newcastle.

Its coming had been long anticipated, and British ports had quarantine procedures in place, but the commercial incentives for diluting these procedures or evading them entirely were too great and in the end they proved ineffective, as such measures inevitably were. In January 1832 cholera erupted in Edinburgh and Glasgow, Scotland, and also in the riverside neighborhoods of London, from where it swiftly penetrated into the English capital's inland parishes.

On January 11, 1832, very early during the epidemic, Dr. William Balfour sent the editor of the *Scotsman* a scientific explanation of the disease and a prescription for its prevention that reflected the miasma model and accommodated cholera's apparent appetite for infecting the poor without his being judgmental:

> Its ravages have been chiefly among the poor, and those of irregular habits, who are ill fed, ill clothed, destitute comparatively (at least the former) of *fire* in their houses, and who have it not in their power, or neglect to maintain that cleanliness which experience has taught goes far in averting the disease; whereas people of condition and of temperate habits, are not only well fed and well clothed, but everything about their persons is clean and *dry*; so that the air they breathe is much more conducive to health, even when no contagion exists, than that which is charged with *effluvia*, exhaled from dirty apparel and persons, and from apartments in which *fire* is almost never kindled. Such circumstances, in combination, are sufficient of themselves to generate disease.

Focused on the wrong contaminated fluid entirely, Balfour's prescription was hot air to dry and rarefy the virus. "*Fires*," he concluded, "should be kept up as strong as can be borne, in every house, and in every apartment of a house, where the disease appears, until there is ground to believe that it has been extirpated. The same precaution should be adopted in every house in the vicinity where the disease exists. Nay, it might be very advisable that strong fires should be kept burning in crowded places of large towns." A lack of heat, he believed, was the problem (that, and the hasty making-up of beds before "all the *effluvia* arising from the body during the night" had been expelled from them), not the absence of morals.

Hot air was useless, though harmless unless it ignited a dwelling fire, but some learned medical prescriptions—bloodletting, opium infused in cold water, saltwater injections, pills of acetate of lead, hot mustard poultices ("remove when the patient complains much of the smarting"), mercury rubs, and boiling water washes (these discontinued because their "application produced great agitation in the mind of patients")—went beyond worthless to dangerous and near deadly.

The epidemic proved to be a bonanza for quacks. Nestled among ads in *The Times* for Read's Patent Stomach Pump and Enema Machine, for Strombom's Incomparable Embrocation for gout and rheumatism (among other ailments), and for J. W. Stirling's Cubebs with Sarsaparilla (described as a certain remedy for gleets, gonorrhea, and other diseases of the sexual and urinary organs), was one for Stirling's Stomach Pills. These, the eponymous "chymist" assured the afflicted, by "keeping the stomach and bowels in proper order" were not only a cure for persons who "have too great a flow of blood to the head" but also the specific for cholera and other alarming complaints.

That July, six months after Dr. Balfour published his diagnosis and remedy, Jane Gibson fell ill, the first cholera victim in Ayr, Scotland, John Hunter's home town. When cholera appeared in Ayr, Hunter, a year away from becoming owner and master of *Amphitrite*, was first mate of another ship, at sea on his first convict transport voyage.

By the middle of August more than two hundred cases had been reported to Ayr's board of health, now operating a cholera hospital and a separate observation house while frantically trying to improve municipal sanitation. Predictably, a disproportionate number of the dead were from south of the river, from the poor, congested areas of upper High Street and Townhead. Before it was over the town had hundreds of cases and had suffered 205 dead, all interred in a special burial ground adjacent to an existing cemetery.[2]

During the several years of this second cholera pandemic some 56,000 died in England, Wales, Scotland, and Ireland, a toll generally believed to have been exacted disproportionately from the among the "destitute, drunken or reckless class" and from "the inmates of lunatic asylums, the fatuous paupers of workhouses, prisoners or other immured [confined behind walls] persons badly housed and ill-fed." The epidemic's unchecked progress prompted the government to announce a country-wide day of fasting and prayer for March 21, 1832, through which it was hoped mass piety would somehow deflect the worst. By the end of 1832, 11,020 cases had been recorded in London, and 5,275 had died from cholera in the capital alone.[3]

From Europe cholera sailed to the New World, where it struck at New York, New Orleans, and Quebec at about the same time. Like everything else during that century, *Vibrio cholerae*, the bacterium that causes cholera, moved long distances fastest by sea.

Astonishingly, some of its victims dropped and died suddenly, like poleaxed cattle, just hours after the first symptom was evident. A New York City apothecary named Horatio Bartley published a small pamphlet in 1832,

Illustration of Cholera Asphyxia in its Different Stages, containing miniature case studies of patients in the hospital on Rivington Street, on the lower east side of the city. Among the pages of sufferers depicted, all sketched with hooded eyes, mouths agape like suffocating fish, and skin tinted a spectral gunmetal gray (from cyanosis), was the local record holder, a fifty-six year old from Barbados, dead just four hours after diagnosis.

Three transports sailing from England in 1832 (*Fanny, Katherine Stewart Forbes*, and the female convict transport, *Hydery*) took cholera on board together with their convicts.[4] *Katherine Stewart Forbes* suffered thirteen deaths from the disease, for which her surgeon, John Stephenson, drew sharp criticism in Plymouth (where the ship put in) and London for doing too much to report the outbreak and too little to control it. Unfairly maligned or not, Stephenson seems to have been a very unlucky man. His next warrant, in 1833 as surgeon-superintendent in *Waterloo*, was also marked by cholera. Eleven died then, roughly one-third of those afflicted. *Surry's* experience that same year, during one of the last of her eleven voyages as a convict transport between 1814–42, was even worse: forty-two cases.[5]

In 1833, however, London was finally on the back side of the epidemic. Even so, according to an 1894 study, *A History of Epidemics in Britain*, during the several weeks surrounding *Amphitrite's* sailing date (August 11–September 7) there were 1,454 cholera deaths in the city.[6] That count suggests as many as 3,000 new cases might have been diagnosed in those twenty-seven days. More than 100 every day, and certainly enough to sharpen the impulse to flight. But the worst was over. In mid-September British newspapers announced that cholera had left London on September 9. Continental port cities were slow to lift their quarantines of shipping from affected areas. For some months thereafter they continued to impose restrictions on shipping from the British Isles.

Parisians, especially, had good cause to be skeptical of British health assurances. Cholera had appeared in a nervous Paris at the end of March 1832, less than two years after the July Revolution ousted Charles X, the last of the senior Bourbon kings, and made Louis Philippe king of the French. By the time the epidemic was over that October, some 35,000 to 40,000 had caught the disease, of whom perhaps 18,000 had died miserably. Most of the dead were the desperately poor living in the foul central and eastern *quartiers* of the city.

The epidemic in the French capital tipped its fragile society toward renewed class warfare. "The lower classes rose up in bloody riots against what they perceived to be a massive assassination plot by doctors in the service of the state," Catherine Kudlick wrote in her cultural history of cholera in nineteenth-century Paris. "Believing that the wealthy had invented cholera as a pretext for poisoning them, they took to the streets and literally tore apart the bodies of several suspected poisoners. . . . In 1832 cholera could

easily become fused with France's violent revolutionary past, while threatening to propel the capital into a perhaps even more terrifying revolutionary
future."[7] With this bloody history—some "suspected poisoners" were beaten
to death in the streets by assailants wielding wooden shoes—not even a year
old when *Amphitrite* disgorged her dead at the end of August, French sanitary
laws were still being observed attentively.

Cholera aside, past experience indicated that *Amphitrite*'s convicts (not
"passengers," that word was correctly reserved for people who paid for their
ocean passage) could expect to disembark in better health than they had coming on board, thanks to regular rations and the sanitation routines of life at
sea. Not so their infants and young children. The nineteenth century had no
treatments for the great killers of children—measles, scarlet fever, whooping
cough, and diphtheria—nor did convict (or, for that matter, immigrant) vessels carry foodstuffs suitable for infants and toddlers until after midcentury.
Mortality rates among the youngest people on board such ships, consequently,
were the highest of any age cohort.[8]

II

The process that plucked *Amphitrite* for this mission out of the host of merchant ships that flew the British flag and prepared her for sea had been polished, if not completely perfected, by the Navy Board during the 1770s and
1780s. This board was the body that had been responsible for the movement
of men and most war matériel from Europe to North America during the
whole of the American Revolution, and the scope of its achievement becomes
clear with the recognition that the board managed intercontinental military
logistics, with quill pens and under candlelight, on a scale that would not be
approached for another seventy years and not exceeded until the early decades
of the twentieth century. In mid-1776 the board had nearly 420 vessels simultaneously under charter operating in three oceans, and at the peak of the con-
flict in the American colonies, 63,000 deployed soldiers and countless horses
relied on the board for practically all their support. In general the board (after
1794 the Transport Board and after 1817 a part of the Admiralty) performed
this essential mission superbly. The same tested charter policies, contracting
procedures, and planning factors were applied largely verbatim to the transportation of convicts to New South Wales and would be used again in the
Black Sea during the war against Tsar Nicholas in the 1850s.

Amphitrite's complement of crew and convict loading was established by a
formula that prescribed the numbers of each based on a vessel's register mea-
surement tonnage, confusingly an approximation of total enclosed volume
and not of weight carrying capacity.[9] The charter contract (called a "charter

party of affreightment," meaning a contract for charter of the vessel for a voyage to a specific place) typically permitted one convict for each two tons and required a crew of seven men and a boy for every hundred such tons. Similar ratios had been used as far back as the Seven Years' War (1756–63), one soldier-passenger per ton and six or seven crew members per hundred, although occasionally when shipping was in short supply the required crew manning was reduced in lieu of an increase in the freight rate paid.

Based on this formula, *Amphitrite* was approved for charter with a crew of fourteen and for carriage of just over one hundred convicts from the Royal Navy Dockyard at Woolwich (downriver from the dockyard at Deptford, the headquarters of the naval transport service and the site of the ship's most recent soundness inspection) to New South Wales.

Convict transports were required to have a poop, an after-cabin, on the main deck. The structure provided topside space for relatively more comfortable berthing for officers, but its chief function was to serve as an elevated island, an "after castle" from which the ship could be defended in the event that prisoners mutinied. The requirement for such a structure to strengthen the ship's defenses dated back to 1822 and to one of three inspection reports filed by Commissioner John Bigge right after his protracted and turbulent inspection tour of the prison colony. Although mutiny wasn't feared on board female convict transports, Royal Navy contracting officers still required a poop to be built atop what had been until then *Amphitrite*'s flush main deck, and it was done.

12

As the mortality data illustrate, well before 1830 the Admiralty and its contract ship owners generally knew well how to ship convicts from the British Isles to Australia and Tasmania economically and in good health. When *Amphitrite* sailed in the summer of 1833, the charter party contract and the Admiralty's instructions to masters and surgeon-superintendents, governing what Captain Hunter and Doctor James Forrester, the ship's surgeon, were to do and how they were to do it, contained the wisdom of more than fifty years of practical experience. That practical experience was of two kinds: that coming from the lessons learned during the course of some 430 previous round-trip voyages carrying 70,000 convicts across two oceans (literally millions of miles of sailing day and night through the seasons of the year) and from dealing during five decades with ship owners, agents, masters, and crews, men whose motives and actions reflected their financial or other interests.

By the 1830s the charter party had become a five-page (single-spaced), fill-in-the-blanks contract between the Admiralty board, styled as "the

Commissioners for executing the Office of Lord High Admiral of the United Kingdom of Great Britain and Ireland (for and on the behalf of His Majesty)," and the ship owner tendering his vessel "for carrying Passengers Soldiers *Convicts* or other persons . . . from the Rivers *Thames* and *Medway* . . . to *Port Jackson* in *New South Wales* or *Hobart Town* on the *River Derwent* in *Van Diemen's Land*."

The contract's terms and conditions required that the ship be "tight strong and substantial both above water and beneath," manned with seven men and a boy "fit and capable to manage and sail her all of whom are to be constantly on board except when their duty requires their absence on shore" ("none of whom shall be *Lascars*," sailors native to Indian Ocean ports) for every hundred register tons and "fitted and furnished with Mast Sails Yards Anchors Cables Ropes Cords Apparel and other Furniture fit and needful for such a voyage." A hired transport was also required to carry "not less than Three proper Boats."

Amphitrite had a longboat on deck, one capable in a flat calm of carrying something less than half of all those on board. We know nothing about *Amphitrite*'s other boats, the usual ship's cutter and at least another small boat stowed on deck to meet the prescribed total of three. These were workboats not lifeboats, not intended to accommodate everyone on board the ship at once in an emergency. Nearly a century would pass before that requirement was written into regulations. Apparently all of *Amphitrite*'s boats broke up on the deck of their mother ship as the night of the storm progressed. Nothing of them is mentioned in reports of the wreckage found on the beach.

Amphitrite's crew, all young men, probably studied the arriving human freight with interest as the wherries pulled alongside one by one, the women dazed—some teary-eyed, some defiant, and some silent—and small children crying or clinging quietly to their mothers. In an earlier era adults of both sexes would have expected some pairing up during the voyage to come, and these first few minutes of eye contact might have been the awkward start to that process. Given a ratio of eight females to each male and—for the women anyway—the unfamiliar shipboard environment, the dynamics of coupling during those first few days would have been unlike anything either side had ever experienced. The outcome would not: short-term marriages of convenience for both sides. (Once ashore in Australia that ratio of the sexes would have been nearly reversed, to 1:5, changing everything yet again.) By 1833, however, casual sex in convict transports had been suppressed below the levels that had made the crossing years ago in *Lady Juliana* so randy.

With a single exception we don't know the names of the ship's "people," her crew of seaman, landsmen, and boys. Thomas Langdon, twenty-five and the fourth son of Rev. Thomas Langdon of Leeds, was described in an obituary as *Amphitrite*'s third mate, which might have made him chief of one of the ship's two watch sections while underway. Ordinarily the ship's crew list, left ashore upon sailing, would have provided a full roster of all those on board. For *Amphitrite*'s August 1833 sailing that list is unaccountably missing, although muster rolls from the vessel's voyages during 1829–31 are in the National Archives at Kew.[10] Those rolls tell us that none of the men we know were on board in August 1833 had ridden the ship before.

Seven was the maximum age of children permitted to accompany their convict mothers to the prison colony, and so all brought on board were supposed to be that old or younger. (Children of volunteer settlers could be of any age.) The Admiralty's prescribed "scales of victualling" reflected the expectation that convict transports would have children on board. Children under ten years of age received a slightly reduced convict ration.[11] Those over ten were counted as adults for this purpose. These older boys were victualed, as were their fathers, and older girls as their mothers. Every convict and each convict's child also was to receive two gallons of wine during the course of the voyage, supplementing the butt of potable water (126 gallons) required by contract to be loaded on board on departure for every man, woman, and child. (Distilled spirits and beer were issued only to the surgeon-superintendent and soldiers of the guard, if embarked.)

Amphitrite, like her sister ships, also carried clothing for children of convicts, a single outfit and pair of shoes for each boy and girl with two spare cotton shirts for boys and a spare linen shift for girls. (Younger boys were expected to wear the same clothes as girls, so the practice was to stock twice as many outfits for female children as male.)

Older children of convicts were to be left ashore in the United Kingdom, some with fathers or other family members, the rest to cope with life adrift and alone. Based on her detailed review of convict indents, the manifests that accompanied convicts to exile, Deborah Oxley says that 4,864 children were left ashore when their mothers sailed away.[12] The precise figure is almost certainly too small, indents were not delivered in the case of convict transports lost at sea, but the order of magnitude number of children left motherless by transportation—thousands rather than hundreds or tens of thousands—seems correct. The count provides a scale to lend dimension to a great human tragedy.

Ann Tolley, forty-seven, tried in Worchester on April 8 for the theft of a coat and some silver a few weeks earlier, might have known this tragedy personally. Upon conviction she "prayed that the court would be merciful, as she had four fatherless children, her husband having been killed in a pit [mine] some time since." Court records showed him alive as recently as late February, when the couple had claimed three small children, not four, so everything she said might have been fiction. It was not her dubious plea, however, but Tolley's poor reputation that drove the outcome. After the local constable's report, "the Chairman remarked that he had been in hopes of hearing something favorable to the prisoner's character, but such not being the case, for the sake of the children, and for the sake of the community, he could not do better than transport her for seven years." There is no record that the Tolley children (Sarah, six, James, three, and William, one) sailed with their mother from Woolwich, but it's possible they did.

Boarding *Amphitrite* and getting settled must have been especially difficult for Louisa Turner, thirty-four, from St. James Parish, London, sentenced in April to seven years transportation for stealing twelve yards of silk waistcoating and four handkerchiefs. Identified in her trial record as a spinster, Turner nevertheless appeared on deck with three children, among them her nine-year-old son, who had somehow evaded the age restriction. At sea his mother would have had her hands full caring for him, his six-year-old sister, and an infant. All four would have been assigned to a single berthing space on one of the outboard platform bunks that together with a long table amidships served as the ship's principal below-decks furniture in the common between-decks cell the convicts shared.

Amphitrite's convicts slept three to a bed, in legless, open boxes on the lower deck, with children plussed into the mix with their mothers. A division board stood between every three beds.[13] When dry and in moderate temperatures and gentle seas, *Amphitrite*'s convict accommodation was not appreciably worse than Newgate's cells, where mats moved to the floor at night had served for beds and all the upright furniture was reserved for prison matrons' use. In rough, wet weather the same enclosed space, peopled with more than one hundred women and children, many of them seasick, and thick with the smell of their vomit and waste, would have been unspeakably foul.

Child labor was a familiar element of Georgian society and the national economy, and most of those left behind or orphaned when *Amphitrite* sailed would have been absorbed into the hordes of "pauper apprentices," who peopled the factories, mines, and slums in the places where their mothers had lived before trial, confinement, and transportation. The jobless remainder would have survived like their elders did, or did not, through scavenging, begging, and crime, or in the workhouse.

The image of childhood that this era brings to mind comes from Charles Dickens' *Oliver Twist*, the nightmarish and melodramatic novel serialized in *Bentley's Miscellany* beginning February 1837 and then published as a book in three volumes the next year. Nothing like the award-winning musical that opened on London's West End in 1960 and—sweetened up even more for its American audience—played on New York's Broadway three years later, but something much closer to its source, perhaps director Roman Polanski's 2005 gritty film version of the story.[14]

Dickens came by his bleak descriptions of waifs adrift in London honestly. He'd been one. In 1824, while (and after) his unemployed father was jailed in Marshalsea Prison for a forty-pound debt, the twelve-year-old Dickens had lived alone in London and worked six days a week in a warehouse at 30 Hungerford Stairs, off the Strand, affixing labels onto bottles of Warren's Jet Blacking boot polish. This embarrassing family history was a secret while Dickens lived, but prisons and prisoners appear and reappear throughout his work.

Two Germans living in England at roughly the same time as Charles Dickens took the novelist's raw material and did something very different with it.[15] Neither man could see how the tensions in the society they were observing could be relieved without explosive change into an altogether different construct. Extrapolating in 1848 (a year of revolutions on the Continent) from the "filth and tottering ruin" they saw in urban slums, Karl Marx and Friedrich Engels confidently predicted a proletarian revolution followed by the inevitable, global victory of communism over capitalism. Their manifesto eventually became one of the seminal documents of the nineteenth and twentieth centuries. In the same year *The Communist Manifesto* was first translated (badly) into English, 1850, fifteen British transports landed their convict cargoes on the other side of the world.[16]

Through the early years of the nineteenth century, children age seven and older were commonly deemed old enough to work for a living anywhere their small size, small hands, and small appetites afforded advantages, just as they had on family farms preindustrialization. At first this meant a move from open fields and barnyards into the water-powered mills of the new textile industry, the harbinger of a larger migration over the next century to cities and onto factory floors. Until coal-fired steam power, rising wages, prickled consciences, and restrictive legislation finally eased them out, a process that took much of the nineteenth century, children comprised a significant part of this new industrial work force.

Some scholars argue that the end of exploitative child labor happened in just that order, that economic processes were already working to replace children with women and women with men on the factory floor when, beginning in 1833, the Factory Act first restricted the widespread use of child labor in textile manufacturing.[17] Most economic historians' judgment is, however, that industrialization first fell most brutally on the very youngest laborers, and that their abuse continued as long as the early captains of industry managed to get away with such unconscionable exploitation.

An 1834 amendment to the Poor Law admitted children into parish workhouses, where they were to be fed and schooled part time but, in common with the other residents, deliberately maintained there at a standard lower than that available to the working poor. An incentive to go elsewhere. The fear was that anything less onerous would be an encouragement to idleness or crime. Charity was to be served up in small portions and under "intensely disagreeable conditions," motivated only by a desire to provide the minimum aid necessary to avoid "criminality, mendicancy, and death from starvation."[18] Critics called workhouses "prisons for the poor." The same pinched philosophy operated to guarantee, in turn, that conditions on board the convict hulks were worse than in the parish workhouses.

1 3

Shepherding the small, ragged convict processions across *Amphitrite*'s deck, down a steep ladder, and into the claustrophobic space between decks that was to contain them for the next four months could not have been a swift or smooth process, despite the fact that the women came on board with little baggage, not much more than a bag of new clothes and a small kit of personal and sewing materials from Elizabeth Fry and her partners in the British Ladies Society for Promoting the Reformation of Female Prisoners.

Prison-issued clothing was probably better than most had worn while at liberty, but it constituted each woman's entire wardrobe for the indefinite future. Every woman received one woolen and one cotton jacket or gown, three petticoats, three shifts, three pairs of stockings, two pairs of shoes, two colored neckerchiefs, a cap, and an apron. The sewing kit, a gift to each woman from the seventeen-year-old Quaker benevolent organization, included pins and one hundred needles, scissors and a thimble, white and colored sewing thread, and two pounds of scrap cloth pieces. Enough stuff to make a patchwork quilt during the voyage, but little enough to wean someone permanently from a life of crime.

Transportation Board practice required vessels offered for charter to have not less than 4 feet 10 inches between decks, meaning a minimum deck-to-overhead clearance about the height of a twelve-year-old boy today. Although many ships slipped through inspection that had an inch or two less standing room, *Amphitrite* was scaled more generously, with five and one half feet of head space from the lower to the main deck.

Not all of *Amphitrite*'s new passengers were docile. Some of the women, full of resentment and hostility, were disciplinary problems almost immediately. Six weeks after the wreck, Boatswain John Owen was quoted in *The Times* as saying some had been confined on deck "into a thing like a watchbox for being riotous. . . . It was very strongly built; no opening except some small holes at the top to admit air. The women were sometimes shut up in this for hours at a time." This even before *Amphitrite* reached blue water.

The box and its intended use were obviously new to Owen, who, if he'd ever been in a convict transport, would not have been surprised that there was such a cell on the ship. The crate Doctor Forrester resorted to, to encapsulate "riotous" women one at a time, was not the surgeon-superintendent's innovation. All convict transports were required to carry one such "Box for solitary Confinement," as well as eighteen pairs of handcuffs and one hundred pairs of ankle fetters ("bazzles," leg irons), for every hundred convicts carried.[19]

Restraining and disciplining convicts took not only hardware but also a certain perverse imagination, as Lieutenant Charles Wilkes, USN, found out when his squadron called on Sydney at the end of 1839, during its historic, four-year-long expedition of exploration in the Pacific. As part of the hospitality program ashore, Wilkes toured a convict transport floating in the harbor. "This punishment is said to be effectual in reducing the most refractory male convicts to order;" he wrote about confinement in the curious box he saw on deck, "but it was not found so efficacious in the female convict ship, for, when put in the box, they would bawl so loudly, and use their tongue so freely, that it was found necessary to increase their punishment by placing a cistern of water on top of the box. This was turned over upon those who persisted in using their tongues, and acted on the occupant as a shower bath, the cooling effect of which was always and quickly efficacious in quieting them. I was informed that more than two such showers were never required to subdue the most turbulent."[20]

14

Captain John Hunter, *Amphitrite*'s new master and owner, had never before set sail with a cargo of women, so he probably felt some trepidation on August 25, when the anchor was lifted from the river bottom sludge, the sails filled, and his ship headed down the Thames toward the Nore light vessel and the North Sea, to be gone for the better part of a year alone on deep water. Long sea voyages were not new to Hunter. He had commanded ships out of his home port on the west coast of Scotland for a few years in the 1820s. Later he was the first mate on several trips to India. Most recently he had been the mate on a passage to Sydney and back.[21] In the next several days Hunter would sail one-fifth or so of the full length of London's great artery to the Nore light, forty-one nautical miles downriver. This small step was the first in a round-trip voyage that would more than equal a circumnavigation of the globe.

The First Fleet had departed Portsmouth in May 1787 and sailed to Botany Bay via stops in the Canary and Cape Verde Islands, and at Rio De Janeiro,

Brazil, and Cape Town, South Africa. It arrived, after a passage of more than 15,000 miles, on Australia's southeastern coast the following January after eight months gone and six underway at an average speed of about eighty miles per day. Charles Bateson described its voyage, fairly, as "a magnificent feat of navigation and seamanship." The First Fleet's route—a sort of one-cushion bank shot off the South American coast—and two months in port along the way reflected the requirements for recuperation and resupply in transit. Carrying provisions and equipment for the new colony, its vessels had insufficient space to stock enough food and water for the passage, which would in any case have been inedible and not potable after so long in carriage.

The track also illustrated the great deal that was known at the end of the eighteenth century about global wind circulation. That knowledge was the general product of nearly three centuries of seafaring, since Columbus' first expedition rode the prevailing easterlies away from the Iberian Peninsula heading, he thought, for the Orient. But it drew directly upon Portuguese expeditions around Africa and later Dutch voyages, especially those directed by Antonis Van Diemen, who fifty years after Columbus first sailed sent a countryman, Abel Tasman, east across the Indian Ocean hoping to reach Chile and the sources of Spain's great wealth.

By 1833 three of the four impediments to generally safe, long ocean passages had been cleared for decades:

1. Mariners now had a general knowledge of the prevailing oceanic winds that defined sea lanes, information that was necessary not only to get them to their destination but also, and more important, to get them back home. This knowledge would become more like a product of science and less like the lore of a guildhall in another few decades, after Lieutenant Matthew Fontaine Maury, USN, began to publish his pioneering wind and current charts.

2. They could usually survive the diet of long months at sea in reasonable health, thanks to Dr. James Lind, a Scottish surgeon who in the 1740s discovered lemon juice to be a prophylactic and cure for scurvy, a life-saving find not effectively promulgated to mariners until fifty years later.[22] Before then the wasting disease, caused by a vitamin deficiency, had weakened and then killed a large fraction of most crews on extended voyages. Some crews were pared to the point that survivors of several ships had to be consolidated, depopulating and abandoning a part of the fleet so that what remained could sail on.

3. They could fix their position on the globe more or less accurately. Establishing one's latitude was easy and familiar, requiring not much more in the Northern Hemisphere than a calculation incorporating

as one term the observed elevation angle of the star Polaris at night. Although other, meticulous astronomical observations ("lunars") could yield an observer's longitude, in practice such observations were best done on land. At sea, where it really mattered, the determination of longitude required knowledge of the time at home port with an error of no more than several seconds per day. Only after John Harrison's accurate and portable chronometers and their derivatives became available was that possible. Before Harrison's chronometers, the usual technique had been to sail east or west along a latitude line, calculating distance made good through an estimate of speed, and then turning north or south to the destination. Some places on the planet, the reefs off Western Australia, for example, were littered with the wrecks of ships whose captains had mistimed that all-important final turn and run out of water under the keel.

The last bar still in place was an inability to predict dangerous weather, which often came, literally, like a "bolt from the blue." In the late seventeenth century the connection between atmospheric pressure, as measured then on a mercury "stick" barometer, and weather was being actively explored, the first step in a process that would eventually see meteorological science replace folk sayings. Soon after the turn of the eighteenth century, standard terms began to appear for the description of the strength of the wind, the fall of precipitation, and the appearance of the sky, permitting crude data to be collected and compared.

By the 1830s the idea that weather phenomena had a coherent structure, that, for example, the Indian Ocean monsoon winds reversed themselves seasonally or that "whirlwinds" (hurricanes) spun about a central core while they proceeded down track across the Atlantic, and could be comprehended, was well established among those who styled themselves "meteorological philosophers." Not until 1854, however, after one had been recommended for years, did the Board of Trade establish a meteorological office, official confirmation that weather was predictable and that its prediction was the responsibility of government.

The First Fleet's indirect route to New South Wales was abbreviated as time went on to a single stop in Rio de Janeiro. By the 1820s, however, many transports were going direct, with no stops on the way at all. Hunter's intentions cannot be known, but it's almost certain that on August 25, while he contemplated what lay ahead, Hunter planned to follow what was by then the familiar, direct track to Port Jackson. It would take *Amphitrite* through the South Atlantic and around southern Africa, eastward across the Indian Ocean to beneath Australia, and finally up the tricky nine-mile passage into the harbor, this with the assistance of a pilot. Departing in the last week of August, he could have anticipated arrival before Christmas, near the start of summer down under.

In 1833, the peak year of convict transportation, twenty-eight transports left Great Britain for the penal colonies on mainland New South Wales and Van Diemen's Land, departing during nine of the twelve months. Only March, November, and December saw no sailings. *Amphitrite* was one of three convict transports that put to sea in August, bracketed by the departures of the other two. The ship-rigged (three masts, square sails) *John*, under Samuel Lowe's command, left Spithead with 260 male convicts on August 6 heading for Hobart Town, capital of Van Diemen's Land. The bark *Lloyds*, with Master Edward Garrett and 201 male convicts on board, left the Downs roadstead headed to New South Wales on August 26, sailing one day after Captain John Hunter left Woolwich in command of *Amphitrite*. The former arrived on December 1, the latter December 18.

Sailing in August, *John*, *Amphitrite*, and *Lloyds* fell in at the tag end of a stream of eleven convict transports from five different British ports already underway for the colonies on the other side of the world. All the others, and the more than 2,900 convicts they carried, were expected to arrive while these last three vessels were still at sea. *Captain Cook*, out of Portsmouth on May 5, was by many miles the lead ship in this slender, four-month-long queue. She arrived in Sydney after 113 days at sea, one day after *Amphitrite* left Woolwich. The ten other transports (including two with women on board, *Buffalo* and *William Bryan*) were afloat somewhere between *Captain Cook* and *John*. As the statistics for 1833 suggest, nearly fifty years into the process the transportation of convicts had become long since a smoothly running industry, a pipeline of ships siphoning convicts in substantial numbers from the British Isles and depositing them in generally good condition thousands of miles away.

Presumably, while *Amphitrite* was still negotiating the upper reaches of the Thames, *Lloyds* lay in the protected anchorage between the Kent coast and the Goodwin Sands, exposed only to the south, awaiting a favorable wind to take her through the Dover Strait in daylight and then down channel past Land's End to the open ocean. Her final departure point was several days down track from the start of *Amphitrite*'s voyage, and this head start kept *Lloyds* ahead of the great gale that during the last weekend in August swept the strait behind the bark clear of shipping, and pummeled the shore on both sides of the Channel with powerful winds and torrential rain. *John* and *Lloyds* arrived safely on the other side of the world, both after a few days short of four months at sea.

15

Although relatively young, John Hunter was no novice merchant ship master. On September 4, four days after the wreck, when newspapers were just beginning to fill with the story, Joseph Lachlan, the prominent Irish ship broker who had served as *Amphitrite*'s charter agent in London, wrote *The Times* to explain that the ship had been sound and Hunter was an experienced mariner. The captain, Lachlan wrote from his office on Great Alie Street, "had been regularly brought up to the sea, and commanded a ship as far back as eight years ago." "Commanded a ship," perhaps, but Hunter seems to have been new to *Amphitrite*. This voyage as her master was almost certainly his first. When *Amphitrite* sailed as a hired transport between 1828 until at least sometime in 1831, her master then was not Hunter but one John Murray, commanding a crew of ten or eleven: one or two mates, a carpenter and a cook, several seamen, and two boys. Lachlan also did not reveal in his letter to the editor, as he might have in the spirit of full disclosure, that *Amphitrite* had been the collateral on a loan he had made days before to her master.

Captain Hunter's financial interest in his ship must have shaped his decision making later, so it's worth noting. Merchant ship masters usually had some share in the vessel they commanded, sometimes mates did, too, but Hunter's was more than just an interest; he owned *Amphitrite*. Registration records indicate that on August 17 Hunter purchased *Amphitrite*, all of the usual sixty-four shares, from William Pearson, her fourth (or perhaps even later) owner.

Evidently Hunter needed working capital to get to New South Wales and back, because three days later, in a transaction recorded in a "deed of mortgage" dated August 20, Hunter borrowed money from Joseph Lachlan against the ship as surety for the loan. Their deal was not a "bottomry bond," an old and common practice in admiralty law (the ship's "bottom" standing in for the whole vessel) that permitted masters to raise money in foreign ports to complete an interrupted voyage. Such a bond would have had Lachlan repaid with generous interest "on the prosperous conclusion of the voyage" but not able to recover his loan if *Amphitrite* went down anywhere out of Woolwich.[23] A deed of mortgage, instead, gave him an insurable interest in the ship, but there is no evidence that he had her insured.

Doctor James Forrester, the surgeon-superintendent in *Amphitrite*, had sailed in a convict transport twice before. From early October 1826 until early February 1827 he'd been in charge of the 161 female convicts being transported in *Brothers* from Cork, Ireland, to New South Wales. Among the thirteen women who reported to him unwell during *Brothers'* 122 days underway, four died during the crossing and three others were transferred still ailing to hospital ashore at voyage's end, meaning that fewer than half recovered their

health thanks either to Forrester's care or to natural process. That mixed result
prompted no special attention to Forrester's forty-eight-page, handwritten
journal report of *Brothers'* voyage, filed the following October. His next such
report, submitted five years later after a second crossing, provoked a threat to
his future employment as a convict transport surgeon.

During the first half of 1832 Forrester was responsible for the health and
good order of the convict women in the transport *Southworth*, Cork to New
South Wales in 129 days. (Four free women and their twelve children also
rode the ship to Australia.) Although he recorded treating only six patients
while *Southworth* was at sea, Forrester managed, nevertheless, to use up nearly
the entire stock of medicines the ship carried. The obvious inconsistency
prompted an unsolicited explanation in the remarks pages of his otherwise
nearly blank journal of the voyage, dated December 2, 1831–June 8, 1832:

> Received on board the convict ship Southworth from the peniten-
> tiary at Cork on the 14th day of January 1832, 134 female prisoners
> varying in age from 13 to 70. They were, generally speaking healthy
> and (except in a few instances where emaciation had been induced
> by long confinement) robust, consequently, there was a correspond-
> ing paucity of complaints during the voyage as the scanty contents
> of this journal demonstrates, indeed so meager are these as scarcely
> to account for the general and nearly total expenditure of medicine,
> etc., supplied for the use of the prisoners, so that I deem it incumbent
> on me, both for the satisfaction of the board, and my own credit, to
> set this apparent discrepancy in a clear point of view.

Introduction accomplished, Forrester now presented a preemptive self-
defense:

> I would state that the general and severe sea-sickness incidental to
> people not habituated to sea voyages induced a dejection so deep &
> obstinate as to resist every mode of consolation I could devise. This
> state of prostration & abandonment naturally included an apathy
> and aversion to exercise which only yielded to coercion. This slug-
> gishness and subsisting for the first time in their lives on salted & dry
> provisions was followed by torpor & irregularity in the digestive pow-
> ers ending (of course) in almost general and obstinate constipation
> which long required numerous & daily exhibitions of all the variet-
> ies of [?] medicines in my charge. In the 2nd place I would observe
> that at a more advanced stage of the voyage, it having been neces-
> sary from the winds to go an unusually long way to the southward

before getting the usual trade wind to enable us to proceed eastward the prisoners were thereby exposed much sooner and longer to the rigors of a lower temperature than generally happens in these voyages. This added to the deteriorated state of their clothing, especially shoes, induced an almost general (and from a continuance of the causes) very intractable catarrhal afflictions, which although not put upon the sick list, from their being so numerous, required throughout the rest of the voyage, daily and attentive treatment and naturally caused a heavy expenditure of medicine indeed, so complete was this, that had I not found sufficient in the ship's chest to warrant my proceeding, the ship must have put into the Cape of Good Hope for a fresh supply & thereby incurred a heavy demurrage. Trusting that this explanation may prove as satisfactory as it is true, I have the honor to be

YOUR OBDT. & HBL. SERVANT
J. FORRESTER
LATE SURGN.-SUPERINTENDENT OF THE
CONVICT SHIP SOUTHWORTH[24]

Sir William Burnett, the physician-general of the Royal Navy after mid-1832 and its senior medical officer for the next twenty-three years, wasn't that gullible.[25] Accepting Forrester's explanation would have required Burnett to believe that the undocumented exhaustion of the ship's inventory of medicines was not only entirely warranted but had in fact saved *Southworth* a stop in South Africa and costly charges for time in port while drugs were replenished. Sir William didn't believe it. The more credible explanation was that Forrester had abstracted the stock, taken it all to resell or use in his own medical practice. "Inform Mr. Forrester," a skeptical Burnett wrote on the cover of Forrester's journal on March 29, 1833, "that I am by no means satisfied with the reasons he has given for inserting so few cases in this journal & that if anything of a similar nature should occur again, the certificate to enable him to obtain the remainder of his pay will not be granted. W. B."

Burnett divided his list of unemployed navy surgeons ashore eligible for assignment to convict transports into three groups. He put Forrester into the last group, those described as "not so well calculated" to serve credibly in the post.[26] Evidently the flow of convict transports in 1833 was so great that Sir William came to the bottom of his roster of better qualified surgeons and was at midway through the year forced to send to sea some from among those he judged least proficient. And so, five months after Burnett penned this acerbic note, Surgeon Forrester assumed overall responsibility for a small, wooden

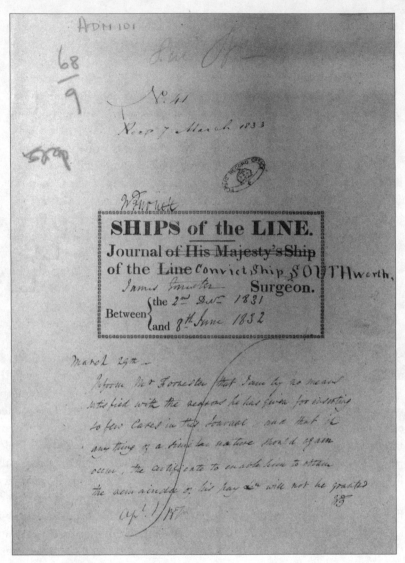

FIG. 7

"Journal of the Line Convict Ship SOUTHWORTH," 1832. Surgeon James
Forrester's journal reporting on medical events during the passage of the transport *Southworth* between Ireland and Australia, December 1831–June 1832,
was received in London, March 7, 1833. Three weeks later, when Sir William
Burnett personally reviewed Forrester's report of services rendered and medicines expended on the way to Australia, he found it incomplete and unpersuasive. This is the cover of that report, as annotated by Sir William.

NATIONAL ARCHIVES OF THE UNITED KINGDOM, REF. ADM 101/68/9.

empire at sea for the third time and ventured out to test Sir William's patience again by practicing medicine.

Four women had died during *Brothers'* voyage, a little worse than average for the year; in *Southworth* only one had expired. The days of terrific convict mortality on the passage were mercifully long since past, so these scant losses were no direct reflection on Forrester's professional ability. The nadir had been more than forty years earlier, illogically not with the first group of some 760 convicts shipped to Botany Bay in 1787 (and landed near there with 40 dead en route) but with the second group of just under 1,020 that left England in 1790.

Two hundred seventy-three male and eleven female convicts had died on board *Neptune*, *Scarborough*, and *Surprize*, sailing in company during the Second Fleet's passage. Another five hundred or so of the roughly seven hundred convicts finally off-loaded in Port Jackson after that voyage went ashore critically ill. A fearsome total of nearly eight hundred of one thousand convicts either dead or debilitated during five months at sea.[27] Those who lived through the passage disembarked at their destination like the stupefied survivors of some great battle at sea.

The loss of life, and the convict's abuse and suffering in vessels of the Second Fleet, was so appalling that going forward the navy line officers who had been on board transportation ships as His Majesty's government's representatives were replaced first by naval surgeons and later by surgeon-superintendents with executive powers, initiatives designed to ensure more responsible care of the human cargo.

The effort to reduce attrition by improving attention to convict well-being and defining the authority of the responsible officer over the ship's master and the chief of the guard detachment was successful. By the 1830s even double-digit convict deaths on a single passage had become uncommon, but they still happened: 11 of 214 died in *Waterloo* in 1833, 13 of 222 in *Katherine Stewart Forbes* the year before, and 11 of 220 in *Asia* the year before that.[28]

As time went on, conditions at sea improved further. When Henry Richardson finished his first and only passage from Deptford to Fremantle in May–August 1859 as the surgeon-superintendent in *Sultana*, he was able to note in his journal that none of the 224 convicts embarked had died during the nearly twelve-week voyage, that none had received corporal punishment, and that only two had been delivered to a hospital on arrival.[29] *Sultana's* crossing saw the hours at sea tick away as smoothly as a metronome, from 5:00 AM, when the galley fires were lit, to 7:00 PM, when, after a bed check, the prison was locked down for the night. Eighty-two days punctuated by only a handful of minor incidents and three births to settlers' wives. Richardson's results flowed from the good health of his charges at departure and also from his good

sense in transit. Fifteen ships followed *Sultana* into Western Australia between
1859 and the end of 1868, when the business of transportation finally ended.
Only 12 among these last 3,300 convicts died on the way.

Describing to its readers the unusual chain of command on board a convict transport, the *New Monthly Magazine and Literary Journal* wrote after the
wreck of *Amphitrite*,

> When the ship is taken up [placed under charter], a naval surgeon of
> experience and certain standing in the service, is appointed "Agent
> for Convicts" on board of her, and to him is delegated a very con-
> siderable power, commensurate indeed with the importance of the
> charge with which he is intrusted.
>
> This agent of convicts is, in fact, the viceroy over the king; the
> captain over the master of the vessel; and, as it is necessary that such
> power should be deposited somewhere, it has been thought right,
> upon a principle of humanity and economy, to place it in the hands
> of an officer who is supposed to blend with the authority absolutely
> necessary on such a service, the medical skill which may be required
> upon so long, and in some cases, so trying a voyage. To the charge of
> the officer the convicts are consigned; he becomes responsible not
> only for their health, but their security.

"Viceroy over the king," maybe, but despite the magazine's flattering characterization of the job, away from their ships and off the waterfront surgeon-
superintendents had none of the prestige that attached to assignment to one
of His Majesty's ships in a squadron at sea. Even Forrester's last active duty,
supernumerary surgeon in HMS *Talavera*, a third rate based at the Downs as
part of the antismuggling effort, had more status than did sailing in a convict
ship. Surgeons were not commissioned by the Admiralty in the name of the
King, but held their positions by virtue of warrants issued by the Navy Office.
The distinction was significant in this intensely status-conscious age.

But more than simply ego gratification was at work here. Status involved
other considerations than a place in the pecking order; most especially it had
to do with promotions and pay. By these measures, navy surgeons were inferior not only to executive branch officers but also to their counterparts in the
British army, whose free access to an "abundance of nutriments, condiments,
and stimulants" provoked intense interservice envy and in 1840 resulted in a
commission to investigate naval and military promotion and retirement.[30]

Still, for grounded, surplus Royal Navy surgeons after 1815, assignment to convict ships opened up employment opportunities in otherwise
very austere times. The Royal Navy immediately after Napoleon's surrender

was a naval force nonpareil.[31] That great fleet was swiftly reduced: from 127 ships-of-the-line (first, second, and third rates) in 1809 and 109 in 1815 to only thirteen in 1817. Nowhere was this decline expressed more succinctly or poignantly than in Turner's 1838 painting of *The Fighting Temeraire Tugged to Her Last Berth to Be Broken Up*, the decayed veteran of Trafalgar being towed upstream to a ship breaker's yard behind a steam tug, like an old beast being led off to slaughter. Likewise, the enlisted strength of the Royal Navy and Royal Marines was slashed by roughly 85 percent from its peak. Similarly, a proportionate number of officers, surgeons included, were sent home on half pay. For more than 100,000 former enlisted sailors and marines, demobilization meant poverty. For midcareer officers it meant indefinite unemployment on miserly allowances of £90–130 per year, paid quarterly.

A few surgeons found full careers in convict transports, making the long voyage to New South Wales or Van Diemen's Land and back six, seven, eight, or nine times. Others used the opportunity to relocate their lives and practices elsewhere, adding to what eventually became a glut of medical men in the small colony. While some ship masters must have resented the change in status and the lost opportunities for personal profit that a surgeon-superintendent presented, others clearly welcomed their reduced role. It freed them to focus on sailing and navigating their ships, and left entirely to the doctors on board the nettlesome problems of preserving order and good health below, and managing convict stores. Hunter seems to have adopted this hands-off attitude. As Owen testified, "The Captain never interfered with them in any way; it was not his business."

16

This time, Forrester was sailing in *Amphitrite* with his wife sharing his cabin, a privilege—or possibly an abuse of office, which was never made clear—even though he was probably obliged to pay for the food she consumed, seventy-eight pounds for the passage if she were charged the same amount he paid for his place at the table. She was the only civilian woman in the ship, the only female traveling to New South Wales not under sentence to transportation. Immediately after the wreck, the same *New Monthly Magazine* delicately questioned Mrs. Forrester's presence on board:

> One thing strikes us as being imprudent in the arrangement; we mean the permission granted to the surgeons to carry their wives with them. In time of war such an indulgence is not granted to the captain of a king's ship, because it is most wisely and naturally believed, that the presence of a woman so nearly and dearly connected with

him would influence his conduct in a very important degree. . . . We
are quite sure it would be for the benefit of the service if a restriction
were laid upon the agents for convicts, who are upon their voyages
in the exercise of a very arduous and responsible duty, similar to that
affecting a captain in wartime.

Moreover, the column's author continued, "It would seem as if the very circumstance of a crowd of depraved convicts forming the great body of passengers would of itself preclude the chance of a lady of delicate habits and
respectable connections from embarking in such vessels."

Probably even without this public prompting the Admiralty moved to
ensure that henceforth surgeon-superintendents were not distracted by their
wives from their duties. Article 44 of the March 1838 version of *Instructions for
Surgeons-Superintendent on Board Convict Ships* made the prohibition explicit:
"He is not, on any account or pretence whatever, to take his Wife or Family,
or any part of his Family, to Sea with him; nor to allow either the Wife, or any
other Relation of the Master or other Person, not forming a part of the Crew,
to be taken to Sea, in the Ship, without our special Authority." Five years too
late for *Amphitrite*.

If there were any questions ashore about Mrs. Forrester's habits and connections, there could have been none at sea. On land, her husband's professional status put him, and therefore her, in the midrange of medical persons.
Not as elevated as physicians but not as common as apothecaries, druggists, or
chemists. These were men who sold things for a living from inside of a shop,
mere tradesmen. Once established onboard, she played the lady.

The doctor's wife promptly selected one of the English convicts, Sarah
Poole, aged forty and the only one from Nottingham, to be her maid servant.
After that she spoke only to Poole and to none of the other women. Later
Boatswain Owen described Poole as being "very quiet and steady" and own-
ing "a great quantity of clothes." These distinctions might have been the reasons for her selection. Without a single lady's maid, even one recruited under
such sketchy circumstances as these, Mrs. Forrester would have been forced to
make do for herself, nearly erasing the line that separated her from the unfortunate females on board.

As the wife of a part time, half-pay Royal Navy surgeon now on a convict
transport, Mrs. Forrester's grasp on solid middle-class gentility must have been
weak. As the only respectable woman among a shipload of those who had
been "living on the town," a euphemism for amateur or professional whoring,
she must have been desperate to avoid any possibility that her status could be
confused for theirs. This upsetting sense of teetering on the edge of class could
explain her later response to disaster as it unfolded.

Mrs. Forrester's new servant pro tem was a thief, charged with and convicted in Nottingham Borough Quarter Sessions Court the April just past of two counts of stealing clothing, household linens and furnishings, and forty pounds of butter. (As suggested by their name, quarter sessions courts sat before a county's assembled justices of the peace four times per year. Capital and other serious civil and criminal cases were referred by quarter sessions to an assizes court, meeting twice each year under the authority of a circuit-riding superior common law court judge from London.) In April 1833 at Nottingham Quarter Sessions Court, the theft of a hat or a single pair of shoes was enough to merit seven years transportation.

One month later, in a story about the grounding of a Scottish smack, *Earl of Wemyss*, down sailing between London and Leith in the same storm that sank *Amphitrite*, the *New Monthly Magazine* revealed "by the way" (and without substantiation) that Mrs. Forrester had been on board *Amphitrite* without permission.[32]

It's possible that Doctor and Mrs. Forrester were emigrating from England, sailing to start life over in the antipodes. If so, they were not the only voluntary settlers in the ship. Young James Towsey, who it later developed knew the Forresters socially, was working his passage to New South Wales to join two older brothers. Perhaps, however, Forrester's wife just didn't want her husband alone at sea again with a shipload of nubile women in his charge. As far back as when *Lady Juliana* sailed for Port Jackson such vessels were regarded by the courts, their crews, and general society as filled from stem to stern with incorrigibly promiscuous women who would spend the voyage swearing and fighting and fornicating with sweaty abandon.[33] The lurid accounts of debauchery at sea that later seeped from New South Wales seemingly confirmed the scandalous, and delicious, worst. They included, inter alia, the stories of an assault on Surgeon-Superintendent James Hall in 1823 in *Brothers* by six women convicts and of Surgeon-Superintendent Matthew Burnside's ribald lifestyle in the female convict transport *Providence* in 1826.

Forrester's wife (her first name has been lost) could have believed all this—she soon behaved as if she did—and for this reason might have boarded *Amphitrite* in an informal role as her husband's chaperone. In a few days some would accuse Mrs. Forrester, posthumously, of personal responsibility for the terrible loss of life.

17

John Hunter was thirty-three when he sailed, just two years older than his ship. Thirty-three would have made him almost certainly the oldest member of the ship's crew, with the exception of Forrester, who was probably in his forties, and possibly Forrester's wife. Going to sea was generally a young man's business. Merchant ship junior officers (even those of the East India Company, which attracted the best) typically were in their twenties. Their sailors were usually in their twenties also, or younger still, and several boys in their teens or even younger rounded out the complement. The oldest *Amphitrite* deckhand whose age we know was the boatswain, Owen, only twenty-two. For the most part, being a convict sentenced to transportation was also reserved for the young. Among *Amphitrite*'s convicts, the women from London averaged under twenty-three years old; the women from places outside the capital twenty-eight, and those from Scotland twenty-nine.[34]

Captain John Hunter is a wraith. Dead three months after his thirty-third birthday, his body lost at sea after the wreck of his ship, only a few sources exist to help flesh out the man. They lead to no obvious explanation for his actions—or inaction—on *Amphitrite*'s deck the night he died.

Hunter was born June 2, 1800, in the royal burgh of Ayr on the southwestern coast of Scotland, where the "Water of Ayr" flows into the Firth of Clyde. Ayr was then a town of several thousand. He was baptized five days later in the Auld Kirk on the river. Hunter's older sister Thomasina Grace was baptized there, too. Their names appear just a few lines apart on the same page in the register. A disapproving Dr. William McGill, the senior minister, wrote there that her late baptism was due to "parents neglect." McGill's notoriously liberal views got him in serious trouble with more orthodox Calvinists, but he clearly was hard line on the question of parental responsibility for timely baptism. (Sister and brother were born only seven and a half months apart, which could explain something.)

On the coast to the north of Ayr, capital of its parish and shire, lies the port of Greenock, and farther north still is the mouth of the River Clyde. For some years in the nineteenth century Ayr was western Scotland's principal port (an important cargo was coal exported to Ireland), a manufacturing center (chiefly soap and tanned leather), the site of a healthy salmon fishery, and a town well known for its academy, fine horses, and tony horse races every fall. Later in the nineteenth century the Clyde became the center of Scotland's (and the world's) iron shipbuilding industry. Not surprisingly, the entire region was awash then with fishermen, merchant sailors, and shipbuilders.

According to Groome's *Ordnance Gazetteer of Scotland*, Ayr commanded a "brilliant and exquisite view" over "the Firth of Clyde, to Ailsa Craig, the Alps of Arran, the Cumbrae Isles, the Hills of Bute, the Mountains of Argyll, and the hanging plains of Cunninghame," place names that sound like the topography of J. R. R. Tolkien's fantastic Middle Earth.

By the early 1830s Ayr's population was just over 7,600. The town's better parts, clustered around the new municipal buildings beneath the great stone

FIG. 8

The Hunter family memorial tablet in the churchyard of the Auld Kirk in Ayr. Photograph by Carol Young, 2010. The family's memorial lies between the north wing of the Auld Kirk and the River Ayr, among the eight hundred or so other old stone markers that surround the church. Much of the original inscription on the tablet, a listing of the dates of birth and death of the ten Hunters of these two generations, has been lost to weather. Some of family Hunter, perhaps all but John, are buried near the stone. The last date on it, December 1886, marks the death of his youngest sister, Agnes. She was twenty-five when John drowned off Boulogne and seventy-nine when she died. The Auld Kirk dates to 1658 and is well known in Scottish history, in part because the national poet, Robert Burns, was baptized there.
COURTESY TOWNEND CAMERA CLUB, DREGHORN, SCOTLAND.

spire rising above Wellington Square, were handsome in their own right, but the place boasted other attractions, too. Its history stretched back to Roman times, and just enough of the intervening centuries remained in place to move the author of Pigot's 1837 directory to prose that was over the top even by the nineteenth century's lofty standards. "Ayr still retains some lineaments of antiquated grandeur," he wrote proudly, "on which the lover of ancient lore may dilate with exquisite sensation," vocabulary that might have alarmed some. Development accelerated after 1840 with the opening of a rail connection to Glasgow.

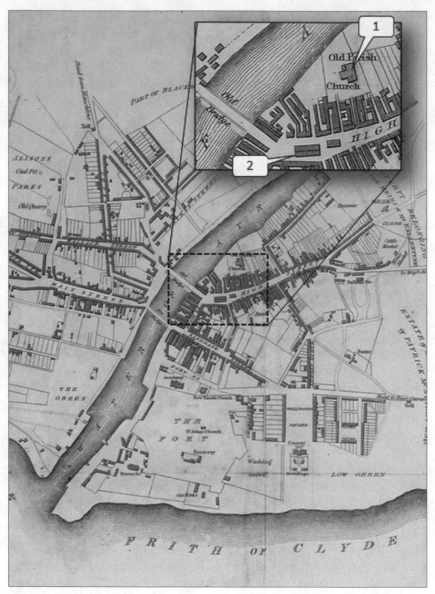

MAP 1

A Ground Plan and Various Views of the Town of Ayr. From *Ayrshire: Containing Map of the County*, William McCarter 1832. Downtown Ayr, Captain John Hunter's home town of 7,600, as it was in the early 1830s. The numbered sites in the map inset are (1) the Auld Kirk and (2) the High Street neighborhood of the Hunters' home and ironmongery.

Hunters were thick on the ground in Ayrshire early in the century. McCarter's 1830 business directory of the town, its first, lists nineteen Hunters in the index. In that directory Hunter's widowed mother, Janet Donaldson, appears as an "ironmonger," a hardware merchant with her home and shop at 68 High Street, near the head of the street and just a short walk from the Auld Brig (bridge) across the river. Boots Opticians today.

When Janet's husband, John Hunter Sr., died in May 1815 at fifty-seven, he left to her shop goods, household furnishings, and other stuff appraised at £893 18s. 11 1/2d., a substantial inheritance. The legal proceedings that followed the widow Hunter's death in May 1851, at eighty-one, appraised her estate at £297 16s. 4d., which included household furniture, the shop stock of the ironmongery, and fully £90 on deposit in the Union Bank of Scotland.[35] Her savings hint that hers was not life on the edge. In an era when women's employment was usually confined to underpaid household service or child care, Janet's bold decision to play the merchant in direct competition with four male ironmongers on the same street seems to have been a successful one.

Janet Hunter's will, written in February 1834 and almost certainly prompted by the recent death of her last living son, suggests that she was married and widowed twice, the first time to an Ayr ship master named Thomas Reid with whom she had a daughter, Christian. Her second marriage, in 1789 to the merchant John Hunter, was much more fecund. Beginning with the birth of their first son in March 1792, the Hunters had seven more children in the next fifteen years, three other boys and four girls. Their sons all died young, the first John Jr. and James before their first birthdays, and William when he was eleven. The Hunter daughters were much more durable. Elizabeth, Thomasina Grace, and Agnes (the youngest) lived into their seventies. Janet, born in 1795 and named after her mother, was eighty-three when she died.

The second John Hunter Jr., later Captain Hunter, shared the house with his mother and four sisters after his father died until he went to sea. Seafaring was not a family business (unless Janet's first husband counts as family), but it was an obvious choice for any young man of Ayr. If Joseph Lachlan knew the truth and wrote it to *The Times*, Hunter first sailed out of Ayr as the master of a ship in the mid-1820s, in his own mid-twenties. The weekly *Ayr Observer* described Hunter posthumously in 1833 as "a regularly bred sailor" and continued the sketch in what passed for an obituary: "For several years he commanded a vessel out of this port, and since he left Ayr, he has sailed as first mate of several vessels trading to India, and in his last voyage was in that capacity to Botany Bay with male convicts. He was an open, generous-hearted man, and much respected, and deeply regretted by his friends." He died a bachelor. (Confusingly, another Captain John Hunter, this one a married sailor from Greenock, also died at sea in August 1833.)

Two convicts on board *Amphitrite* were tried in the Ayr Court of Justiciary on the same day in April, Agnes McMillan (or McGinnis) and Agnes McKissock. Their trials' venue hints that Hunter might have recognized the women or known of them as they came on board his ship for transportation, but that's unlikely. Neither one was a native Scot; both were Irish and Catholic. McMillan was from Bangor, Ireland, and lived not in Ayrshire but in the next county south, in Wigtownshire, where known as "Supple Nancy" she was a notorious thief. McKissock had no fixed address in 1833 when she was convicted of stealing from Peter O'Hara. She was lodging on Isle Lane in Ayr at the time, having moved into the town from Kilmarnock, elsewhere in the county, after a conviction the year before for "aggravated robbery."

18

Surgeon-Superintendent Forrester's professional life left a denser paper trail than has Hunter's because Forrester was a naval officer and subject to Royal Navy record keeping, from which merchant seamen were free. Less, however, is known of Forrester the man, and nothing is known of his wife, not even her first name. So perfect is this lack of family information about the Forresters that one of *Amphitrite*'s first scholars, Eleanor Finlay, has mused that perhaps the two were not married, which would account for the lack of a marriage certificate filed in the obvious places but not for the absence of other documents.

During the nineteenth century there were ten medical colleges at a like number of British universities, five in England, four in Scotland, and one in Ireland. A graduate of one of these schools would have sought licensure as a physician, not a surgeon, and spent his time in the higher status and more lucrative business of examining patients, diagnosing disease, and prescribing medications. In early Victorian times this would have been done during the course of parlor conversations with all interlocutors fully clothed, and nothing more overtly medical happening than, perhaps, a diagnostic glance into a chamber pot. A surgeon, in contrast to a physician, worked with tools in hand and ended the day splattered with blood—or worse. In time surgeons' status would rise above that of physicians', but that promotion was not to come until after the inauguration of sterile operating theaters and the routine use of anesthesia, both decades in the future.

There is no record that Forrester attended any university. (In that he was a Scot, the medical schools at the universities of Edinburgh, Aberdeen, Glasgow, and St. Andrews were the most probable candidates.) More likely Forrester completed a surgeon's apprenticeship somewhere, several years of hands-on training under the tutelage of a licensed surgeon.

On October 15, 1813, Forrester passed the professional examination of the English Royal College of Surgeons, one of the nearly two dozen licensing bodies certifying health-care practitioners and competing for members and influence. After a few preliminary administrative questions, an examiner would have quizzed Forrester about anatomy, physiology, surgical practice, and patient care according to the standards of the day. This brief oral exam constituted the entire licensing requirement. Exam completed and the necessary fee paid, Forrester became qualified to serve as a surgeon in Royal Navy ships of the first through sixth rates, meaning any man of war carrying more than one hundred guns or as few as thirty-two.

Consequently, 1813 was an important year in Forrester's life. That's when, joining more than eight hundred other surgeons in the Royal Navy, he gained admission to what must have appeared to be a solid future of lifetime professional employment. The next month, November, Forrester went to sea for the first time, as assistant surgeon in the frigate HMS *Bedford*. (Probably as her second or even third assistant surgeon. A 74-gun, third-rate ship would ordinarily have carried a surgeon and as many as three assistants in wartime.)

With his warrant as an assistant surgeon in hand, Forrester's first responsibility would have been to proceed promptly to join his ship with a complete kit of required instruments available for an inspection of their quantity, quality, and condition. Although the navy provided "Medicines, Utensils, and Necessaries" for a practice afloat, Royal Navy surgeons, in common with their counterparts ashore, were expected to own the tools of their trade, altogether seventy-nine different items for a surgeon and only thirty-three for an assistant.

Among those required tools were the amputating knives and saws, the scalpels, razors and bone nippers, and the tourniquets and bandages that hint how bloody the business of being a navy surgeon could be, but surgeons were expected to tend the sick as well as the wounded and injured. Reports to the fleet's physician required statistics to be collected not only on the number of victims of combat and accident (in one category) but also on those suffering from any of twelve different diseases, among them "intermittent fever" (malaria), typhus, pneumonia, dysentery, scurvy, and venereal disease. Upon sailing, every one of His Majesty's ships carried a two-year supply of seventy three different medicines, everything from *Acaciae gummi* (gum acacia) to *Zingiberis Rad. Pulv.* (dried ginger extract), specifics thought to cure or treat these twelve and other diseases.

The year 1813 was important in the history of Europe, also. The year before Napoleon Bonaparte's Grande Armée, a juggernaut until then, had been destroyed in Russia. Some 600,000 men and 200,000 horses (and tens of thousands of camp followers, including women and even children; Stephen Talty called the armed assembly "a portable metropolis") crossed into Russia beginning at the end of June 1812. Their objective was defeat of Russian armies and subjugation of the tsar, but it's possible that even as Napoleon crossed the Nieman River from Poland with his private entourage of three hundred coaches, the emperor of the French was looking beyond that, all the way to India.[36] The proud parade ended far short of the Ganges, and if the Grand Armée marched toward Moscow in the summer of 1812, it can only be described as hobbling back that winter in one of history's most wretched retreats. By the time the campaign's survivors returned to the east bank of the Nieman, more than three hundred thousand of its men were dead from diseases, exposure, and combat. Another two hundred thousand had deserted or been captured. Almost a million dead in the campaign if one added the Russian lives lost to the French total.[37]

Reversing his record of the dozen years immediately after he was chased out of Egypt, excepting a few bright months in 1814, Napoleon did almost everything important wrong after 1811 until he died ten years later: He alienated his key subjects, abused his allies, provoked his enemies, lost in the field, and even failed (in April 1814) two attempts at suicide.[38] Napoleon's first humiliation, kingship over tiny Elba's 12,000 citizens, ended in spring 1815 when he came ashore on the Continent near Cannes and promptly raised another army. In early summer this army met one under the command of the victor of the Iberian campaign, Field Marshall Arthur Wellesley, in Holland and lost. The defeat at Waterloo (now in Belgium) on June 18, 1815, triggered his final humiliation.

The contribution of the Royal Navy to victory in this world war was wonderfully, if coincidently, symbolized by Napoleon's final surrender a month later, not to any of the many generals who had fought against him in the field but to a navy officer instead, Captain Frederick Maitland, RN, commanding officer of HMS *Bellerophon*. (One Napoleon biographer, Frank McLynn, says that in Maitland's enthusiasm to be the one to deliver the great ogre to England, he deliberately deceived a remarkably trusting Napoleon about British intentions.) In August, after an idle month in *Bellerophon* during which his future was finally decided, the former emperor and his small court were packed on board HMS *Northumberland* and transported to St. Helena Island, exile, and his death.

The long war now really over, realists in London moved quickly to shrink the Royal Navy to something England could afford. Many of the fleet's storied warships were unsentimentally stricken from the navy list. HMS *Bellerophon*, one of the frigates at Trafalgar and Napoleon's temporary home cum prison afloat, became—disarmed and dismasted—the hulk for convict boys. The sharp reduction in the size of the fleet prompted a proportional shrinkage in the number of navy officers on active duty. Even so, Forrester did manage to wrangle other assignments and a promotion. On September 11, 1820, he was promoted to surgeon, and several days later Forrester joined the Bermuda-built sloop HMS *Morgiana*, almost four hundred tons and eighteen guns, then operating off Sierra Leone on antislavery patrol.

Royal Navy surgeons practiced their trade at sea generally under the remote supervision of physicians of the fleet, senior medical men charged with the oversight of health-care services at sea and in naval hospitals ashore at foreign stations. From their vantage point on board hospital ships or fleet flagships, physicians of His (or Her) Majesty's fleet were more administrators than practitioners. For the most part the care of the wounded, injured, and sick in the Royal Navy at sea was the business not of physicians but of ships' surgeons and their assistants.

The usual image of a nineteenth-century Royal Navy ship's surgeon has him standing in a smoky, lantern-lit charnel house in the forward part of his ship, literally amid buckets of blood and piles of hewn limbs, but the 1825 edition of "Instructions for the Surgeons of His Majesty's Fleet" suggests a very different kind of practice. A peacetime practice in which he was charged to ensure that assigned nurses drawn from the ship's company were "not negligent or wanting in Tenderness, in the Performance of their Duty" and "to give the most positive Directions, that the Nurses and Attendants offer, and gently press [Medicines and proper Drink] upon the Patients every hour or oftener . . . although the Patients may not ask for it."

"As he has the charge of the Lives of so many Persons," paragraph 11 of the postwar instructions read,

who from crowded Accommodations, the Nature of their Diet, the Variation of the Weather and Climate, and numerous other circumstances, are liable to infectious Fevers, as well as Scurvy and Chronic Complaints, and also to accidents from Wounds, or Hurts, &c. incident to the Mode of Life, the guarding against and counteracting of which Evils, will depend very materially on his own Resources and Promptitude, in applying the most speedy Remedies, according to circumstances; and as Sickness (which in the most favorable situation on Shore, in some degree depresses the Spirits) will much more affect his Patients on board Ships of War, who labour under so many Inconveniences which cannot be remedied—under all these circumstances, it will become his Duty to soothe and cheer their Minds by the most humane Attention and every expression of conciliatory Kindness—to hear with Patience all their Complaints, and redress all real Grievances—which will naturally inspire them with Confidence, exhilarate their Spirits, and add to their Hope of Recovery.

Just ten years after the defeat of Napoleon, Royal Navy surgeons were being enjoined by the Admiralty to exhibit a standard of sympathetic care that would be uncommon a century later.

During the last decade of his life Forrester served in three more Royal Navy ships (the sloop HMS *Alacrity* and two 74-gun third rates, HMS *Ramillies* and HMS *Talavera*), and in three convict ships (*Brothers, Southworth,* and *Amphitrite*).

On November 8, 1823, while serving in *Alacrity*, Forrester was tried by court-martial on two charges of improper conduct. The charges reveal either a becoming humanity in a medical man or a disturbing lack of discipline on the part of an officer who, it was alleged, had given Thomas Williams, a marine, a bottle of wine to drink just before he was flogged ("in consequence of which he appeared in a state of stupor and intoxication"), and then compounded the offense by shaking hands with the anesthetized and bloody Williams after he was cut from the grate following punishment.[39] Forrester was acquitted for lack of evidence, an unusual outcome that raises questions about the charges. Only a handful of the nearly 2,700 Royal Navy courts-martial held between January 1812 and December 1855 ended in acquittal with charges not proved.

Forrester's assignment to *Alacrity* had a second distinguishing moment two months later. In January 1824 the sloop was in the eastern Mediterranean. Lord Byron, the romantic poet, was there, too, camped in swampy Missolonghi, Greece, in his quixotic campaign supporting the Greek independence movement. On January 23 *Alacrity*'s captain and Forrester called on the famous man, an extended visit recorded in two lengthy letters by Forrester describing the poet and his boggy quarters at the mouth of the Gulf of Lepanto. Before the month was out Byron was showing symptoms of malaria, perhaps diagnosed in passing by Forrester, who had commented on his lordship's trembling hands.[40] In mid-May, while *Alacrity* was at Malta, Forrester learned that Byron had died the previous month.

Approaching five years later, in September 1828, Forrester's lackluster career was derailed by "a paralytic affliction of the left side," perhaps Bell's Palsy. A short while later he claimed restored health, and asked for but was denied assignment to HMS *Alligator* in the Mediterranean. When not at sea, Forrester was ashore on half-pay, anxiously awaiting assignment, the usual career pattern for most naval officers after the Napoleonic Wars.[41] Half pay meant six shillings per day, or seventy-two pence, in a time when a loaf of bread cost ten pence and a copy of *The Times* seven. Discomforted and embarrassed by the necessity to live on the cheap, many army and navy officers on half pay became expatriates, living on the Continent in austerity, out of sight of others more fortunate than they or with more influential friends. Forrester's mysterious palsy triggered a period of idleness, broken first by the warrant to *Southworth*, and then the next year to *Amphitrite*.

Later, as some of Forrester's charges were milling about on *Amphitrite*'s deck, it would have appeared to the modern eye that the ship was carrying not a cargo of harlots but a contingent of munchkins: girls (some prisoners barely in their teens) and small women, many not more than five feet tall, and some elfin children, all marked by the tight, translucent parchment skin that signified poor health, scant nutrition, and chronic fatigue.

19

Amphitrite was also small. From the very first, most convict transport vessels were barely chips of wood by today's standards and nothing so grand as contemporary Royal Navy first rates, or the handsome armed East Indiamen that sailed between Europe and Asia carrying the treasure of two continents. The six transports, three supply vessels, and two men of war of the First Fleet— the convoy that in January 1788 carried the civil servants, military units, and roughly one thousand male and female convicts who established the colony that became Australia—averaged not much more than 100 feet long and 30 feet abeam, not so long as but a little wider than three city busses end-to-end or side-by-side. Each ship loaded probably drew less than 16 feet of water, equivalent in height to a bus with a sliver of another stacked on top.

Even after she was lengthened in 1824 *Amphitrite* was less substantial than any of them, smaller, in fact, than all but one of the convict vessels that followed the First Fleet to Port Jackson and all that would follow her in the years to come: 92 feet long overall, 23 feet abeam, and 14 feet below the waterline.[42] The key dimension was not, however, length, beam, or draft but "burden," expressed in tons but really a calculated measure of the ship's below deck volume. The concept was simple but complex in practice because at any one time there were several ways to calculate tonnage, none of which encompassed the advanced mathematics required to compute accurately the volume of such a complex three dimensional shape as a ship's hull. What emerged from all of the simple formulas was a number that could be used only to compare one ship to another but in fact was used for much else besides; ships were designed, contracted and paid for, manned and loaded, and charged fees and leased on the basis of their notional register tonnage. Expressed in words, the most commonly used formula required three steps: first, the length of the keel was multiplied by the breadth of the beam; next, that product was divided by one-half the breadth of beam; and, finally, the resulting quotient was divided by a constant, ninety-four, to yield the answer.

Once *Amphitrite* had been even smaller. She was English-built, in Bideford, North Devon, near where the Torridge and Taw Rivers meet at a swirling sandbar just below the Bristol Channel at 51 degrees north latitude. Only tiny, stony Lundy Island protects the towns of Appledore and Bideford, upriver, from Atlantic surf and Canadian winds running across an unobstructed 1,800-mile fetch from Newfoundland to Bideford Bay. Because of the danger of being blown or pushed onto a lee (downwind) shore, the entire coast from the bay's southern jaw down to Land's End in Cornwall was famous as a ship trap in the nineteenth century. The rugged conditions along the Cornish coast and the Bristol Channel produced durable ships and doughty seamen, and a nasty reputation, too, for some of the villages that clung precariously to dry land. Among their denizens were many believed to be ship wreckers, cruel men who lured vessels in extremis ashore, there to strip the wrecks of cargo, furniture, and fittings, and the beached bodies of their valuables.

Amphitrite came off the building ways at Bideford sometime in late 1801, a time frame suggested by the first survey of the ship, by Laurence Pridham, done in connection with her registration in that port on March 3, 1802. The ship's building yard is unknown, but there are only three candidates. Shipyards in operation at Bideford that year were William Clibbett's, Edward Jenkins', and Richard Chapman's. The first two, the Hubbastone and Lower Cleave Yards, closed in 1804 and 1805, respectively, so if *Amphitrite* came from one or the other, she was one of the last vessels built there. The third yard, Chapman's Higher Cleave, continued building ships until 1814. Her first registration document lists nine partners in ownership. Among the nine were three Hoggs, including *Amphitrite*'s first master, Robert Morgan Hogg, of Appledore. In time, *Amphitrite* would be owned by a half-dozen or so groups and individuals and registered in several English and Scottish ports.

Pridham's survey reported the bare essentials. As built, *Amphitrite* was 75 feet 10 inches long, 22 feet 10 inches in beam, and drew 14 feet. Her "tonnage" (a measure of interior volume as described earlier), calculated by the formula then in use, was 158. She had a single deck, two masts, and was rigged as a snow, meaning she mounted a small, vertical spar on the after side of the main mast and could carry a gaff-rigged fore and aft "spanker" sail.

In the eighteenth and nineteenth centuries "Amphitrite" was a popular name for a ship. Amphitrite, the consort of the Greek's sea god, Poseidon, and the mother of Triton, evoked just the right images for something as important during those centuries as the name of a ship. The reference was at once classical, nautical, and feminine, a learned allusion to the queen of the sea and a nice charm to carry during times when a long sea voyage still defied the odds.

The name "Amphitrite" might have held an honored place in U.S. Navy history, too, if events in 1777 had worked out differently. That May the

Continental Congress ordered Captain John Paul Jones to sail in the French armed transport *L'Amphitrite* from South Carolina to France, taking command in mid-Atlantic from her French master when opportunities arose to capture British prizes. Only the refusal of her captain to share command stymied this irregular scheme. *L'Amphitrite* was a substantial vessel—480 tons, 24 guns, a crew of 160—and had Jones been in command and had a little luck at sea, who knows what damage he might have caused. In 1833, *Lloyd's List*, the society's shipping newspaper, showed six merchant vessels with the same name, John Hunter's and five others. Popular not just for merchant vessels. The Royal Navy has had seven ships named *Amphitrite*: the first a sixth rate of 24 guns lost in 1794; the last a four-stack, protected cruiser launched in 1898 that fought in World War I. In between were clustered a miscellany of fifth and sixth rates of no particular distinction.

And popular with republicans as well as with royalists; the United States Navy commissioned three ships with that name. The first USS *Amphitrite*, a wood-hulled ironclad designed by John Ericsson, fought in the Civil War. Seduced after USS *Monitor* met CSS *Virginia* in Hampton Roads by the idea that turreted, armored warships were the combatant ship of the future, in the 1870s the U.S. Navy started construction of a post–Civil War class of these low-freeboard gun platforms. The new monitors finally went to sea almost twenty years later as coastal defense ships, in essence, floating forts. The second USS *Amphitrite*, lead ship of her class, was a miserable product, insufferably hot below decks, dangerous in any sea, and short-legged to boot.[43] An evolutionary dead end despite her apparently imposing four 10-inch diameter rifled guns, this *Amphitrite* spent her last thirty years off the navy list and disarmed, afloat ignominiously as a hotel. The last USS *Amphitrite* was a repair ship that appeared briefly in the Pacific during World War II.[44]

Off the ways and in the water, with her carvel-built (smooth-sided, planked) hull prudently sheathed in antifouling copper sheets, Captain Hogg's *Amphitrite* was representative of the state of the art in marine architecture, materials science, and construction practices of her time. A more impressive exemplar would have been one of the proud East Indiamen that plied regularly between England and India, or a 110-gun first rate, but when she was launched the little unarmed, two-masted vessel reflected good contemporary shipbuilding practice, the high technology industry of the age.

Amphitrite's thirty years afloat spanned the golden age of fighting sail and the introduction of steam propulsion at sea. Not until near the end of *Amphitrite*'s life did any ship on salt water promise more capability than a well-built sailing vessel manned by an experienced crew. When she broke apart on the sands at Boulogne, *Amphitrite* unwittingly represented the approaching and inevitable end of an era.

FIG. 9

Model of a snow-rigged merchantman. As built in 1802, *Amphitrite* would have resembled this small snow, running before a light wind with all possible sails aloft. In 1824 she was lengthened and rerigged as a three-masted bark. This model's hull form, proportions, sail plan, boats, and deck furniture suggest *Amphitrite* before these changes, and before the addition of a poop just before she sailed. The model, in the collection of the National Maritime Museum, Greenwich, England, was built circa 1840. Its sails were added in 1963.

© 2010 NATIONAL MARITIME MUSEUM, GREENWICH, LONDON, SLR 0142.

The first true steam-propelled crossing of the Atlantic, eastbound by Quebec-built *Royal William* in the same year *Amphitrite* was lost, had been anticipated in 1819, when the paddle-wheel steamer *Savannah* crossed the Atlantic from Savannah, Georgia, to Liverpool, England, with a four-day assist from her boiler during a thirty-day passage. In 1840 the British government contract for a new subsidized bimonthly mail service between England and the Caribbean and South America prescribed steam propulsion. But not until six years later, during a two-part competition (prompted by the brilliant engineer, Isambard Kingdom Brunel) that pitted the screw sloop of war HMS *Rattler* against the paddle sloop HMS *Alecto*, did the precise shape of the future became certain: steam propulsion through propellers, not paddle wheels. In 1846, in a contest that might have been rigged, *Rattler* handily beat *Alecto* over thirty-four-, sixty-, and eighty-mile courses. When the two were tied stern to stern and powered up, she towed *Alecto* backward at two knots.

It is possible to extract the outline of a nineteenth-century ship's biography from port registers and customs and excise shipping records. From these sources *Amphitrite*'s registration can be traced from Bideford in 1802, to Glasgow in 1815, and then to London in 1824, and her ownership from the Hogg group, through Liddle and Company of Greenock and Lyall and Company of London, to William Pearson in 1832, and finally to John Hunter in 1833, where everything ends. After her launch and over the course of the next twenty-five years and in the service of these owners, *Amphitrite* sailed the coast of the British Isles and between the British Isles and the Caribbean Sea and Baltic Sea.[45] A few years later, as a "hired transport" under contract to the Transport Board, *Amphitrite* went into even more distant waters.

In 1824 Liddle had *Amphitrite* stretched to 92 feet 10 inches, resulting in an increase in tonnage by a third, to 209 tons (208 and 73/94ths, more precisely), and rerigged into a three-masted bark carrying square sails on her fore and main masts and fore and aft sails on the mizzen mast. Early-nineteenth-century ship designs were driven by several rules of thumb, derived in the first instance by the size of sailors and by the strength of wood in tension and compression, and once enlarged *Amphitrite* continued generally to comply with these fundamental ratios: her beam roughly one-quarter of her length, and her draft roughly one-half of her beam.

The 1824 rebuilding was a major piece of work, possibly done in connection with a sale to George Lyall in that same year. *Amphitrite* emerged from it 17 feet longer but still not especially pretty. With a standing bowsprit, square stern, no galleries, no figurehead, and a flush deck, she would have appeared dowdy and utilitarian. Even stretched, which made her original matronly lines appear a little sleeker, there was nothing about *Amphitrite* that evoked the romance of the sea. Nothing alike (and not one-half as long as) the elegant warships off Holland that Turner painted, but more substantial than the hoys in his picture. In this enlarged configuration, and boasting an expanded suit of sails, the coaster's conversion to a true blue water vessel was complete, and she became eligible for government charter.

The average tonnage of convict transports chartered in 1833 was 418, which meant that even after this work *Amphitrite* was still less than half scale compared to most ships sailing to Australia that year.[46] There was no doubt about her being undersized. On June 11 the Admiralty solicited tenders for a three-hundred-ton vessel for this contract. The fact that the contract was then awarded to one of only two hundred tons raised questions later. (The downsizing might have reflected that only 100 or so female convicts were ready for transportation. A three-hundred-ton vessel could have accommodated 150, at a higher lease rate.)

The decisions in 1824 to stretch *Amphitrite* and to offer her for government charter service were good ones. Two years after Lyall bought her, *Amphitrite* appears in the record as a government transport in London for the first time, now styled "His Majesty's Hired Transport *Amphitrite*." Admiralty charters sent *Amphitrite* to Bombay and back, loaded with British army soldiers, and on a round trip to Portugal to repatriate released prisoners of war from the campaign in Iberia.

Lloyd's surveys of her in 1802 (at launch), 1812 and 1830, and her inspections at the Royal Dockyard in Deptford in connection with government charters, all seem to have been unexceptional. Through most of her years *Amphitrite* was listed by Lloyd's as having an "E1" classification, the second of Lloyd's four survey classes. Class A1 was supposedly reserved for the best British-built vessels in their first years of service, for example, *Amphitrite* when new was a "first class vessel built of first class materials."

In fact Class A1, as Parliament learned some thirty years after *Amphitrite* was launched, reflected not much more than where a ship was built and her age.[47] Initially a vessel built on the Thames held on to an A class rating for twelve years, while those built in Bristol were A class for eleven, in the northern ports for ten, and in the out-ports for six to eight, or even as few as four years.

What had begun in the early eighteenth century as an effort to evaluate seaworthiness and so to establish a rational basis for charter rates was quickly gamed by ship builders. "All new vessels, however slightly constructed," an 1836 House of Commons committee report lamented, "were entitled to be registered in the First Class for a given number of years, ranging from six to twelve, after which, the strongest ships were placed on a level with the weakest, being excluded from the First Class when the prescribed period of years had expired: the tendency of this system of classification being to induce shipbuilders to build their ships in the cheapest manner and with the least degree of strength that was sufficient to sustain the vessels through the shortest period named . . . after which period their value would be greatly reduced by their exclusion from the First Class."

After Class E1 came Class I1. It identified those ships suitable for the carriage of cargo that would not be damaged if it got wet. Class O1 warned shippers and seamen that the vessel was suitable for coastwise sailing only, not for overseas voyages. As a registered E1 vessel *Amphitrite* was judged to have no defects and to be capable of carrying cargo safely and dry in transoceanic commerce.

On August 17, 1833, John Hunter had *Amphitrite* registered in the port of London, number 251 on that port's registry. When she sailed for New South Wales a week later, *Amphitrite* was over thirty years old. Her age did not make her exceptional; the service life of carefully maintained wooden ships could easily extend to three, four, or even more decades. Nelson's fleet in 1805 at the

Battle of Trafalgar, a mix of British and captured French-built warships, averaged seventeen years of age, but several were much older. HMS *Britannia* had been launched in 1762, and his flagship, HMS *Victory*, had been launched in 1765, forty years before challenging and defeating the continental allies in the decisive sea battle of the Napoleonic Wars.

The generally high quality of charter ship inspections at Deptford is borne out by the superb safety record of convict transports over eighty years. Whether *Amphitrite* had been put through a sufficiently rigorous inspection was the question in the days immediately after her loss. The answer would prove to be inconclusive, but there is no question that the Deptford imprimatur usually signaled a sound ship. In the year that *Amphitrite* sailed, Granville Mawer wrote in *Most Perfectly Safe* (1997), "convict passage to Australia was arguably better managed and unarguably safer than any other trans-oceanic passenger voyage."[48]

Lachlan said nothing about *Amphitrite* when he wrote to *The Times* in early September to establish Captain Hunter's bona fides posthumously, but he could have. Demonstrably—by her long service—sound from the beginning and apparently well maintained during many years at sea, there was no obvious reason why *Amphitrite*'s crew could not have challenged open water with confidence. A confidence bolstered by the knowledge that no chartered convict transport had been lost in the half-century since the first felons were shipped to Botany Bay. Leaving Woolwich for a night on the river at anchor in Margate Roads, Hunter and Forrester would have anticipated arriving in Port Jackson just before Christmas, at nearly the same time as summer came to the antipodes.

THE WIND DID ROAR, THE SEAS DID RUN, THE VESSEL SPLIT IN TWO,

And floating on the watery main, Were passengers and crew;

The Captain, Surgeon, and his wife, All perished in the sea,

Out of one hundred and thirty-six, Were saved only but three.

CHAPTER 4

The Convicts

20

Convict transports usually sailed for New South Wales and Van Diemen's Land with a detachment of guards on board. These men, an officer and thirty to fifty "other ranks" from regular army regiments posted to the colony or on their way to India, were on the ship to give the master the disciplined muscle (and firepower) he might need to control the convicts and to deter or defeat mutiny should one suddenly flare out of the locked compartment between decks to threaten the ship. As the published REGULATIONS *to be observed by Detachments of Troops embarked on board* CONVICT SHIPS made clear, theirs was a serious business.[1] "There is no Duty which can occur to a Regimental Officer, (whatever his rank)," the Regulations intoned soberly, "in which unceasing Vigilance is more required, than that connected with the command of a *Convict-Guard.* . . . Any laxity of discipline or deficiency in the exercise of proper Vigilance and Caution might be attended with most serious consequence, and entail disgrace on the Officers and Soldiers, and also on the Regiment to which they belong, by whose remissness and neglect such consequences may have arisen."

Having first summoned the mortifying specter of personal and professional disgrace to concentrate the reader's attention, twenty-seven numbered regulations followed. These prescribed the guard detachment's organization and its daily routine and outlined ship security procedures. One-third of the detachment was to be on duty with firearms at hand around the clock, atop the poop in daylight and on the quarterdeck at night. No watch-stander was to speak to any convict. One sentry, armed with a pistol and a cutlass, was stationed day and night at the windward gangway. Two others similarly equipped were posted beside the poop in daylight but down the hatchways at night (from where they were "to report any sounds they may hear, which appear to proceed from sawing planks, filing iron, or from any other cause of a suspicious nature"). Every half-hour the three were to report, "All is well." Every hour they were relieved.

The tactics to suppress a convict uprising at night differed from one in daylight, but the goals were the same: to control the high ground at the ship's stern and to block convict access to her helm, to weapons, and to officers' quarters—all separated from the open deck amidships by a stout defensive barricade penetrated by firing ports (the "barricado," a structure borrowed from slave ship practice). At night, this was to be done by flooding the hatchways with armed soldiers and sailors, thus avoiding a nightmarish hand-to-hand melee aft that could let a horde of convicts reach the main deck and overwhelm guards unable to bring firepower to bear:

> In case of Alarm during the Night, the Guard on Duty is to immediately occupy the Hatchways, and if necessary, employ their Arms to repel any attempt by the Convicts to gain the Deck. The Soldiers of the next Relief are to hasten to the Barricado, and to occupy each Gangway. The remaining Watch is to proceed to the Poop and act as a Reserve. The Sailors, armed with Cutlasses, are to proceed to the Hatchways, or assist in defending the Barricado and Quarter-Deck. If necessary, men on the Quarter-Deck are to retire into the Cuddy, and fire through the windows; the Reserve is then to fire from the Poop.

In daylight, when friend could be distinguished from foe at a distance and musket fire was more effective, the defense collapsed immediately to behind the barricade, where it was to be reinforced by men from the next watch, while the reserve mustered on the poop.

Soldiers must have loathed guard detachment duty at sea. It coupled the usual miserable conditions prescribed for deploying army units—close, damp shipboard quarters and scant rations, foul water and motion sickness, and enervating boredom, conditions almost indistinguishable from those experienced by convicts—to around-the-clock supervision of potentially dangerous young men very much like them.

But no guard detachment was assigned to *Amphitrite*, indeed, none had been assigned to any female convict transport in nearly four decades, not since the summer of 1797, when *Lady Shore*'s embarked guard detail hijacked its own ship. In what was the worst disciplinary problem on board a female convict transport (and the only successful mutiny on any transport), her New South Wales Corps guard detachment—a mixed bag of native felons, former foreign prisoners of war, and assorted other villains chased into British army uniform by the threat of something worse, and under the command of a very junior officer—seized *Lady Shore* approaching Brazil. After murdering Captain Willcocks and his first mate and later setting some two dozen loyal crew members adrift, the army mutineers took the ship up the Platt River into Montevideo, apparently ignorant of the fact that England and Spain had been at war for the past year. In Montevideo the sixty-seven convict women on board "were distributed as servants among the Spanish ladies," upon whom the convicts' seductive powers would presumably have no great effect.[2] What happened to the mutineers isn't clear, but it's unlikely to have been pleasant.

The *Lady Shore*'s experience duly absorbed, the transportation board decided that a shipload of women was less of a threat to vessels under charter than was an accompanying small, armed band of bored and horny men. The board accordingly eliminated such detachments. That conclusion—correct as it turned out—freed up space below deck for the carriage of additional female convicts that an army detachment would have otherwise filled, thus improving the economics of the passage. Reducing the number of young men in heat sailing for months in a ship full of young women, moreover, eased the sexual tensions that inevitably complicated the preservation of discipline on every female transport. Oddly, the requirement for a poop, irrelevant in the absence of a guard detachment, remained intact.

A lurid broadsheet circulating in Edinburgh in 1830 gave "an ACCOUNT of the Dreadful MUTINY that toon [took] place on board the Convick Transport Hope having on board 291 Female convicts many of whom belonged to Edinburgh, Leith Glasgow, &c" out of Deptford on March 20, for Swan River under the command of Captain James Murray. The story, quoting James Maitland, identified as a *Hope* crewmember from Leith, was that one month underway and a thousand miles from Gibraltar the transport's women mutinied and murdered seventeen of the crew (among them the captain, drunk at the time), at the price of thirty-nine of their own killed or wounded. The mutineers then put the rest of the crew in irons in the hold. "The rush now was for the spirit room," reported the narrator, "and after procuring a quantity of the beverage, [the convicts] began to Song, dance and use all the extravagance of victors wholly relieved from bondage. . . . The Ship was allowed to drift unheeded in the wild deep without even a sailor on deck." Nine days later, that initial alcohol-soaked celebration long over and the ship again under sail, *Hope* was deliberately run aground at "Barbaty" (Barbate, on the Spanish Atlantic Coast), where the mutineers scattered inland and from where the surviving members of the crew eventually left for London in the brig *Galadon*.[3]

Maitland's account of hundreds of criminal Amazons wresting control of his ship from an improbably large crew probably guaranteed the broadsheet was a sidewalk best seller, but convincing details aside, "Mutiny & murder aboard the transport Hope" seems to have been fiction, conjured up to enrich printer McMillan of Lawnmarket. No description of this mutiny appears anywhere else. The first convict transport to Western Australia—Perth and Fremantle are on the Swan River—didn't sail until 1850. Although a transport named *Hope* is mentioned several times in the records, none with that name sailed in 1830. One vessel called *Hope* was wrecked on the Tasman coast in 1837. Another *Hope* sailed between Dublin, Ireland, and Van Diemen's Land five years later with 139 female prisoners, 77 settlers, and 44 children. She arrived without incident (but suffered a few deaths from disease on board) at her destination August 23, 1842. Surely had such a mutiny happened the response would have been the prompt reinstitution of armed guard detachments in female convict transports. That never happened.

2 1

So ineradicable was "indecent and licentious intercourse" between members of the crew and convicts on board *Friendship* in 1817 that her captain's only response was an attempt to restrict such "connexions" to someplace out of his sight. In *Janus* and *Providence* even "see no evil" was an unworkable solution because of the enthusiastic participation of both ships' senior officers in socializing with the women. *Janus'* master, Captain Thomas Mowat, and her first mate, John Hedges, both impregnated convicts during a voyage in 1820. Six years later the scandalous behavior of Surgeon Matthew Burnside of *Providence*—he hosted sex and drinking parties in his cabin—confirmed that right conduct had not yet come to stay the transport fleet.[4]

Offense to morals aside, the fear was that unless controlled, female convicts and crewmembers would trade sex for favors during the long crossing to Australia, an exchange that carried far enough could threaten the discipline essential to safe, successful passages. Perhaps that actually happened. Writing in the remote southern fastness of Launceston, Tasmania, in 1852 and looking back more than half a century, the Reverend John West attributed the uprising and seizure of the *Lady Shore* (he called her *Jane Shore*) to the women and not to their guards. Reverend West knew something about female convicts.

His home town was the site of the Launceston Female Factory, one of several government workhouses for fractious women in Van Diemen's Land. At peak occupancy in the 1840s, the Launceston factory employed or farmed out more than 250 female convicts. He was, however, a leader in the philosophical opposition to transportation.

In West's story the "persuasion of the women accomplished what the male prisoners rarely attempted, and when on this passage to the colony have never been able to effect. The soldiers and sailors, seduced by their caresses, seized the vessel, and having shot the captain and the chief officer, steered into a South American port."[5] But perhaps not. No other historian has attributed the *Lady Shore* mutiny to the wiles of her convicts.

The Admiralty's solution to the problem was an obvious one. It determined to pay sailors, or at least their officers, *not* to have sex with the women. Given that the untoward behavior was happening in a ship at sea, no other incentive for right conduct could be imagined that would operate from afar.

The subject was forthrightly addressed in instructions to the surgeon-superintendent and the ship's master. Article 13 of the surgeon's instructions directed that he was to use his "utmost endeavours" to prevent the prostitution of female convicts with officers, passengers, or crew, "showing a good example himself in this particular, and not failing to report to the Governor any instance of improper intercourse with Women which may be detected." Further, as "an inducement to the Mates of the Ship to support the Surgeon-Superintendent in his exertions to attain this object, a Gratuity of twenty pounds to the Chief Mate and of Fifteen Pounds each to the Second and Third Mates, will be respectively paid to them at the termination of the Voyage, on their producing certificates signed by the Surgeon-Superintendent as to their having conducted themselves to his satisfaction."

The economic pressure on the ship's captain was greater still. Article 7 of his instructions provided that unsatisfactory conduct on his part in this particular (or in any other) sacrificed his eligibility for the usual end-of-voyage master's gratuity of fifty pounds: "No gratuity will be granted to him unless the Governor's Certificate be explicit as to the fact of his being satisfied that all practicable means had been taken to prevent prostitution."

Through the nineteenth century and into the twentieth, female convicts under sentence of transportation were thought likely to be prostitutes, if not full-time professionals then part-timers, supplementing their income from crime by selling themselves. That belief was common as late as 1985, when in *Naufrages et Fortunes de Mer* author Christian Gonsseaume described *Amphitrite* as carrying "118 prostitutes, their 12 children, a crew of 14 men, Captain Hunter, and Dr. Forster [sic] with his wife." By then, however, the rise in universities of an academic specialty in women's studies had already prompted a much more sympathetic scholarly reexamination of the identities of these women, one that gained adherents to the view that female convicts were victims, not just of their bedfellows but also of the social order and its criminal justice system. Some scholars further concluded that given economic reality in the colonies, prostitution represented "a sensible, self-directed choice by the woman concerned," an entrepreneurial business decision, not a moral failing.

In the late 1970s Deirdre Beddoe asked the obvious question at the outset of *Welsh Convict Women: A Study of Women Transported from Wales to Australia, 1778–1852*: "Were women, like men, transported simply because they had committed crimes, or was there a more sinister reason behind the transportation of females?" Beddoe's instant answer: "There is ample reason to confirm that the main reason women were transported was for the sexual gratification of both free and convict males. . . . The decision whether to transport individual women, including first offenders, depended on the colonial balance of population. . . . When [a female convict] reached Australia the role expected of her was clear and consequently her chance of reformation minimal."[6]

Nearly twenty years after Beddoe, Kay Daniels posed the same question in her *Convict Women* (1998). "Why were convict women sent to the new penal colonies?" Daniels asked. "Are the reasons advanced for sending male convicts sufficient to explain the sending of women too? Were they sent because they made up a part of the criminal population and there was as much need to find a new place to send female criminals as there was to send males? Or did the colonial administrators take a broader view, looking beyond exile and punishment and mindful of what was necessary to sustain life and civilised society in a colonial outpost?"[7] The answer, of course, is both. The three, generally similar national criminal justice systems of the British Isles had little capacity for the long-term incarceration of women and no substitute for hanging apart from the solution for men—transportation. From the outset, however, officials in all four principal places (London, Dublin, Edinburgh, and Sydney) saw the penal colony as something more than a prison camp.

Sex and alcohol were the two great lubricants of crime. Sex (or its promise) brought people and property together, reduced natural wariness, and made it easier for criminal acts to be committed by strangers upon one another. Prostitution was not a transportable criminal offense. It was, however, an easy avenue to robbery, which was among the more serious transportable crimes because it encompassed theft from a person rather than a place and posed the possibility of physical harm. Mary Brown, age forty, and Caroline Smith, age twenty, both of St. Pancras Parish, provide an example. The former was a brothel keeper, the latter a prostitute. In February Brown and Smith had lured John Gates "to a house of ill-fame" in Somerstown, where they "violently and feloniously" stole six shillings from Gates with "force and arms," putting him in "corporal fear and danger of his life." Both were sentenced to death after a trial in the Old Bailey on April 11, 1833.

Sophia Gough, twenty-four was described in the *Worcestershire Herald* of July 8, 1833, as one of the "frail inmates" of a "house of rather questionable character." Her crime also was typical: Gough and Francis Jefferies, her male accomplice, lured a man to the place and later stole twenty-one pounds and seven shillings from him while he lay asleep. Gough was sentenced to seven years transportation, the court remarking that "it was notorious she had been long engaged in a life of infamy and there were no hopes of her amendment" in England.

Amphitrite carried seven other women identified in court records as prostitutes: Janet Turnbull, Eliza Smith (eighteen), Caroline Ellis (twenty-seven), Jane Huptain (twenty), Ellen Bingham (twenty-two), Agnes McKissock (twenty), and the aptly named Hannah Tart (twenty-five). The trial records of two other women, Elizabeth Clark (twenty-four) and Mary Pettingall (twenty-five), suggest that they, too, were prostitutes. Several academic surveys of female convict records indicate that one-fifth to one-quarter of all women transported had "been on the town." If that estimate is correct, then prostitution was an underrepresented trade in *Amphitrite*.

2 2

There was roughly one woman to every eight or so men in New South Wales when *Amphitrite* left Woolwich on the tide bound for the growing colony at Port Jackson.[8] That ratio condemned most men there to monastic bachelorhood and set a sharp limit on the rate of natural population increase, putting a premium on the continued importation of female convicts and prompting a long-running campaign to attract other young women as volunteer settlers. Not until the 1820s, however, did free immigrants begin to appear in New South Wales, and through that decade and into the beginning of the next they arrived in small numbers. Only after the 1850s and the gold rush were most male Australian laborers not convicts and former convicts.

From the very beginning the Australian convict colony was meant to be self-sustaining economically, but the metropolitan objective—no cost, essentially permanent incarceration of its exiles—which had been so easy to achieve in the relatively mature society and economy of the American colonies, was to prove more elusive here, never mind Joseph Banks' expectations drawn from his several weeks ashore collecting botanical specimens and misimpressions during autumn 1770. There was no private market for convict labor in Australia during the early years as there had been in America.

Moreover, reality at Botany Bay was not what Banks had recalled and reported, but instead "a flat heath of paperbark scrub and gray-green eucalypts stretching featurelessly away under the grinding white light." Relocation north to Port Jackson made survival possible, but that just barely.

Although Banks had suggested less, the planners at the transportation board had been conservative, they thought, and provided the First Fleet with stores for two years. Accordingly the first ships out carried substantial, albeit what turned out even so to be inadequate, stocks of foodstuffs and start-up livestock, seeds, tools and equipment. (In fact even the most austere self-sufficiency took decades to achieve, and the early arrivals suffered through grim deprivation. The final months before the arrival of the Second Fleet saw the colony pushed hard against the edge of mass starvation. For months after April 1790, the individual ration stood at just over a pound of unprepared food per day.)

Among other things self-sustaining meant "self-reproducing," and so a significant number of women of child-bearing age necessarily had to be a part of the colony's population mix. Some 70 percent of all females transported were between fifteen and thirty years of age, with forty-five established as the upper limit for transportation. In part these limits reflected expectations about strength and vigor as well as fertility. (Granted that limit was occasionally exceeded. A small percentage of all the women exiled were in their fifties, sixties, and seventies, and at least one eighty year old, Catherine Finn, was among the convicts transported. She died in 1826, soon after her arrival.) Condemned by society, if not explicitly by the courts, for their supposed sexual accessibility in the home islands, once ashore in exile the same female convicts were valued largely for their ability to reproduce.

The first all-female transport left Plymouth at the end of July 1789, only eighteen months after the First Fleet arrived in Botany Bay and six months ahead of the departure of the Second Fleet from Portsmouth. From then on women went ashore either as part of mixed sex transports or, after 1811 (with a few exceptions), in all-female vessels. Between 1812 and the end of transportation in 1868, 161 female convict transports sailed from the British Isles to Australia.

23

Overall, some 90 percent of the female convicts sentenced to transportation were sent from England and Ireland. Women from Scotland comprised fewer than 10 percent, roughly 2,300, supporting the view that Scottish courts were more reluctant to sentence women to transportation than were English or Irish ones. The relatively few women Scottish courts exiled to Australia were, however, thought to be "the most abandoned," incorrigible hard cases fit for

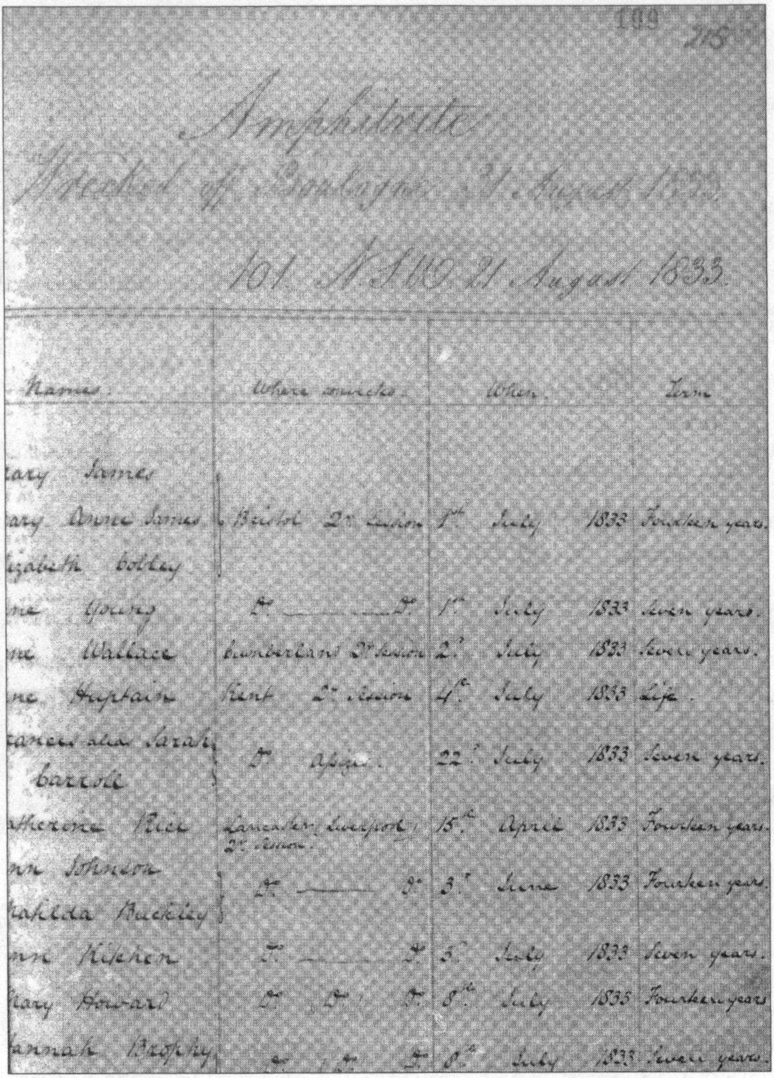
109 215

Amphitrite
Wrecked off Boulogne 31 August 1833

101 N.S.W. 21 August 1833.

Names.	Where convicted.	When.		Term
ary James ary Anne James izabeth Colley	Bristol 2d Session	1st July	1833	Fourteen years.
ne Young	Do. —— Do.	1st July	1833	Seven years.
ne Wallace	Cumberland Qr Session	2d July	1833	Seven years.
ne Huptain	Kent Qr Session	4th July	1833	Life.
ances alias Sarah Carroll	Do. Assizes	22d July	1833	Seven years.
atherine Rice	Lancaster Liverpool Qr Session	15th April	1833	Fourteen years.
nn Johnson athilda Buckley	Do. —— Do.	3d June	1833	Fourteen years.
nn Kitchen	Do. —— Do.	5th July	1833	Seven years.
ary Howard	Do. Do. Do.	8th July	1833	Fourteen years
annah Brophy	Do. Do. Do.	8th July	1833	Seven years.

Fɪɢ. 10

Amphitrite's convict indent, 1833. This first page of the convict manifest lists details about sixteen of the women embarked. Among the names here is Jane Huptain's. She was sentenced on July 4 in Kent Quarter Sessions Court to transportation for life. Nineteen others of those named on the indent were also tried and sentenced in the month before *Amphitrite* sailed. One, Elspet Fraser, had been sentenced as long ago as the previous September. There were possibly as many as 108 female convicts aboard the ship when she left Woolwich, but only 101 names appeared on the Home Office manifest.

Nᴀᴛɪᴏɴᴀʟ Aʀᴄʜɪᴠᴇs ᴏꜰ ᴛʜᴇ Uɴɪᴛᴇᴅ Kɪɴɢᴅᴏᴍ, ʀᴇꜰ. HO 11/9 215.

no lesser punishment, among whom those convicted by the Glasgow Court of Justiciary were generally believed to be "the worst of a bad lot." The remaining percent or so came from Wales.

The Home Office's indent for *Amphitrite*, the transport's convict manifest, listed 101 women. The indent's four, carefully handwritten columns—beginning with Mary James from Bristol (a one-woman crime wave, sentenced July 1 to fourteen years) and ending six pages later with Ann Thompson from the Isle of Man (sentenced May 21 to seven years for shoplifting thirty-seven yards of lace edging, twenty-five shillings worth)—listed the name or names, court and date of conviction, and term of transportation of almost all the convicts on board. Another woman, Margaret Dunbar, a horse thief from Keith, Scotland, must have been taken on board at Woolwich in the few days immediately prior to *Amphitrite*'s sailing. Her name was not on the indent, prepared four days before the ship headed downriver, but instead was mailed in a dispatch to the colony's governor, Richard Bourke. Dunbar was the 102nd convict embarked. If there were other women on board, and Boatswain Owen said there were six more and some counts went even higher, then their identities have been lost.

Amphitrite's convicts came from four rootstocks native to the British Isles: English, Welsh, Irish, and Scottish. Together they formed a microcosm of the impoverished womankind of the home islands, unusual only in the high percentage of convicts from Scotland in the mix, almost one-third of the total, and the low percentage of those from Ireland. Most came from a city or had moved to one. Eleanor Finlay's 1991 census of the convicts indicated that fifty lived in London or Edinburgh and almost as many came from English or Scottish provincial cities.[9] Only a few were from the country and still living there or, like Margaret Dunbar and Agnes McMillan, had committed distinctly rural crimes.

These were hard women, many of them. Owen later testified that he overheard several wish aloud that Elizabeth Fry would tumble off the hoist—a barrel with its top removed and sides cut down into a kind of cramped bucket seat—and drown in the Thames while she was being lifted from a wherry onto *Amphitrite*'s main deck during one of several presailing visits to succor the convicts. Fry, "the angel of Newgate" and then fifty-three, deserved better than that. She and the other ladies of her reform society had been the chief source of what little kindness was shown during years past to British female convicts in prison wards or on board transport vessels at anchor. It was she, for example, who in 1818 had induced an end to the humiliating practice of hauling open wagon loads of female convicts in chains between prison and port, ensuring that the enthusiastic abuse of passersby would form their last memory of home. After that date, these women were moved from one place to the other in closed hackney coaches, protected from insult and weather alike.

In the early nineteenth century two rival models of confinement vied for endorsement in Great Britain. Fry, generously described as "'tall and majestic,' blonde and pretty" as a young matron, was the most articulate and influential among those who argued that the purpose of prison was convict rehabilitation, and that this goal could be realized only through a regime that featured kindness, secular and religious instruction, productive employment, incentives for good conduct, and the strict separation of the sexes in confinement.[10] Arrayed against her, and the ultimate victors in the policy debate, were those who believed that deterrence of crime and not reform of felons was the chief object of prison sentences and that solitary confinement, exhausting (and otherwise meaningless) labor at the treadwheel or the capstan, and "a spare diet" were essential to deterrence. The Prison Act of 1835 signaled the victory of the hard liners. When it was enacted Fry's influence on policy, although not her personal reputation, had been in decline for a decade.

Fry was a pioneer reformer, but she wasn't alone. Thinking about prison reform was in the European air in the 1820s and 1830s. In May 1831 two young aristocrats, Gustave de Beaumont, twenty-eight, and Alexis de Tocqueville, twenty-five, left France for the United States, ostensibly to study rival penology practices in Pennsylvania and New York. During the course of their nine-month tour (they stayed until late February 1832), the pair inspected Auburn Prison and Sing-Sing Prison and along the way visited fifteen more of the twenty-four American states, where they met citizens of every description.

Few today have read their resulting report, *On the Penitentiary System in the United States* (1833), but de Tocqueville's *Democracy in America* (1835), the first of his two volumes of thoughtful observations during the tour, became an immediate classic in two languages and still spangles high school and college required reading lists.

Devout Christian and impassioned reformer, mother of twelve and proto-feminist, articulate advocate before parliament and opium addict, Elizabeth Fry has been the subject of a handful of admiring biographies, most of them written by fellow Quakers.[11] By 1827, when she published her seventy-six-page booklet, *Observations on the Visiting, Superintendence, and Government, of Female Prisoners*, Fry had been visiting prisons (most often London's notorious Newgate, where, by Owen's count, forty of *Amphitrite*'s convicts had been confined pending transportation) and convict transports at anchor, and lobbying officials to improve the conditions of confinement for women for nearly fifteen years.[12] *Observations* distilled her long experience, filtered through great piety and a missionary impulse, into a ten-chapter, how-to manual that concluded with an appeal for an end to the death penalty.

Fry's example was a powerful one. It animated Quaker ladies in Philadelphia to make regular weekly visits during the 1820s to women confined in that city's Arch Street Prison. Farther afield it prompted a short-lived prison visit program in Van Diemen's Land in the 1830s, led by Lady Jane Franklin, wife of the colony's new governor.

Elizabeth Fry was wrestling with a problem that penologists have failed to solve in the many intervening decades: how to make incarceration a reformative experience and so to reduce recidivism among "the helpless, the ignorant, the afflicted, and the depraved." More challenging still, she was trying to do this on the cheap, with a corps of volunteer ladies sustained only by their piety and good will, all presumably intent on "becoming the faithful, humble, devoted followers of a crucified Lord, who went about DOING GOOD." On the cheap and also in the context of a system that, in G. Allen Mawer's words, "seemed poorly designed for reforming its prisoners but well calculated to degrade the society in which it operated."

Her solution to the problem was to add two innovations to the thinking of England's first great prison reformer, John Howard, who raised reform to national consciousness in the years before his death in 1790. To Howard's prescriptions Fry added volunteer boards of lady "visiters," which made prison visits fashionable (and abuses of convicts visible outside the walls), and the idea of exclusively female administration of women's prisons.

There is no reason to doubt Owen's short story about sullen hopes "that she might fall overboard and be drowned" muttered and overheard while Elizabeth Fry swung in a crude chair above *Amphitrite*'s rail, but there's a small question whether Fry ever was on board the vessel at all. Two sources (or perhaps one, with the later referring to the earlier) say that Fry was never on board *Amphitrite*. In 1853 Susanna Corder, a biographer, wrote that between 1818 and her death in 1841 Fry visited every other female convict ship before sailing, but that "neither Elizabeth Fry or any of the Committee ever visited this ship." Corder probably took that from a sentence in Elisabeth and Katharine Fry's memoir of their mother's life, published in 1847. Fry almost certainly did visit the ship, as she did 106 others. It appears that her supporters, mortified by the reported ingratitude and hostility of *Amphitrite*'s Newgate alumnae and by this evidence of the failure of Fry's efforts at convict reform, tried to discredit Owen's story to protect her reputation.

24

Five of the convicts, Mary Constable, Eliza Smith, Mary Brown, Jane Huptain, and Charlotte Smith, shared a special distinction: They were heading for sea and a life sentence in New South Wales. Thirty others on board *Amphitrite*, nearly one-third of her passengers, were going under a sentence of fourteen years transportation. The remaining two-thirds or so were banished for seven years, the minimum and usual sentence for women.

Mary Constable's crimes were three instances in February and March 1833 of "larceny from a dwelling house," the home of her employer, during which she took linens and clothing, a lamp, and two five-pound banknotes. Among these five her sentence was something of an anomaly. Constable was one of the two nonviolent offenders in the group, but because she was a servant stealing from her master, a crime that threatened not only property but also the natural order of society, she was treated with special severity. The other nonviolent offender, Eliza Smith, age eighteen and described in the *Morning Post* as "a mere infant," was found guilty of snatching a watch and fob from the owner. Because such crimes had the potential of injury to a person they, too, were judged especially harshly.

Something similar happened to George Day, a milk carrier, who went with Jane Huptain to her lodgings in Deptford to have sex. When he refused to pay Huptain anything until after he "had connexion with her," a brawl ensued during which he was thrashed by Huptain and her accomplice, James Perry, and robbed of a silver watch worth forty shillings. Day, face "black with blood running down it," was spared worse only by the timely intervention of Police Constables Rixon and Maher from the force's Greenwich Division station.

Rixon (No. R125) and Maher (No. R132) were members of the new Metropolitan Police Force, the professional constabulary established several years earlier by Sir Robert Peel, the home secretary, to fight crime and preserve order in greater London. Peel's "bobbies" at first supplemented but eventually supplanted the ad hoc watchmen, thief takers, and runners who had been their predecessors. By the date of Day's beating, 3,300 bobbies, each assigned to one of seventeen station houses, were responsible for crime prevention and law enforcement across an area of more than 1,500 square miles.

Constable Rixon's testimony at trial in Kent County Quarter Sessions Court described the crime scene on Effington Place, in Deptford, four days earlier:

> About 12:00 o'clock last Monday morning [July 1] I saw George Day go into lodgings with Jane Huptain. Five minutes after I saw [James Perry] place himself at the door and ten minutes later he went in. I heard a cry of "Murder" in two to three minutes and ran in with a brother policeman. A woman opened the door and said "for God's sake Police come in for they will murder the man." I rushed in and saw [Huptain] beating the man who was stooping down in a corner by a cupboard. [Perry] was close by. I did not see him strike [Day]. . . . I took

[Huptain] forcibly out of the house. [Perry] at first defied me to take her but did not prevent it. Both were taken to the Station House.

Perry was sentenced to life in the hulk *Retribution*, which he went on board at Sheerness on August 3. Huptain was sentenced to transportation for life. She joined *Amphitrite* in the Thames off Woolwich on August 14.

Everyone understood that the chance any of the sixty-seven convicts sentenced to the shortest term would return to the British Isles and to home after serving their time was vanishing small. Return fares were prohibitively expensive, and women, unlike some of the men, could not work passage home as a member of a returning ship's crew. This fact made meaningless the distinction between seven-, fourteen-, and twenty-one-year sentences. All of them were for life.

25

Amphitrite's convicts spanned nearly three generations in age. They ranged from sixteen prisoners under age twenty being transported for their crimes to the senior felon on board, a woman approaching sixty. Some who appear to us today like children were not seen so then. If the world of work began very early for the poor of Great Britain, so too did family life. Beginning ten years before *Amphitrite* sailed, a fourteen-year-old boy could marry legally without parental consent, and so could a twelve-year-old girl, middle schoolers today. (Not until 1885 was the age of consent for girls raised to sixteen.) Overall, nearly one in six of all those sentenced to exile were teenagers or younger. Some years into the program an occasional transport sailed from the British Isles with a convict indent comprised largely of adolescents.

Margaret Knight, thirteen, seems to have been the youngest convict on board *Amphitrite*, but she was not new to the Scottish justice system. Passing sentence, a judge described the young teen as "by habit and repute a common thief." That phrase, "by habit and repute," was a legal shorthand for "repeat offender." It appeared often in the court books of the time and frequently in the trial records of these convicts. Knight was convicted of several thefts between November 1830 and March 1832 while a preteen and sentenced to sixty days each time, once with hard labor. Then, in December 1832, when "betwixt thirteen and fourteen years of age," she stole a calico printed gown and apron from Helen Stratton's fence in Aberdeen, hoping to sell them, she said, to buy whiskey for the woman who looked after her. Sixteen witnesses testified against her. Upon conviction, the sentence of the Aberdeen Justiciary Court was four years transportation, after first serving "sixty days hard labour with the last fourteen days to be spent in solitary confinement and fed on only bread and water."[13]

The dreadful consequences of indiscriminately mixing young and presumably naïve offenders with old, hardened ones was a frequent subject of commentary on the transportation system. Most often the topic was the danger of mingling boys with men. "If a boy be convicted of a trifling misdemeanour," wrote The Times on October 16, 1833, "let him undergo imprisonment when so ordained, but let him not, under the name of correction, be condemned to a life of incurable guilt, ending almost of necessity in some extreme and ignominious punishment by being plunged into compulsory association with the most depraved and hardened and infamous of the human species."

In that same opinion piece about Amphitrite's wreck, The Times sermonized at length about what the editor had learned "from a person of strict veracity, who was present on the beach of Boulogne . . . who displayed the most active benevolence on that occasion":

> So if men, but more especially if women, and more than all if girls, —nay, female infants of 12 or 13 years of age, be transported for offenses not apparently the results of inveterate practice, or in their nature and incidents of the deepest dye . . . —if, as we say, it be judged right that very youthful female culprits should be banished to the other side of the globe for such transgressions, let the authorities of the state be content with strictly executing the judicial sentence, but let them, in the name of all that is just and merciful, not superadd the most grievous of punishments—namely, that of destroying the mind of the young offender, and so saturating the child's whole being with depravity, as to cut off every hope of her future purification. . . .
>
> If the sketch which our correspondent presents to us, of the terrible intermixture of heinous with slight offenders on board that fatal vessel to which it applies, be equally true of all ships of the same description, what a mass of unredeemed iniquity and barbarity has the British Legislature to answer for every year! When we see that young and inexperienced females, in whom the virtuous sensibilities are obviously not yet extinct, although they may in some moment of sudden temptation have subjected themselves to the stern rebuke of justice— when such young persons are linked inseparably with old, inveterate, desperate, and incurable malefactors—confined in the apartment with them—nay, forced into the same loathsome bed, what can be thought of such arrangements, but that they have been purposely designed to convert, as against the most venial class of offenders, a sentence of

transportation to a colony into one far more vindictive and awful than death upon the gallows?

The author of these views is anonymous, but it was probably Sarah Austin, an Englishwoman living in Boulogne-sur-Mer at the time who could have been rightly described as having "displayed the most active benevolence on the beach that night." We meet her later.

26

Ann Lewis was, together with Margaret Knight, among the fifteen or so teenagers embarked in *Amphitrite*. Lewis was the lone convict from Wales on the ship, and she seems to have been the only one on board who spoke no English. For her, to be transported in the company of incomprehensible strangers to exile in Australia must have been tantamount to a death sentence. It turned out to be just that.

This perfect separation from home and everything familiar by open water and from everyone afloat by language happened occasionally to convicts. John Nichol, the *Lady Juliana*'s cooper (barrel maker), whose 1822 memoirs of her 1789–90 crossing are the only participant's published account of the first female convict transport's voyage to New South Wales, described an unnamed "young and beautiful . . . but pale as death" Scottish girl who could have been a model for Ann Lewis. "Her eyes red with weeping," she sat in the same place speaking to no one and eating nothing, Nichol wrote, and "at length sunk into the grave of no disease but a broken heart." Nichol inclined toward romanticism, however, so his account may be overheated. During the voyage he fell in love with a convict, reluctantly left her in Australia promising to return, and then pined in public the rest of his life for the marriage and life that might have been. His beloved, Sarah Whitelam, was less the romantic than he. She married another the day after Nichol reluctantly sailed away in *Lady Juliana* for Canton and then home to England.

Ann Lewis was from Dolgellau in northwest Wales, a center then of weaving and tanning on the River Wnion, some 230 miles and twenty-four hours northwest from London by fast stage to the Golden Lion Inn (now rental flats). The town—one-, two-, and three-story, rough-cut gray stone buildings rising from a warren of narrow streets—was also the seat of Merionethshire and the site of the county's general and quarter sessions courts. Her name was (and still is) such a common one in northwestern Wales that it's not possible to pull genealogical threads unambiguously related to her. Boatswain Owen said Lewis was nineteen, which would have put her birthday in 1814, but her age is uncertain. It is probable that she learned to read and write in Sunday school; many in this part of Wales were literate in their native language thanks to Thomas Charles, a Methodist preacher, who decades earlier had fostered a vigorous literacy program to enable people to read scripture for themselves.

On July 5, seven weeks before *Amphitrite* sailed, Lewis and her accomplices were tried in Merionethshire Quarter Sessions Court for theft. The indictment read, "That Ann Lewis, late of [parish] Dolgellau, stole 3 hats, value £5, one umbrella, value 7s., 3 shawls, value £10, the property of Hugh Price, her employer. And that Catherine Humphreys did incite her to steal these items, whilst Mary Ellis accepted the 3 shawls and Jonnet Rees, the umbrella and 3 hats, knowing them to be stolen." Lewis pleaded guilty to stealing from Price's draper's shop on Skinner Square. Her sentence was transportation for seven years. The unfortunate young woman was doubly unlucky. Although she and her two receivers, Ellis and Rees, were all sentenced to transportation, only Lewis' sentence was executed promptly, and only she left the British Isles in *Amphitrite*.[14] Ellis' and Rees' convictions came despite their pleas of innocence and each was sentenced to fourteen years, but they escaped transportation.

Lewis was robbed by some of her shipmates soon after she stepped on board *Amphitrite*. After that initiation to the rest of her life, the Welsh teenager stood at the ship's rail sobbing for the remainder of the short voyage. According to Owen, she ate practically nothing, "a drink of cold water, or now and then an apple or pear." This might have been her second time afloat on salt water. Over the years instead of being moved overland, some of Merioneth County's convicts were floated down the Mawddach River to Barmouth, a port on Cardigan Bay, then shipped around southern England and finally up the Thames to London and to Newgate Prison, where they were held awaiting transportation. (Only after the coming of the railroad later in the century did cross-country travel become generally easier and cheaper than sailing in coastal shipping.)

Lewis' plight inspired a typically melodramatic memorial poem in the *London Monthly Magazine*, a riff in rhyme on Owen's deposition. The anonymous poet of "The Convict Girl" assumed (perhaps rightly) that Lewis passed her time on deck staring at the sea and contemplating suicide. Just so her connection to the wreck was clear, Boatswain Owen's investigation testimony about poor, pathetic Lewis was quoted at the top of the page. Farther down, the second stanza began with what must have been a reference to Lewis' tough shipmates:

Around me crowd strange things of crime,
Pollution meets mine eye,
But not a look of childhood's time—
Nor tone of home is nigh;

And this, aye this, they mercy call
For her who sought a grave;
Homeless they hold me still in thrall—
An outcast, yet a slave!

Dark wave! Dark wave that roll'st in pride
To lash yon distant shore,
Oh! Bear my spirit on thy tide,
To visit it once more:
If but my tears could there find rest.
To mingle with thy spray;
I'd fling my fondness on thy breast,
And weep this heart away.

Nearly three hundred women from Wales were shipped to Australia during the years of convict transportation. The first two were exiled to New South Wales in 1778 on board *Friendship* and the *Prince of Wales*, and the last eight arrived together sixty-four years later in *Duchess of Northumberland*. Many of them spoke only Welsh.

Bridgett Glynn, also nineteen, was another of the several convicts who had been afloat on blue water. Like the other women originally from Ireland on board *Amphitrite*, Glynn had crossed the St. George's Channel to England at least once. Neither she nor any of her countrywomen in *Amphitrite* were sentenced to transportation by an Irish court. Glynn's trial, for the theft of almost thirty pence from William Gunston, had been in Westminster Sessions Court in May.

27

"It is a melancholy reflexion, that so large a proportion of the inhabitants of this country . . . are still left in a condition of almost extreme ignorance," Elizabeth Fry wrote in 1827. "This observation applies with particular force to those who are in the habit of breaking its laws." If Fry's population sample at Newgate was representative of female convicts in general, one-third of the women on board *Amphitrite* were illiterate and another third could read very little. Because none of the convicts from Scotland claimed at trial to be able to read, it is more likely that in this ship only two dozen or so could pick their way through the Bible or another book.

Most female convicts, like their male counterparts, were thieves. The goods these women took, and often pawned for very little, were generally the bits and pieces of everyday life, snatched from dwellings or workplaces, lifted from small shops or befuddled drunks, or taken while drying on hedges or from public bleaching greens. The era's unfortunates usually had access to little else of use or value other than this stuff or someone's pocket change. Far from threatening the law-making class, Great Britain's poor generally preyed on one another.

Pawnbrokers' shops acted as community banks for the impoverished, but their proprietors also served as receivers of stolen goods and made possible the easy conversion of such swag to money. When one especially practiced female criminal went to trial in Bristol on July 1, 1883, eight pawnbrokers, the men (and one woman) among whom she had scattered her gleanings over a long criminal career, were called to testify against her. All eight spoke at her trial in quarter sessions court, opening their own behavior to examination. As the *Bristol Mirror* reported, these enablers of crime frustrated court officers:

> The town clerk asked the pawnbroker if it did not occur to him extraordinary that a woman who appeared to be poor should be in possession of a quantity of fine glass, colored plates with engraved armorial bearings, etc. The pawnbroker replied that he asked the usual questions required by the act, viz; was the property her own? And that she replied it had been left to her by an aunt in Bath. The town clerk rejoined that no pawnbroker could screen himself from the consequences, whether moral or legal, of conniving and encouraging theft by merely confining himself to asking that question. In the present case the glass was packed in straw, and evidently came out of a dealer's shop and the pawnbroker had behaved most culpably in not detaining the prisoner. He [the pawnbroker] would however lose the whole of the money he had leant and if he acted in the same way in the future he would expose himself to serious responsibility.[15]

Two imaginative thieves bound for *Amphitrite* had laid their hands on more unusual booty. "Supple Nancy," the nickname was Agnes McMillan's, for her fifth crime stole a grip of herring nets from a rope maker in November 1832. "It appears that the accused and her family are bad characters," Wigtonshire's prosecutor then wrote to the sheriff, "and as the stealing of fishing nets has often been practiced here it would benefit the community if 'Supple Nancy,' as she is locally known, was sent out of the way." She got seven years.

Another, Jane Young, managed to steal and pawn, one after another, nineteen sets of polished fireplace irons, valued at one pound each, and loose pokers, tongs, and fire shovels worth another eighteen all together. The hardware was taken over some months from her employers, Price and Company, Firemongers, concealed under her dress, and delivered item by item to James

Stone, pawnbroker. She, too, got seven years. Stone, who watched these items pass one after the other through his shop, only got "cautioned by the court not in the future to afford facilities for the disposal of stolen property by persons like the prisoner."

Surprisingly, foodstuffs appear to have been uncommon objects of crime. Sarah Poole, as mentioned, ran off with several years' supply of butter as her ticket to Australia. Janet Becket, twenty-one, a weaver, caught first at nineteen stealing from her sister, managed two years later to gather up "six pounds or thereby of mutton ham" together with the clothing and jewelry she took from a house in Glasgow. She got seven years. In May, Ann Rogers, a cook, stole five pounds of bread and plum cake, six one-pound jars of jam, and two pounds of sugar. Two months later she was sentenced to fourteen years for the crime, and a month after that Rogers was on the way to Australia.

Most thefts and robberies were sudden improvisations offering slender rewards. Very rarely is a criminal found like Janet Struthers, forty, who in mid-1832 with several accomplices broke through two sets of doors into a warehouse in Glasgow, and then "wickedly stole and theftuously carried away" three hundred printed shawls and another hundred handkerchiefs, the property of Fotheringham and Buchanan, calico printers. Her crime, obviously, was a carefully planned burglary. Glasgow Justiciary Court sentenced Struthers, separated for four years from her husband, a fish peddler ("hawker"), to fourteen years.

Less often still did the crimes of women involve violence, like the robbery of four pounds and four shillings committed by Mary Lochie and Margaret Henderson. The charge was that "they did wickedly and feloniously attack and assault Alexander Wright, feuar [land tenant] and weaver, residing in Alloa by striking him one or more blows with an iron poker and did knock him to the ground and otherwise maltreat him." In her defense Lochie claimed that Wright deserved the beating. Drunk after downing more than a mutchkin (an imperial pint) of whiskey, he had tried to enter her bed and she had struck him in defense of her virtue. Unfortunately Henderson, Lochie's sister-in-law, didn't corroborate the story. Lochie got seven years transportation; Henderson got nine months in prison.

Amphitrite's many convicts from Scotland came via trials in all six national courts, from those in Edinburgh, Glasgow, Aberdeen, Ayr, Perth, and Stirling. In the relatively few days the thirty-two were on board *Amphitrite* and alive, the older Scots, seven women in their forties and fifties, gained a reputation for being obstreperous that has survived until today. At the other end of the age spectrum, the nine youngest Scots were teenagers, among them three thieves, aged thirteen, fourteen, and fifteen, and a sixteen year old (Margaret Johnston, convicted and sentenced March 11 in the Edinburgh Court of Justiciary) who preyed on small children by stripping them in the street and pawning what she had taken.

One of the Scots, Mary Clark, alias Donaldson, sentenced in mid-April in the Perth Court of Justiciary for her thirty-sixth larceny, was a recordholder. No one else could boast of such an impressive life of serial crime. Her previous sentences had included imprisonment, once for two months on bread and water, and banishment from her home county for five years, which she ignored. It was not family ties that kept her in County Forfar. Although married, her husband was a sailor, and at the time of her last trial she had not seen him for six years and was uncertain if he were alive. Surprisingly, this practiced criminal from Dundee (perhaps not "practiced," as she'd been caught committing every one of these three dozen transgressions) was sentenced to only seven years transportation. Clark made Margaret Robertson, fourteen counts of theft heard by the Edinburgh Police Court beginning with a first crime in September 1815, look like a good citizen. In common with most of the others, Robertson got seven years.

Another Scot, Elspet Fraser (or Elspet Smith, she was manifested on board under both, presumably one was a married name), forty-two, held a morose record, too: She'd been locked up for almost a year by the time *Amphitrite* sailed. Fraser had been convicted in the Aberdeen Justiciary Court on September 27, 1832, of four acts of "falsehood, fraud, and willful imposition." Although no one else was held in post-trial confinement nearly as long as she, those eleven months in jail got her no reduction in time to be served "beyond the seas."

Fraser had a criminal record going back at least until December 1822, when she apparently first developed what was to become her modus operandi for the next ten years, claiming others' property—clothes, money, food, wool, and other goods—by pretending to be someone else. By the time she was sent to Newgate to await transportation, Aberdeen officials were out of patience with her. "The accused has long been a pest in this quarter," one wrote to another; "it were well if this county could now be got rid of her."

Elizabeth Jackson, twenty, sentenced to fourteen years transportation by the Glasgow Court of Justiciary on April 26, 1833, was yet another recordholder: She boasted the most aliases, four, suggesting if not so many marriages then at least four accommodations with different men, named successively Barr, Cunningham, McKellar, and Campbell. Jackson was tried and convicted five times between November 1831 and March 1833, usually for "wickedly stealing and feloniously carrying away" the property of others from their homes—miscellaneous used clothing, shoes, dry goods, tableware, bedding, books, and even the pistol of one James Jackson, who might have been her husband in 1832. During her last trial, on March 20, 1833, Jackson said she was tired of Scotland and wished to be transported.

To a knowledgeable observer on the embankment when *Amphitrite* sailed, her disproportionate population of Scots, including fully ten from Glasgow, foreshadowed certain trouble during the long crossing to come. "There were 18 women from Scotland," *The Times* of London quoted John Owen, miscounting badly, on October 16, now six weeks away from his ordeal. "These were the worst and most ferocious and hardened on board. They were almost all above 40, only one young woman among them. There was not one tolerably decent. Their language was the most disgusting that can be conceived, and they were always quarreling and fighting and stealing from the other women."

There was a mother-daughter team in *Amphitrite*'s convict hold: Mary Ann James, fifteen, of Bristol, England, sentenced to fourteen years with her mother, forty-one, also named Mary and also exiled for fourteen years. The first was the thief, the second the fence, disposing of the stolen goods by pawning them at any of eleven pawn shops she regularly visited. All eleven proprietors, only one of whom was upbraided by counsel for the obvious role all played in abetting crime, testified for the prosecution at the James' trial. Mary's and Mary Ann's haul in the spring of 1833 was impressive and eclectic: carpet and linens; china place settings and silver service pieces; nearly ninety pounds of fat, tallow, and grease (stolen from an employer, a tallow chandler and candle maker); books and Bibles; and all manner of other things extracted from the homes of neighbors in St. Paul's Parish.

Stealing, receiving, and pawning stolen goods seems to have been the James' family business. Henry, nineteen and Mary Ann's older brother, also got fourteen years for his part in the crime wave. Henry James worked for a shoemaker on 4 Mary Port Street, in St. Marywhile's Parish, where he lightened his employer's extensive stock of three pairs of boots and twenty-two pairs of shoes, which his mother promptly pawned. Only their husband and father, Richard, escaped transportation. Mother and son tried hard and apparently successfully to isolate Richard James from their work, or else his own crimes were never discovered.

28

For many decades the usual answer to questions about the identity of these women (and of their many more fortunate sisters who survived the voyage to Australia and Tasmania) was simply that they were felons—the fraction of criminals culled by several criminal justice systems from among the many robbers and thieves who constituted the female half of the British Isles' criminal class. This was the contemporary view in the late eighteenth and nineteenth centuries, and it prevailed largely unchallenged through much of the twentieth century. That assessment was close to unanimous. The only early dissenting voices, heard first in the United Kingdom and later from the distant settlements themselves, came from social reformers philosophically opposed to transportation or from people unwilling (as the American colonies had become by the mid-1700s) to host any more of the mother country's criminal class.

In 1965 the Melbourne University Press published Lloyd Robson's *Convict Settlers of Australia: An Enquiry into the Origin and Character of the Convicts Transported to New South Wales and Van Diemen's Land, 1787–1852*, a pioneering, pre-computer attempt to plumb the entire convict database to learn what kinds of people convicts were and about the lives they led on arrival from other than anecdotal accounts. Robson first compiled a random, 5 percent sample from roughly 150,000 transportation records and then, threading carefully punched data cards with sorting sticks, he drew his conclusions. (The resulting semiscientific sociology book, buttressed by eleven tabular appendices, reads very much like the doctoral dissertation it once was. Despite that, *Convict Settlers* has been reprinted several times.) Robson's sample included 1,248 female records, from which he concluded that the "female prisoners had little to recommend them, and, in the early years especially, they included many Londoners who had led dissolute lives in a Hogarthian capital. . . . Careers of the women convicts in Australia confirmed the impression that, although not surrendering themselves to abandonment completely, they yet were an indifferent group of settlers."

That almost reflexive answer to his question reflects public opinion at the time and the perspectives of the almost exclusively male scholarship of Australian history as it was written well into the twentieth century. Later, alternative descriptions gained adherents. One of these saw the crimes committed not as the natural employment of a criminal class but as trivial misdemeanors, the reasonable responses of people driven into crime by soul-killing want and hunger. More recently the answer has become much more nuanced. Not necessarily more descriptive of reality, but more complex.

29

From the beginning—and that's all there ever was to this voyage—Doctor Forrester took a very light strain on the line. This from Boatswain John Owen describing *Amphitrite*'s few days underway: "The women had the range of the ship," *The Times* of October 16, 1833, quoted him as saying:

The doctor let them go where they liked: he never took any notice, if they did not make a riot. The doctor had the sole management of them; never heard him expostulate, advise or in any way converse with them. There was no attempt at restraint, instruction, or government of any kind; only if one was riotous he had her brought upon deck, and put into a thing like a watchbox, in which they could not sit, and could only just stand upright. . . . This was the only punishment. There was no reward or encouragement for good conduct. No attempt to keep them employed. . . . The only order he ever gave them was to bring their beds up on deck every fine morning. That was the only thing they were ever set to do. All the other employment was at their own pleasure.

It is not easy to imagine the end point of such a laissez-faire regime, to picture what conditions on board might have been like in December while *Amphitrite* finally threaded her way northward through the approaches to Sydney Harbor after four months of "no government of any kind" between decks. It's possible to foresee the emergence of something like a state of nature in the convicts' spaces, a society dominated by the appetites and morals of the clique of hardened old crones, but something more benign might also have emerged from Forrester's abdication of responsibility. Still, Owen's glimpse of Surgeon-Superintendent Forrester at work confirms Sir William Burnett's tepid assessment of the man.

Had the Captain yielded to their cries, Alas! they might them save,

The women, children, and crew, All from a watery grave;

And numbers on the shore did weep, And bitterly did mourn,

To see them on the briny waves, Would pierce a heart of stone.

CHAPTER 5

Underway in Thick Weather

30

Her second survey in dry dock that year successfully completed, and newly adorned with a poop atop the quarterdeck aft, *Amphitrite* moved downriver from Deptford to Woolwich. There, during several weeks in midsummer, she completed final preparations for sea. The short transit between the two royal dockyards, passing in a slow, looping S-turn first the east side of the Isle of Dogs on the left hand and then around the Bugsbys Marshes on the right, moved *Amphitrite* from one historic naval base to another.

Despite its name, the swampy and foul-smelling Isle of Dogs beyond London's East End was not a natural island. It was a low-lying peninsula bound by the arc of a tight meander of the Thames at its last great bend as the river left London for the North Sea, made into what could pass for an island by a cut excavated across its narrow neck. The sale of this cut, originally the Limehouse-Blackwall Canal, to the West India Company and its conversion into a proprietary dock heightened the efficiency of the company's cargo handling facilities dramatically, but it also forced river traffic into once more sailing the long way 'round the Isle of Dogs.

For a brief while this place was the center of British iron shipbuilding and marine engineering.[1] On what had once been windswept and boggy pasture land drained by windmill pumps there eventually stood more than two dozen shipyards, dry docks, and steam engine manufacturing factories, all served by "slushy, ill formed roads" and located amid stunted trees and "tumble-down buildings, stagnant ditches, and tracts of marshy, rubbish-filled waste ground." By midcentury a great industrial complex employing fifteen thousand men and boys working six long days a week was spread along the shoreline of this unlikely place, protected from regular tidal flooding by raised embankments and apparently extruding oceangoing ships from little more than smoke and noise.

In 1833 Woolwich and Deptford had been Royal Dockyards for several hundred years. They were opened by Henry VIII in 1512 and 1513, respectively, on the south bank of the Thames. Both were conveniently near to Henry's capital, to his palace at Greenwich, and to the armory and arsenal just upriver in the Tower of London. In the late eighteenth century the two yards stood among the largest industrial properties in the British Isles, complete with moorings in the river and slips and docks on their waterfronts, and backed up by clusters of red brick shop and storage buildings inside of cantonment areas.

After proximity to London became less important than proximity to the sea, both yards' missions were taken over by larger and more accessible navy bases closer to open water, bases that could handle deep-draft first rates and didn't require the occasional long wait for favorable winds so that ships could sail upriver.

Shipbuilding was suspended at Deptford in 1833. Although it was briefly resumed in the 1840s with construction of a steam-powered, paddle frigate, and Deptford continued on as a repair and inspection facility through midcentury, the yard's future was already cloudy when *Amphitrite* went into dry dock there for her second inspection in a year. Approaching fifty years later, part of the property became the site of the Foreign Cattle Market, huge holding pens and slaughter houses. "In the vast shambles," one history of the Thames said, "which no person of nice tastes should think of visiting, beasts are being killed and dressed and quartered from morning to night, with a expedition which strikes the beholder as something unnatural and amazing . . . evidence of the vast capacity of Englishmen for the consumption of animal food."[2]

Not far downriver, Woolwich looked for a time to have better prospects. In the 1830s that yard began to develop expertise in the new steam-propulsion technology. It gained two new dry docks and, in 1842, saw the construction of what turned out to be an underutilized steam engine factory. In 1869 both yards were closed, their futures finally choked off by development around them and by their dependence on the shallow, sinuous Thames.

Beyond the Isle of Dogs, and safely by the shelves and shoals of Bugsbys Reach, *Amphitrite* drew up at Woolwich to take on board stores, cargo, and convicts. The only places at Woolwich where the water was deep enough for a vessel drawing fourteen feet were the anchorages at the Bell Water Gate and Broad Street. Both offered sixteen to eighteen feet of water at low tide, as much as four feet of clearance beneath *Amphitrite*'s keel. Not far away, several prison hulks squatted near the bottom in fifteen feet (and delivered hundreds of convicts daily to hard labor in the yard), but at low tide along this reach of the river there was no more than nine feet of water anywhere else.

Shallow water was not the only threat to shipping near Woolwich. Ordnance vessels with gunpowder on board, occasionally with hatches open and loose black powder dusted about their decks, were anchored there, too, close to the arms depot adjacent to the dockyard. The great danger Ordnance Board vessels posed to others afloat was marked by a red flag at their masthead, a signal to captains, masters, and pilots of passing ships to remain well clear of these floating bombs.

After the stores for *Amphitrite*'s passage to New South Wales were stowed safely below and the last convicts had been taken on board, her master and the surgeon-superintendent would have wanted to get underway as soon as possible. Once the wind and tide permitted a safe departure downriver, nothing good could come from further delay, and the standard charter contract set a limit on demurrage, the daily payment for time in port: Thirty days were allowed for installing the required modifications to house the convicts and loading them and provisions; only twenty days were permitted for disembarkation at voyage's end. Perhaps this explains *Amphitrite*'s unusual Sunday sailing.

If Saturday night were clear of clouds, a three-quarter moon (it would be full at the end of the month) would have shed some light on deck. Any last minute work required before sailing could have continued through the night, but as it developed there probably wasn't much left to do. One of the crew's three survivors, James Jones Towsey, later said that all stores for the crossing were loaded and secured below when he joined the ship, a week or so before she sailed. Clear or cloudy, morning twilight came before 5:00 the next morning, the first glimmer of nearly fourteen hours of late summer daylight to come at this latitude. Hunter's crew would have been fed, on deck or aloft, and well into final preparations to get underway before four bells, at 6:00 AM.

31

Amphitrite was no Royal Navy first rate carrying acres of canvas sails on a thicket of spars trussed with forty miles of standing and running rigging, lines passed through more than a thousand blocks, some larger than a man's head. But despite her relatively small size and simple sail plan, making *Amphitrite* move on command with a crew of few more than a dozen men and boys, and with usually only half that many on deck at any time, was a complicated business. The necessary skill set is largely unknown today, outside of the pages of Patrick O'Brian's novels, and unfamiliar even to most people who actually spend time on salt water in addition to reading about it. Not many sailing vessels anything like her still exist, and few of them ever leave their berths. When one does, watching landlubbers inevitably are awed and mystified by the near-magical progress of a "tall ship" from place to distant place propelled by the unseen wind.

There is no record of what time that Sunday *Amphitrite* sailed from Woolwich, but because much of the River Thames was dangerously shallow at low water and the incoming tide ran upriver at about four knots, it's reasonable to assume that Hunter timed his departure just after the morning high tide on August 25, riding the receding waters downriver, to add their speed to his own under sail. The tide was the great master clock of the Thames, fixing the rhythm of all motion on the river. Anywhere within sight of land the state of the tide was essential knowledge, as Captain Hunter would soon relearn in peril. So, too, would Captains Nesbitt and Compton, masters of *Earl of Wemyss* and *Ann & Amelia*, respectively, both soon to go aground in the same storm that would destroy *Amphitrite*.

High tide at North Woolwich that long-ago Sunday was at 9:10 in the morning and at 9:57 in the evening, slightly upriver at the dockyard on the facing riverbank both might have come a minute or two later.[3] Accordingly, Hunter probably got underway around 9:00 AM, two bells. The prevailing, contrary wind that often made progress up the Thames slow and frustrating might have eased *Amphitrite* under her topsails alone along the first few dozen miles of the thousands to follow. (Alternatively, *Amphitrite* might have been towed down the river by a steamer. That's how in mid-December 1834 *George the Third* got from Woolwich to Margate, when she left London on her only convict charter.) On deck Hunter would have been attentive to the river pilot's instructions after he clambered on board at Gravesend, to ride the ship until sometime Tuesday, when he was to be put ashore at the Downs. Where he could, the pilot most likely took *Amphitrite* down the middle of the river "with the tide up her skirt," where the helpful current was strongest.

Locked beneath the main hatch, the women and children below deck would have seen nothing, not the water—here brackish and more than one mile wide—not the bobbing hulls and forest of masts in the anchorage, and not, if any happened to be present, some of the many steam packets now spinning their paddle wheels on the river and hinting, to the far sighted, how the future was going to look. (Sparks blown carelessly downwind from their stacks were a great threat to ordnance vessels.)

Early Sunday, while *Amphitrite* shook out her sails and got underway, if the wind were out of the west everybody on board could have heard some of

the bells of London's churches ringing to announce Morning Prayer. An echo
from parish churches downriver might have reached the ship hours later, calling the Anglican faithful to the evening service. Late in the day, as *Amphitrite*
left Gravesend behind to starboard, several of those churches would have been
visible, bell towers emerging one after the other from a vista of reeds swaying
in salt marshes. Finally let out on deck but still in sight of land, *Amphitrite's*
women could see their familiar lives slipping away behind them, at the rate of
a few miles per hour.

This was a God-fearing age. Reportedly all of *Amphitrite's* convicts, even
the several dozen who could not read, went on board with a Bible in their
personal kit, a gift from prison reformers ashore and very likely the only book
any of them ever owned outright. (Mary James had taken four "printed books"
from John Naish, part of a mixed pile of things she'd been caught stealing
from her employer. James later pawned them for one pound to a fence on
Redcross Street, Bristol, but no one counted those volumes as hers. *Harvey's
Meditations*, *Edward's Sermons*, and *Brown's Dictionary of the Bible* were some
of Elizabeth Jackson's loot from a robbery in Glasgow. They were of no use to
her; she couldn't read. Ann Brown also had stolen some books. For all three
women books were just things to pawn.)

Amphitrite also carried the usual convict ship library of Books of Common
Prayer, Psalters, New Testaments, and Bibles. Several of each were to be distributed to every mess of eight convicts, the goal being the promotion of "a religious and moral disposition in the Convicts" during their long voyage. Once
landed in Australia, the most worthy of the women were to receive these good
books as presents. (Potential rewards for good conduct were not limited to
books or all delayed for months. The tidiest mess among those groups of eight
women preparing their food and eating it together was to be rewarded with
tea and sugar every day. The same had been the reward for good conduct in
prison ashore.)

Absent an ordained minister on board, Doctor Forrester was required
by Admiralty instructions to read the church service every Sunday during
the ocean voyage and to deliver either a sermon or "some well selected parts
from the [ship's] Religious Tracts" to convicts assembled on deck. Later, during the wreck investigation, Boatswain's Mate John Owen said that no religious observances had been conducted on board *Amphitrite* in the weeks
immediately before the ship left Woolwich other than some Bible readings by
Elizabeth Fry. In fairness to Forrester, getting underway and navigating downriver would have left little time for church services during the vessel's only
Sunday afloat, and massing the women on deck in sight of the passing shore
might have provoked hysteria or worse. If Forrester were present much before

sailing, the several Sundays at anchor after convicts started embarking were missed opportunities.

In any event, whether in a convict transport, merchant vessel, or a man-o'-war, authentic godliness was often in short supply at sea during the early nineteenth century, as the Reverend Edward Magin had ruefully observed during his three months and two weeks of service as chaplain in HMS *Gloucester* some years earlier. "Nothing," he wrote in his brief journal about his very brief experience, "can possibly be more unsuitably or more awkwardly situated than a clergyman in a ship of war; every object around him is at variance with the sensibilities of a rational and enlightened mind; amidst preparations the most complex and ingenious for the purpose of plundering and murdering his fellow-creatures, he must act and speak as becomes the promoter of 'peace and good-will towards men.' . . . He is, besides, by his instructions, enjoined not only to preach and pray, at stated times, but is also exhorted to do some things which are improper, and some which are impossible."[4]

32

A safe departure from Woolwich was no mean feat it itself. Between *Amphitrite* at anchor and the North Sea lay ten bends in the Thames, called "reaches," each one dotted with mud flats, sands, shelves, and shoals that could quickly put the unwary or inexperienced into low water, adhesive mud or atop hard ground. J. W. Norie's published sailing directions, the period's popular guide for English mariners, took five printed pages to describe the passage between Woolwich Reach (the eighth on the Thames downriver from the "Upper Pool" around the London docks, where the river was some six hundred feet across) and Sea Reach (the eighteenth) where the Thames, here five miles wide, opened to salt water across its broad delta. That whole, sinuous stretch, end to end and from bank to bank measured at high water, constituted the Port of London.[5]

Only scrupulous compliance with sailing directions could get a ship dropping down the Thames from London and drawing near fourteen feet past, for example, the twin hazards of Gray's Reach at low water:

> In this reach are two shoals: one beginning at the upper point, a little below *Broad Ness* and extending down the west side. It projects about a cable length [some six hundred feet] from shore, and has only 3 or 4 feet on it. The other shoal begins a little above *Tillbury Ness* and runs down to the point; it is about a half cable's length from shore, and has only 5 or 6 feet on it. *Gravesend Mill* open to the westward of *Northfleet Ness* will clear it. As the ebb tide sets strongly in toward

Northfleet Creek and upon the three upper *Chalk Wharfs* at *Northfleet*
you should be careful when coming down with the wind, to guard
against its operations. Between *Northfleet* and *Gravesend* the ground
is hard and bad.

The same ebbing tide that Norie cautioned against would have given
Hunter a valuable extra few feet of water beneath his keel while *Amphitrite*
approached Gravesend Reach heading practically due south.

A three-masted bark had an ideal sail plan for a small crew, but every reach
would have required *Amphitrite*'s yards to be rebraced, to trim her sails to the
changed direction of the wind relative to ship's course as she eased her way
downriver. Perhaps helped along by a southwesterly wind, but possibly drifting with the tide with her topsails barely full enough to give her steerage-way,
Amphitrite's head passed through more than 90 degrees of arc, from northeast
just beyond Woolwich almost to south and back to east again, while she moved
slowly through the Thames' serpentine bends. Nothing suggests that Hunter
and his pilot had any difficulty maneuvering *Amphitrite* to the river's mouth.

From the three survivors of the wreck we know that after two days dropping down the Thames, *Amphitrite* spent Monday night at Margate Roads, a
busy anchorage off the southern channel through the river's broad estuary.
She left Margate for the Downs in darkness at 4:00 AM Tuesday, half an hour
before morning twilight, her departure timed to catch the early high tide at
the mouth of the Thames. Had all gone well, Hunter's course would have
taken him around the North Foreland, then through the narrowest portion
of the Dover Strait between Dungeness, England, and Cap Gris Nez, on the
French coast, and finally out the English Channel to the Atlantic.

Once underway from Margate, Hunter took several hours to leave the
river behind. He then spent the rest of the day threading his way past shallow sands, sailing generally south to *Amphitrite*'s next overnight anchorage in
the Downs, off the town of Deal and in sight of the ruins of Henry VIII's twin
coastal defense forts. The two, Sandown and Walmer Castles, had for centuries overlooked the adjacent water, good holding ground for vessels coming to
anchor—or to invade.

According to *Lloyd's Shipping News*, *Amphitrite*, "a barque, from London
for New South Wales," arrived in the Downs August 27 and anchored overnight in that sheltered place. *Amphitrite* spent Tuesday night in the Downs,
there in company with an impromptu flotilla of merchant vessels and warships, the others planning, like her, soon to go somewhere or to do something. Even more than leaving Woolwich behind, the routine act of putting
the pilot off at Deal before *Amphitrite* started through the Strait marked the
true beginning of her voyage to Sydney. With him gone, *Amphitrite* was on her

own. Now everyone on board, willing or not, was bound for New South Wales, and Hunter, who had sailed to Australia once before as first mate of a convict transport, was responsible for getting all of them there safely.

After a night in the protected roadstead waiting for favorable conditions to help her through the Dover Strait, *Amphitrite* weighed anchor and got underway late Wednesday, August 28, on the afternoon tide propelled by a "moderate breeze." Angling through the strait on the larboard tack, the wind coming across her bow from the west southwest, the ship's long voyage to Australia had finally begun in earnest.

Once in the Strait many of the women, perhaps even most of them, became seasick, lying below in the convicts' compartment and being tossed about on their pallets by the ship's irregular rolling and pitching—a twitchy, corkscrew motion that would have nauseated any landlubber, male or female, and raised ripples in the bilges. After her shipwreck a Royal Navy surveyor asserted that even while laboring through a very heavy gale, *Amphitrite* was not strained and shipped no water. This might have been a falsehood. Between departing from Woolwich and leaving the Downs, her bilges had to be pumped out twice for ninety minutes at a time.

Through the rest of Wednesday *Amphitrite* sailed off the English coast, tacking as necessary while heading generally down-Channel toward distant Lizard Point and, beyond that, the mouth of the Atlantic Ocean, more than three hundred nautical miles away.[6] It is possible that Hunter planned a last stop in England at Portsmouth; Towsey thought this was the captain's plan. If so, the next, short leg in the Channel would have taken him less than half way to Land's End, a small second step on a long trip.

Three days behind the transport *Lloyds*, *Amphitrite* passed Thursday unknowingly falling farther behind the last of the good weather, with a killer storm brewing not far off.[7] The day had dawned uneventfully, hinting at an easy day of sailing. Presumably the next fifteen Thursdays at sea would be tranquil as well. What began as a moderate breeze from the west southwest on this first full day out of the Downs, however, strengthened gradually as the weekend approached, forcing Captain Hunter progressively to reduce sail. Thursday night he sent the crew aloft to double reef *Amphitrite*'s fore and main topsails; by then everything but the foresail had already been furled. She remained under this short canvas—reefed topsails and the foresail—for the next twenty-four hours, into Friday night, while the seas rose and clouds lowered.

Later that year, long after *Amphitrite*'s dead had been recovered and buried in France, the *United Service Journal and Naval and Military Magazine* published "The Shipwreck," an article critical of everything and everybody connected to the catastrophe, especially French authorities, whom it charged failed to provide "those common assistances which the most inferior watering-place

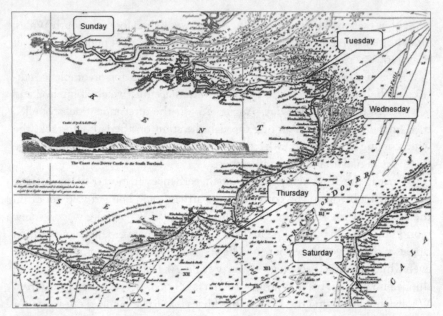

CHART I

Detail from The Entrance to the River Thames Exhibiting the Various Channels from
the River Nore to the Downs. J. W. Norie, hydrographer, 1817, corrected to 1832 and
1837. On Sunday morning, August 25, *Amphitrite* left Woolwich on the morning tide.
Until late that Thursday, her departure for Australia was entirely routine. Monday
night was spent on the Thames, Tuesday night at anchor in Margate Roads, and
Wednesday night at anchor in the Downs, off Deal. On Thursday, while the ship was
passing Dungeness heading down-Channel, the weather began to deteriorate swiftly.
Saturday midafternoon, after two nights and a day under reefed sails and later bare
poles in mid-Channel, *Amphitrite* found herself off Boulogne, blown inexorably toward
a lee shore by a great storm. It's possible none of the crew recognized where they were
when the French coast first came into sight.
© THE BRITISH LIBRARY BOARD, SHELFMARK 1240 (97) 13.

in England might have supplied" to the unfortunates washed up on shore.
According to the *Journal*'s count, there were 137 on board *Amphitrite*: 100
women, 23 infants, and 14 crewmembers, a census that was almost certainly
incorrect.

    In a snarky paragraph on the third page, the article's unidentified author
spent a sentence or two comparing the seamanship of vessels of the Royal Navy
and the merchant fleet before getting into his narrative. On Friday, two days
out of the Downs anchorage and in a freshening breeze, he wrote, *Amphitrite*'s
crew began to reef her topsails and "courses," the mainsails, reducing the canvas aloft to match the growing strength of the wind. "Although in men-of-war

half an hour at the very utmost, even in ships badly disciplined, would have been ample time for the performance of such duties," he continued, "yet on board a merchant-ship it not unfrequently, especially in squally, rainy weather requires the whole night for such a reduction of sail." The jab was unfair, and the author must have known better. Warships were overmanned for anything but war at sea; their complement was fixed by the requirement to serve the guns, not what was necessary to sail the ship. By comparison, merchant ships carried the minimum number of hands possible because the economics of their business (and the terms of the charter party) permitted nothing else.

Early Saturday the weather went from thick to violent. At 2:00 AM the crew was back in the rigging close-reefing the topsails, taking in the last reef-band and leaving only a single horizontal ribbon of sail on the fore and main masts to maintain steerageway. When the main topsail sheet went out later, taking with it control of what little main mast canvas had been left in the wind, Hunter was forced to send men aloft to furl that sail, too. *Amphitrite* then hove to, pitching and rolling atop the waves under bare poles alone, from just after 3:30 AM Saturday until 10:00 that morning. After many hours on deck and aloft, everyone in her small crew must have been exhausted and soaked, the women and children being thrown about in the darkness below not much more comfortable than the watch exposed at the ship's wheel.

Nearing midday Saturday Hunter had a single triangular storm trysail put up, heavy canvas rigged fore and aft between the fore and main masts and designed for nothing more than keeping the ship's head into the wind and seas, safe from broaching. Unable to see the shore and with the sky obscured for more than a day, none of her officers knew the ship's position.

In the absence of any alternative—a practical shipboard anemometer to measure wind speed at sea wasn't developed until 1846—we can use Royal Navy captain Francis Beaufort's wind force scale as a guide to what *Amphitrite* was enduring. In 1833 Beaufort was the Royal Navy's hydrographer, well known and widely admired not only for his seamanship but also for his survey-ing and cartographic skills. Beaufort's twelve-point scale, an improvement of one he adopted from Alexander Dalrymple, used the maximum amount of sail a "well-conditioned" frigate could carry as an indicator of the strength of the wind she was experiencing. Up through Beaufort Force 5, defined as a "Fresh Breeze," for example, such a ship would carry courses, topsails, topgallants, and royals, four tiers of canvas rising from the deck. The scale was not formally adopted until 1838 by the Royal Navy (and not until decades later for mer-chant mariners), but it was in general use years before then.

Based on Beaufort's scale (which might credit the convict transport with a more experienced crew than she had), *Amphitrite* on August 31, with only her trysail up, was likely sailing through a Force 11 "severe storm," winds more powerful than any of the four "gales" Beaufort had defined, and inferior in strength only to Beaufort Force 12, a "Hurricane," with a force of wind "no canvas could withstand." Force 11 translated to winds around sixty knots, roughly seventy miles per hour. Even blowing over the confined waters of the English Channel, northerlies at this speed could push up seas approaching thirty feet high. On board *Amphitrite*, with her low freeboard (the distance from sea level to the deck), such waves would have appeared mountainous and been life threatening.

Sometime on Saturday the wind that had been tearing at her since Friday swung farther around the compass. What had started as great discomfort now became mortal danger: *Amphitrite* was being shoved by the storm toward the unseen French coast.

33

The murderous storm of late summer 1833 was not unique. The "dreadful tempest" that blew across the British Isles and toward Scandinavia at the end of November and beginning of December 1703 was the archetype of a perfect storm in the eastern Atlantic. Dazed survivors' accounts reported thunderstorms, at least one tornado, possibly a waterspout, and, very improbably, an earthquake as part of the "Commotion of the Elements of Air, Earth, and Water" that had fallen upon them. Surveying the broad path of death and destruction the storm left behind, stunned residents of Wales and England understood their battering as the wrath of God expressed in wind, rain, and temblor. For the next two centuries the devastation was recalled in sermons and prayers on the storm's anniversary.

Hundreds died ashore, most felled by flying bits of roofing and chimney pots or uprooted trees, and perhaps thousands drowned off ships underway or caught at anchor in coastal roadsteads. In a span of hours the Royal Navy lost twelve ships and 1,700 men and, reportedly, seven hundred other vessels were piled in a raft of wreckage in the lower reaches of the Thames. One colorful report had it that HMS *Association*, flagship of Vice Admiral Sir Stafford Fairborne's squadron, was torn from her anchorage at the entrance to the Thames and blown all the way to the coast of Norway, where she fetched up unexpectedly without anchors or cables on board—and, worse yet for her crew, without any beer to drink. "The most remarkable of the many edifices destroyed during that dreadful night," wrote Robert Chambers in his 1869 *Book of Days*, "was the first Eddystone lighthouse, erected four years previously by an enterprising but incompetent individual, named [Henry] Winstanley. . . . It was built of wood and deficient in every element of stability. . . . When the fatal tempest came, it swept the flimsy structure into the ocean, and with it the unfortunate Winstanley, and five other persons who were with him in the building."[8]

The best known contemporary description of that late autumn 1703 hurricane is former Newgate prisoner-turned-author Daniel Defoe's *The Storm; or, a Collection of the Most Remarkable Casualties and Disasters which happened in the Late Dreadful Tempest, Both by Sea and Land,* printed in 1704. Not Defoe's first published work, it was his first full-length book, out fifteen years before his much better known *Robinson Crusoe.* A flood of his novels and other works followed into the 1720s. *The Storm*'s structure is remarkably modern: an introductory essay in several chapters by the author followed by edited "authentick Accounts" written by eyewitness survivors in various places whom Defoe had solicited through newspaper advertisements in the *Daily Courant* and the *London Gazette.* Some sixty of these contributions were used, a few surreptitiously substantially revised, each describing one facet of a calamity marked by general "Horror and Confusion."

Catastrophic storms on this scale are uncommon over the British Isles, visiting them perhaps several times each century, although episodes of harsh weather in Europe appear to have been more frequent during the centuries of the "little ice age" (1550–1850) than before or since. The great gale of 1833 must have been much like that of 1703. It might have been spun up from whatever atmospheric energy and instability remained from an Atlantic hurricane that had passed off shore the American mid-Atlantic states and near the Crown Colony of Bermuda about the time *Amphitrite* departed Woolwich. Late on Thursday, August 29, the former tropical storm began to blow over the English Channel and its eastern littoral. It spent itself some four days later, finally drained of energy by cold temperatures over Scandinavia, leaving in its wake churning seas and terrific damage ashore and afloat.

Unfortunately, no early-nineteenth-century author had Defoe's good instincts and compiled a book of survivors' impressions. What we have instead is journalists' reporting. Everywhere the storm was described by them in superlatives. Newspapers seemingly competed to see whose was the most colorful or most dismal description of the tempest. At Hull: "In the memories of the widow and orphans of the shipwrecked voyagers those days will form an epoch not to be forgotten." At Flushing, Holland: "Our seamen declare that they do not remember to have witnessed so severe and long-continued a storm. The night of Sunday in particular the weather was most terrible; the violent gusts of wind, the awful claps of thunder, the incessant blaze of the lightning, the rain pouring down in torrents, with the frightful raging of the sea, formed altogether a scene which it is more easy to conceive than to describe, exhibiting to the mariner a war of elements threatening to involve all nature in destruction." Down the coast at Ostend, in newly independent Belgium, less colorfully but to the same effect: "For the last 48 hours a most frightful storm has been raging. Such a one has not been known here within the memory of man." A gourmet in Somerset, England, offered his special perspective of the calamity: "Immense heaps of apples have, within the last few days, been blown down in the orchards throughout this county. The process of cider-making will, in consequence, be prematurely commenced, but the beverage thus made will prove to be of inferior quality."

Imbedded in the published accounts of dikes topped and polders flooded, ships blown aground and piers washed away, roofs lifted and pigs drowned, hop grounds flattened and orchards stripped of their fruit, flying chimney pots and eight hundred dead sparrows found under a single tree near St. Ives, is the bare outline of a tight, deep low-pressure center and trailing fronts passing suddenly and swiftly over the central British Isles. Late summer temporarily obliterated by a "severe visitation" of howling winds, rain, sleet, and even snow. The *Norfolk Chronicle* compared the resulting destruction ashore to that of a West Indian typhoon. "Such a storm, at least one so fatal in its consequences," wrote *The Times* of London on Saturday, September 7, "has seldom if ever been known at such a period of the year. The oldest underwriter at Lloyd's remembers nothing of the kind."

The author's reference to Lloyd's as an authority was natural.[9] In the 1830s Lloyd's underwriters knew all there was that could be known about hazards to global shipping. Although perhaps not the preeminent commercial intelligence collection business in the world—that title probably belonged to the Rothschild banking empire, with its centers in London, Frankfurt, Naples, Paris, and Vienna—Lloyd's had no rival for second place. Comprehensive marine intelligence (information about ship specifications and their material condition, sailing departures and arrivals, the names of masters, cargoes on board, port operations and quarantine requirements, and hazards and catastrophes along the sea lanes) to satisfy the risk management requirements of Lloyd's many insurance syndicates flowed into London from sources in the British Isles and dozens of agents abroad. The information was published in proprietary registers and subscription newsletters that made Lloyd's underwriters uniquely well informed and wonderfully wealthy while commerce boomed around them. *Lloyd's List* was already ninety-nine years old when news of the wreck of *Amphitrite* appeared in its pages. The issues of September 3 and 10 would become the authoritative inventories of the weekend's destruction at sea.

If Lloyd's oldest underwriter, the aged keeper of the institution's collective memory, didn't remember as powerful a summer storm as this, most were willing to believe that was because there had not been one such. That conclusion was consistent with an appraisal in *Nautical Magazine* that in its issue of

October 1833 footnoted a two-page, small-print table of shipwrecks with this
sober commentary:

> It has not fallen to our lot before, to record such extensive losses of life
> and property as have been produced by the severe gales which took
> place in the end of August , and the beginning of September; and it
> has been generally allowed by seamen, that they were the severest
> within the their recollection in these latitudes. They commenced in
> the S.W. on the 29th of Aug., and hauled gradually around to N.W.
> and N.E., lasting throughout the first week in September. Their con-
> sequences have been sad and depressing. Our shores have been liter-
> ally strewed with wrecks, and many vessels have foundered unheard
> of and unseen. To relate the several accounts which we have, would
> fill a volume of our work with a lengthening tale of sorrow and suffer-
> ing. We shall therefore leave our table of wrecks to impart the mel-
> ancholy facts, adding one or two of the most important particulars
> concerning a few of the vessels, and we fear that even the extensive
> list it presents does not include the entire loss of British shipping.[10]

Lloyd's was the authoritative source for the identity of ships lost or damaged in the gale, and for whatever snippet of amplifying information might be
attached to the name of each vessel sunk, grounded, or damaged. But Lloyd's
was imperfect. There was no mention in *Lloyd's List*, for example, of the disappearance of *Lady Emma Wemyss*, foundered on Sunday some six miles off shore
with the loss of four lives. She left three widows and eight fatherless children.
No mention either of the steam packet, *Ardincaple*, a day late underway and ten
hours out of Leith for Newcastle midday Sunday with thirty-two passengers on
board when "a most dreadful sea struck her upon the larboard [port] quarter . . .
and made a clean sweep of everything off the deck, tore away the whole of the
bulwark stanchions and paddle-casing on the starboard side, and we lament to
add, carried overboard Captain McLeod [and four others]." Before *Ardincaple*,
with her fires out and her stack gone, made it to the lee of the rocky Farne
Islands under a jury-rigged sail, the remainder of the crew had been washed over
the side. She stayed afloat long enough to get under tow only because among her
surviving male passengers were several sailors, including Captain Pearson of the
steam packet *King of the Netherlands*, who in the crisis assumed command.

Other's accounts were also flawed and included some catastrophes that
never happened. That's the case with an unnamed American vessel, described
in Bell's *Life in London* of September 8, "which went on shore at Dunkirk with
180 passengers, all drowned."

34

Notwithstanding what old underwriters and veteran sailors might or might not remember, reliable historic information about severe weather in European waters wasn't available in the early nineteenth century. The process through which governments slowly assumed the responsibility for weather forecasting and for data collection and dissemination was paced by progress in science and pressure from shipping and agricultural interests. Enabled by the former, impelled by the latter, and impeded by limited funds (and until the invention of the telegraph by slow communications), national meteorological offices were not opened until after midcentury. The first, in 1854, was the United Kingdom Meteorological Office (successor to the Board of Trade's meteorological department), but it was not until years later that historic weather phenomena could be spoken of in any but anecdotal terms.

In 1991 the Cambridge University Press published climate historian Hubert Lamb's *Historic Storms of the North Sea, British Isles and Northwest Europe*, a study of four centuries of bad weather across an enormous area spanning 25 degrees of latitude and 40 of longitude. The study catchment area was centered on a point in the North Sea roughly one hundred miles east of Aberdeen, Scotland. It encompassed more than 2 million square miles, including a slice of the eastern North Atlantic Ocean, the entire English Channel and Celtic Sea, and bits of the Baltic, Greenland, and Norwegian Seas.

Lamb and his colleagues had begun their research for the book some fifteen years earlier, funded initially by a grant from Shell Exploration, Ltd., which wanted to learn about possible risks to the oil platforms their company had under construction in or planned for the North Sea. Study completed, the scholars identified fourteen "class I storms" (the most severe) and twenty-eight "class II storms" (the next most severe) among the 166 that passed through this vast space between 1509 and 1990. Sadly, the great gale of 1833 was not among them.

The only remaining possibility to learn about this particular storm from scientific data rather than contemporary journalism might have come from an unusual database called CLIWOC, the Climatological Database for the World's Oceans, a digitized compilation of centuries of observations at sea as recorded daily in the deck logs of ships from four nations. The logbooks come from the navies and merchant fleets of the United Kingdom, Holland, France, and Spain. (Historic logs from Europe's other great seafaring nation, Portugal, were largely lost in the great earthquake, tsunami, and fires of November 1, 1755, that one after the other destroyed Lisbon and its archives. More than 30,000 died in the catastrophe. The principal temblor was felt as far away as Germany.) These data are now being mined by an international consortium for insights into global climate and climate change preindustrialization, but they are useful, as well, for point data on specific events—some specific events.

What is unusual about CLIWOC is not the use of ships' logs. Deck logs were a source for the analysis that underlay Royal Engineer Lieutenant Colonel William Reid's pioneering 1838 book, *An Attempt to Develop the Law of Storms by Means of Facts, Arranged According to Place and Time and Hence to Point Out a Cause for the Variable Winds, with a View to Practical Use in Navigation.* Some twenty years later, Lieutenant Matthew Fontaine Maury's oceanographic research also drew on ships' logs, in his case to postulate prevailing winds and currents in the North Atlantic by month during the year. CLIWOC's enormous scale is what makes it unique, that and the fact that it is digitized. Unfortunately, the database uses only data from the deep oceans, to avoid boundary layer effects resulting from vessels being close to land. Accordingly, the study area excluded the Mediterranean, the Caribbean . . . and the English Channel.

35

"From an examination of Lloyd's List, from the year 1793 to the commencement of 1829," reported an anonymous tract several years later, "it has appeared that the number of British vessels alone, lost during that period, amounted, on an average, to not less than one and a half daily."[11] Just over ten ships every calendar week, year in and year out for thirty-five years. According to the author, warships fared no better than merchant ships:

> Out of 551 ships of the Royal Navy of England, lost to the country during the period above-mentioned, only 160 [fewer than one-third] were taken or destroyed by the enemy; the rest having either stranded or foundered, or having been burnt by accident—a striking proof that the dangers of naval warfare, however great, may be far exceeded by the storm, the hurricane, the shoal, and all the other perils of the deep. . . .
>
> To this immense loss of ships of war and commerce, the imagination must be left to supply the incalculable amount of wealth swallowed up with them, and the thousands of human beings who thus found a watery grave.

With this as his depressing introduction, the author launched into a sermon constructed like a Socratic dialogue, with a naïve shipping clerk asking questions of a worldly colleague, whose answers educated the reader about the evils of the British ship classification system and the corrupting effects of maritime insurance.

This text could have served equally well as an introduction to a broader inquiry into the causes of these sad statistics. By the mid-1830s the loss of British lives and property at sea year after year had become so substantial, and so visible, that in 1836 Parliament empaneled a select committee of the House of Commons to "inquire into the causes of shipwrecks," to calculate (or at least estimate) the swallowed wealth and numbers of drowned human beings, and to suggest what might be done in remedy.

Under the leadership of James Silk Buckingham, MP for Sheffield (himself a sailor, a prodigious foreign traveler, and a sometime journalist), the committee met often during June and July to take the testimony of dozens of witnesses, after which it published a 450-page report, one that went beyond establishing causes and included a list of specific "remedies proposed or suggested." The report was not only voluminous but also candid. In three instances (ship construction, crew performance, and sobriety at sea) it compared British practices unfavorably to American, which must have rankled its readers.

Buckingham's committee first scoped the problem through an analysis of Lloyd's underwriters' data from six sample years, 1816–18 and 1833–35, recognizing that these numbers understated reality because they included only insured vessels (for this reason, e.g., neither *Amphitrite* or the *Earl of Wemyss* were included in the 1833 data). Even so, the results were sobering. Study completed, the select committee concluded that British shipping wrecked or foundered at sea during the early 1830s represented an annual property loss of some £3 million sterling, and the extinction of not fewer than one thousand lives every year from drowning. (Some ports suffered hugely and disproportionately. In the five years 1832–36, more than one-quarter of ships home ported at Tyne—272 of approximately 1,000, colliers for the most part—were lost at sea, leaving behind, the report noted precisely, a surprisingly few 147 widows and orphans.)

Buckingham and his colleagues identified not two but ten principal causes of shipwreck that could be eliminated or reduced:

1. Defective construction of ships
2. Inadequacy of equipment
3. Imperfect state of repair
4. Improper or excessive loading
5. "Inappropriateness of forms" (meaning bad ship design)
6. Incompetence of masters and officers
7. Drunkenness of officers and men
8. Operation of marine insurance

9. Lack of harbors of refuge
10. Navigation chart errors

The reason for *Amphitrite*'s sad fate had been sought several years earlier in several of these causes, but not in the most relevant one, poor performance upwind, which is what forced Captain Hunter's decision to run his ship ashore.

"Inappropriateness of forms," the report explained three years after *Amphitrite* broke up, "often incapacitates [British vessels] from beating off a lee shore, and consequently leads to their being wrecked." Bad merchant ship design, Parliament learned in 1836, was

> partly the result of the nature of British maritime trade and partly of the defective systems of measurement and the heavy tonnage duties formerly levied on British ships; many vessels being necessarily constructed of a flat form of bottom to adapt them to the shoal harbours of England, and enable them to lie in safety while aground, but though these last are cases which no reform of fiscal regulations could remove, yet it is established and admitted that the system of measurement and heavy tonnage duties which formerly existed [before 1834], presented a strong inducement to shipowners to build ships of such forms and dimensions as should write a small nominal tonnage by admeasurement with a large actual capacity for carrying a cargo considerably above the tonnage at which she might be registered which [?] qualities could only be obtained at the sacrifice of speed, buoyancy, celerity of evolution, and consequent incompetency to escape from the dangers of a lee shore.

Curiously, weather was excluded as a cause in Buckingham's report, presumably because it was not subject to either elimination or reduction. But if poor upwind performance is what forced Hunter to put *Amphitrite* on the Boulogne sands, the wind he was desperately resisting came from a furious, unexpected storm, and the low clouds that had obscured the coast until too late also came from that storm.

Despite the committee's efforts and insights, solutions came hard. Twenty years later, during the mid-1850s, the statistics on ships and lives lost were not appreciably better, as two ships and nine lives lost on average every three days, despite the passage of the Merchant Shipping Act of 1850, which assigned regulatory oversight of the industry to the Board of Trade.

3 6

On Sunday, September 8, Bell's *Life in London*, looking back at the great gale from the perspective of one week, recalled that "the loss of life and property in all parts of the country presents a dreadful catalogue of calamities, which must fill the minds of our readers with horror. . . . On Monday the public mind was shocked by the description of the disaster of the most appalling description, and every day since has produced some new account equally heart-rending." So it was, for example, that readers learned of dead bodies floating ashore through-out the storm "from one end of the Norfolk coast to the other." The small town of Cromer at the tip of the peninsula reportedly collected eighty-four from its waterfront over the weekend. The unfortunates were buried in the church yard on Sunday.[12]

Published reports after the storm's passage from English towns inland emphasized the damage to homes (roofs and chimneys, especially) and to fields and orchards. At 8:00 Saturday evening, according to the *Cambridge Chronicle*, the rain- and tide-swollen Ouze River breached its banks, and "such was the immense body and impetuosity of the water, that in a few hours upwards of 1,500 acres of land were laid under water . . . many acres of standing corn are irretrievably lost and many head of cattle drowned. . . . The damage sustained by the lamentable event has not yet been ascertained, but it is much to be feared that it is to a considerable extent, nor is there any prospect that the water can be got off before the next spring."

Similar accounts from ports along the North Sea and Channel coasts nat-urally focused on the destruction of ships, sailors' lives lost, and harbor infra-structure damage. "The whole coast is strewn with vessels, parts of vessels, boats, goods, &c.," said *The Times* of the shore around Lynn in a report unusual for its consideration of the human cost of the calamity. "The brig *Margaret*, [Captain] Osire . . . went down on Saturday afternoon, near Whiting Sand and all hands perished. By this awful circumstance there are four women left with-out husbands, and 22 fatherless children." Better luck attended the crew of the brig *Waterloo*, like *Margaret* carrying a load of coal. After *Waterloo* went down, "the crew ascended the rigging at 8 on Saturday night, and remained lashed in that perilous situation, the sea breaking over them mountains high, till 1 the next day, when they were taken off by our fishermen, several of whom manned their boats and succeeded in rescuing eight individuals."

In some places, the effects of the storm were as weird as they were devas-tating. From the same September 8 account in *Bell's*:

In the metropolis [London] and its vicinity the effects of the Tempest were everywhere visible. . . . The wind, as the sailors say, blew all the water out of the Thames, and persons were seen fording the river at Waterloo-bridge. The tide has not been so low in a great many years. The shoal just below London-bridge was high out of the water, and the Margate and Gravesend steam-boats were for a short time hard aground and unable to get away. The return of the tide was truly remarkable; for, without any previous indication whatever (for it appeared to be running down with great velocity the instant before), it rose at once nearly a foot, rolling in like a wave, and in less than three minutes after the persons on the shoals took to their boats, the shoals were under water, and the steam-boats afloat and under weigh.

L'Annotateur, Boulogne-sur-Mer's newspaper, inventoried the losses to the French city's important fishing fleet, seventy-four of which boats were working the waters off Scotland, not far from where a Scottish smack named Earl of Wemyss was assailed, when the storm struck. Seven of the French boats were sunk (their crews were saved), and another eighteen lost their catch and their equipment and were damaged so badly as to require reconstruction prior to sailing back to France. Captain Guillaume Huret's boat had left the grounds early, only to be lost with her crew of seven en route home.

Most of the losses compiled by Lloyd's disappeared quickly from public attention, largely unnoticed and unmourned amid the great fleet lost at sea during the weekend. One did not, the Earl of Wemyss, of Leith's Old Shipping Company. In common with Amphitrite, the Earl of Wemyss' tragedy was much more durable than all the others, in part because it exposed the failure of men to act in manly fashion.

37

Early morning February 26, 1852, Her Majesty's Troopship Birkenhead, almost two months out of Portsmouth and under way at full speed for Algoa Bay, South Africa, ran aground on an uncharted rock two miles off the South African coast. The ship, an iron-hulled, paddle-wheel steamer built by John Laird in 1845 in his busy yard across the Mersey River from Liverpool, England (and designed originally as a warship), was carrying nearly 650 passengers. Among those on board were officers and men from several British line infantry regiments ordered to fight in the Xhosa Wars and a small number of women and children, members of their families.

The impact tore open the several largest of Birkenhead's twelve hull compartments, instantly drowning many sleeping below. In the twenty minutes after the grounding and before Birkenhead sank, the women and children on board were loaded into the few boats safely launched and sent toward shore.

There were not enough boats for all the others embarked, and so the officers and men of the regiments stood frozen in ranks and files on deck watching the others pull toward shore. Standing fast as their ship sank beneath them, they quickly become the legendary model of British heroism and sangfroid in the face of certain death at sea.[13]

But the tradition of "women and children first" predated the wreck of HMT *Birkenhead*. So it was that thirty years earlier, in September 1833, the news that the crew and all the male passengers on board the *Earl of Wemyss*, sailing between London and Leith, had survived her grounding in the great gale at the end of August but that women and children on board had drowned was met with disbelief and anger.

Some sixty vessels registered in Great Britain were reported to Lloyd's as having been lost in the same gale, caught in the North Sea and the English Channel by the sudden storm and driven aground or sunk outright. Perhaps an equal number on the ship registries of other European states went down, too, as must have countless small fishing boats and miscellaneous small craft on no register at all. Among all these and including *Amphitrite*, the wreck of the *Earl of Wemyss* briefly became the most notorious. The smack's story unfolded through the last months of 1833 in a dozen long pieces in *The Times* and Edinburgh's *Scotsman* and in occasional periodical articles, more attention by far than that focused on any other aspect of the freak storm.

Leith, Edinburgh's port on the Firth of Forth, was a busy place in the 1830s. Four hundred hard miles overland by horse, carriage, or wagon separated the Scottish capital from London, so the preferred route between the two places was by sea. Later in the decade, most scheduled service to and from the Leith and Berwick Wharf on the Thames in London was powered by steam, but in 1833 packet lines operating smacks (nearly two-hundred-ton, oceangoing vessels with a distinctive cutter rig carrying a huge mainsail) were still eking out a profit competing against steamships on the same route.

Those of the Old Shipping Company, berthed at the foot of Queen Street, were called "white siders," distinguished from the rival "red siders" of the London and Edinburgh Shipping Company and the "green siders" of the London, Leith Edinburgh, and Glasgow Shipping Company, by their stripe of white paint on the hull. All three companies carried passengers and freight and hauled convicts sentenced to transportation or the hulks, as many as thirty at one time, from Edinburgh to London. The Old Shipping Company sailed on Tuesdays and Thursdays for the English capital.

On Thursday, August 29, while *Amphitrite* was off Dungeness, the *Earl of Wemyss* (named for the eighth earl himself, a sometime-passenger on the line; his name is pronounced "weemz") left London for Leith with Captain Henry Nesbit in command. Not the same Captain Nesbit who almost thirty years earlier had been master of the Old Shipping Company's smack *Queen Charlotte* when she was attacked by a French privateer. Her successful defense earned that Nesbit a £105 reward from the owners. Common name aside, the captain of 1833 doesn't sound much like the hero of 1804.

Ahead of the *Earl of Wemyss* was a 417-mile passage that, depending on the weather, could take as little as several days or as much as two weeks, but usually took one. Nesbit later said he had nineteen passengers on board, eight men and eleven women and children, but his count didn't include several passengers not traveling business class in the compact men's and women's salons but traveling economy in steerage. A substantial load of cargo was on board, too, including pockets (man-sized bales) of hops from Kent. After the wreck fifty or sixty men worked for hours to unload the ship's hold of the now-sodden stuff packed inside, none of it insured.

Late afternoon Saturday, Nesbit testified at a hearing later, a northeaster blew up in the North Sea and "continued to freshen until it became a hurricane." Others on board said that the gale had been blowing since before 6:00 that morning, when the smack was off the Spurn Light. By midday Saturday, an anonymous survivor told the editor of the *Scotsman*, *Earl of Wemyss* was adrift out of control on seas "like mountains of snow," all her canvas shredded and her stern boat gone. The wind, rain, and sleet must have been ferocious. David Reid, Nesbit's first mate, had little to say to the magistrates investigating the wreck beyond confirming the captain's self-serving account, but he did volunteer that "had leather been on board for sails, instead of canvas, it would not have stood the gale."

By 10:30 Saturday night—an hour or so into full darkness and soon after *Amphitrite* had been battered to death a few hundred miles away at Boulogne-sur-Mer—the *Earl of Wemyss* was in extremis: She'd lost both anchors in a failed attempt to wait out the storm in place and was now aground on the North Norfolk coast off Brancaster, some four hundred yards off shore atop the "scurves," outcroppings of mud and peat. An effort after sunrise on Sunday to launch another boat quickly failed, and soon thereafter the smack flooded with water, either from below through a ruptured hull (the captain's story) or from above by storm-driven seas breaking over unprotected skylights and shattering their glass (the survivors' consensus story), drowning everyone in the ladies' cabin below. But not before one of the men had time to observe "Mrs. Cormack, a young lady about 19, with her child 18 months old lying in the upper [berth]. She looked up—shook her head—held up her child—kissed it—pressed it to her bosom, and lay down to die—for the returning wave, now awfully increased by what poured in at the broken sky-light of the ladies' cabin suffocated all but *one* in an instant. I heard but one shriek."

The still-living now fled on deck, "where we found the captain and crew, with all the steerage passengers, including three females, secured to the rigging and the winch. We lashed ourselves in the same manner, and continued there with the sea breaking over us for about four hours." Their rescue came later.

Captain Nesbit missed at least two opportunities to save his passengers. A chance to wade ashore at 2:00 Sunday morning during a lull at low water passed when he misread a nautical almanac and confused the flow of the tide with its ebb. He then offered the "fatal advice" that sent his female passengers and children into their berths. The failure to protect his ship's four skylights, glass-covered chutes through the main deck into the spaces below, set up the drownings that soon followed.

Two weeks later a magistrate's inquiry was convened by the Home Office to determine "whether there had been any loss of life by culpable negligence, or loss of property by dishonesty." The captain's incompetence was made manifest. So, too, was evidence that the dead, "whilst their bodies were yet warm," had been ghoulishly stripped of their valuables by one William Reeve (in some sources "Joseph Newman Reeve"), son-in-law of the aged lord of nearby Brancaster Manor, soon after it became possible to move between the wreck and the shore. Nesbit lost his job and was ejected by his guild. Reeve was tried in March 1834 at Norwich assizes before a Judge Vaughan but escaped conviction on two charges of felony thanks to representation by Sir James Scarlett, a local MP and famously able lawyer. He might have been helped by the still general sense, in France as well as in England, that coastal residents were "the lawful heirs of all drowned persons" and so entitled to the property a generous Providence had cast at their feet.

All that is left of the wreck of the *Earl of Wemyss* is a gravestone inscription in a Brancaster churchyard: "Sacred to the memory of Susanna Roche aged 32 years and also to her nephew Alexander David Roche aged 4 years, who were unfortunately drowned with many others in the cabin of the Earl of Wemyss, Leith packet, which was stranded on this coast during the dreadful gale on September 1st 1833 on its passage from London . . . no attempt was ever made to rescue them from their situation, and in continuation of such inhuman conduct their persons were stripped of every valuable and their property plundered."[14]

Coming upon beached bodies while they were, allegedly, "still warm" is one of the clichés of nineteenth-century shipwreck narratives, akin to the frequent discovery of drowned mothers and babes tied together. That latter image, of maternal devotion and childish innocence devoured by the heartless sea, appeared in accounts of the wreck of the *Earl of Wemyss*, and in poems and ballads describing the wreck of *Amphitrite* and French newspaper accounts of the tragedy. A better-than-usual example is in these stanzas from the middle of "Verses on the Loss of Amphitrite . . ." in the March 1, 1834, issue of the *Court Magazine and Belle Assemblée*, a ladies' magazine published in London:

> Men awe-struck gaz'd, yet not unpleas'd to see,
> O'er man's own work, the tempest's mastery,
> But other thoughts to all of us belong'd,
> Who at the hospital, too curious, throng'd
> To see the drowned women's bodies there,
> Outstretch'd in rows, their ghastly faces bare.
> Such sudden death the sinful crowd o'ertook,
> That life's last impulse spoke in every look.
> As though just hush'd to nature's needful rest,
> An infant nestl'd on its mother's breast:
> To part those forms the winds and waves had fail'd,
> A mother's love had over all prevail'd;
> She held in death the being priz'd on earth,
> Though guilt and shame had waited on its birth.
> Some youthful faces kept their beauty still—
> That beauty cause of each succeeding ill;
> While others, worn by passions more than time,
> Told fearfully of unrepented crime.[15]

Like *Amphitrite*'s, the *Earl of Wemyss*' story combined elements certain to fascinate: evidence of grotesque incompetence at sea, the suffering to death of innocents, and a suspicion—soon more than that—of crime inflicted on the dead. The reason for such persistent coverage, however, was that unlike *Amphitrite*'s convicts, all the dead in the *Earl of Wemyss* came from the same propertied class as did readers of *The Times* and the *Scotsman*.

On May 16, 1834, the rebuilt *Earl of Wemyss* went back into service for the first time, carrying passengers and cargo for London under the command of a Captain Brown. Eventually chased out of packet service by steamers, the *Earl of Wemyss*, now twenty-five years old, could still be found at sea fifteen years later sailing between Aberdeen and the Baltic for new owners.

38

Through a midsummer marked by smooth seas and blue skies, but also by unremitting heat, the idlers at Boulogne enjoyed "gypsy parties" on the cliffs, out-of-town picnics at Souverain-Moulin, boat rides up the Liane River to Pont de Briques, and splendid evening soirées in the town's handsome beachfront spa.

More athletic tourists wandered hand in hand along one or another of several popular walking tours, north toward Napoleon's column at Wimile or east in the direction of St. Omer.

At first, while the final weekend in August approached, the lowering clouds and the rising wind from the west might have appeared as harbingers of a belated blessing to the farmers of Boulogne, Dieppe, and other places along the Pas-de-Calais and Normandy coast, if not to fishermen, signs of the end of a summer drought in northeastern France that had dried up ponds, shrunk streams, and opened cracks in the desiccated ground.[16] Soon, however, what had seemed like welcome relief turned into something that resembled the sudden arrival of winter, or worse. A week or so after the storm, Paris newspapers began to run lists of ships and boats damaged or destroyed during two days by the tempest, aggregated under each of the region's chief ports: Dunkirk, Calais, Boulogne, and Saint-Valéry-sur-Somme.

In the early reports eighteen vessels were listed as wrecked, grounded, or seriously damaged near these four ports and twenty-nine lives lost for certain (all from the wrecks near Calais). The unfortunate eighteen included several vessels lost of substantial size, among them the ship *Hylaa*, 340 tons, Captain Heidlman, with timber from Sweden to Portugal; ship *L'August*, 420 tons, Captain Remquet; ship *William*, 500 tons, Captain Friends, carrying timber from Canada to England; and ship *Ann & Amelia*, 587 tons, Captain Compton, India to England with a fortune in indigo and silks on board.

In the 1830s the Dover Strait was probably the world's most congested waterway. Its only possible competitor was the Dardanelles and Istanbul's Golden Horn, the busy maritime junction between Asia and Europe. The great late August gale blew onshore during the second, most violent, half of the storm, inexorably pushing vessels in the Channel toward the French coast. From reports in the French press, the destruction and damage to shipping on the southern shore of the Channel was apparently not so great as on the northern, but the count is certainly too low. It excludes, for example, several vessels listed by Lloyd's as lost off Calais (*Helen* and an unnamed packet from Hull) and Dunkirk (*Chevington Oak*, with her entire crew drowned).

An explanation for the short count might be found in the fact that Bureau Veritas, the French counterpart in Paris to Lloyd's, was only five years old in 1833 when it moved its headquarters from Antwerp to Paris. The company had not developed the information collection apparatus of its much older and more established rival in London; hence French newspapers could not present ship losses as compiled by a single, expert commercial party. Instead, they published what amounted to statistical samples gleaned from waterfront reports.

"All the practical seamen understood," Alexander McKee wrote in his thrilling 1975 story of the wreck of *Medusa* off Senegal, West Africa, in July

1816, "that it is not the sea which is a danger to ships, it is the shore."[17] This truth was surely known to Hunter, whose years afloat and in command would have taught him the same lesson. Saturday afternoon after 3:00, more than an hour following *Amphitrite*'s last depth sounding—after which the clumsy mate lost the deep water line over the side and failed to bring up the hand line to replace it—those on deck suddenly saw land close up on the lee (downwind) beam. All hands turned to again, back up the ratlines and out the foot ropes, to set sail in an attempt to claw her off upwind. The attempt quickly failed. *Amphitrite* was out of sea room.

Roughly eighteen months later Commander William Moriarty, the port officer at Hobart Town, capital of Van Diemen's Land, in an aside on the results of his investigation into the recent wreck of the female convict transport *Neva*, wrote that "a lee shore to a sailor should be an object of the holiest dread; its dangers are seldom to be overcome, its horrors are not to be imagined." Moriarty was a former Royal Navy officer. He was also a shipwreck survivor, so his observations about marine horrors carried special authority. In August 1828 the brig *Letitia*, out of Dublin for Hobart with Moriarty, his wife and two children, and some fifty other Irish emigrants on board, was wrecked on the rocks of Porta Praya at St. Jago in the Cape Verde Islands. The family hitchhiked with little more than what they were wearing in *Hesperus* to Rio de Janeiro, and on from there sailed to Hobart in February 1829 in *Anne*.

Some time around 4:00 PM, several hours before low tide, on August 31, 1833, Captain Hunter deliberately put his ship onto the Boulogne sands, not because it was a good idea but because he had run out of alternatives. *Amphitrite* could no longer escape the horrors of a lee shore, and Hunter would soon experience Moriarty's dread.

FRIENDS, PARENTS, AND RELATIONS, THAT DAY WILL LONG DEPLORE,

That fatal night just sixty-six were washed upon the shore;

It would cause the hardest heart to ache, To see how they did weep,

But death was near & they were plunged, Into the briny deep.

CHAPTER 6

Boulogne-sur-Mer

39

Twice, while the eighteenth century rolled over into the nineteenth, Boulogne briefly found itself at the epicenter of world war. Both times the small town, some 140 road miles northeast of Paris, where the Liane River flowed into the Pas-de-Calais (the Dover Strait) was to be the principal embarkation port for a French amphibious invasion of England commanded by Napoleon. His selection of Boulogne followed encouraging, albeit ancient, precedents. In 55–54 BC and again in AD 43 the Romans (Caesar and later Claudius) chose the Liane estuary as the launch site to mount their own invasions of Britain, whose white chalk cliffs rising tantalizingly in the distance must have made the intervening miles of open water appear less intimidating to the thousands of legionnaires massed on the coast.[1]

Much later, in 1588, that same temptation called out to the king of Spain. Supported by King Philip II's great armada, the Duke of Parma's army in the Spanish Netherlands was to cross the Dover Strait and take England back to the Catholic faith from Anglican apostasy. The Spanish failure to seize Boulogne denied Philip's fleet and Parma's army a safe embarkation port on the Channel from which to work their bold plan, but the armada's dispersal in a storm made everything moot.[2]

Soon after the Directory in Paris first resolved in 1797 to invade Great Britain and to put him in command of the effort, Citizen General Napoleon Bonaparte, then twenty-eight, was seemingly in the middle of serious preparations for his new mission. On February 12, 1798, after a very quick search for suitable invasion bases along the coast from Étaples northeast to Dunkirk, he directed a subordinate to "repair at once to Boulogne and take measures for the improvement of the harbour; it must be capable of accommodating 50 gunboats, from six to nine divisions of fishing-boats, with a draft of 7 to 8 feet; one or two divisions of horse transport, 50 to each division; six ships of 100 tons for the staff; six ships for artillery; six ships for the official management; six ships for hospitals."[3]

In the same directive Napoleon commanded the chief engineer to "start the works at once." In addition to strengthening the defenses of Boulogne, this worthy also was to "send privateers with engineer officers to reconnoiter the English coast from Folkestone to Rye, to ascertain the real conditions of defense on that part of the coast, and take note of the batteries which it would be necessary to carry [overwhelm], or take by surprise, so as to effect a landing." Meanwhile French troops from many places were converging on the city, where they were to assemble and constitute the invasion force, "the Army of England."

Although this first cross-Channel invasion plan was publicly abandoned several months later, in January and February 1798 Napoleon appeared to be intent on attacking England in 1799 after a year's preparation. The idea (never formed into a workable plan) was to have the Army of England, 50,000 to 60,000 men and all their equipment, loaded into open assault boats and towed across the English Channel . . . on a single tide . . . during a long night in winter. (Darkness in summer would be too brief to cover the movement across.) Once on the other side, if, improbably, the army had survived the crossing reasonably intact, it was to fall upon a monarchy ripe—the French trained themselves to believe—for its own republican revolution.

But amid all the port improvements; the slow collection of men, horses, and cannon; the building of boats; and the concentration of munitions, foodstuffs, and other matériel, no one (Napoleon included) figured out a way past the Royal Navy. All the order writing might have been a sham. During or very soon after his hasty port survey, Napoleon decided the mission could not succeed—he wrote the Directory to that effect on February 23—and not long thereafter the planned invasion of England quietly deflated. Instead, at the head of another army, one loaded in an enormous fleet in the Mediterranean, Napoleon sailed from Toulon for Alexandria in May, the first step in a fantasy to gain a strategic colony and to spread French culture to Ottoman Egypt on the way to seizing the real prize: British India. Eighteen months later he was back in Paris; his supporting fleet under Vice Admiral François-Paul Brueys shattered at Aboukir Bay by Rear Admiral Horatio Nelson, his plague-ridden "Army of the Orient" repulsed from Syria and stranded, and France herself in terrible danger.

A second plan to invade England was drafted following the collapse in April 1803 of a halftime break in the fighting after the Treaty of Amiens over arguments about Holland and Malta. The result was the formation of yet another—the third (there would eventually be seven)—international coalition to defeat Napoleon, soon no longer a mere *citoyen* or first consul for life but (after December 1804) the emperor of the French. This time the French assault force was to be much more robust, more than 160,000 men and nine thousand horses. Despite Napoleon's miserly support of his navy, the invasion fleet that was to float the army across the Channel was impressive, too: nearly 2,300 *prames, chaloupes cannonières, bateaux canonnières, péniches*, and miscellaneous other armed and unarmed vessels.

To support this enormous invasion force, Boulogne and its neighbors became host to a cluster of six military camps, and the city's port and six others nearby (among them Étaples, Wimereux, Ambleteuse, and Calais) were transformed into an extensive naval complex, all defended by coastal batteries located many places where there was a clear shot to seaward. The concentration of gun tubes pointing over the Channel merited a new, temporary, name for the area, the "iron coast."

Napoleon visited Boulogne often while the preparations for the assault continued, so often that the great man had several residences there, one in the upper city on the Place des Armes (now Place Godefroy de Bouillon), another a chateau on the road to Paris, and a third a prefabricated, single-story, wooden "pavilion" in one of the army camps. Enormously proud to be hosting the general, Boulogne provided a suitable ceremonial guard at its expense: young locals outfitted in the height of early-nineteenth-century military fashion. White waistcoats over tight scarlet jackets. A sky blue silk sash beneath a sword belt with its suspended sabretache. Buff trousers decorated with a black stripe down each leg. Knee-high Hussars' boots. The entire splendid uniform capped off by a yellow-plumed hat. The occasional changing of the guard at the Place des Armes must have been a full color marvel, prime entertainment for country yokels in town to watch how war was waged by experts. As it developed, however, everything else turned out to be for show too, despite two boat-boarding rehearsals held in summer that seemed to indicate everyone and everything was ready for the great adventure.

The second invasion plan, like the first but more serious, likely would have quickly collapsed of its own weight had the Army of England ever manned its boats. Not until well into the next century was an opposed amphibious landing of such size and complexity feasible (and that one, Gallipoli, ended horribly). In 1805 available French shipping was inadequate to load and lift so huge an army across open water as swiftly as required. Moreover, command arrangements designed for land warfare would likely have yielded to chaos once the invasion began. Finally, despite conceiving a head fake across the Atlantic by allied ships, intended to lure the Royal Navy out of position, Napoleon and his admirals were again not able to come up with a way to seize control of the Channel from Great Britain for the few magical hours—only six, he once boasted to Admiral Latouche-Tréville (later the requirement crept up to two months)—that the emperor believed would have permitted certain victory over the English and made him master of the world. This plan, too, became the preface to something very different: ten years of combat on a twentieth-century scale in Austria and Prussia, on the Iberian Peninsula, in Russia, and finally, in Belgium.

40

Two subsequent invasion plans, in 1807 and 1811, came to even less. At war's end in 1815, with Napoleon safely confined on remote St. Helena in the South Atlantic, all that Boulogne had to show for its recent prominence were some harbor improvements, war surplus fortifications, and a handsome, unfinished monument, the towering Colonne de la Grande Armée, built in premature celebration of the great general's greatest success. During the era that followed, the city, the capital of its arrondissement in the Département du Pas-de-Calais, grew steadily. From perhaps 13,000 residents at the end of the war in 1815, its population increased to nearly 21,000 in 1832—for scale, several thousand fewer than contemporary Albany, New York, or Cincinnati, Ohio.

Paradoxically the city that was twice to have been the springboard for unrivaled French domination of Europe evolved instead into an outpost of Englishness on the Continent. "It is a busy and populous place, the shops presenting an appearance of great opulence, and the numerous hotels indicating a place of considerable resort." This from Irish artist Clarkson Stanfield's short description of Boulogne that served as a caption to three of his steel engravings, from a collection published in 1836 depicting scenes "in the British Channel." His admiration was ambiguous, however. Boulogne, Stanfield went on to say, "is much frequented by the English, and particularly by that class whose moderate incomes are sufficient to indulge a taste for luxury when it is to be procured for a reasonable amount. It is also an asylum for those who love England so well, that they are not easily prevailed upon to take up a more distant abode, yet are not sufficiently attached to their country or loyal to their

king to covet a residence at the expense, or in obedience to the summonses of
His Majesty issued from the [law] courts at Westminster."⁴

When *Amphitrite* sailed from Woolwich during the last week of August
1833, summer was in full heat on the beaches of Boulogne, where sea surface water temperature was about 65°F, near its annual high. Salted among
Boulogne's natives and visiting vacationers from many places was a large
community of Britons, most of whom were seeking not life on the edge in
the resort town but respectability on the cheap. Its members lived out their
days in an English-speaking enclave complete with hotels, clubs, schools, a
library and reading room, and a newspaper. (Off and on. The first English language paper, published in 1834, was the short-lived *Boulogne Literary Album &
Weekly Advertiser*. Its successors lasted only a year or two.) They left this life
for the next through the portals of the six-hundred-seat chapel of the Church
of England on rue St. Martin, to be interred among their countrymen in the
nearby Cimetière des Anglais. Dispatched toward eternity to be spent with
God in heaven, who, like everyone else, was expected to speak to them in
their mother tongue.⁵

From the *haute ville*, the old fortified town on the bluffs above the port,
one could see England's Kent and Sussex counties and imagine oneself to be
there. Until the Chemin de Fer du Nord's rail connection to Paris via Amiens
(157 miles) was completed in 1848, it was easier to travel between Boulogne
and London, 105 miles across the strait and up the Thames, than it was to go
overland from Boulogne to Paris by coach.

More than an outpost, Boulogne-sur-Mer was the busiest French port trading with Great Britain as well as a holiday destination. The 1838 *Almanach de
Boulogne-sur-mer*, looking back five years, reported that in 1833 some 15,600
travelers had passed through the port on the way to and from France. Its shipping basin next to the *basse ville* handled fully a quarter of all tonnage flying
the British flag entering France in the early 1830s. On average a British registry merchant vessel sailed into Boulogne every working day of the year.⁶
During the last six months of 1832, the resident consul reported to the Foreign
Office, twenty-eight different English ships had entered Boulogne a total of
173 times, ten times as often as those of five other nations combined. The
trader *Liberty*, from Rye, helped inflate the number. Carrying English eggs in
and French wine out, she came to and went from Boulogne an average of once
each week. The traffic must have kept His Majesty's consul and the Lloyd's
agent in the city busy.

By 1833 J. W. Norie and Company of London had published nearly a
dozen "pilots," individually bound books of sailing directions for the world's
principal seas and oceans, and had already released and superseded the first
nine editions of its 1805 navigation textbook, *A Complete Epitome of Practical*

Navigation, proudly described as "containing all necessary instructions for keeping a ship's reckoning at sea." The book followed by several years the first edition of its transatlantic counterpart, Nathaniel Bowditch's now-famous book, *The American Practical Navigator*, itself a revision of an earlier text by another author. These two volumes became the foundation of an enormous English language library of texts on seafaring, detailed how-to guides to mastery of the industry that underlay the global commerce of the era and enabled nineteenth-century capitalism.

A *Complete Epitome* contained (in what eventually swelled to nine hundred–plus pages of text and tables) all the book knowledge necessary to navigate the globe, an "oblate spheroid" Norie helpfully explained to his readers, whose circumference was nearly 24,869 miles and whose "polar and equatorial diameters are, respectively, 7898 and 7924 English miles, being nearly in the ratio of 304 to 305." The effective edition in 1833 was the tenth. The book was revised and republished at roughly four-year intervals into the next century.

Before his death at seventy-one in 1843, John Norie saw his company, conveniently sited down the street from Lloyd's and the Honourable East India Company's monumental headquarters on Leadenhall Street, rise to become the principal vendor of navigation instruments and publisher of charts and maritime ephemera in the United Kingdom and, arguably, the world. It was possible to sail the world's oceans and seas in the early nineteenth century with substantial if not necessarily complete confidence by referring exclusively to Norie pilots.

Norie's popular *British Channel Pilot* included directions for sailing both English and French sides of the Channel. England from the North Foreland (where traffic leaving the Port of London for points west turned sharply south from the mouth of the Thames toward the Dover Strait) to beyond Lizard Point, and the "coasts and harbours of France" from Calais, facing Dover, southwest to Brest, on the Atlantic.

In describing Boulogne, after first cautioning sailors about the dangers of a strong westerly wind to ships at anchor in St. John's Road below Cap Gris Nez, at the western end of the Strait of Dover, Norie sounded for a few sentences like a practiced tour guide:

> The TOWN OF BOULOGNE is divided into the upper and lower town; the latter is commonly distinguished by the title of *Boulogne sur Mer*; it lies along the shore and it is better built than the upper town. A considerable trade is now carried on at this port in fresh and salt fish, especially herrings and mackerel, which are caught in great numbers in the vicinity; its exports also are coal, salt and fresh butter, soap, and earthenware, as well as silks, linen, and woollen stuffs, which are

FIG. 11

Boulogne-sur-Mer, vue prise au dessus de la côte de la fontaine Hulain, d'après nature.
Artist and lithographer G. Muller, ca. 1846. Boulogne-sur-Mer on the Pas-de-Calais,
as seen looking northeast across the Liane River from overhead the farms and estates
of Outreau. The mouth of the Liane River divides this bird's-eye view of the French
coast at Boulogne in half. The upper, *haute*, and lower, *basse*, halves of the town lie
beyond the ship basin, with the leafy upper town rising in the distance on high ground
behind its ancient wall masked by trees. The three prominent structures in the lower
town are (*right to left*) the Church of St. Nicholas facing Boulogne's market square, the
theater, and the Hospice de St. Louis, where the bodies of *Amphitrite*'s dead were prepared for burial. Muller's aerial views of French cities appeared in a collection titled
Tour de France à Vol d'Oiseau published by Dopter of Paris. This print was registered
in *La Bibliographie de la France* in January 1847 and was probably done by the artist the
year before. Progress on the construction in the upper town of Notre Dame's drum col-
onnades also dates the scene to just before midcentury.
COURTESY OF ALAIN EVRARD AND THE BIBLIOTHÈQUE DES ANNONCIADES, BOULOGNE-
SUR-MER.

manufactured in the town. This place is also the channel of conveyance for Champaigne, Burgundy, and other French wines, to England.
It is a favorite resort of the English, more than 6,000 having taken up
their residence at this place since the peace. . . .

BOULOGNE HARBOUR has of late years been considerably improved;
new piers have been built, and the bason much extended, it being
now capable of containing many hundred sail of small vessels. Vessels
may anchor off the harbor, at half or three-quarters of a mile off shore,
in 6 to 9 fathoms.

FIG. 12

Boulogne-sur-Mer, vue prise à vol d'oiseau. Artist Alfred Guesdon, lithographer Louis Jules Arnout, 1863 (?). Michael Barry's Hotel de la Marine stood at the foot (north end) of rue de Boston, to seaward of the Imperial Hotel, facing the beachfront and the rooms and bathing machines of Monsieur Mancel's celebrated spa, L'Établissement des Bains. Because of its proximity to the wreck, Barry's hotel became the center of the rescue and body recovery efforts. In 1833 two small structures (not visible here) were at the end of the rue de Boston beyond Barry's, a customs guardhouse and the Boulogne Humane Society's one-room shack. Guesdon's and Arnout's professional lives overlapped through much of the mid-nineteenth century, so this lithograph might have been done anytime during those decades, but the unfinished towers and the completed dome atop the Notre Dame Basilica date it to after midcentury.
LIBRARY OF CONGRESS, 2003688886.

Curiously, Norie didn't describe the most important characteristic of Boulogne's harbor, the fact that twice each day for several hours around low water it was too shallow to be entered by a ship with *Amphitrite*'s draft, pilot or no.

A much more colorful description of the town and its English residents than Norie's appeared in the August 24, 1834 issue of the *Satirist, and the Censor of the Time*, a weekly London newspaper first published in 1831 by Bernard Gregory, the journalist and sometime-actor. (He and his paper soon became notorious for extorting money from their targets and for libeling public figures who didn't pay hush money. For a time, Gregory's formula was a winner: prepublication extortion paid much better than more pure journalism. His idea was not original, however. Around the same time the publishers of New York City's "flash papers," soft-core pornographic weeklies that provided such

CHART 2

Detail from Plan du Port de Boulogne et de Ses Environs, Levé en 1835 par les
Ingénieurs Hydrographes de la Marine. Au Dépôt-Général de la Marine en 1840.
During low tide at Boulogne the water was only a few feet deep out as far as five cable
lengths (a half nautical mile) from shore. Admission into the harbor was via a narrow dredged channel between two manmade jetties each six hundred meters long. A
red light on the seaward end of the north jetty and two white lights on the end of the
south jetty were illuminated when there was sufficient water to permit safe entry into
the channel. (North is to the top.) Work on the jetties began in 1829 and took ten
years to complete. This detail from a French Navy chart is centered on Barry's Marine
Hotel. The walled, upper town is at bottom right and the Colonne de la Grande Armée
(Napoleon's column) is at top right.
LIBRARY OF CONGRESS, FRANCE, 192 (1840).

titillation in print as there was during that more innocent age, were doing
the same thing. The *Satirist* finally collapsed under pressure in 1849 after its
proprietor had been jailed several times for his crimes.) In a single short column Gregory managed to denigrate Boulogne's attractions, to abuse a dozen
or so of its expatriate residents individually by name, and to describe the
town more generally as headquarters for Britain's single ("unmarketable")
women, whom he tarnished as "a collection of ugly, ill-dressed, trolloping,
awkward, impudent looking girls . . . accompanied by their fat, frowsy mamas
and dirty-looking red-nosed papas."

Boulogne was, Gregory's correspondent reported in his antidote to Norie's bland description of the port city, "long and justly celebrated as a place of refuge for 'gentlemen in embarrassed circumstances,' that is to say, men who dread the gripe of the bailiff or the persecutions of the police in their own country":

> The society of Boulogne, as you may suppose, is not therefore very select, being chiefly composed of smugglers and swindlers, pauper peers, beggar baronets, half-pay officers, and spendthrift parsons, lawyers, and doctors, and swarms of insolvents, the very "scum of Britain's rascal runaways, whom the o'ercharged country vomits forth," and who here inhale, in peace, the sea breezes and laugh to scorn the "the world and the world's laws." The Boulogne people may be classed under two heads, the ridiculous and the notorious, and in truth there is no lack of either. . . .
>
> Boulogne can boast also of its club. The world will pronounce easily on the respectability of its members. Suffice it to say that all who can muster five francs are admitted; the pigeons to be sure are few, and those not over rich, but they still afford a livelihood to the sharps.

One resident expatriate, Robert Coates, the now-destitute but formerly fabulously wealthy dandy from Antigua by way of London, came in for special scouring in the piece:[7] "'Romeo' Coates, once the laughing stock of London . . . has recently got a new set of teeth, which, he told me, in consequence, once ornamented the head of one of the unfortunate convicts lost in the Amphitrite. . . . By the way, this shipwreck was a God-send to the dentists, as they bought permission to extract the teeth from the dead bodies!"

The revelation that Amphitrite's dead had been plundered for still serviceable parts by French dentists reads like just another off-hand slap shot by Gregory, but it might not be. It's possible, even likely, that teeth were extracted from some of Amphitrite's dead for use in dentures. Until the invention of "patent masticators," false teeth, the practice of recycling human teeth was not unusual in the nineteenth century, and the low-mileage teeth of young women would have been attractive source materials to the dentists of the city. ("Waterloo teeth," extracted from a battlefield's dead and formed into dentures, had appeared on the market soon after Napoleon's defeat, and similar sets of false teeth from cadavers were sold through dental equipment catalogues into the 1860s, when the stock was extracted from American Civil War dead.)[8]

Gregory's disclosures about teeth were nine months too late to be a scoop. The previous November *Fraser's Magazine for Town and Country* had published the same story. The interment ceremony for the dead, *Fraser's* correspondent

explained near the end of four pages of fulminating about the French, began at
2:00 PM on Monday, September 2. That's when sixteen "wretched" carts stacked
with cheap coffins wound uphill in solemn procession from the Hospice de St.
Louis on the rue de l'Hôpital, to the Protestant portion of the graveyard outside the eastern wall of the upper town. Sixty-four were then interred in two
trenches there, "but as they were generally young, and had good teeth, the nuns,
who had charge of them at the hospital, I am told, allowed (without much scru-
ple) the dentists to draw the 'heretic' teeth, which were too good a prize to be
lost, and which will probably adorn some Catholic jaws, when cleaned and filed
by the French dentists. Thus was plunder carried out to the last extremity."[9]
Fraser's had the part about the nuns correct. In 1833 the hospital was staffed by
twelve Augustinian sisters, but whether or not they cooperated in "plunder to
the last extremity," or even if it ever happened, is unknown.

In the 1830s Boulogne was an almost irresistible punching bag for English
periodicals, even those that didn't write much of their own copy but lifted
most from others. Thus in March 1838 the *Idler and Breakfast-table Companion*
(described by its editor as "a new and fashionable weekly journal of literature,
fine arts, satire and the stage," and then less than one year old) quoted verbatim a page-long denigration of the small city written by one "Captain Orlando
Sabertash" that had appeared earlier in *Fraser's*.[10] After conceding that "the
time when you could not walk the streets of Boulogne without a pack of cards
in one pocket and a pair of pistols in the other has passed away," Sabertash
concluded, "English life in Boulogne is a poor affair. . . . It is the life of a second rate watering place continued, not for a few weeks . . . but continued for
months and years." His review might have slightly thinned the crowd planning to cross the strait to enjoy the city's attractions.

British tourists were hardly new to France in the nineteenth century.
During the years of peace in the second half of the eighteenth century, several
thousand Britons a month had crossed the Channel eager to sample something
new. Many carried one or another of the popular guidebooks to France and the
Continent available, among them *Observations on the Customs and Manners of
the French Nation*, the practical *Gentleman's Guide in His Tour through France*,
or the critical *Travels through France and Italy*. By the early 1830s packet boat
(meaning scheduled) service between England and Boulogne from London
and Dover was on a near daily basis, either every day to Calais (and then on
to Boulogne in three and a half hours by twice-a-day, horse-drawn passenger
coach en route to Paris) or several times weekly directly. By 1835 steam power
had displaced sail on the popular tourist crossings.

Sufficient Britons were interested in Boulogne specifically, either as a place
of refuge or vacation destination, that there was a market for English language
guidebooks to the town. In 1835 James Clarke, an author of other tourist

guides, published one, *Bononia: or a Topographical and Historical Description of Boulogne and its Vicinity*. ("Bononia" was the Romans' second name for the place, and its inclusion in the book's title hinted at the town's antiquity and at the brief history and geography lessons contained between the covers.) Clarke's attractive, small volume containing an excellent fold-out street map of the port and city provided a more complete and better balanced sense of *Amphitrite*'s final destination than either Norie's short, workmanlike description or Gregory's hatchet job.

Clarke soon had a French competitor. J. Brunet, who described himself as a "professor of languages and literature at Boulogne," wrote a guide to the city in English that first appeared the year after Clarke's and went on to be republished by a local printer several times. Brunet later claimed that his book was plagiarized verbatim by Francis Coghlan in *Coghlan's New Guide to Boulogne* (1838), a third entrant into the English language Boulogne guidebook market.

Unlike Brunet, Clarke did not include Michael Barry's Marine Hotel among the eleven he listed by name in his guidebook, their appearance there an implicit recommendation as suitable places for touring Britons of the gentler classes to stay while visiting the city and enjoying its popular beach, hot salt water spa, and sulfur baths. Barry had been an hotelier in Boulogne-sur-Mer since 1820, when his tidy four-story building was built across from the spa in the *basse ville*'s northwestern corner, almost the last house at the harbor's mouth. Even without Clarke's endorsement Barry evidently enjoyed strong summer business, but the omission from Clarke's book suggests that the Marine Hotel occupied a humbler tier of accommodations for transients than did the elegant places bunched along rue de L'Ecu. Though not as humble a tier as the one that included Thomas Collett's Boarding House, another economy accommodation for tourists that Clarke neglected to mention.

Perhaps the omission arose because Collett's was on rue Tant Perde Tant Paie, in the city's gambling and red light district. This sporty neighborhood near the quays enjoyed a cross-Channel reputation. "Gentlemen who love darkness rather than light—a species lately known by the cognomen of Black-leg, are said to very much abound in Boulogne," cautioned Stanfield, elaborating on his description of the city, "though we believe that of late years, their numbers have something diminished. Be that as it may, those who are fond of play will not find any great lack of opportunity; and, as dueling is rather prevalent, they may finish with that unusual accompaniment."

"Black legs" were not exclusive to Boulogne's high life. They could be found at both sides of the channel. A cautionary tale in rhyme printed in an 1851 edition of *Punch* began by describing

FIG. 13

Barry's Marine Hotel and Family Boarding House, from the first, 1836, edition of J. Brunet's *New Guide to Boulogne-sur-mer and Its Environs*. Frederic Jorieu artist, B. Kaeppelin and Company, lithographers. "This hotel," Brunet wrote in his guidebook, "is delightfully situated on the port directly opposite the Bathing Establishment and commands a most picturesque view of the Harbour, the sea and surrounding country. Families and single gentlemen may be accommodated with board and apartments by the day, week or month. During the bathing season, this hotel is much frequented by the most respectable French and English visitors. Table d'hote every day. Warm baths and showers are now attached to the Establishment." B. Kaeppelin and Company were in business at 20 rue du Croissant, Paris, between 1832 and 1856.

> a restless young heir
> deficient with brains, but with money to spare
> 'Mong sharpers and black-legs, who spends his last crown
> then goes to Boulogne or is flung upon town.

Four attendants, touring French officials, miscellaneous curiosity seekers, and the first bodies recovered from the shipwreck filled the nearby Humane Society shack quickly, so almost from the beginning Barry's hotel became the center of the effort to revitalize *Amphitrite*'s victims. Many of the Britons and some of the others who testified at the shipwreck investigation to come were residents who had watched the tragedy unfold directly in front of them, through the hotel's dining room windows or its door toward the beach. "The critical situation of the Amphitrite," Consul Hamilton wrote days later in a defense of his performance that evening, "does not appear to have been known at the period when effectual assistance might have been afforded but to some few persons living at Barry's Hotel & the sailors and Customs Officers about the port. Very few of the British naval or military or other British residents of Boulogne were aware of the fatal occurrence until Sunday. . . . Even the English officers and persons living at Mr. Collett's boarding house immediately at the port and having a view of the sea & within sight of the very spot where this wreck occurred were not apprised of the circumstances till next morning."

If the expatriate scene in Boulogne were too louche for someone with Gregory's elevated tastes, the bathing season of 1833 in the city was, nevertheless, especially brilliant by local standards, carried along day after summer's day without rain or even clouds. The beach-going vacationers included members of the French aristocracy, chief among them the new King Louis-Philippe's eldest son, his Serene Highness Ferdinand Philippe, Duc d'Orléans, as well as powerful commoners, including the current and a former French navy minister and the minister of justice, all three cabinet officers escaping the heat of the capital. "La célèbre tragédienne," Melle Duchesnois, the enormously talented and remarkably ugly marvel of the Paris theater, was also in town, representing the artistic demimonde, as was her polar opposite, Hyacinthe-Louis de Quélen, the upright archbishop of Paris. The quality of Portugal was there also, in the person of the Marquise de Loulé, aunt of the young queen, who with her impressive entourage was ensconced in a hotel on rue Neuve-Chaussée, in the *basse ville*.

The glitterati were about the city in such numbers that Monsieur Mancel's Bathing Establishment (L'Établissement des Bains) could not keep up with the demand for horse-drawn machines to drive his clients to the water's edge for a swim. The crush must have gratified the man, the bath's new proprietor. Although the Humane Society provided lifesaving services on the beach, Mancel was a forward thinker: among his staff of spa attendants and wagon drivers was a "master swimmer," Pierre Hénin, who watched over those among the establishment's clients who were bold enough to enter the water more than ankle high.

Built originally in 1824, L'Établissement des Bains housed "a handsome saloon, a pavilion for balls and fêtes," and rooms for reading or playing cards and billiards. During a four-month-long season, from mid-June through mid-October, Mancel hosted children's balls on Mondays, *soirées dansantes* on Wednesdays, and grand balls on Fridays. Fun for everybody, never mind what the *Idler* said about "a second rate watering place."

"One saw on the beach," wrote an observer, "Spectacles, balls, entertainments of every type followed one another without interruption" that summer.

In short, Boulogne, "the city of debt, peopled by men who have never understood arithmetic" (the skewering phrase was Canon Sydney Smith's), shone in 1833, despite what uppity foreigners thought.

41

"The night of the 30th of August, 1833, had been tremendous," wrote an eyewitness to the storm on the French coast in a description quoted at length in the Royal Humane Society's annual report for 1834. The author is not identified, but it was almost certainly Sarah Austin, one of Barry's more interesting guests:

> The house in which we lodged, the Marine Hotel, had rocked sensibly with the violence of the wind, and the morning [Saturday] was ushered in with every circumstance calculated to depress and alarm. The storm, far from abating, continued to increase: from our darkened windows, the Venetian shutters of which we dared not unclose, lest the glass should be shivered by the wind, we saw only the ceaseless lashing of the sea, and the currents of the peculiarly fine sand of Boulogne beach, sweeping up the Port with blinding violence. . . . About five p.m., we heard (for we could not see, the shutters still being closed) that a vessel of considerable size had just come on shore. . . . At this time, the tide was going out; it was within an hour of low water. On going to the door we saw her, as well as the lowering sky and the driving rain mixed with sand would permit.[11]

"I walked down to the port with a friend—no, not walked—my progression cannot have that name," wrote another of the expatriates in November, recalling that Saturday evening on the Boulogne-sur-Mer jetty:

> I strained my limbs, arms, and legs, and with difficulty I had not before conceived could be required, I slowly advanced to the end of the pier. Thousands have reason to remember that awful storm! The wind blew most ferociously, drifting the sand along with vengeance, and directly in our faces. We held on our hats with one hand, and shaded our eyes frequently with the other. Tall men and strong men stood still at times, and turned their backs, unable to proceed an inch, and holding fast by the railing along one edge of the pier, to prevent their being blown over. We at length arrived at the extremity of the pier. . . . There was a vessel about half a mile along the coast northward. . . . It was now past seven o'clock, and it had been stranded at half-past five.

FIG. 14

The Amphitrite Wreck'd off Boulogne Augt 31st 1833 (108 Females on Board). Artist and lithographer N. E. Deey, 1834. James Towsey described *Amphitrite*'s last minutes this way: "About 9 PM the ship beating very heavy on the ground sprung a leak, the water washing up the lower deck. We all ran up the fore rigging the spray then running over us. She filled and in about 10 minutes a sea struck her on the larboard beam, washed the poop off her and all the women overboard. Their screeches were horrible." Deey's colored lithograph was published in London by T. Gillard the year after the wreck. Its title was a marketing exercise, designed to boost sales of what is otherwise a generic shipwreck piece apparently drawn entirely from Deey's imagination by tying it to a current event. Other printmakers and publishers did this, too, and so did painters. Ferdinand Victor Perrot's huge *Wreck of Amphitrite*, done the year before the young French artist left home on a last, fatal trip abroad, for example, is fiction described in oil paint. The painting was exhibited for years in Boulogne-sur-Mer's town hall. It now hangs neglected in La Chapelle, a library building of the Université Saint Louis in Boulogne.

© 2010 NATIONAL MARITIME MUSEUM, GREENWICH, LONDON, PAF 8062.

It is easy to imagine watching the shipwreck of *Amphitrite* in high definition video on a news or weather channel. A reporter doing a standup near the hotel, with his back to the wind and the water, holding his mike like something to eat. Spent waves now just inches high washing up practically to his shoes. Sheets of rain pelting him in the dark. What remains of the ship mostly unseen behind lines of towering whitecaps running in from open water.

Shadowy clusters of men here and there on the beach congregated around yet another body discovered on the sand. Others picking up bits of flotsam. Armed customs officers chasing still others away from the shore.

While the reporter speaks he is conscious of the great drama inherent in the setting and in his exclusive story about the mass drowning of young women and children at the edge of town. He revels in the attention being its narrator has given him, and is loathe to put down the microphone. The commentary, however, has none of the detached professionalism characteristic of today's better television journalism, none of its graphics gimmickry, either. Instead, he is outraged, and his evident anger—directed almost indiscriminately at everyone other than the storm's victims and possibly entirely feigned—is audible in his commentary and powerfully sways his audience.

That, minus the technology, is what happened. *Amphitrite*'s agony played out in front of a large audience and mobilized public sentiment in a way that shipwrecks usually did not. Most occurred in distant places and even the most horrific ones lost their power to appall over time and distance and sank into the statistics of what everyone accepted was inherently a dangerous business, sailing a ship between continents. This wreck, however, was seen by hundreds, and one of its most impassioned observers was John Wilks, the Paris-based correspondent for London's *Standard*.

42

Under certain weather conditions, the narrow, relatively shallow strait (twenty-one nautical miles across and generally less than twenty fathoms deep, 120 feet) acts like a funnel to focus powerful tidal currents that spin up steep, short period seas to beat upon the shore. Augmented by an onshore wind, these waves can reach enormous size. In time, if *Amphitrite*'s hull were not quickly crushed first by the pounding, then ranks of storm-driven waves seconds apart, growing taller as they pushed up the beach one after the other like pistons, would knock down the poop, wash over her main deck, flood everything below, and drown everyone not aloft in the rigging. As soon as her masts unshipped, or broke off at the deck line, even that last refuge would be lost, throwing those few still alive into the water, too.

The special heroes of the night of the shipwreck were a dozen or so of Boulogne's *matelots*, fishermen, who at risk to their own lives tried twice to alert Captain Hunter to the terrible danger his ship was in, hard on the sandbar off shore with little time before the wind-whipped tide began to come in. Twice they told him to abandon ship. They knew, although Hunter clearly did not, that the rising tide—usually sixteen feet above low water at its peak, but on August 31 sucked even higher by low barometric pressure and a full moon, invisible above the first deck of clouds—would not float *Amphitrite* off the bar and set her free to work toward open water behind the storm. Exactly the opposite was going to happen that Saturday night. Her hull embedded deep in fine sand carried in by the surf, *Amphitrite* would be held fast in position while the Dover Strait rose furiously around her. Under unrelenting battering by tons of salt water, *Amphitrite*'s deck would inevitably collapse and her disassembly would quickly follow.

Harbor pilot François-Augustin Huret's brave act, collecting volunteers, launching his boat, and pulling it alongside *Amphitrite* to alert her crew they were in mortal danger, is diminished by comparison with the near-suicidal courage of Pierre Antoine Hénin's nude swim to the ship towing a lifeline a little while later, but it should not be. Huret was first to act in the crisis, and what he and his crew did could have—should have—triggered the rescue of many on board.

Boulogne's fishing fleet provided a large pool of small boat handlers. Dozens of stout fishing vessels were home-ported there, so many that they were accounted for prosaically by number, not by name. Under its characteristic brick red sails, the fleet crowded the basin when ready for sea. The port's many *matelots* were real seafarers. Although the whiting, sole, and flounder fisheries were in local waters, among these men of Boulogne were also some who worked in distant water for herring and mackerel, and in the North Sea beyond Scotland for cod. From among their number Huret had managed quickly to recruit Jean-Charles Testard and nine others to row out to the grounded vessel: Antoine Heret, Jean Coquelin, Louis Testard, Pierre Huret, Jacques Delpierre, Adrien Danger, Joseph Verdière, Louis-Joseph Flahutez, and Napoléon Ducarne. We know their names (and their ratings: Pierre Huret was an "aspirante [candidate] pilot," Coquelin a quartermaster, Ducarme was master of fishing boat number 53, and the others were common *matelots* of the second or third class) because Paris newspapers later carefully and proudly identified each man.

This pick-up crew manhandled Huret's nearly new pilot boat, *L'Espoir*, from the port over the sand to a launch site, and pushed it into the surf. Boulogne's ten-year-old newspaper, *L'Annotateur, Journal Politique, Commercial et Littéraire de l'Arondissemt de Boulogne-sur-Mer*, described to its readers what happened next (and miscounted the number of would-be rescuers at the oars):

> During this time a canoe [the pilot boat] had been brought up opposite the vessel: the pilots Huret and Testard, along with eight other brave sailors on board. After extraordinary efforts they were finally able to approach the ship and take the end of a rope and signal for it to be attached, and they would lead the vessel to shore. The rope

stayed attached for a while, and a second attempt was made, but
suddenly the canoe's bow dove under a wave, and began to fill with
water. Our brave mariners, for their own safety, were forced to give up
and abandon their courageous undertaking.

Huret's crew's confidence in small boats on rough water and their respect
for the terrible strength of the sea might account for the fact that they made
it out to *Amphitrite* and back. They were followed into the water by another
well-known figure, the lifeguard Pierre Hénin, who struck out alone, alternately swimming and wading, toward the beached vessel in an act of almost
lunatic bravery.

43

Although life ended badly for her—dead of tuberculosis in 1869 at age
forty-eight in Cairo after seven years as an invalid at Luxor on the Nile, surrounded by devoted Egyptian attendants but otherwise alone, having suffered
from the disease for nearly twenty years—young Lucie Austin must have been
a delightful child. When she was not enchanting Heinrich Heine, who while
they relaxed together in August 1833 at the end of one Boulogne jetty told
her beautiful stories in German, she charmed local fishermen and their wives.
One especially was captivated, the same Pierre Hénin who had taught her to
"swim admirably."

The day in 1836 when father, mother, and daughter decamped from
Boulogne for the next to last time after a long, third stay in the city, Lucie
wrote a friend, "I went over to Pierre Hénin's (the man who swam out to the
Amphitrite). . . . He . . . said he could not bear my going away, saying that I had
been '*si bonne*' to him, and that he loved me as much as his own daughter, and
wanted to know whether there was nothing in the world he could do to serve
me and to show me how much he was attached to me." Hénin's attack of separation anxiety might have been a foreboding; he never saw Lucie again. When
the Austins returned to Boulogne for their final visit in 1843, he already had
been dead one year.

That mildly spooky farewell by the father of ten- and eleven-year-old
daughters to a fifteen-year-old schoolgirl suggests Hénin might have been well
known to the children of expatriates. William Clark Russell, an American-
born British journalist and author of many popular nineteenth-century sea
stories, lived in Boulogne for a while as a preteen before he went to sea at thirteen in 1857. Years later he wrote, "I remember [Hénin] very well; he was a
large, fat, cheery man; he taught me to swim when I was a child, and in memory I can see him now lying upon the water as buoyant as a grampus that has

risen to breathe."[12] Maybe Hénin truly was as buoyant as a dolphin—that would explain his swimming skills—but he died in 1842 and Russell was born in 1844, so Russell's memory of a plump and happy Hénin afloat is fiction. Fortunately, we have another, much more flattering portrait of Pierre Hénin than the picture in words conjured up whole from Russell's imagination. This one is part of the collection of the Château-Musée de Boulogne-sur-Mer.

L'Annotateur began its account of Pierre Hénin's brave attempt at 6:00 PM on Saturday, about the time that François Huret's pilot boat turned for shore to escape capsizing and the failure of its crew to carry with it a line from the doomed ship became obvious to those watching. Stripped naked and carrying a line, Hénin then plunged into the water. "No one dares follow him," wrote the paper:

> We see him struggle against the waves, but what strikes us is the inaction of the crew, who gives him no signal. We asked ourselves the possible motive. These unfortunates, have they no more strength? Is the captain hoping to save the ship?
>
> Around seven o'clock we saw the courageous Hénin touch the vessel. We saw a sailor throw him a line, then the line was pulled in. Hénin, being at the point of expiring himself, was forced to let go and then get back to shore. He wants to dive back into the sea, but he is completely exhausted. . . . All hope of rescuing those unfortunates is lost; night falls, the sea starts to rise, the noise of the wind, the waves prevents us from hearing the screams of the victims.
>
> How can I depict the anxiety of the crowd that has gathered on the beach exposed by the tide? A large number of hardy mariners throw themselves into the sea, with the goal of collecting the shipwrecked. [Visibility drops,] the wind rages with more violence than ever, the waves arrive quickly and with great force, and we can barely make out the ship. The sea forces the less ambitious to retreat. Then all of a sudden a mast is washed up at the feet of the spectators, then barrels, then debris, then bodies.

What happened when Hénin arrived alongside the ship can be pieced together from the accounts of two survivors, Owen and Towsey. "When he came alongside he asked, as well as I could understand, for a cord," Towsey recalled. "I had seen one of the men getting a rope up the fore hatchway previously to this, and knowing it was a long one, I gave about 18 or 20 fathoms to the man in the water on the starboard bow." Someone, Towsey says the mate, Owen says the captain, now ordered Towsey aloft and the rope was forgotten and the exhausted Hénin left to make his way to shore.

Fig. 15

Pierre Antoine Hénin, 1804–1842, Chevalier de la Légion d'Honneur.
Attributed to the English School, oil, 1833. Hénin, matelot de 3e
classe, holds over his shoulder a jacket adorned with the handsome
cross of the Legion of Honor and two lifesaving medals. *Amphitrite*,
barely visible in the right background, provides the context of the portrait. The Legion d'Honneur probably was presented to him during
an audience with King Louis-Philippe on December 18, 1833. (Huret
received a Croix d'Honneur for his brave act, Testard a gold medal,
and the other nine in the boat a silver medal each.) By the time of
his death nine years later, Hénin had been awarded four more lifesaving medals and the Monthion Prize. He died in his home at 25 rue de
Boston on September 3, 1842, at age thirty-eight, and was buried the
same day in the Cimetière de l'Est. In March 1893 the city council honored Hénin's memory by agreeing unanimously to a perpetual, no-cost
extension of the rental term of his cemetery plot. The plot's location
has since been forgotten. This portrait was added to the collection of
the Castle Museum, Boulogne-sur-Mer, in 1913. The museum fills several floors of the walled city's medieval citadel with an eclectic collection that includes Egyptian, Greek, Roman, and Inuit artifacts as well
as the abstract calligraphy of a local artist, Georges Mathieu.
Courtesy Château-Musée.

Around low water, after both attempts to alert the crew of their danger had failed, an observer asked one of the men of the Humane Society, both were watching the drama in front of them from inside the hotel, what he thought. "In two hours she will be all to pieces," was the reply.

"Probably the captain knows what he is about. Perhaps she'll get off."

"Not if she were of iron."

Hénin's heroic, failed attempt at the rescue of the unfortunates on board *Amphitrite* brought him general admiration. (It is possible that his act was the model for a scene in "the Tempest" chapter of Charles Dickens' 1850 novel, *David Copperfield*, in which a schooner is driven aground during a great storm. The wreck prompts Ham Peggoty to tie a line about his waist and plunge into the surf in a dramatic but fatal attempt to affect a rescue just before the vessel breaks up.) Accolades from the press of both nations were accompanied by tangible rewards from the grateful governments concerned. Hénin, only twenty-nine and still a junior sailor as the French ordered such things when *Amphitrite* was driven aground, was awarded membership in the Légion d'Honneur in the degree of *chevalier*, knight. Although *chevalier* was (and is still) the lowest of the five degrees of this national order of merit, such royal recognition was nevertheless a great distinction for a common *matelot*.

On October 3 the Humane Society of London granted Hénin a silver medal and 250 francs, then equivalent to £10, for his "courage and humanity." He received another £16 from the £184 pot raised by private relief drive in Boulogne. (The three survivors split £60 from the same source, with an unexplained £15 tip awarded to Towsey. The balance went to Huret and his crew, to five members of the Humane Society, and a few others. Hotelier Barry was presented a £10 silver cup.) Another relief subscription in Great Britain raised another £100 for the hero swimmer.

These same traits attracted other civilian attention, too, none more extraordinary than that from the members of the Phrenological Society of Paris, whose agenda during the society's annual meeting ten months later, in August 1834, included a discussion led by the society's secretary, Monsieur Broussais, on the physiognomy of Hénin and another man, both then well known for exhibiting courage in marine disasters.[13] The month before the group met, Hénin had distinguished himself as a lifesaver yet again, rescuing two Frenchmen in trouble on the beach not far from where *Amphitrite*'s victims had washed ashore one year before.

The Phrenological Society's meeting at the Hôtel de Ville (city hall) had opened with the society's president, "the celebrated M. Andral," expressing his great satisfaction that the basis of their science—elucidating the imaginary relationship between the topography of a skull and the moral and intellectual faculties of the man who inhabited it—was "supported by so many strong presumptions as to nearly merit the rank of a certainty."

Andral and the other disciples of Franz Joseph Gall (1757–1828), the father of "cranioscopy," thought that by examining distinctive bumps in the skulls of subjects one could identify various "organs" of the underlying brains, each organ responsible for a different propensity, sentiment, perception, or reflection—these four constituting the "powers" of the mind. Cranioscopy, its adepts believed, revealed not only capacity but also character. It could help one select a profession, choose a spouse, even educate a child according to his aptitude. Especially useful, it appeared that criminals could be identified by the shape of their skulls, as confirmed by a blind experiment briefed to Andral's group in Paris, which established the existence of an "organ of rape" in the posterior region of the head—not where one would expect the French to locate such an organ. (Years earlier Gall had demonstrated his ability to identify malefactors at first sight, as many as hundreds during a single day, during walking tours of prisons in Berlin and Spandau. The exercise sounds suspiciously like working backward from the solution.)

Craniologists' palpitations of the skull were worthless and Doctor Gall's "science" was entirely bogus, but, curiously, given the bizarre path he took to it, Gall's key insight, that different regions of the brain performed different functions, was not. Magnetic resonance imagining and even more sophisticated scans of the living brain have confirmed that certain of its nodes, parts, *are* associated with specific tasks, with, for example, attention, decision making and planning, memory, and sensory processing. There are indications, moreover, that the volume of the frontal cortex is somehow related to general intelligence, although other factors are relevant, too. If so, this would mean, as Gall fervently believed, that size does matter (the example of Albert Einstein's first-class but relatively small brain aside). Nor was Gall's idea that personality resided in the meat of the brain and not in an insubstantial soul wrong. In 1805 that heretical conclusion, right or wrong, got Gall ejected from staunchly Roman Catholic Austria. He soon resettled in France.

Gall's work was elaborated by Dr. Johann Kaspar Spurzheim, one of his first students and his chief collaborator, in *Phrenology, or, the Doctrine of the Mind; and of the Relations Between its Manifestations and the Body* (1825). It was Spurzheim who renamed cranioscopy as "phrenology" and reported the existence of fully thirty-five organs resident in the brain.[14] (Gall had managed to find only twenty-seven, eight of which were unique to humans.) Hénin's heroic performances were attributed to a well-developed organ of benevolence, number thirteen on Spurzheim's list.

Alas, Andral's happy expectations aside, after a golden age in the mid-1800s in Great Britain and the United States, his new science slowly went into eclipse, condemned as quackery. Learned journal articles written during phrenology's ascendancy read today like loopy science fiction. Not much is left of phrenology beyond part of Gall's collection of specimen human skulls, on display at the Rollet Museum in the Austrian spa town of Baden bei Wein: a number of glossy, full-scale "Fowler" china heads scored to indicate where beneath the skull various organs of personality were believed to reside, once used as three dimensional study guides; and some miniature heads for the same purpose made by William Bally. (This special purpose pottery is now cherished by collectors of the outré, so much so that there is a good market for reproductions on eBay.)

In 1837 the *Monthly Instructor*, the journal of London's Religious Tract Society, published yet another report about Hénin's irrepressible heroism, this time in connection with the rescue of three drowning sailors near Ambleteuse ("one after another . . . borne to the shore in safety by the protecting arms of this philanthropic fisherman, this hardy wrestler of the sea") and two others at Boulogne. The author satisfied himself by crediting Hénin simply with "generous impulses and noble daring." Nothing was said in the article about any well-developed organ of benevolence.

44

Some few victims of wrecks, such as those from *Ann & Amelia*, aground that same night down the coast at Berck, managed to wade ashore unassisted, but most could not. Hénin's brave goal had been to string a stout line from *Amphitrite* to dry land. (That must have been Huret's goal, too. *Amphitrite* aground could not have been led to safety into the harbor at low tide.) Once in place and at low water, the line could have been used as a handrail for a risky escape from the ship on foot through the surf. It might have worked, for the adults at least, had Hunter, Forrester, and the weather cooperated.

The problem of getting survivors off their grounded ship and safely to shore before the vessel broke up bedeviled would-be Samaritans through much of the nineteenth century. It prompted the development and patenting of bizarre devices (among them a lifesaving hat) as well as genuinely useful things, such as buoyant, self-righting surfboats and ingenious rescue apparatus—some with a distinctly Rube Goldberg quality—that could shuttle one or several survivors at a time from a stricken ship over the surf to the beach. Technical solutions were accompanied by the development of private and government institutions to organize and perform rescues and resuscitation.

In January 1850 one such invention, the American Joseph Francis' patented life-car, proved to be a famous success. Over the course of two stormy days near midmonth, Francis' life-car (a sausage-shaped, enclosed vessel with a capacity of four riding on a line rigged between ship and shore) hauled 201 of the 202 on board from the wreck of the immigrant transport *Ayrshire* safely to land at Squan Beach, New Jersey. Until she was shoved on the offshore sands by a violent nor'easter, *Ayrshire* had been on the way to the port of New York from Newry, one of several emigration ports in Northern Ireland. This rescue, by the men of Station No. 5, was the first at any of the six new U.S. government–funded lifesaving stations along the New Jersey shore, and the first anywhere by a Francis life-car.

In 1833 Boulogne was marginally better prepared to respond to a marine catastrophe offshore than anyplace on the French coast. The port city was home to France's first marine lifesaving organization, the Société Humaine de Boulogne. That July the society's president, the elderly John Larking, one of the men who was credited with creating the charity eight years earlier, had been honored for his role and leadership with a lifelong seat on the board of directors of its model and counterpart in London.

The Humane and Shipwreck Society of Boulogne-sur-Mer was born September 8, 1825, at a meeting of the resident subscribers to the English Chapel, who, after completing the regular semiannual audit of the chapel's accounts, acknowledged, "Many lives having been lost on this coast for want of the measures pursued by the Royal Humane Society in England for restoring life to the apparently drowned, it has been thought expedient to apply to the mayor of this town for a proper building to receive the bodies of the drowned or apparently drowned, and a house by the seaside has been granted for this purpose." The necessary funds to move the initiative forward—five hundred francs to pay off the current tenant and to fit out the building, to buy the necessary "apparatus," and to print materials required—were unanimously voted from chapel accounts. A meeting of the same group three weeks later established a schedule of rewards for bodies brought to the shack that were subsequently revived (three hundred francs) and those that could not be (fifty francs), and with that done, but no lifeboat, the society began its "laudable" work.

The connection between the society and the chapel's congregants remained very close through the next decades, but Boulogne's French citizens adopted lifesaving as their cause, too. Although in 1833 the society's president and three members of its executive committee were English, everyone in the other eight leadership positions was French, and three-quarters of the donors to the 1833 fund drive were also French.

The Boulogne society's "receiving-room" for "persons drowned or apparently dead" occupied the last building at the foot of the rue de Boston, between Barry's hotel and the sea, down slope of the hilly fishermen's quarter. The receiving-room was a common beach shack, "consisting of a small room, with a door and window fronting the pier, and, behind it, a long shed, opening to

the sea, and long ago destined . . . for the reception of a Life Boat. In the room
are one bed with blankets, &c., one bath with a pipe for conveying hot water,
and, in short, such arrangements for the purposes of the Society as their very
limited means allow."[15] Even eight years later those limited means had not yet
provided a lifeboat, although one was allegedly under construction at Calais.
The shack was usually manned during swimming season by four uniformed
watch-standers.

Later a critic would sniff that *Amphitrite*'s would-be rescuers in the beach
shack and at the Marine Hotel had no access to an "apparatus for restoring
circulation or restoring warmth," nothing but "warm cloths, warm water, and
a few similar things." Access would itself become an even larger problem:
Saturday night the shack and the dunes around it became so thick with aspir-
ing do-gooders and curious gawkers that the British consul William Hamilton
later complained he had been unable get through the crowd to satisfy himself
that everything possible was being done to treat the still-living and deal with
the dead.

The archetype for a well-equipped humane society "receiving house" was
built by the Royal Humane Society in London's Hyde Park in 1794, one of
eighteen in the capital alone. It was perhaps this handsome brick structure,
close to the Serpentine River through the park, against which Boulogne's hut
was being measured and found inadequate. According to the *Illustrated London
News* in 1844,

> The interior of the receiving-house consists of an entrance-hall, with
> a room for medical attendant, on the left; and waiting-room on the
> right; parallel with which are two separate wards for the reception of
> male and female patients. Each contains bed, warmed with hot water,
> a bath, and a hot water metal-topped table for heating flannels, bricks,
> &c.; the supply of water being by pipes around the stalls and beneath
> the floor of the rooms. Next are a kitchen and two sleeping-rooms for
> the residence of the superintendent and his family; adjoining is the
> furnace for heating water. . . . In the rear is a detached shed, in which
> are kept boats, ladders, ropes, and poles; wicker boats are likewise in
> constant readiness.

Hot water, apparently the panacea for near-drowning in either swimming or
skating accidents on the Serpentine, was available "in a minute" from sunup
until 11:00 PM. The Société Humaine de Boulogne, soon to confront dozens of
British dead simultaneously, had a supply of hot water too, but it boasted nothing comparable to the amenities in London's opulent temple of resuscitation.
Like Hyde Park's receiving houses, however, it was scaled for the rescue of an

occasional swimmer in distress, not for the sudden appearance of an entire shipload of drowning candidates.

Once Hunter put his ship hard aground, there was no way to save her; nevertheless *Amphitrite*'s crew and her unhappy human cargo still had a chance to survive the gale, even if their vessel did not. Bernard Gregory's characterization of the port city and its French and English residents might have been good for subscription sales, but it was unfair. With the possible exceptions of the ghouls scavenging after teeth and other plunder, a few unnamed types who during the storm refused a desperate request to move Huret's boat along the beach in their horse-drawn wagon, and perhaps officials of both governments, Boulogne's residents attempted to come out in force to help at the scene of disaster. The party of impromptu, would-be rescuers on the beach was thickened for a while by forty soldiers of a battalion of the 5e Régiment d'Infanterie de Ligne (Fifth Line Infantry Regiment), based in Boulogne. (The regiment later contributed generously to a fund for the victims.) Almost everyone ashore exhibited remarkable courage, humanity, and determination, until most were chased off the beach by customs officers, who feared an orgy of looting and saw prevention of that form of smuggling as their sole mission.

Although their presence appears to have gained no press attention, the British Admiralty's investigator (whom we will meet soon) reported that seven French medical men were also near the scene of the wreck Saturday night. Presumably they were working at water's edge or in the humane society's crowded shack. They were not at the impromptu morgue set up in Barry's hotel, where two English women volunteers and their lady's maids labored bravely and apparently unassisted amid the dead. Nothing known about the background of these two (Mrs. Sarah Austin, Lucie's mother, and the more obscure Mrs. John Curtis) suggests that either one knew anything about resuscitation, but the several French doctors almost certainly did know.

By the early 1830s their attempts to revive the drowned would have been informed by two centuries' worth of solid science, beginning with William Harvey's brilliant insights into human anatomy. In 1628 Harvey, fifty, published his now-famous "Anatomical Essay" and upended conventional wisdom about how the human body worked. Before Harvey, professors and practitioners believed that there were two distinct types of blood, venous (originating in the liver) and arterial (originating in the heart) that moved through the body via separate, one-way plumbing lines. In this classical model, blood didn't circulate. It rose from one of these two organs and was consumed entirely as it flowed downstream, pushed along by pulsating blood vessels. Harvey described how human circulation really worked, the heart pumping a fixed quantity of blood around a closed system. Beginning with Harvey, and for the next three hundred fifty years, a beating heart was the very definition of life.

After Harvey, and particularly after 1668–69, when two Englishmen, John Mayow and Richard Lower, published seminal treatises on respiration and the heart, the blood's circuit through the lungs and the process through which venous blood turned into aerated arterial blood became generally understood. Roughly one hundred years later oxygen was isolated from the atmosphere and recognized as the gas essential to respiration and life.

Thus by the first decades of the nineteenth century, resuscitation from drowning had moved much of the vast distance from efforts to relight a mysterious, spiritual spark believed fundamental to life to mechanical manipulation of an inert body, whose purpose was to restart the reasonably well-defined process of respiration. The debate between "vitalists," those who believed in a life force that animated flesh and encompassed the possibility of a human soul, and scientists who did not was still ongoing. But at that debate's margins and theology aside, technicians continued aggressively to explore methodologies of resuscitation.

When *Amphitrite* broke up, three generations of European physicians had been familiar with all manner of rhythmic manipulations of a drowning victim's torso and with mouth-to-mouth resuscitation, techniques of revival possibly hinted at in I Kings 17 and II Kings 4. The Royal Humane Society had distilled this accumulated wisdom into a five-step procedure summarized below:

1. Convey the body to a dry, warm place, "avoiding the usual destructive methods of hanging it by the heels, rolling it on a barrel, or placing it across a log on the belly."
2. The body should be stripped, swathed in blankets and well-warmed, on its back with head slightly raised.
3. "The whole body should be rubbed with the hand or with hot woolen cloths . . . particularly around the breast. . . . The immediate application of frictions is of the utmost importance."
4. "A bellows should be applied to one nostril, whist the other nostril and the mouth are kept closed. . . . When the breast is swelled, an assistant should press the belly upwards, to force the air out . . . twenty to thirty times a minute, so as to imitate natural breathing as nearly as possible. . . . If a bellows cannot be procured . . . [some person] should blow into the mouth, while both nostrils are closed."
5. "Ashes, water, salt, or sand should be heated, and as soon as it is milk-warm, the body should be placed in it."

"These methods," the society continued, "must be continued for three or four hours. . . . After life has returned, if convulsions come on, blood should be taken by direction of a physician." The protocol did nothing to restore circulation, which was assumed to be coupled in some way to breathing.

Despite the existence of this practical wisdom and the substantial medical talent assembled on the beach at Boulogne, there is no evidence that any of *Amphitrite*'s drowning victims was actually brought back to life by resuscitation. The three survivors came out of the water alive, and all the dead remained dead.

Ordinary Seaman John Richard Rice, eighteen, was said to have ridden a ship's ladder through the surf where he was rescued by Louis Bourgain, who pulled him from the grasp of the breakers. *The Times* reported that James Jones Towsey, nineteen, floated ashore supported by a ship's timber, a board he said he'd shared for a brief time with the captain, until Hunter was flushed from it to drown. Young Towsey later got credit in London for an attempt at heroism. "A very good thing is told of him," *Fraser's Magazine for Town and Country* reported, "—that he fastened the hair of a young woman around his arm, and swam ashore safely with her; but she died, in a few minutes, from exhaustion." It is difficult to picture how such a lifesaving drag might have been done in real life (or to believe that a female convict was permitted such long hair). Feasible or not, Towsey never claimed that he did this and *Fraser's* story is fiction. A French sailor, Jean Nicholas Lépine, pulled Towsey alone from the water.

Boatswain John Owen, twenty-two, reportedly dropped into the water after forty-five desperate minutes aloft in *Amphitrite*'s foremast rigging and then, in what might have been a familiar act, swam to shore. (Familiar because *The Times* told its readers that Owen had now been wrecked a total of thirteen times. He told the Admiralty investigator the same thing, which suggests that Owen was very durable but a slow learner and unlucky. Nearly one shipwreck a year.) He was fished from the surf and taken up the beach by Louis-Joseph Caboche, one of Mancel's bathing machine drivers.

Given their youth, the amount of experience at sea claimed by the three survivors is impressive, and in at least one case improbable. Owen claimed sixteen years in the merchant fleet, meaning he first went to sea as a child of six. Towsey was a veteran of six years in the Royal Navy, including four with Admiral Sir Thomas Baker in *Warspite* beginning as a thirteen year old, and two with Captain William Canning in the sloop HMS *Alligator*. Rice had sailed five years in merchantmen. Of the three survivors only Owen was described as having been injured, experiencing swollen and lacerated hands and a "contusion in the knee." Owen and Rice recovered in the Marine Hotel, Towsey in the hospital.

Quoting their correspondent again, *The Times* went on to say that Rice was "brought in a state of insensibility to the hotel," probably by Bourgain.

Sarah Austin then described Rice's arrival at Barry's. Some time about nine, she wrote,

> A young man was brought into and deposited on a sofa in Mr. Barry's private room. He was not insensible, but nearly so; trembling and speechless with cold, he was soon wrapped in blankets, hot bottles were applied to his feet, stomach, and arm-pits, a warming pan was passed over the blanket, and the feet, hands, and arms rubbed. In about half an hour the cold shuddering went off, and he began to feel warm. Almost the first words he uttered were, "I hope some more will be saved—a hundred women!" I could not conceive what he meant. He said, "She was a convict vessel." The horrible truth now burst upon us.

Until then the expectation ashore had been that the ship had twelve or fourteen men on board.

There is slender evidence that some others could have been saved from the breaking surf. Various secondhand accounts describe several convicts reaching the water's edge still alive, if just barely, and these few—if they existed—might have survived had they received prompt medical attention. Two master fishermen, Achille Leprêtre and Nicholas Huret, reportedly "drew from the waves a woman with signs of life, who even grasped the hand of Huret! They were carrying her to a place of shelter and safety, when two of the superior customs-house officers came, and, pointing the bayonet against them, compelled them to abandon her!" Baron le Schacht deposed during investigation that he, together with Captain Fourmentin (both men seemingly well known in Boulogne-sur-Mer in 1833), were turned away by a sword-wielding customs officer from going "to succor the unfortunate" just before they heard a cry from the beach.

45

The story of *Amphitrite*'s destruction appealed to more than ghoulish fascination. *L'Annotateur* featured extensive, thoughtful coverage. The wreck on their city's waterfront might have been presented to *L'Annotateur*'s readers simply as an example of British incompetence coupled to proof of French heroism, granted courage frustrated in its purpose by the doomed ship's officers. Because charges in the English press assailed the performance of customs officers at the port, *L'Annotateur*'s editor also could have responded with an automatic, nationalistic defense of the French civil service larded through with the usual clichés about tragic loss of life. Instead, he took a much more introspective

approach to the story. The paper's investigation subsequently seemed to confirm some charges.

Other French newspapers also highlighted the story of the wreck, exhibiting no less proprietary interest in the catastrophe than did the British press.
Coverage in Paris was substantial, especially so in *Le Journal des Débats Politiques
et Littéraires*, a forty-four-year-old capital daily with its origins (as the name suggests) in political reporting. Shipwrecks and marine malfeasance were old subjects for the paper. In 1816 it had extensively covered the sensational story of
the wreck of *Medusa*, the torments suffered by those abandoned on the make-
shift raft, and the courts martial and royal cover-up that followed.

A week after the wreck of *Amphitrite*, *Le Temps*, another of the capital's
several daily newspapers and then only four years old, also began to tell its
five thousand or so subscribers about the many recent disasters at sea, and this
one in particular. Its story could have been written with more authority, with
the extra credibility that comes from eyewitness reporting if Jacques Coste, *Le
Temps'* editor and one of the paper's two founders, had waited one day, until
September 8 to print his piece. That's when Coste received a letter from a foreign friend who had witnessed the drama unspool in front of him.

In August 1833 Heinrich Heine, the German romantic poet cum political journalist in exile, was on vacation in Boulogne, staying in oceanfront
rooms at the Marine Hotel. He planned to return to Paris before summer's end
and to his young shopkeeper girlfriend, later his wife. Heine had moved to
France some two years earlier and was to spend the rest of his life in the country, where he was to die miserably and impoverished in February 1856, having
passed the last twelve years disabled and nearly blind but still writing. (During
the final eight years Heine was bedridden, confined to what he described his
"mattress tomb." His death is variously attributed to ALS, syphilis, opium, or
a combination.)

On September 5 Heine, then thirty-five and healthy, wrote a letter to
Coste reporting on the "sad spectacle" he had seen several days earlier through
his window.[16] "Undoubtedly you already know the story of the wreck of
Amphitrite," Heine surmised, "a horrible accident which struck horror into
the hearts of all in Boulogne." He then elaborated:

> As I was living in the Hotel Marine, the closest to the beach, I could
> observe from my window the unfortunate vessel, whose crew could
> have been so easily saved, yet nevertheless was to perish so miserably,
> with an inconceivable loss of life. I don't recall the number of vic-
> tims, but there were more than 150 women, several small children
> and a dozen sailors. It was a sad spectacle, to witness some 50 cadav-
> ers that the waves tossed on the beach, tossed to our feet! The hostess

at the Marine Hotel and two other women who were lodging there showed such charitable courage on this occasion, which is scarcely found except amongst the fairer sex, as while the men were stupefied with horror and grief, the women strove to find every imaginable method to revive the shipwreck victims. But their efforts would benefit only two sailors who, along with a third, were the only survivors of the whole crew. One of these women passed me the note enclosed, to have it entered in a French newspaper. In sending it to you, I am fulfilling this errand. I am writing you in haste, and request that you not tell anyone that it was I that sent this note. This unfortunate accident will probably cause the loss of the English Consul, who resides here in Boulogne, to whom we had notified of the desperate situation of the British vessel, and who nonetheless did nothing to save his countrymen. But they were in reality the victims of the scruples of the Captain, for as long as he had the slightest desire to be set afloat, he did not wish to abandon his ship and disembark the women he had been entrusted by the Government to deliver to Sydney. (They were almost all young creatures condemned to deportation for poor morals, and amongst them were some of rare beauty. I saw one woman emerge from the foam of the sea who was an absolute Aphrodite, albeit a dead Aphrodite.) Before dying these poor, unfortunate women passed two entire hours in the most horrible agony. (Their cries pierced the noise of the storm.) When they noticed no help was forthcoming, many of them undressed in order to save themselves by swimming, but the tide rose too violently, and the sea showed them no mercy, coldly sacrificing them. After such a cowardly event (murdering such beautiful and unfortunate women) the sea today is so calm, so gentle, so lighthearted, it seems to be even innocent. What a cowardly and hypocritical event! To what can it be compared?

46

Before the calamity Heine had been enchanted by twelve-year-old Lucie Austin, the daughter of John and Sarah Austin from England and the same sprite who later captivated Hénin.[17] The Austins had lived in Germany during 1826–28, and that's where young Lucie (after her marriage in May 1840, Lady Lucie Duff Gordon) learned the language that her mother knew well and where she adopted the German spelling of her name. The family was in Boulogne for several weeks over the summer, John Austin newly unemployed after three frustrating years attempting to teach law in London. In time he would prove himself incapable of any employment.[18]

John and Sarah were an unlikely and unhappy couple, although nothing in their bizarre five-year-long engagement seems to have warned either of them that was going to be the case. They were married in 1819, he fearful that her racy reputation was deserved, she after determined study to match her learning to his and expecting marriage to be a blissful, intellectual partnership.

The accepted model for successful marriage in that age, however, was nothing like Sarah's fantasy. It contemplated, instead, the wife's near complete submergence beneath husband and home. For the benefit of young women and new wives, newspapers occasionally printed advice columns, including one regularly reprinted titled "Maxims for Married Ladies" featuring strictures that could have been written in the first century AD by the Apostle Paul. Devoutly observed, these twelve rules were presented as guarantees of domestic tranquility; among them was such counsel as the following:

> Occupy yourself only with household affairs; wait till your husband confides to you those of higher importance, and do not give your advice till he asks it.
>
> Never take upon yourself to be a censor of your husband's morals . . . practice virtue yourself to make him in love with it. . . .
>
> All men are vain; never wound this vanity, not even in the most trifling instances. A wife may have more sense than her husband, but she should never seem to know it. . . .
>
> When a husband is out of temper, behave obligingly to him; if he is abusive, never retort; and never prevail over him to humble him. . . .
>
> Seem always to obtain information from him, especially before company, though you may pass yourself for a simpleton. Never forget that a wife owes all her importance to her husband. Leave him entirely master of his own actions, to go or come whenever he thinks fit. A wife ought to make her company amiable to her husband, that he will not be able to exist without it, then he will not seek for pleasure abroad. . . .

"Two people more unlike it would have been difficult to find—John Austin, habitually grave and despondent; his wife, brilliantly handsome, fond of society, in which she shone, and with an almost superabundance of energy and animal spirits," so wrote Sarah Austin's memoirist and granddaughter, Janet Ross, in 1893, tiptoeing down the crevasses of her grandparents' relationship, one that she learned had been a sad mismatch almost from the beginning.

Sarah Austin was beautiful, adorned with almost "hectically intense, warm blue eyes," vivacious, fluent in four languages and literate in five, and wonderfully well read, a woman who throughout the best parts of her life was at the center of a salon of educated people, held together by their extensive correspondence.[19] John Austin—briefly a British army officer in Sicily, then a lawyer, later a university professor, and later still a senior civil servant in Malta, all unsuccessfully—suffered from something that sounds today like a blend of the worst symptoms of acute depression and obsessive compulsive disorder. The condition, whatever it was, frequently disabled and immobilized him for long periods. In his 1873 autobiography John Stuart Mill, a sympathetic family friend (whose own depression lasted for years), described John Austin this way:

> He hardly ever completed any intellectual task of magnitude, He had so high a standard of what ought to be done, so exaggerated a sense of difficulties in his own performances, and was so unable to content himself with the amount of elaboration sufficient for the occasion and the purpose, that he not only spoilt much of his work for ordinary use by overlabouring it, but spent so much time and exertion in superfluous study and thought, that when his task ought to have been completed, he generally worked himself into an illness. From this mental infirmity . . . combined with liability to frequent attacks of disabling, though not dangerous, ill-health, he accomplished, through life, little in comparison with what he seemed capable of.[20]

In 1831 Sarah Austin translated a book by Prince Hermann Ludwig Heinrich von Pückler-Muskau, one curiously titled *Letters from a Dead Man*, from German into English. Its four volumes constituted a candid travelogue, the edited product of a stream of diary entries and daily letters from the prince to his former wife, written while Pückler-Muskau trolled for two and a half years through the British Isles in open search for a wealthy woman to marry, whose money could rescue him, his divorced wife, and their country estate from austerity.[21] (Pückler-Muskau's divorce *invitus invita* in September 1826 from Princess Lucie, nine years his senior, daughter of the Prussian chancellor and widow of a wealthy German count, was their contrivance to free him for the treasure hunt.)

Austin had come upon the book and been fascinated by it and the free spirit visible behind its pages. Her translation, *The Tour of a German Prince*, was published in 1832, and the breezy, rakish memoir quickly became a sensation in England and the United States, despite her having pruned out the seamier parts, which he characterized as its "salt" but she inelegantly called "dirt."[22]

The same year Sarah began what grew into a torrid correspondence with the prince, a forty-six-year-old Saxon aristocrat described dismissively in 1981 by John Austin's biographer as "only a moderately successful heiress hunter." In fact, he was an entirely unsuccessful one, returning to Muskau and to his complaisant ex-princess in February 1829 alone and empty-handed. Eventually, however, book royalties and the sale of his estate eased the reunited (but never remarried) couple's financial anxieties.

In its own way the Pückler-Muskaus' relationship was as weird as was the Austins'. Weirder still after the prince began a campaign in 1838 to set up a ménage à trois in which his first wife, who had until then agreeably tolerated his dozens of affairs and her own unofficial status, and a teenage Ethiopian slave girl whom he purchased in Africa would have shared his presence and attention on the estate. Only the girl's death from tuberculosis in October 1840 ended that princely initiative.[23]

Sarah Austin must have seen more in the man than did his stuffier English critics. During most of the three years immediately following her work as a translator, 1832–34, Prussian embassy couriers carried in their weekly diplomatic pouches a stream of personal letters between her and the prince. Her letters reveal deep unhappiness and frustration with her arid marriage to Austin and much more, unsatisfied appetites that make them sound occasionally like Victorian versions of telephone sex scripts. ("Cleopatra herself could not excel me as a bedfellow," she wrote to the prince in one letter; "all that is beneath the petticoat is worth one thousand times the rest," she wrote in another.)

A careful, offhand comment by Ross half a century later suggests Sarah's frustration had been fermenting for a decade by the time Pückler-Muskau materialized as a pen pal. There is no evidence that their relationship ever went beyond passionate letter writing—she declined her first opportunity to meet Pückler-Muskau early in the 1830s; they finally met in late 1842 in Berlin, perhaps more than once—but while their astonishing correspondence continued, her many letters to Pückler-Muskau radiated an almost adolescent heat in response to his wolfish encouragement.

Austin's debility accounts for the family's presence in Boulogne-sur-Mer in 1833. Paying students had stayed away in droves from his lectures in law during his prior three years as professor of jurisprudence at the new University of London. By the end of 1832 that failure was complete, but before the Austins were forced to recognize they could not manage in England on a yearly allowance of four hundred pounds from their parents plus the one hundred or so pounds annually she was able to earn as a translator, their prospects brightened, briefly. Austin senior promised further financial support and two offers for lucrative positions for John Austin materialized unexpectedly. Under pressure to prepare to perform, Austin collapsed at the good news. The

FIG. 16

Sarah Austin, Boulogne-sur-Mer, September 8, 1835. Wilhelm Hensel, engraving, 1835. "I am exactly 5 feet 6 inches," Sarah Austin wrote to Prince Pückler-Muskau, describing herself, ". . . my shoulders wide and well formed and my waist extremely slender in proportion to the expanse above and below. My bosom is not extremely large and prominent but round and firm. But I tell you [the hips] and all below them are singularly handsome, I believe I might say perfect. . . . Knee and ankle sharply turned, and calf and thigh firm, round and accurately formed." Not visible in this drawing is the faint mustache her good friend, Scottish author Thomas Carlyle, described to his wife in an August 1831 letter. Hensel (1794–1861) was a well-established court portraitist and member of the academy in Berlin in the 1830s. In Germany the Austins and Hensel traveled in the same social circle, one that included the composer Felix Mendelssohn, whose sister was married to the artist.

BILDARCHIV PREUSSISCHER KULTURBESITZ/ART RESOURCE, NY.

FIG. 17

Prince Hermann Pückler-Muskau. Franz Krüger, oil, 1819. In February 1833 the *Court Journal: Gazette of the Fashionable World* described Pückler-Muskau as "tall and well made; his countenance is full of intelligence and expression. There is a certain originality in his manners, as well as in his character." Pückler-Muskau (1785–1871) was more than a shameless voluptuary, enthusiastic solo tourist, and author of several commercially successful travel books. He was also a pioneering landscape architect whose handsome estates at Muskau on the Polish border and later at Branitz became models of very large scale landscape design in Europe and the United States. Pückler-Muskau's influence grew following publication of his *Hints on Landscape Gardening* (1834) and in English translation in 1917. Franz Krüger (1797–1857) was a Berlin painter whose portraits were especially popular in the Prussian and Russian courts.

COURTESY HERMANN GRAF PÜCKLER, MUNICH/BRANITZ.

small family retired to Boulogne in August, where he could recover strength and steel himself for the challenges to come in autumn. And so it happened that in the late summer of 1833 Sarah Austin, aged forty, was living with her husband and daughter in the Marine Hotel when *Amphitrite* sailed out of the storm and ran aground on the sands in sight of all inside. Soon the dead were floating ashore.

There is no reason to doubt Sarah Austin's dramatic (and flattering) description of that ghastly night in the hotel on the strand, spent trying to bring corpses to life:

> I saw nothing, felt nothing, conceived of nothing else but the pres-
> ent—the tremendous present; human beings brought into this
> house whom it might yet be possible to wring from the iron grasp of
> death. Had I been told that I should turn from one dripping corpse
> to another, tear off their clothes, think of every thing, order every
> thing, order every body, rub them with my hands, take their feet in my
> bosom nay once even *lift* a full grown man, and never once feel faint-
> ness, never lose my presence of mind for a moment and not suffer in
> health afterward, certainly I could not have believed it—but it is true.
> I don't mind saying to you that I am still astonished at what I did—the
> promptitude with which I recollected everything and did it.

The effort was courageous and remarkable. Manipulating, even just touch-ing, bodies of the dead brushed up hard against powerful taboos. None of the hotel's chambermaids would touch the dead, Sarah wrote, but "in the hotel was a pale, delicate, quiet young English lady. She had a nursemaid. . . . I had my good, faithful Elizabeth, my femme de chambre. . . . We four did every-thing. Mrs. Curtis kept imploring the men to bring us more bodies. Something was said about the naked bodies of men. She said, we know no difference, we cannot think of those things. I looked at her with surprise and admiration. She was in all common things full of English reserve. The French girls kept pulling my clothes, entreating me not to touch the bodies. . . . We saved two men— they are alive and well."[24] For Mrs. Curtis the catastrophe was a chance to dip into her family history for a brief, horrific moment. By coincidence she was, *Le Mémorial Dieppois* told its readers, the granddaughter of the man who had established the Société Humaine at Boulogne, John Larking.

The British Royal Humane Society thought that Sarah Austin responded to the catastrophe heroically, crediting her with all three lives saved. Months later the society presented her with a vellum certificate, marking "its grateful and sincere thanks . . . for the lively solicitude which she manifested . . . on the occasion of the calamitous wreck of the British convict ship *Amphitrite*, off the port of Boulogne-sur-Mer, on the night of the 31st August last; when, by her presence of mind, perseverance, and humanity, in conjunction with that of Mrs. John Curtis, she had the happiness, under Divine Providence, to recover three of the mariners of the above vessel, who were washed on shore by the violence of the gale, and taken to the Marine Hotel in a state of insensibility."

The story of the wreck and her dramatic part in it, as it was passed around the Austins' circle, had Sarah "standing wet through on the beach, receiving survivors" and responsible for the rescue of one woman "by dashing into the sea and pulling her to land." In fact, no woman survived the wreck of *Amphitrite*, and Sarah's own account says she labored in the hotel and not on the beach, but to be generous to her memory it is not impossible to imagine that one convict emerged from the surf and was alive for a brief time. It is also not impossible, although mentioned nowhere else other than in Ross' memoir, that one of the convicts as her last act in life somehow presented Sarah with a book washed up from the wreck, *The Mirrour of the Magistrates*, which "although sadly torn and battered" was later restored. There was such a book, a three-volume poetry collection about the lives of great men last published in 1815, even if there were not such a convict.

Nothing so thrilling happened to Sarah Austin again. After 1834 her odd romance with Pückler-Muskau slowly lost heat, and a decade after its incendiary beginning, when the two finally met, even the embers were cold. Through the next thirty years, while they both aged (he outlived her by three years), Sarah slowly accommodated herself to life as it was, spared humiliation because her letters to him remained private. During eight years as a widow Austin edited and published her husband's class notes as a book titled *Lectures on Jurisprudence*, giving the man the posthumous success he could never achieve on his own in life.

By this time Sarah Austin's great beauty was long gone. The enchantress who had sat for a portrait by John Linnell in 1834 (the sketch is part of Britain's National Portrait Gallery collection today), hair crowned atop her head and her gown draped artfully to expose the points of her shoulders, was no more. In her place was the fleshy matron of Lady Arthur Russell's ca. 1867 oil painting, obviously weary and overweight, and for the first time exhibiting the hint of a mustache that even her admirers had observed in her youth.[25]

She died on August 8, 1867, "after an acute attack of a malady of the heart with which she had long been afflicted," less than two years before the death of her daughter and only child. "Ever since John Austin's death eight years earlier," Lucie Duff Gordon's biographer wrote in 1994, "her life had been a sad, dreary, posthumous existence. The main thing that had kept her going was her 'sacred work' of editing and reissuing her husband's works. Once this was accomplished and once, too, she had brought out Lucie's [books] and seen her dying daughter for the last time [in Germany, in 1865], Sarah had no reason to linger."[26]

That same month *The Times* printed what amounted to Austin's obituary in an advertisement for Sarah's last book. "To the attractions of great personal beauty in early life," wrote the newspaper,

> and of a grace of manner undiminished by years, Mrs. Austin added a masculine intellect and a large heart. It was not by the play of a vivid imagination, or by an habitual display of what is termed wit, that she secured the affections and the friendship of so many of the wisest and noblest of her contemporaries. The power she exercised in society was due to the sterling qualities of her judgment, her knowledge and her literary style—which was one of great purity and excellence— and above all, to her cordial readiness to promote all good objects, to maintain high principles of action, and to confer benefits on all who claimed her aid.

The Times said nothing about Sarah Austin's exciting night on the beach at Boulogne nearly thirty-five years before, but those few who remembered *Amphitrite* on the sands at the edge of the town would have assumed it was implied in the general praise of her character.

47

It does not take long to drown, to suffocate under water, not much more than several minutes. The final breaths come at the same time as do brief upticks in heart rate, blood pressure, and cardiac output, but all three begin to decline soon after the last gasp. Five to ten minutes later, the heart stops completely. After a short time submerged, authorities now say approximately ten minutes, "it becomes progressively more difficult to achieve a recovery," and that's with modern resuscitation protocols and equipment.

One hardened researcher (his subjects were animals, not people) identified five distinct phases during fatal submersion: A short struggle to remain above the surface. Swallowing to prevent inhalation of water. More struggling. Convulsions, gasping, and water inhalation. And death. *Amphitrite*'s human victims would have passed through something very like that sequence, complicated and accelerated by the powerful seas churning around them.

No one from *Amphitrite* was alive in the water long enough to suffer death from exposure, even though water at 65°F (18°C, and not commonly thought of as "cold") sucks away body heat with potentially lethal efficiency. A core temperature drop of relatively few degrees below normal (98.6°F, 37°C) induces significant physiological effects that accumulate as the body cools. A further drop through 86°F (30°C) is often fatal for adults. At 82°F (28°C) a final threshold is crossed; that's when the heart's pumping chambers begin to flutter (fibrillate) instead of beating regularly and effective circulation ceases. Hénin, the brave swimmer, spent an hour and a half, perhaps longer, unprotected in the water during his failed effort to connect ship to shore with a life line. He emerged from that experience exhausted and chilled practically speechless, but still mobile.

But just as the waters of the Dover Strait were too warm to kill quickly, they were also too warm to trigger a potentially lifesaving reflex called "the mammalian diving response." This mysterious leftover of human evolution accounts for the occasional, astonishing survival and recovery to health of ice skaters, sailors, and aviators down in cold water, in rare cases some with submersion times longer than one hour. The chief mechanism appears to be a reflexive constriction of peripheral blood vessels. Operating through slightly different physiological processes, hypothermia and the diving response would have led to a sharp metabolic slowing and a concomitant reduced requirement for oxygen.[27] Without this metabolic reset, even a short period of oxygen deprivation and cardiac arrest in 1833 meant almost certain death.

Although drowning in salt water is different from drowning in fresh water—the former thickens the blood, reduces its volume, and increases all blood electrolyte levels; the latter does the reverse—these differences were not significant to medical men of the nineteenth century, and they are not clinically significant today. Submersion is what killed *Amphitrite*'s victims, not sea salts.

Not all would have died with their lungs full of water, the idea most people have about what drowning does and is. A small number, ten or fifteen, would have experienced an involuntary convulsion of their vocal chords triggered by the first few drops of water inhaled, a "laryngospasm" that would have closed their airways and blocked further inhalation of water. These few would have drowned "dry." Most, however, would have inhaled some water during their frantic fight for air and life, some as much a quart or so, the fluid whipped up in their airway and lungs into frothy foam.

"Wet" or "dry," to a clinician all the dead would have exhibited the same signs of asphyxiation and sudden circulatory arrest: low blood oxygen and high blood carbon dioxide, and high blood acidity. Modern emergency medical care in the event of drowning calls for immediate mouth-to-mouth rescue breathing to resume ventilation, supplemented as soon as possible by additional oxygen, and prompt cardiopulmonary resuscitation through chest compressions to restore circulation. Only in rare instances is defibrillation required.

Approaching the 1820s the Royal Humane Society for the Recovery of the Apparently Drowned or Dead (one form of the charity's name) already could, and did, boast of thousands of saved lives in and around London alone since its founding fewer than fifty years before. Its record was confirmation of the hope expressed in their official seal, a pudgy boy puffing on an almost extinguished torch, beneath the Latin motto *Lateat Scintillula Forsan*, "Perchance a spark may be concealed."

Among its triumphs, the society reminded the general public during its annual fund raising campaigns, were not only revivals of would-be victims of accidental immersion in water but also the recovery of "many persons who, forsaken by reason, and driven by despair, would otherwise have rashly rushed, unrepented and unprepared, into the presence of their Maker, but who were recalled to a sense of their duty, and reclaimed from a life of wickedness" or a wicked death. To those snatched from successful suicide by the intervention of a society member could be added many others "interred as dead when breathing only was suspended (a fact too shocking for contemplation!)," one of the era's more baroque fears, and still more who had escaped death by, for example, "noxious air—lightning strike—suspension by the cord, &c." Other national societies had similar catalogues of success.

By the 1830s resuscitation techniques had advanced significantly from the methodology introduced by the Dutch Society to Rescue People from Drowning (the *Maatschappij tot Redding van Drenkelingen*, established in 1768, well before counterparts elsewhere in Europe and the United States). The early Dutch method comprised three elements: warming the body, providing mouth-to-mouth ventilation, and infusing tobacco smoke up the rectum of the victim—perhaps the most imaginative of the beneficial medical properties tobacco enthusiasts have claimed for their plant over time. By 1861 there were so many rival techniques, and so much uncertainty about what worked best, that the Royal Medical and Chirugical Society of London established committees to consider and evaluate the alternatives.

So to conclude this mournful tale, Those tidings for to hear,

It cannot fail from high and low, To draw a silent tear.

This wreck will never be forgot, This dreadful tale of woe,

We hope their souls in heaven rest, While their bodies rot below.

CHAPTER 7

The Admiralty Investigation

48

On December 31, 1812, Lieutenant Henry Ducie Chads, RN, then just twenty-four but already a dozen years into what would become a very long navy career, sent John Wilson Croker, the "famously unpleasant" first secretary of the Admiralty, the most painful report of his life:[1] "It is with deep regret that I write you . . . that His Majesty's Ship *Java* is no more, after sustaining an action on the 29th Inst for several hours with the American frigate *Constitution* which resulted in the Capture and ultimate destruction of His Majesty's Ship. Captain [Henry] Lambert being seriously wounded in the height of the Action, the melancholy task of writing the detail devolves on me." Chads had been second in command of HMS *Java*, the frigate whose loss two days earlier he was now reporting to his masters in London.

Writing such a report to the Admiralty would have been difficult for any ambitious Royal Navy lieutenant, made more so by the fact that he did it while embarked in USS *Constitution*, a prisoner of the victorious Americans until he was paroled and put ashore in San Salvador, Brazil, two days later. The knowledge that the letter's addressee was a powerful, vindictive man despised by his enemies and feared even by his friends should have made drafting and dispatching it even more of a trial for Chads.[2] Captain Lambert's fatal wounding, moreover, was likely a special burden.

Chads had served with Lambert for three years (1808–11) as his first lieutenant in HMS *Iphigenia*, a tour of duty that was interrupted for several months in 1810 while he was ashore on Mauritius as a prisoner of the French following the Battle of Grand Port, the Royal Navy's worst defeat during the Napoleonic Wars. Chads then served briefly in HMS *Semiramis* until August 1812, when he and Lambert were reunited in *Java* at Lambert's personal request, when she was commissioned in the Royal Navy.

Spotting an unknown sail on the horizon in the South Atlantic off Brazil on Tuesday, December 29, Captain Lambert interrupted his passage to India and sent *Java* in that direction, instinctively exhibiting the aggressive spirit and self-confidence bordering on hubris typical of a Royal Navy captain in command of a warship. (Typical since March 14, 1757, anyway. That's when Rear Admiral the Honorable John Byng, RN, was executed on HMS *Monarque*'s quarterdeck after being found guilty by a court-martial of failure "to do his utmost to take or destroy enemy ships" in an engagement the previous May against a French squadron before the walls of Fort St. Philip, Minorca.)[3] Lambert was bolder than many, rash even. His crew, mostly landsmen, had left Portsmouth, England, only six weeks or so earlier and since departure had little experience in loading, laying, and firing *Java*'s great guns.

At first Lambert did not know that his intended prey was USS *Constitution*, the American frigate that five months earlier had made quick work of HMS *Guerrière* and now, under a new commanding officer, was prowling the area with USS *Hornet* looking for British merchantmen to ambush. Shortly after 2:00 in the afternoon, with the ships now a half mile apart and the South American coast out of sight to the west, *Constitution* fired the first of two port broadsides into *Java*'s rigging. *Java* replied with her starboard guns a little later, after the ships had closed to near pistol shot. By every conventional measure *Constitution* was the superior ship: bigger, stouter, and better armed, albeit not as swift as her French-built opponent. Fresh out of a shipyard and under an able captain leading an experienced crew, and absent either freakish accident or grotesque error, *Constitution* was certain to defeat *Java*.[4] And that's how the engagement ended after four hours of gunfire and maneuver.

The rest of Chads' letter described the duel between the two ships during which the outmatched, heavily laden, and badly overmanned *Java* (49 guns versus *Constitution*'s 54 and crowded with nearly seventy supernumeraries) was first dismasted and then shot near to pieces. Lambert's only realistic hope had been to close with *Constitution* and board her, submerging the defending Americans on deck beneath a storm of pistol-, cutlass-, pike-, and axe-armed British sailors and marines. That never happened, but once during the battle the ships were so close together that *Java*'s jib boom fouled *Constitution*'s mizzen rigging.

Although the precise numbers are still uncertain, at least 120 of *Java*'s officers, men, and ship riders were killed, died of wounds, or were wounded in battle, and possibly as many as 160 were. Captain Lambert was at first counted among the wounded, shot off his quarterdeck in midafternoon by a musket ball fired by a Marine sharpshooter from *Constitution*'s fighting top and like Nelson, a victim of the tradition that required Royal Navy officers to expose themselves even in furious close combat. The ball punctured a lung and shattered Lambert's spine; he lived in pain for a week and died the evening of January 3, 1813, in San Salvador (now Bahia).

"I then consulted the Officers," Chads continued in his New Year's Eve letter to Croker, "who agreed with myself that on having a great part of our Crew killed & wounded our bowsprit and three masts gone, several guns useless, we should not be justified in waisting [sic] the lives of more of those remaining whom I hope their Lordships & Country will think have bravely defended His Majesty's Ship." The next day, after officers' baggage and all the defeated survivors had been removed to *Constitution*, the British frigate was set afire and sank. *Guerrière* had suffered the same fate.

Looking to salve British pride after this third single-handed defeat of a Royal Navy frigate, Chads' letter concluded with a postscript describing the loss of life and very substantial damage USS *Constitution* had suffered in the engagement. He exaggerated slightly, and perhaps unknowingly, the price his foe had paid for victory.[5]

We know the details of this battle at sea from excellent sources, the descriptive reports of the surviving senior officers, Chads in *Java* and Commodore William Bainbridge, USN, in *Constitution*, written soon after the fight, and other official records of both navies.[6] In 1882 from these materials Theodore Roosevelt, then twenty-three, drew his description of the battle in his book-length tactical study, *The Naval War of 1812*. From the same sources, the late Patrick O'Brian did even better in 1997. That's when he wrote *The Fortune of War*, the sixth of twenty volumes of fiction in which he recreated a world at war around the friendship of Captain Jack Aubrey, RN, and his ship's surgeon, close companion, opium addict, and sometime master spy, Doctor Stephen Maturin—a literary partnership as durable, but more egalitarian, as that of Sherlock Holmes and Doctor John Watson.

In *The Fortune of War* HMS *Java* is at sea in the South Atlantic and crammed to her gunwales with her crew, the future governor of Bombay and his entourage, men slated for assignment to three Royal Navy ships under construction in India and—here the first bit of fiction—with Aubrey and Maturin and ten other survivors of a ship-killing fire in HMS *La Flèche*. *Java*'s captain is described as a good seaman but without private means and unlucky; her first lieutenant, Chads, is "a very scientific officer," a wizard at gunnery and the inventor of a gun sight, and a man who has married into great wealth. O'Brian's brief sketch of Lieutenant Chads is not so much fiction as forecasting. Chads was single when *Java* challenged *Constitution* and lost. He did not marry until November 1815, when he wed Elizabeth Townshend from Fareham, on the northwestern corner of Portsmouth Harbor in Hampshire County and his father's home town.[7] Similarly, Chads developed his gunnery skills later in life than O'Brian would have us believe, not until after he joined HMS *Arachne*.

In O'Brian's tale, as in history, *Constitution* leads *Java* ("a fine dry quicksailing weatherly ship") away from shore and into the open ocean. Lambert's plan when he overhauls his target is "to batter 'em yardarm to yardarm for a while, and then board in the smoke." Once in range of their guns, the ships exchange fire, *Java*'s eighteen pounders gamely responding to *Constitution*'s twenty-fours. Sometime early in the fighting Chads gets "a nasty swipe." (In fact, he was seriously wounded during the battle.) Later *Java* crosses *Constitution*'s stern close aboard to starboard—potentially a ship-killing maneuver—but, terribly, that broadside's guns have not been reloaded. Here the second bit of fiction, as in fact, Java fired two broadsides into *Constitution*'s stern. The first destroyed the wheel, killed all four helmsmen, and forced the Americans to jury-rig steering gear.

The second, and last, chance at victory is lost when *Java*'s boarding party is trapped on board their ship, smothered under her collapsed foremast and sails:

> The boarders swarmed on to the forecastle, cutlasses, pistols, axes ready. Chads was there again, pale at his Captain's side; both of them caught Jack's eye—a savage, eager grin. A few yards more and there would be the crash of impact, the spring aboard, the hot work to hand . . . the furious impatience of the crowd of men poised for their leap.
>
> But then . . . the mast, the towering great edifice of the foremast with all its spreading yards, its fighting-top, its sails, its countless ropes and blocks, came crashing down, the lower part kicking aft to cover the main deck, the upper covering the forecastle.

The best opportunity to board has been lost in a shower of masts, yards, and canvas. And at the end, after *Constitution*'s long 24-pound guns have bludgeoned *Java* to near immobility, perforated her hull, and turned her gun deck into an abattoir, the two ships lie apart just outside hailing distance. In Patrick O'Brian's imagination, the larger of the two makes her move:

> Deliberately and under perfect control she crossed the *Java*'s bows at rather more than two hundred yards, shivered her main and mizzen

topsails, and lay there, gently rocking, her whole almost undamaged larboard broadside looking straight at the dismasted *Java*, ready to rake her again and again. With her single sail right forward the *Java* could not move into the wind—could no longer approach the *Constitution*; all she could do was to make a slow starboard turn to bring her seven port guns to bear: by the time they could fire she would have been raked three times at point-blank range—in any case, the *Constitution* would not wait until they bore, but fill again and circle her. The *Constitution* lay there: with evident forbearance she did not open fire. Jack [Aubrey] could see her captain looking earnestly at them from his quarterdeck.

"No," said Chads in a dead voice. "It will not do." He looked at Jack, who bowed his head: then walked aft, as a resolute man might walk to the gallows, walked between the sparse gun-crews, silent now, and hauled the colours down.

The victory was a great triumph for Commodore William Bainbridge and his crew, but it was not the payday for which they had hoped. For that, Bainbridge needed to capture plump prizes that could be sold whole, not to pick over battered hulls to salvage bits of intact cargo and baggage. *Java*'s charred timbers on the seafloor inflated the commodore's reputation but did little to increase his net worth.

The Royal Navy's surprisingly poor performance against the U.S. Navy's 44-gun frigates disconcerted Britons, who were inexperienced in combat losses at sea. Their usual calculus had one British tar worth two Frenchmen or three Spaniards. Nearly ninety years after HMS *Java* was put to the torch, William Laird Clowes in 1900 introduced the fifth volume of his magisterial history of the Royal Navy, noting a distinct performance decline in the years after Nelson's triumph at Trafalgar. After that bit of candor, Clowes turned to tribal arguments in further explanation. Britain, he observed, had "forgot, however, that her new enemy [the United States] was of her own blood; and she did not then know that the old blood in the new land had lost none of its old virtue, and, like all the blood of the stock, would be stimulated rather than weakened by the prospect of a really serious struggle. And so there came the American War, with its early defeats and various disappointments."[8]

On April 23, 1813, Chads and all the other survivors of *Java*'s fatal battle were summoned before a court-martial on board HMS *Gladiator* in the port of Portsmouth, Rear Admiral of the Blue Graham Moore, RN, presiding. Such a trial was the form of the usual investigation conducted after the loss of one of his majesty's ships. At proceeding's end the "board was of the opinion that the cause of the capture of the said ship was her being totally dismasted in a long

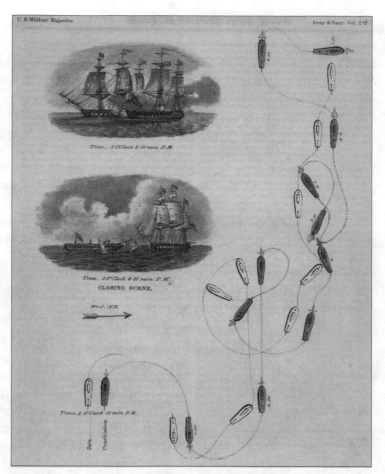

FIG. 18

Diagram of the Action between the U.S. Frigate Constitution Com. Bainbridge and H. M. Frigate Java Capt. Lambert. James Queen, artist, and Peter S. Duval, lithographer, 1840. In this illustration the wind is from the left. After her defeat of HMS *Java* in December 1812, handsomely but imperfectly represented here, USS *Constitution* remained in commission through much of the nineteenth century. "Old Ironsides"—the nickname is an admiring reference to her tough, live oak hull—was restored 1927–30 at the Boston Navy Yard and recommissioned in 1931. She lies pierside in Boston Harbor today as a revered tourist attraction, still in commission. This illustration is from the November 1840 issue of William Huddy's *United States Military Magazine,* vol. 2. The magazine, a pioneer in high-quality color lithography, was published in Philadelphia between March 1839 and June 1842. Duval was Huddy's partner in the venture.

COURTESY OF THE NAVY ART COLLECTION, NAVAL HISTORY AND HERITAGE COMMAND.

and spirited action with a far superior force, that the conduct of all the Officers and Ships Company was highly conspicuous & honorable and equally so after the death of her captain; that they only yielded when continuance would have been a useless sacrifice, and the Court therefore most honorably acquitted all the surviving Officers and Ships Company."[9]

Admiral Moore went out of his way to be solicitous. "I have much satisfaction in returning you your sword," he told Chads at trial's end. "Had you been an officer who had served in comparative obscurity all your life, and never before been heard of, your conduct on the present occasion would have been sufficient to establish your character as a brave, skillful and attentive officer." (The loss of *Java* aside, by early 1813 Chads was hardly an unknown lieutenant. He had served on salt water in three oceans, led an amphibious raid ashore near Mauritius, and been for several months a prisoner of war of the French.)

Real absolution came the next month, when Chads was ordered to take his first command, HM sloop *Columbia*. Orders to command at sea marked Chads as a star among the Royal Navy's 3,268 lieutenants that year.

49

Henry Chads joined the Royal Navy in October 1800 at twelve—soon after the death of his father, and now orphaned—then spent the next three years as a student at the Royal Naval Academy before going to sea for the first time in HMS *Excellent*. The sea service was in his genes: He was the eldest son of a Royal Navy captain from Hampshire, also named Henry Chads, and became father to another with the same name. Chads remained in uniform and on active duty or half pay ashore for the next fifty-five years. During those many years he commanded successively HMS *Columbia*, HMS *Arachne*, HMS *Alligator*, HMS *Andromache*, HMS *Cambrian*, and the Royal Navy's gunnery school HMS *Excellent* and flew his flag as a rear admiral in HMS *Edinburgh* and HMS *Nile*.

Promotion to flag rank in the Royal Navy was strictly on the basis of seniority, less a selection process than an endurance contest. As in a tontine, after others fell along the way, the last man (men in this case) standing got the big payoff. In 1854, during the Crimean War, the Royal Navy's five senior commanders at sea were from sixty-four to sixty-nine years of age. Chads, flying his flag in HMS *Edinburgh* and in command of a squadron in the Baltic, was sixty-six. "From officers of such advanced life," Sir William Clowes wrote, thinking back almost fifty years, "it was perhaps unreasonable to look for the energy, activity, and mental suppleness that distinguish capable younger men."[10]

FIG. 19

Admiral Sir Henry Ducie Chads, RN. Lieutenant Henry Ducie Chads assumed command of HMS *Java* when her captain was fatally wounded, and it fell to him to surrender his ship to USS *Constitution* after their duel in the South Atlantic. Midway through his long career in the Royal Navy, Sir Henry (1788–1868), then a captain, was appointed to conduct the Admiralty's one-officer investigation of the wreck of the convict transport *Amphitrite*. He did that during three weeks in September 1833, absolving practically everyone from responsibility for the "melancholy event" that saw 133 on board drown. After twenty-nine years as a captain, Chads was promoted to rear admiral in January 1854, to vice admiral in November 1858, and finally—when he was seventy-five—to admiral in December 1863. The artist and date of this engraving are unknown.

In late summer 1833 Captain Chads, forty-five, was ashore between *Alligator* and *Andromache* and impatiently at home in Portsmouth awaiting assignment when he was commissioned by Sir James Graham, then First Lord of the Admiralty, to investigate some circumstances of the wreck of the convict transport *Amphitrite*. Chads' biographer, Montagu Burrows (a three-time former shipmate and later a renown professor of history at Oxford), wanted his readers to believe that Graham's commission was meant to be a favor to Chads, who had been ashore at half pay and unemployed for nearly seven years, ever since paying off the crew of HMS *Alligator* in January 1827 following two cruises in the Indian Ocean. That was his second extended period ashore. The first had been the eight years between *Columbia* and *Arachne*.

If so, Chads had finally recruited a powerful friend. Sir James would later repeatedly demonstrate no talent whatever for electoral politics—his switch from one side to the other in the House of Commons exasperated both parties, and his speeches before that body were notoriously unpersuasive—but in the early 1830s he was in his first term as the cabinet officer in charge of the Admiralty and in a position to provide the necessary political impetus to revive any officer's stalled but otherwise successful career. (Graham would be First Lord of the Admiralty again twenty years later, his last government service.)

A successful career in the Royal Navy such as Chads' had been and would remain usually reflected more than good seamanship and courage; it also required "interest," the support of powerful mentors. Supplicants for assignment and promotion were immodest about their ties to power, and their supporters were, too. A typical phrase from one petitioner's mentor to an Admiralty figure had him "avail myself of old friendship as well as the family connection that exists between us to write a few lines in favor of . . ." in pressing a case for his client.

Interest, but also a deft touch navigating the bureaucracy. Since *Java* went down during the last week of 1812 Chads had enjoyed the admiration of Major General Sir Thomas Hislop, the commander in chief designate then sailing to Bombay with him, but now Chads had the personal interest of someone potentially much more useful than a baronet in the British army, however supportive: the Right Honorable Sir James Robert George Graham, Bart., MP. An officer who depended on official favor for his next assignment to active duty could have been expected to tread delicately through the minefields of Foreign Office and Admiralty sensitivities. Conducting such an important inquiry would increase Chads' visibility among hundreds of unemployed captains, and perhaps restore him to active duty.

With more than three decades in uniform behind him, including service at sea in ten of His Majesty's ships, ranging in size from a sloop of war to a 74-gun frigate, and eight years as a captain, Chads appeared to be the perfect choice to investigate a shipwreck. Whether or not these many years of distinguished navy service prepared him to navigate the political issues the investigation inevitably would turn on—questions about what the British consul and French Customs (Douane) officers at Boulogne did or didn't do during the night to ease the suffering of *Amphitrite*'s victims—the next several weeks would tell.

50

Chads' mission was triggered by John Wilks Jr., the Paris correspondent of the *Standard* of London, in Boulogne for the past four days when Hunter deliberately put *Amphitrite* aground. Wilks' agitated letter writing and newspaper reporting from the scene over several days in early September transformed the wreck of *Amphitrite* from a maritime tragedy into a national scandal. But Wilks was more than a crusading journalist appalled by human failure and its ensuing catastrophe, or perhaps he was less than one. It all depends on how you measure such things. Like "Romeo" Coates, John Wilks, forty, was "a gentleman in embarrassed circumstances" in France when he seized on the wreck of *Amphitrite* to restore his visibility to English society, which he had left in disgrace some five years earlier. He was living in France on an annuity from his parents, provided on condition that he stay out of England.

Wilks was a lawyer, an author of books, and an occasional journalist, writing for newspapers and periodicals when he needed the money, but in his prime his profession was committing what is now called securities fraud.[11] His entry by Richard Davenport-Hines in the 2004 edition of the *Oxford Dictionary of National Biography* described Wilks in a single word, "swindler," before going on in a long paragraph to detail the many imaginative cons he committed in London and Paris, and his near ejection from France for cause.[12] Before 1844 and passage of the Joint Stock Companies Act there were few controls on British capitalism other than the natural (and very elastic) limits of human gullibility. Wilks managed during the mid-1820s in England and Wales and the early 1830s in France to create, plunder, and then abandon a string of ventures, in each instance enriching himself and conniving corporate directors, and leaving his gulled investors holding worthless stock in mining, gas lighting, railroad, publishing, or coach companies, among others. Eventually his victims numbered in the thousands. The collapse of the British stock market under such manipulative pressure was so complete that the privately managed, semiofficial Bank of England was forced to seek assistance from its counterpart across the Channel, the Banque de France.

Wilks' opportunity arose because while industrialization accelerated during the early nineteenth century, the traditional sole proprietor and private partnership business models became unable to finance and operate enterprises large enough to exploit new technology or satisfy new demand. (Example: The rail line in Scotland between Ayr and Glasgow that opened in 1840 required some £550,000 to construct. This fortune was raised through the sale to investors of 11,000 £50 shares.) The solution was to pool the capital of investors in joint stock companies, a Dutch invention. Most Victorians viewed the structure with skepticism, if not outright hostility, because it separated ownership from control, risk from reward, and labor from income. It all looked immoral. Conservatives feared—rightly, as it developed—that such impersonal, large companies lacked the ethical compass that proprietors and partners brought to their businesses, and that the new model would encourage speculation and its attendant crimes.

The range of offerings promising fabulous wealth from brilliant innovation demonstrates early-nineteenth-century capitalism at its most inspired. Real ventures (the East of England Screw Coasting Company, the London Genuine Wine Company) sounded no less bizarre than did invented ones (the Resurrection Metal Company, recovering spent cannon balls from the sea floor for reuse; the Galvanic Navigation Company, powering oceangoing vessels electrically). Soon joint stock companies were thick on the ground, up and running (and imploding) long before laws and institutions that could protect investors from stock manipulators and greedy insiders were in place.

One Wilks obituary reports that after 1825 he "lived in a state of siege in consequence of the Sheriff's-officers," but in fact his humiliation came a little later than that. During 1825–26 the thirtysomething entrepreneur was at the top of his form: chief of companies whose imagined collective wealth was compared to the contents in the vault of the Bank of England, proceeding between his "sumptuously furnished" town house at 36 New Broad Street and a "splendid mansion" at Mill Hill in a flashy four-horse coach with liveried outriders, and, when on foot at either place, often in the company of "Lords, Ministers of State, Members of Parliament, [and] a large portion of the aristocracy."

Propelled by his celebrity, Wilks then took a seat in the House of Commons as one of two members from Sudbury, having received half the votes in a field of three in the general election of 1826. (The "ancient and loyal" borough of Sudbury's famously corrupt balloting might have played a role in his short-lived political success. Years later the open buying and selling of votes in two Sudbury pubs, the Black Boy and the Swan, finally resulted in the borough's disenfranchisement.) In a society that equated human worth with financial success, Wilks was for a few years in the mid-1820s the young lion of London, but his election to Parliament marked the peak of his trajectory.

As he passed through apogee, perceptive (or embittered) observers marveled at Wilks' continuing machinations, and at his brass. In September 1826,

just as a Wilks mining venture deflated, "Anti-Humbug" signed two letters to
the editor of *The Times* about Wilks' schemes, writing in rhyme in one:[13]

> Come with me, and we will blow
> Lots of Bubbles, as we go;
> Bubbles, bright as ever Hope
> Drew from fancy—or from soap:—
> Mix the lather, Johnny Wilks,
> Thou who rhyms't so well with 'bilks,'
> Mix the lather—who can be
> Fitter for such task than thee,
> Great M.P. for *Suds*bury.

Anti-Humbug's poetry muse had been brought to life by a Wilks prospectus for the Provincial Bank for England and Wales, circulated to the public
and to members of Parliament after his other ventures, said the letter writer,
had "vanished into thin, thin air. . . . Mines, whether of coal, iron, copper, or
tin, had all exploded—their railroads were impassable—their gas-lights had
become darkness visible—their Paddington stages were at a dead standstill—
their metropolitan fish actually stunk in the market—and their Alderney cows,
every one of them, fairly a-dry." The bank's prospectus solicited distinguished
"patrons" to lend their names and auras to the scheme without further obligation and investors at two pounds sterling per share. (The Provincial Bank for
England and Wales was a long way from Wilks' very first fund raising attempt,
the Joint Stock Sunday Company. Its curious purpose had been to finance
a solicitor, himself, through "parochial subscription" to lobby Parliament for
legislation enforcing observation of the Sabbath.)

Anti-Humbug's last item in his doleful roster of scams was a reference
to the Metropolitan Alderney Dairy Company, which Wilks concocted in
January 1825 ostensibly to supply unadulterated, cream-rich milk to London
from cows native to tiny Alderney in the Channel Islands. By mid-1827,
£141,200, of the original £150,000 subscribed by its investors had vanished,
leaving little behind but the company's deputy chairman sputtering about false
statements in the prospectus and disastrous results, dairy cows with depleted
udders, and investors also holding empty bags.

Status and fortune quickly unraveled after yet another of his schemes, the
Welsh (sometimes "Welch") Iron and Coal Mining Company, caved in, taking with it £250,000 from investors, who until then had stoutly believed Wilks
was an alchemist, capable of turning base metal into gold.[14] When the company's shareholders met in January 1827 it was to listen to a report of losses
"owing to the conduct of Mr. Wilks" that required the immediate infusion of

180 CHAPTER 7

a further £25,000 and to recommendations for the suspension of certain directors for speculation in company shares.

By the time Welsh Iron's collapse was complete, Wilks' reputation was, finally, in ruins. Presumably still hounded by creditors and embarrassed by parliamentary debate in 1827 about his Cornwall and Devonshire Mining Company swindle, Wilks resigned his seat in April 1828, one step ahead of ouster and just in time to be suspected of embezzlement from a church fund. A cascade of other failures and exposures followed, and it was only because his seat in the House of Commons had brought with it parliamentary immunity from imprisonment that he had not already been jailed for debt.

An indictment on forgery charges came next, and this saw Wilks, now in between Parliament and France, briefly confined in London's Giltspur Street Compter (Jail), a forty-year-old lock-up conveniently down the street from the much better known Newgate Prison, where in time many of *Amphitrite*'s unfortunates would be assembled.

Debtors were assigned to the compter's ground-floor group cells ("wards"), women in the south wing, men in the north. Felons of both sexes, drifters, children on the loose, and those like Wilks awaiting trial filled in the remaining open space. Confined pending trial, Wilks would not have been put to work dressing flax in the compter's mat room or grinding corn in its mill, dull prison industries for those sentenced to hard labor, but his brief visit inside would have been grim none the less. Annual inspectors' reports of the 1830s read like something by Dickens, describing wards in which Giltspur's inmates are flaunting every imaginable variety of vice, corruption, and dissipation, and where the methods of crime are being taught by the old to the young.

Wilks senior, the son of a Methodist minister and collector of art and ephemera and his wife, Isabella, must have been mortified by the antics of their only son. It was they (or perhaps an uncle) who put up the money in the late 1820s so that he could leave England and live in France. In 1833 there were still many in London who ruefully reminded each other that Wilks rhymed with "bilks."

Wilks died suddenly in January 1846, at age fifty-three, apparently of tonsillitis. Memories of his schemes long outlived him. They were still vital enough eight years later to merit a paragraph in his father's obituary, which in 1854 reminded readers that thirty years ago the junior Wilks had "made himself so notorious by his activity in the concoction of various joint-stock companies in the year 1825 that he acquired the name of Bubble Wilks."[15] (The "Bubble" in his moniker and in Anti-Humbug's poetry was a wry reference to England's largest financial collapse to date, the great crash of stocks on the London Exchange in 1717, punctuated by the spectacular implosion of the South Sea Company.)

FIG. 20

The Giltspur Street Compter. T. H. Shepherd, artist, and R. Acon, engraver, steel engraving, 1838. John Wilks left England for France soon after his release from pre-trial confinement in the Giltspur Street Compter, a small prison for debtors, felons, and vagrants of both sexes on the east side of Giltspur Street, across from St. Sepulcher's Church and close to Newgate Prison and the Old Bailey Court. He escaped trial and almost certain conviction for fraud because of the suspicious failure of one of the aggrieved to appear in court. Thomas Hosner Shepherd (1792–1864) was well known for his architectural watercolors. This hand-colored engraving after Shepherd is representative of the work of Robert Acon (1792–1880), whose plates illustrated many books of the period. COURTESY FRÉDÉRIQUE DECHOW, LE VOYAGE EN PAPIER, HAMBURG, GERMANY.

This was the man who energized enormous public interest in *Amphitrite*'s last voyage. Typical of Wilks, it later developed that at the same time he was writing exclusive columns for the *Standard*, a Tory evening paper, on Mondays, he was also submitting articles under an alias to the Whiggish *Morning Chronicle* for publication on Tuesdays, and to a third paper on Fridays. "When these facts became notorious," *Fraser's Magazine* wrote in 1860, "Mr. Wilks spoiled his literary and political market, and ultimately lost his corresponding engagement."[16]

51

Corpses started floating ashore soon after *Amphitrite* broke up, beginning with the bodies of one man and three women. One report said that between 10:00 PM Saturday and 2:00 AM Sunday the surf brought in thirty-two additional bodies, their great number interspersed with pitifully few survivors. Captain Hunter might have been among the lucky few to live—for several minutes he and Towsey had shared a bit of floating wreckage, before he'd been flushed from that impromptu raft—but he was not. Hunter's body was never found. Nor was Mrs. Forrester's, even though weeks later *Fraser's Magazine* reported that Forrester's body had washed up onto the beach on Tuesday to be "plundered, of course, as his wife had been."

The scene on the beach at sunrise Sunday with the tide running out must have been ghastly: pale human forms not found in darkness now discovered in the half light, lying strewn at random between the high water line and the surf, still breaking on the sand on the backside of the tempest not yet entirely past. Encouraged by the morning's marginally better weather, resident sea gulls would have been back in the air above the waterfront, patrolling low over the sand in a sharp-eyed hunt for anything edible. Their tenor mewing, punctuated every quarter hour by faint basso notes from the Church of St. Nicholas' bell tower, accompanied the search for *Amphitrite*'s dead.

The *Preston Chronicle* described that morning on the beach to readers of its September 7 issue: "The scene presented in the Port of Boulogne on [Sunday] morning baffles any description—corpses strewn here and there along the beach and each advancing wave pouring forth from its bosom some fresh victim of the frightful calamity. Sixty bodies had been washed on shore, one presenting the appalling spectacle of a child, whose mouth was fast locked to the nipple of his mother's breast."[17] Other newspaper stories invariably observed that some bodies were carried up from the water's edge entirely nude, their state suggesting that *Amphitrite*'s victims had undressed before leaping into the waves or been somehow unclothed by the pounding sea. That's what Heine had written Coste in his letter to *Le Temps*' editor about the wreck: victims doffing their clothes to prepare for a swim to shore. Almost certainly Heine was wrong, and these dead had, instead, been stripped in the dark by beachcombers, drawn to the wreck the night before by the expectation of plunder.

That same Sunday morning, the day after *Amphitrite* broke apart on the Boulogne sands, John Wilks wrote a letter to Lord Palmerston, the foreign secretary, to accuse William Hamilton, HMG's consul in Boulogne, of such disinterest and incompetence on the night of the storm as to have resulted in the deaths of almost everyone on board. His letter did not arrive in the Foreign Office cold. Wilks and the foreign secretary knew each other.

Henry John Temple, third Viscount Palmerston (1784–1865), would become a giant figure in nineteenth-century Great Britain. He served in one or another government post for nearly sixty years, capping off his public service with two terms as prime minister, the first beginning when he was seventy, and dying in office at age eighty-one during the second. As foreign secretary in the 1830s Lord Palmerston was famous for his consuming interest in issues for which he was responsible, and for a disinclination to delegate or to permit others to describe, never mind make, foreign policy.

Palmerston's various government posts and the diligence with which he pursued them still gave him time for another of his favorite pursuits, that of women. This enthusiasm accounted for one of his nicknames, "Lord Cupid." There is evidence Palmerston fathered five children by three different women. (To Palmerston's credit, it appears that he generously supported the four children who survived infancy.) The last of the three women became his wife in 1839—after she was widowed—when both were in their fifties. She was Lady Jane Cowper, born Emily Lamb, with whom he had carried on an affair for decades. The Palmerstons remained happily, if not necessarily faithfully, married until Palmerston's death in 1865.

In the mid-1820s Palmerston had been enticed onto a seat on the board of Wilks' Cornwall and Devonshire Mining Company, and when, predictably, the company collapsed the then-fortyish secretary at war spent some of the summer of 1826 trying to distance himself from the wreckage and from Wilks, its solicitor. Palmerston, who rightly believed Wilks to be clever but also knew him to be a rogue, could not have forgotten the man in the seven years since.

"The state of public feeling and of public excitement are so great at this moment on the subject of this most deplorable affair," Wilks wrote Palmerston after first devoting four paragraphs to abusing Consul Hamilton for failing to effect a waterfront rescue, "that I pray your Lordship will *forthwith* send a <u>Commission</u> of naval officers who can speak *French*, to examine on the spot all the circumstances, and make a report to the British Government and the British nation."

Until September 3, a man on the street in Great Britain likely knew nothing about this "most melancholy occurrence which took place during the tremendous storm Saturday night" in Boulogne, although he would have experienced the great gale himself and assumed enormous destruction at sea within the storm's scope. That destruction was catalogued, county by county, port by port, and wreck by wreck, in the pages of *The Times* of London (and in many local weeklies throughout the British Isles) beginning at the start of the week. Even in a country inured to shipwrecks and drownings, this flood of bad news was stunning.

During the same week, while the Foreign Office and the Admiralty were dealing with his letter to Palmerston, Wilks' pen was not still. In two letters printed in *The Times* from Boulogne, dated September 1 and 2 and published on September 4 and 5, that contained his description of the catastrophe and allegations about incompetence and dereliction of duty, Wilks set the terms of the public discussion to come about what had happened and who was responsible.

That Wilks appeared in *The Times* at all is a measure of public interest in his story of the shipwreck. In 1833 *The Times* and the *Standard* (later and still today the *Evening Standard*) were aggressive competitors in London, England's only daily newspaper marketplace. The year before, in June 1832, *The Times* had called the *Standard* "a stupid and priggish print which never by any chance deviates into candour." Two months later the *Standard* struck back, commenting on its rival's "filthy falsehoods and base insinuation."

In the 1830s *The Times*, then nearly fifty years old and midway through the era of editor Thomas Barnes, was not yet the newspaper of record for the capital and its global empire, but alone among its eight competitors in London it was a political neutral, starting on the path to becoming the preferred journal of England's elite. Given this visibility, Bubble Wilks' sensational accounts could not have been ignored. Palmerston took them seriously.

The Times' first report of the wreck of *Amphitrite*, "Dreadful Shipwreck," was published on Tuesday. It and follow-on stories were soon quoted verbatim in other newspapers throughout the British Isles. *The Times'* source for the initial short piece was not Wilks but an unidentified "passenger who arrived in a steam-vessel [late September 2] from Calais." He reported *Amphitrite* had grounded midafternoon Saturday "about a half mile to the right [north] of Boulogne, and within a short distance of the shore." The story went on to describe how later that night "the waves broke through the poop, and swept away in an instant every soul in the cabin . . . in a few moments the ship went to pieces, and out of 154 persons on board, only three escaped to land! And one of these died a few hours afterwards." All the tragic result of the decisions of the ship's master and surgeon, and the fact that their ship was "very old . . . and altogether unfit to have been employed longer in any service."[18]

Under the headline "Dreadful Shipwreck off Boulogne," on Wednesday Wilks anonymously recapped the story and added more details: *Amphitrite* deliberately run up onto the sands during a great gale; François Huret's pilot boat carrying out to her a warning of certain disaster, only to be chased off by Hunter and Forrester; no ship's boat sent ashore because of fears convicts might escape; the naked Pierre Hénin's brave offer to swim a line ashore stymied by the master and surgeon for the same reason. Around 7:00 PM the flood tide begins. Later, while the seas build, frantic female convicts escape the hold and rush about the deck. Fearful crew members scale the rigging to escape the waves, and hang aloft there like strange fruit till shaken loose to drown. Only three wash ashore alive. All the others die when the ship breaks up.

"Whose fault was all this?" Wilks asked. "The captain has been blamed for his obstinacy—but he is dead. The surgeon has been blamed for his tenacity—but he is lifeless." In a *Times* column that appeared the next day, "Further Account of the Wreck of the Amphitrite," Wilks answered by providing his roster of the malefactors. In the author's order, they included:

> French customs-house officers at Boulogne, "harpies," who "put every obstacle in the way of saving the crew and ship," and in one instance "actually prevented by force a woman from saving the life of an unfortunate sailor who was struggling in the surf."
>
> The English consul in Boulogne, who was absent from the scene—allegedly at a dinner party—and so not there during the crisis to grant authority or issue orders to bring the crew and convict women ashore.
>
> The captain, who "appeared to abandon himself to the sole hope of getting off with the flood tide—a hope which was perfectly absurd, placed as the vessel was, with a tremendous gale blowing on the shore, and in the midst of the breakers."
>
> The surgeon and his wife, who between them prevented the launch of *Amphitrite*'s long boat, thus condemning the sixty it might have carried ashore to drowning.

This roster became the punch list for any future official investigation of the shipwreck.

On September 4 Wilks ostentatiously reassured readers of the *Standard*, "Although my health requires repose, and my duties call me away from this port, I shall certainly prolong my stay until something be done by the British and French governments, or one of them, in the shape of a naval commission. The readers of The Standard may be assured the correspondent of that journal will not leave the case in the present situation."

The next day (the same day The Times ran Wilks' second letter) the Foreign Office asked the Admiralty to have a post captain or an admiral "proceed to Boulogne, with a commission to inquire on the spot into all the circumstances attending this melancholy case." Captain Chads' orders to do so left the Admiralty Friday, September 6, signed by Rear Admirals Sir Thomas Hardy and George Dundas, the first and second naval lords. "Whereas Viscount Palmerston, His Majesty's Secretary of State for Foreign Affairs," the two wrote him, has caused to be transmitted to our secretary a copy of a letter from a British resident in Boulogne, detailing the particulars of the shipwreck of the transport "Amphitrite" off that port, and stating that if prompt and decisive measures had been taken by Mr. Hamilton, His Majesty's Consul at Boulogne, the lives of all on board would have been saved; and whereas it is desirable that so grave a charge against a public officer should be thoroughly investigated, and reposing every confidence in your discretion, impartiality and judgment . . . we hereby require and direct you to proceed without loss of time to Boulogne, and to report your opinion with respect to the facts of the case, and the accusations which have been preferred against Mr. Hamilton. . . . Mr. Hamilton will be directed to answer such interrogatories as you may feel it your duty to put to him; and you are hereby empowered to examine His Majesty's Consul himself, and for so doing this shall be your warrant and authority.

Chads' one-man mission quickly expanded to consider other aspects of the wreck, but what sent him to France in a hurry was the central question embedded in the journalist's harangues: Had Consul Hamilton's lapses in fact resulted in the deaths of *Amphitrite*'s victims? "One hundred and thirty-three British lives have been sacrificed off the harbour of Boulogne," Wilks' letter to Lord Palmerston had concluded, "and every one might have been saved if proper steps had been taken." Chads' chief purpose was to determine if that were so.

With Wilks' two midweek blasts still echoing across the Channel, Chads arrived at Hughes' Royal Hotel on Boulogne's rue de L'Ecu midday Sunday, September 8, barely a week after the ship had disintegrated in the surf and Wilks had first accused Hamilton of personal responsibility for the tragedy. Brunet's guidebook described the moderately priced Royal Hotel as "delightfully situated in the most central part of the town" and credited it with "an excellent table d'hote, where every delicacy of the season is served." He was to remain there through September 27, paying nineteen pounds, eight shillings, and four pence for his accommodation, or just over one pound per day.

Standing almost anywhere on the lower city's waterfront as the weekend came to a close, looking past the bathing machines parked in a line upslope from the water's edge, Chads would have seen large pieces of the wrecked transport strewn about the beach, lying there like an unassembled shipbuilding kit or the disarticulated body parts of some stranded leviathan.[19] The *Court Magazine and Belle Assembly* imagined that view this way:

The Sabbath morn it rose upon a scene
Revealing all the fearful night had been;
The ship, hull, rigging, masts, and staves
Lay there, as scatter'd by the wind and waves;
The mainmast's stump stood planted in the sand
Seeming the pastime of some demon's hand.
Men awe-struck gaz'd, yet not unpleas'd to see,
O'er man's own work, the tempest's mastery.[20]

The investigation kept Captain Chads in Boulogne for three weeks.

Amphitrite had been intact with her hold reasonably dry when she was deliberately driven ashore under her foresail, fore topmast staysail, and main topsail, canvas put up a short time before in a desperate and futile effort to escape land by sailing to windward. She lay there now in ten large pieces: the whole length of the vessel's bottom; her sides in four, thirty foot-long slabs; her main deck broken in half; and the newly built poop shattered into three or four other big bits.[21] What remained of Doctor Forrester's "watchbox," the stout, telephone booth-sized container in which the surgeon-superintendent had obstreperous women confined to subdue them, lay together with the other wreckage on the sand, torn from the main deck near where the unused long boat had been stowed.[22] Although anything of obvious value would have long since been gleaned from the foreshore, scraps and bits of worthless detritus lay everywhere.

During the week after the wreck several French sailors found packets of letters and dispatches *Amphitrite* had been taking to New South Wales. Hamilton sent these to London, where they arrived on September 6, their leather cases stiff with dried-on salt. In late November Hamilton deposited 955 francs, 77 centimes (approximately £38) into the consulate's account, proceeds from an auction by the port's Marine Department of spars, some line, and government provisions salvaged from the wreck. Dispatch cases and their illegible contents, the wreckage on the waterfront, some bodies, and these £38 were all that was left of what had been a ship at sea.

Chads began his work on Monday morning. By the time his investigation was finished he had conducted dozens of interviews, thirty or so of witnesses identified to him by the indefatigable Wilks, the others named by Hamilton or walk-ins, and one more—a special purpose consultation rather than an interview—at the end of the proceedings with M. Victor Le Cerf, a local master ship builder he had hired for technical help.

Between Monday, September 9, and Friday, September 20, Chads wrote Captain George Elliot, first secretary to the Admiralty (and since 1830 the long service John Wilson Croker's successor in that influential post, but for

only another year) six times to report on the progress of his investigation.[23]
The first letter, outlining Chads' approach to the investigation, focused largely
on process. It was sent to ensure that his vision of what was to come would
govern, and not Wilks' competing one. "I trust the mode of proceeding I have
adopted and am acting on will be approved by His Majesty's Government,"
he wrote, "or it will lead to endless discussion, and would require a person of
the legal profession, instead of a naval officer (as Mr. Wilks himself required)
to conduct the Commission."[24] Chads' subliminal threat to withdraw if Wilks
were permitted to act as prosecutor and examine Hamilton's witnesses as the
journalist wished, and his implicit suggestion that the government could lose
control of the proceedings, worked. There was no further debate about Wilks'
status; he could nominate witnesses and would be one himself, but he would
not act as Hamilton's prosecutor.

5 2

That issue settled, Chads moved swiftly ahead with the substance of his investigation. The first installment, a judgment of Captain's Hunter's seamanship
and how it related to the loss of his ship, was sent to Elliot on Wednesday,
September 11. "In obedience to the commands of my Lords Commissioners
of the Admiralty," he began this report, "I have made the most minute investigation into the circumstances relating to the melancholy wreck of the
Amphitrite; and as various injurious misstatements have gone forth, I deem it
right to inform their Lordships of my judgment on the case, without waiting
the results of the inquiry I am making into the conduct of His Majesty's consul, and which will probably take some days."

"Most minute" was self-serving at this very early stage in his work. He'd
spent not much more than two days on this part of his inquiry. Chads' sources
for information about the wreck were generally the same as those everyone else
used to draw his own conclusions about the recent waterfront tragedy: a double handful of English citizens of both sexes who had worked unsuccessfully
on the beach or in the Marine Hotel to restore life to bodies washing ashore,
some from among the French medical men and others who'd attempted the
same thing in the Humane Society's beach shack, the three survivors, the several French heroes, and others—a dozen or so of assorted citizenship—from
among the mass of horrified observers who had seen one or another dramatic
bit of Amphitrite's last hours unfold in front of them through the rain and
encroaching darkness. Chads could leaven everything he heard from all of
them with his experience as a seaman under sail in heavy weather.

Also on September 11, three days before Hamilton's statement in self-
defense was written, Wilks sent Chads a lawyerly, nineteen-page letter (by

several pages the longest document related to the investigation) listing thirty-three numbered talking points and conflating charges against Hamilton with proofs, or what passed for them. That same day Chads completed his appraisal of Captain Hunter's exercise of command in crisis, freeing him to examine these other questions.

For an officer raised in the uncompromising traditions of the Royal Navy, one who had seen one ship captured, had another shot out from under him, and who had since commanded three others, Chads' report on *Amphitrite*'s destruction was remarkably phlegmatic. He started by observing mildly that the sea was an inherently perilous place:

> From the very numerous vessels passing up and down the Channel, it ought to be expected that occasional disasters should occur, and that, too, without misconduct being imputable. The present instance of the Amphitrite I consider to have been one of this description. The gale was most violent and unexpected at this season of the year, with a very heavy sea, and the wind veering round from the S.W. to the N.W., placed the vessel on the Lee shore. The ship behaved very well, was well found, had a chronometer on board, and made little or no water.

To lend context to his investigation, Chads had a list assembled of British ships cast on shore near the same port between March 1823, when *Young William*, out of Weymouth, went aground, to just weeks before *Amphitrite*'s wreck, when *Crescent*, of Exeter did. M. Hercule Adam, Boulogne's resident Lloyd's agent and a substantial figure in the city's business community, was the roster's probable compiler.[25] Its tally was sobering: During those ten years eighteen merchant ships representing twelve different British homeports had been wrecked on that short stretch of French coast.

The next ten years were no less perilous. Midafternoon on December 21, not four months after *Amphitrite*'s destruction, a Norwegian trader went aground off Boulogne. "Conceive only the late dreadful scene of the Amphitrite acted over again," *The Times* quoted an eyewitness one week later, "conceive the having before your sight in broad daylight a gallant ship, and in a short two hours a total wreck, and every soul on board lost. . . . Thus we have again been condemned to see our fellow creatures perish in the sight of thousands unable to give any assistance." That decade's marquee shipwreck was the spectacular destruction south of Boulogne on November 12, 1842, of the big East Indiaman *Reliance*, out of Canton for London carrying 27,000 boxes of tea—black congou, green twankay, and other varieties with equally exotic names—1,884,748 pounds of costly dried leaves, insured for nearly £200,000.

Reliance's wreck closely followed *Amphitrite*'s scenario. "The account given by the inhabitants of Marlimont of the disaster," the *Weekly Chronicle* reported on November 20, "is that [*Reliance*] drove ashore between nine and ten o'clock at night, at low water, where she subsequently firmly imbedded in the sand, and, upon the tide rising, the sea made a complete breach over her, carrying with it nearly all the unfortunate creatures on board. . . . Many bodies had been washed on the beach, some of them showing symptoms of life: but although every medical attention was promptly rendered, none of them were restored." *Reliance*'s loss included the 1,500-ton ship and all but 2,050 damaged boxes of tea, as well as the life of her master, Captain Green. One hundred twelve others on board died, too, many of them Chinese and Filipino sailors. Only seven survived.

Consul Hamilton, writing from Marlimont the morning after the calamity, measured the great confusion he saw strewn on the beach against the scale of his experience and concluded in a letter to the East India Company's secretary, "I never witnessed such a wreck during twenty years I have acted as her Majesty's consul at Boulogne."[26] It is at least possible that in this instance, if not in *Amphitrite*'s, that "misconduct was imputable." The *Weekly Chronicle* speculated that the reason *Reliance* ran aground in France was that her deck watch had carelessly mistaken the Boulogne light for the one at Dungeness, across the Channel.

A color print of the wreck of *Reliance* was published on its anniversary in 1843 by George Baxter, an English artist whose patented process involved using multiple engraving plates inked with oil paints. His source for the details was the ship's carpenter, Robert Dickson, the only Englishman among the seven survivors. Baxter's print must not have been a commercial success because a planned partner to it, *Reliance at sea off Hong Kong under full sail in better times*, seems never to have been done.

Buttressed by this proof that occasional shipwrecks were a cost of doing business, and by Towsey's assessment that her sails and rigging were "very good," Chads concluded that *Amphitrite* was sound when she set sail. Better than sound. She was generously equipped, and as proof of that he offered up the information that she'd carried a chronometer, the essential instrument for calculating longitude and fixing position in the open sea, but in fact irrelevant to anything that had happened to *Amphitrite* in extremis. (And with just a single timepiece on board, its accuracy would have to be assumed, opening up an opportunity for navigation error.)

Next he went beyond absolving Hunter of any fault all the way to flattery: "The conduct of the master, more particularly when danger was discovered, was seamanlike, judicious, and decisive, and he was perfectly cool and collected throughout." Chads ascribed to no one the "sad . . . most deplorable error in judgment" that resulted in no effort being made on board to save the crew and helpless passengers.

Hunter had other defenders, including the author of a column that appeared in *Bell's Life in London* the weekend before Chads' report was published. "At this period of the year gales are seldom lasting," *Bell's* reminded its readers, "and the Captain might very naturally, as sailors usually do, conclude that the storm would abate when the tide changed. He relied, therefore, on his ship floating off the shore as the tide rose; he relied on its being only a summer's gale, and his confidence caused his own and his companions' melancholy fate. The very extraordinary nature of the storm, and Captain Hunter's reliance on the ordinary course of events, combined with a very natural desire to do his duty, explain, we believe, without casting censure on any persons, the melancholy results which every man must deplore." And so *Bell's* gave Hunter a bye, just as Captain Chads would do a few days later.

Others, however, were not so certain that the late Captain Hunter was blameless, either because they got important details of the story wrong ("it is said that he even carried a pistol in each hand threatening to shoot any person who should attempt to come aboard"; not true) or because they got them essentially right but were not inclined to be understanding. Still others were more critical still, astonished by what seemed to have been Hunter's inaction in saving his ship, crew, and human cargo. From his ship's first appearance off shore—showing no flags and firing no distress rockets—until her complete destruction hours later, Captain Hunter appeared to them to be sleepwalking through the calamity. One magazine called Hunter's inexplicable indecisiveness during his ship's last hours "the strangest of all infatuations," during which "no boat was hoisted out, no raft was constructed, no preparations were made to meet the worst consequences; we are bound to believe the report, that the captain, who was the owner of the vessel, was so appalled by her danger, that he lost all command of himself and his crew." Not "cool and collected throughout," but catatonic.

Although Hunter's indecision and fatal inaction Saturday night look inexplicable now, once hard aground he was acting on a plan to take *Amphitrite* off the sands on high water behind the storm. Not a routine evolution, certainly, but probably the school solution for the situation he faced and one that any veteran merchant ship master unfamiliar with Boulogne's particular hazards would have accepted. His crew understood what he was doing and expected it to succeed.

So high was their confidence in what their captain had in mind that several climbed into hammocks around 9:00 that evening, even as *Amphitrite* started "beating very heavy" as the tide came in. "The tide rising," Towsey wrote on September 9, "the sea of course made more an impression on her, but we still thought she would hold out the tide, I therefore turned in with several of the rest, thinking to get a little sleep, having had little or none the two previous nights." That the crew was willing to wait out the crisis asleep suggests that Hunter wasn't alone in his appraisal.

But he could have been blinded to the threat embedded in the weather by his ownership of the vessel and by his financial interest in a successful voyage delivering convicts to Australia. Moreover Forrester's exclusive authority over the prisoners might have somehow impinged on Hunter's sense of his own scope of action as the master of the ship. It's also possible his inexperience and a nightmare scenario (aground in the Dover Strait in a powerful storm, in command of this ship for the first time, with a newly assembled crew) underlay Hunter's inaction.

Any one of these explanations could account for Hunter's lack of response to his plight and to the explicit warnings he received, but a fourth should be added to these speculative causes: enervating fatigue. James Towsey's deposition is the best source on this subject. In it he described "thick weather" and very high, adverse winds beginning soon after *Amphitrite* left the Downs on Wednesday afternoon, with no chance during the next two days to make an observation and fix the ship's position in the Dover Strait before the wreck and little opportunity for rest, much less sleep. When the crew unexpectedly spotted land close under the lee beam at around 3:00 PM Saturday (after some hours drifting under bare poles, and now with only the main trysail set), none of the officers knew where exactly off the French Coast they were, and it's certain that none knew the depth of water beneath the keel.

In this near-perfect ignorance, Hunter ordered more sail in a desperate attempt to claw away from shore. With an odd scattering of canvas on two masts—the fore course and foretopmast stay sails, and the trysail and topsail close reefed on the main mast—but without sea room and so unable either to tack upwind or wear downwind, he had to put *Amphitrite* aground instead. Some hours later, with the tide now running in, Hunter's exhaustion might have immobilized him.

In place of Hunter, Chads offered up another villain: Mrs. Forrester, whose "fatal interference" during the crisis prevented dispatch of the long boat to shore when that was still possible. The proof was in John Owen's testimony. "The surgeon called us aft," the mate had told Chads, "and ordered us to hoist the boat out, his wife standing by him; she said that she would not go in the boat with the convicts. The surgeon then said: 'neither the boat nor any person should go on shore that night.'" It was not fear that the convicts might escape once on shore that kept them on board, Owens explained; it only could have been Mrs. Forrester's pride. Although it soon became public,

Chads had meant to keep John Owens' testimony on "the fatal interference of the Surgeon's wife" quiet.

But Dr. and Mrs. Forrester had defenders, too. On September 19 the *Trewman Exeter Flying Post* bent Owen's testimony backward, reporting "the surgeon's wife said to her husband that she would get into the boat. The surgeon replied, 'Do so, but I shall remain at my post. I cannot quit my prisoners.' Upon which the poor woman said—'Well, then, we shall die together!' and she threw herself into his arms." (This error committed, the *Flying Post* segued into a comment on the obvious superiority of steam power over sail in a storm because it allowed progress into the wind.) Other English papers carried the same bit of fiction about the Forresters. The next year it reappeared across the Channel in a French anthology of shipwreck stories, *Beaux Traits de l'Histoire des Naufrages*, published anonymously in Rouen by Mégard et Compagnie, and now enrobed in all the authority that appearance in a hard-cover book brought with it.

In a few sentences the newspaper and its several echoes managed to evoke the gender models of nineteenth-century heroism: a man bravely dying at his post with his devoted wife willingly sharing his fate, the two locked together to face death in a pose any sculptor would admire.

Chads believed that from Saturday midafternoon through 7:00 PM, and perhaps as late as when the first seas broke over *Amphitrite* two hours later—the first of the hammer blows that soon pounded the ship into pieces on the anvil of the bar—no one on board, "neither the master, the surgeon, or the crew had any fears for their safety, or apprehended their *inevitable* fate on the rise of the tide." Left out of Chads' opinion poll entirely were the women and small children confined below deck, terrified landlubbers churned about for the previous two days in tumultuous darkness. Early Saturday afternoon they must have feared they were in mortal danger, a suspicion that would have slid closer toward certainty with every lurch of the hull and groan of ship's timbers. Certainly no one ashore had any doubts that the night was going to end in tragedy. It seems that only *Amphitrite's* officers and crew did not recognize terminal danger.

Well into *Amphitrite's* fatal beating, just before the masts toppled and her hull collapsed, the women reportedly broke out of the hold, animated by fear. Some few found temporary shelter in the poop, most others clustered on the open deck, from where they would soon be swept away. The scene during the ship's last few minutes intact must have looked very much like that depicted in John Cousen's 1859 engraving of the wreck, skeletal faces and all.

53

True to his promise of September 4, ten days later Wilks shared with his readers an appraisal of Chads' first week at work. "I am bound to state that the examination has not been conducted in the way I should have preferred or expected," he told them.

> The Consul has not been examined or cross-examined by any but the Commissioner [Chads]. No one has been allowed to be present at the examination of witnesses but the Consul: the witnesses, who have differed from each other in their statements, have not been confronted one with the other. There has been nothing like a public or open enquiry; &, although I am quite certain from the known integrity and character of the Commissioner Chads, that he has meant well, yet his decisions as to secrecy, &c. as to the examination of witnesses, have all tended to throw great difficulties in the way of elucidating the truth. The Commissioner did indeed yesterday consent, after much previous argument and doubt, to examine some of the poor witnesses, who would have been intimidated by the presence of the Consul, in consequence of his power over their actual means of existence, without him, the Consul, being present. On the whole, I hope much good will result from the inquiry, which has even hitherto been gone into, not withstanding the strong objections I feel to the mode in which the Commissioner has thought it most desirable to conduct it.

Wilks' pot-stirring also included a personal letter of protest to Chads, but nothing came of his rabble-rousing beyond Chads' agreement to hire an interpreter ("gladly, as it will be a relief to me").

What of *Amphitrite* herself, described—maligned, rather—in *The Times* as "unfit . . . for any service" and defended in that paper only by her charter agent, whose self-interest would have been evident to all? "It seems almost incredible," echoed the *United Service Journal* soon after the wreck, "that any vessel deemed by the surveyors as sea-worthy could be beaten to pieces on a sand in the short space of six hours." Consul Hamilton, himself, contributed to this charge, writing the Foreign Office on September 3 to report "that it is the general opinion of seafaring men, French & English, that the ship Amphitrite of London was not seaworthy when she sailed from England." The "seafaring men" to whom he referred included a small constellation of British flag officers, Admirals Lake, Kellar, and Horton, who disbelieved that a sound ship would go to pieces after only five hours on a sandy beach.

"J. C. S., a British Officer," who wrote a long letter to the editor of the *Standard* in September about the wreck, must have been another of Hamilton's skeptics. "She was newly coppered, I admit," conceded J. C. S. (twenty years at sea and "somewhat of an amateur shipwright") "and a fine looking vessel so far as paint and putty were concerned." But speaking for many other anonymous officers "who have minutely inspected every part of the wreck," he found frailty everywhere:

> She was not at all adapted for the service she was selected in as much as her wooden ends were in the last stage of decay, and sheathed over; nearly all her timbers and beams were in the same state, saving a few rough pieces that had been brought on to strengthen and hide the most defective, and some of those only trunneled. The midship part of her keelson has, at some time or the other, been removed and scarfed [spliced], and it appears to me part of some ship's mast has been bolted overall, in doing which the after part of the keelson is split four or five inches deep and evidently appears an old wound.

"It is the general opinion here that the *Amphitrite* was not surveyed," J. C. S. concluded, but she had been.

Chads' commission from the Admiralty had said nothing about inspecting the wreckage to draw conclusions from it about the ship's matériel condition when she sailed. "Various officers of high rank have called on me to beg me to look into the state of the remains of Amphitrite. . . . I beg their Lordships directions on the subject," he wrote to Elliot on September 13, mentioning he thought that Consul Hamilton had already sent a similar request to his masters at the Foreign Office. Chads' idea wasn't new to Captain Elliot. A week earlier Elliot had written to Lieutenant J. H. Bailey, RN, the resident agent for transports at the Royal Dockyard at Deptford, where *Amphitrite* had twice been inspected earlier in the year, to ask about the ship's surveys and anything else that might be relevant.

Sometime early in the week of September 23, Elliot probably had several answers to his questions about the ship's condition; certainly one from Bailey dated September 9 was in hand, likely also one from Chads, dated September 20 and containing an enclosure quoting the French shipwright, Monsieur Le Cerf, of the same date. Bailey, Chads, and Le Cerf could have been describing two different ships.

Lieutenant Bailey, filling a position at Deptford usually assigned to a more senior officer, was quick to reply to Elliot. "The late bark" had been under government charter twice in 1833, he told Elliot, and then he went on to describe

Amphitrite's day-and-a-half-long inspection in February, before the start of her short, first contract:

> In conjunction with Mr. Martin, the shipwright attached to this department, I had the ship laid on Mr. Cardero's ways at Deptford; had her opened, by taking planks off on the outside, as well as a considerable part of her ceiling within [the interior skin], when the whole of the beams were bored, as well as many of the timbers; what was found in anyway defective was made good. Her fastenings were particularly examined, and where any were found imperfect they were removed, and others put in their place, with many additional ones, including three pairs of iron knees.
>
>   During the period these repairs were going on the ship was visited daily by the shipwright, and as often by myself as my other duties would permit, to see the defects properly made good. They were so.

Idled after that contract expired June 10, *Amphitrite*'s next—and last—survey at Deptford began the day after she was tendered for charter to transport convicts to New South Wales. Bailey again:

> I . . . went again with the shipwright, and examined her in the most particular manner, to ascertain if I could find out anything to cause me to reject her. I ordered her to be put into a dry dock, had all her copper taken off, and the bottom particularly examined. The bottom was fresh and perfect: it was caulked from the keelson upwards, and new coppered. Nothing could be discovered to authorize the rejection of the vessel. . . . The shipwright stated to me that her body of timber was considerably larger and fuller that vessels of her tonnage usually are. She was built of oak, at Bideford. In the year 1824 she was lengthened, and had a very considerable repair, and was then refastened from the keelson upwards. . . .
>
>   I can assure their Lordships no ship ordered for survey, since I have held present appointment, was more carefully looked into or examined. . . .

L'Annotateur told its readers that an inspection of the wreckage showed *Amphitrite* to have been in such poor condition it was inconceivable the Admiralty had permitted her to load and sail, but French master shipbuilder Victor Le Cerf's assessment of *Amphitrite*'s soundness was equivocal. In the ageless tradition of hired consultants everywhere, Le Cerf's report comfortably supported incompatible conclusions. Based on his fifteen years of experience,

Le Cerf told his client, *Amphitrite* would have looked good on superficial inspection alongside the dock, but an internal inspection would have revealed timbers and planking destroyed by repairs and by a great number of vacant treenail holes. That said, when questioned by Chads directly, Le Cerf still allowed that *Amphitrite* would have been equal to the voyage to come "if she had not got on shore." Chads also found that *Amphitrite*'s hull was riddled with treenail holes, and like Le Cerf he concluded that these many, empty bores though planking and beams significantly weakened her.

Treenails (or "trunnels"), large hardwood pegs, were the ubiquitous fasteners for most of the age of sail, all-purpose organic counterparts to the rivets, bolts, and welds of a later era. They pinned the hull's load-bearing structure together and attached the planking inside and out to its supporting timbers, the decking to the beams beneath. The best treenails were cut from close-grained hardwood of several species, inch-and-a-half diameter dowels carefully shaved to an octagonal cross-section ("eight square"), used in five standard lengths from one to three feet long, and carefully driven all the way home with an iron maul through prebored, slightly undersize holes. Perfect for their purpose, treenails also offered unscrupulous ship builders and lazy yard workers easy opportunities to save money and skimp on effort by using too few or setting short ones in place of long.

Amphitrite's treenails could not have worked loose in great numbers unless they were undersize or otherwise improperly installed. No shipyard survey could have missed such a lapse. "She was an old ship," Chads wrote to Elliot in what should have been taken as a condemnation of Bailey's work, "having recently undergone considerable repair; and from her repairs the strength of her timbers were entirely destroyed by the very great number of treenail holes although the wood itself was good excepting a part of the topside planking & that she could not have been thoroughly inspected before taken up as a transport."

These inconsistencies were never resolved, but in fact, as Chads emphasized to Elliot, *Amphitrite*'s condition either sailing from Woolwich or a few days later hard atop the bar at Boulogne was irrelevant. "The state of the 'Amphitrite' transport . . . I view it as totally unconnected with her loss, it being abundantly proved that no strength could have saved the vessel or her crew," he wrote. Stronger, she might have "protracted their existence for a few minutes; the result would have been the same." *Amphitrite*'s timbers, riddled through with superfluous treenail holes, and her planking, eaten away in places by decay, might have been fatal somewhere down track on the way to Australia, but she never made it even as far as Portsmouth, possibly her last planned port call after leaving the Downs for Port Jackson. (Where, James Towsey told Chads on September 20, he had intended to leave the ship, because she was "wet and uncomfortable" and because he couldn't get along with the mate.)[27]

That "no strength could have saved vessel or crew" was not universally accepted. In 1833 an anonymous "Surveyor of Shipping," author of the descriptively titled tract *The True Causes of the Numerous Wrecks of Merchant Shipping Clearly Explained: And an Appeal to the Nation, in the Cause of Humanity, to Apply the Remedy*, published his view that the causes of the dreadful safety record of the British merchant marine were two: a merchant ship classification system that encouraged the construction of unsafe vessels and an insurance industry that took the risk out of sending decrepit vessels knowingly to sea.[28] *Amphitrite* was an example of both. "Could the wreck of the *Amphitrite*, convict ship, have been prevented?" asked the author. "No. But the lives of the crew and convicts might have been preserved, had they been embarked on a stronger vessel." Curiously, despite practically weekly evidence of the power of the sea, commentators were very reluctant to credit destructive nature with the blame for shipwreck. Instead, they were quick to conclude that the explanation for ships failing to survive battering against land lay in criminal lapses ashore.

54

Hunter commended handsomely (albeit by then far beyond caring); Forrester and his wife hit by a glancing, posthumous blow; *Amphitrite* and the Deptford Royal Dockyard apparently entirely absolved despite sharply divergent appraisals of both—this left Chads to answer two remaining questions. The first was about the role played by French Customs officials, *douaniers*, at the port, accused by Wilks of inhumanity. The second had to do with the consul's performance of his duty, charged by Wilks with criminal neglect tantamount to murder.

Enforcement questions aside, French quarantine laws were not just another example of nineteenth-century Gallic perversity. In an era when the usual solution to death at sea was to slide the corpse(s) overboard, with the amount of attached weights and associated ceremony varying depending on circumstances and the social status of the deceased, discovering a human body washed up on shore was not uncommon near high traffic waters. A body on a beach fronting the Pas-de-Calais in 1833 suggested contagion, not crime as it would today, and the sanitary laws of the period departed from the notion that every cadaver so found represented an evasion of quarantine. Even basted in salt water, every body was thought to pose the threat of disease. The living or drowning victims of shipwrecks, of course, were something else altogether. Exactly how that difference was perceived and acted upon at Boulogne became the next focus of Captain Chads' investigation.

Wilks' condemnation of the *douaniers* had many echoes. One early critic had special authority. He was the Reverend Jelinger Symons, whose eleven years in Boulogne as the British stipendiary chaplain ("stipendiary," meaning paid, as opposed to "gratuitous," voluntary) overlapped Hamilton's first years in the city. The two contemporaries must have known each other well, given Hamilton's consular duty to audit the chapel's books annually. Symons had since left Boulogne for England and the parish church of St. Mary at Radnage in South Buckinghamshire, but he remained attentive to his former congregation.

The reverend's critique appeared in a letter to the *Globe*'s editor, describing his exchange with the director of the Douane during a meeting of the Société Humaine de Boulogne after the wreck. In reply to Symons' question if there were a French sanitary law prohibiting anyone from helping people trapped on a sunken vessel or one about to sink, the director is supposed to have replied that such a law existed and officers were instructed to arrest any violators. News of this letter drew a quick, somewhat confusing response from the director of customs to Hamilton on September 17:

> If M. Symons asked such a question, as it is reported in the newspaper, I didn't give the answer he is saying for a perfect reason, such a ban doesn't exist in any law, order, or directive whatsoever.
>
> Therefore, it is quite obvious that from me or M. Symons there was a misunderstanding on this occasion, which can easily happen between two people who express themselves in an idiomatic way which might not be familiar to one of them.

But charges similar to Symons' were repeated elsewhere, notably in the *United Service Journal* and *Fraser's Magazine*, which fulminated about "the very gross negligence of the French authorities" and about French laws thought to protect *douaniers* who prevented with determination "any *thing*, be it living or dead," from passing the mean high-water line without prior permission and the payment of duties. "On the night of the wreck of the Amphitrite," charged the *Journal* as proof of its claim,

> a female washed on shore alive; she was carried ashore by Achille Le Prêtre and Nicholas Huret, two Frenchmen who rescued the poor creature from at any rate a watery grave; she was so far sensible, as frequently to grasp Huret's hand; and no doubt exists in the minds of the above-mentioned men, but that had assistance been promptly rendered at the moment, that woman's life would have been saved. Two *superior* officers (these are their own words) of the custom-house

came towards the bearers of the then living woman; they pointed their bayonets, and forcibly compelled the above-named men to abandon the female; *and she died on the beach at the feet of these self-styled human beings!*

Of all the issues raised by Wilks, this one, the allegedly callous, perhaps even murderous, conduct of French officers on the beach Saturday night, was probably of greatest interest to the foreign secretary personally, because it raised potentially awkward questions. What William Hamilton had done or not done that night was Palmerston's business, but the consul was, after all, only one of almost 140 such men in Britain's Foreign Service, spread among nearly as many posts in twenty-eight different countries (and reinforced by twice as many vice consuls—an indication of the enormous vigor of the country's foreign trade and commercial interests in the 1830s). In such a large community a nasty bit of professional delinquency or corruption would float to the surface from time to time. Lapses, even notorious ones such as this might have been, could be corrected in-house when discovered. But if French officers had failed in their duties and so caused English deaths, or worse yet, if they had executed those duties precisely and the deaths had been the consequence, then bilateral issues arose that went beyond a simple internal ministry personnel management problem.

Palmerston, a part-time francophile in the upper pay grades of His Majesty's government—he believed that King Louis-Philippe's new constitutional monarchy helped balance the scales on the Continent against absolutist Prussia, Austria, and Russia—was nevertheless willing to have the charges explored. It later emerged, however, that he wanted the dialogue held in Foreign Office channels under his control, and not initiated by a naval officer interrogating miscellaneous persons in the emotional aftermath of the wreck.

Wilks was not the only commentator horrified by the belief that the *douaniers* had forcibly prevented assistance to victims of the wreck in the surf and on the beach, but in *The Times* of September 5 it was he who had lit the fuse that set everyone else off. "The conduct of the Customs-house officers at this port," he wrote then, "demands the most rigid and severe investigation." His reporting, substantiated by two worthies, Captain Fourmentin and Baron de Chact (or "Schacht"), both long-term residents but otherwise unidentified, who claimed to have been repulsed from the beach by *douaniers* wielding bare *baïonnettes*, ricocheted around Boulogne's tight English community.

That brouhaha prompted a petition to Lord Palmerston, penned on double-wide folio paper and signed by eighty-seven expatriates. "We the undersigned, residents at Boulogne-sur-Mer, respectfully present to your Lordship the following statement and petition, relating to the shipwreck of the Amphitrite," they wrote, "earnestly hoping that your Lordship [will] communicate with the French Government upon the subject and thereby endeavour to affect such alteration and amelioration in the laws and regulations for the conduct of French Douaniers as may, in the case of ships stranded, wrecked, or in distress, appear consistent with the claims of humanity and the principles of the Christian religion."[29] The petitioners included a representative sprinkling of Boulogne's Britons of substance (including the Reverend Symons, preparing to depart France) and one outsider, John Wilks, whose name appeared modestly near the bottom of three columns of signatures.

Chads later explained the petition to the Admiralty and the Foreign Office as arising from the British residents of Boulogne's "deep regret & mortification that they were kept in total ignorance of this mournful occurrence; when, had they been on the spot many of them think from their professional experience & personal exertions they might have rendered essential services." That might be so, but it's difficult to imagine what such "personal exertions" might have accomplished under the circumstances.

The residents' appeal was presented to Palmerston in London on September 25 by two MPs, Lieutenant Colonel Sir William Clayton (member for Great Marlow) and Mr. Benjamin Hawes Jr. (representing Lambeth), in Boulogne at the time of the wreck, who acted as couriers for the agitated expatriates. The next day Messrs. Clayton and Hawes reported to their countrymen in France that "his Lordship . . . said it was a subject deserving the serious consideration of the British Government, and that [it] would enable him to found a communication with the French Government and that he would write to Lord Granville, the British Ambassador at Paris, upon it." "We trust that," the members continued their informal report to the eighty-seven, "when your memorial comes under the consideration of the French Government, the melancholy statement of facts which it contains, now that they are made public, will be the means of preventing similar calamities, which can never occur again without disgrace to a high-minded and generous people, which is impossible."

Some days later Undersecretary of State Backhouse gave Clayton further reason to believe that the petitioners of Boulogne were being taken seriously.[30] "Should it appear that the French Douaniers are acting under such orders as those which the persons who have signed the memorial suppose," he wrote him, "H. M. Govt. will not fail to represent the case to the French Govt., with the view of inducing them to make such modifications in those orders as most naturally suggest themselves to the humane and generous feelings of that govt."

English expatriates and miscellaneous European drifters were not the only people aghast at the idea of armed men pushing would-be rescuers off the beach at the point of a bayonet. Some French citizens were, too. What its government officers had or had not done at water's edge during that dreadful night was reported in *L'Annotateur* and other newspapers in the Département du Pas-de-Calais.

L'Annotateur led the coverage—quite naturally, as it was a local story— describing how Customs officers, determined to prevent *le traditionnel pillage*, restricted the number on the beach first to only twenty-five men and then, after importuning by the master of the port, to fifty. "But twenty-five, fifty people!" *L'Annotateur* lamented, "1,500, 2,000, were required. . . . We don't hesitate to say it: these instructions of Customs were on this deplorable night disastrous beyond all expression. . . . The whole population has risen to lay blame against Customs." Among the would-be rescuers chased off the beach, the paper reported, quoting some of the horror stories spread by English critics, were men of recognized probity whose good intentions could not have been doubted, members of the city council, respected citizens, and fishing boat captains.

Experience with scandalous looting of past wrecks (and the wreck of *Amphitrite*, *L'Annotateur* conceded, was picked over all Saturday night and well into Sunday in daylight) caused a "disastrous" response on the part of Customs in this instance, one that focused government efforts entirely on the protection of property and not at all on the preservation of life.

L'Annotateur's investigation of what happened on the waterfront Saturday night led its editor to hope that *Amphitrite*'s wreck would become the trigger for reform of a system defined by a patchwork of laws, orders, ministerial guidelines, and circular letters dating back to King Louis XIV's historic Ordonnance de la Marine of August 1681, the grandfather of many national maritime codes. From this pastiche, improvised over 150 years, came the procedures in effect August 31, measures the paper characterized as "unfruitful, useless, or damaging," and all implemented by single-minded *douaniers*.

Under the rules, officers from the Douane, from the port authority (the Marine), and from the police—all three independent agencies—had interlocking roles to perform on scene. In theory, the Douane's scope was limited generally to preventing the smuggling of wreck cargo into France. The Marine Department was responsible for the rescue of crew and passengers, and the Gendarmerie was responsible for the preservation of order and the protection of property at the scene.

"But that's not the way things happen," *L'Annotateur* observed. "Customs intervenes in every aspect of the grounding, because this service is usually rather intrusive, and because above all, it has a strong, united, compact, flexible, and dedicated organization supporting its commander." In contrast, the Marine organization is an "old, complicated machine wherein all the wheels are worm-eaten by old age. The result is that [the Marine] almost completely disappears behind Customs, which shows itself very jealous to extend its power as much as possible":

> Very few [M]arine superintendents will open themselves to custom's disfavor. The triumph of tax considerations over more commendable humanitarian ideals is, therefore, made certain from the beginning of every grounding. . . . All errors, all mistakes, all wrong measures which are so often and so unnecessarily mourned flow from this. Customs is strict, dominated by iron rules; it has only one objective, which totally excludes any humanitarian ideas. Consequently, where these ideas should prevail, they come in second. Most often they are not visible through the concerns which occupy customs officers. This is not Customs' mistake . . . it is the Marine's mistake.

Drawing a lesson from the calamity just past, the paper's editor concluded that a new civil organization was required, *un force publique spéciale*, capable of protecting ships' property, aiding crews, and generally dealing with storm damage.

55

Just as Wilks' first letter to Palmerston had triggered Captain Chads' investigation, so too the Boulogne petition set off an exchange of correspondence between the Foreign Office, the Admiralty, and Chads that began with a private note from Palmerston to his senior undersecretary on September 26. "What appears to have been the fact as to the alleged conduct of the French Customs House Officers on the loss of the Amphitrite?" Palmerston asked Backhouse. "Did they or did they not as asserted in the Representation given me by Colonel Clayton signed by some English at Boulogne prevent any Persons from bringing up from the Beach the Bodies that were floated on shore?"

"Nothing appears in Captain Chads' reports, to confirm the imprecations against the French Custom House," Backhouse answered, "but Captain Chads in his Report of the 20th Sept. throws discredit generally on the statements of parties [read "Wilks"] who were most industrious in getting up inculpating statements of various kinds. Captain Chads has not yet sent home the detailed evidence which he had collected. Might it not be well to wait for it, before sending the Representation from Boulogne to L[or]d. Granville, especially as the letter of the Directeur des Douanes to the Consul denies the accuracy of the statements of the Rev. W. Symons?"

John Barrow, second secretary at the Admiralty and a much more influential bureaucrat than his modest title suggested, now joined the exchange by invitation. "I have read over the letters and evidence transmitted by Captain Chads," he wrote to Backhouse on October 9, "and I can find nothing that can warrant the charges made against the French Employees—but if Lord Palmerston thinks it necessary, I can call on Captain Chads either publicly or privately to state what fell under his observation on the subject." Obviously referring to Wilks' accusations, Barrow added "I don't believe a word of it."

In 1833 Barrow, then nearing seventy, had been second secretary nearly thirty years and would be for another dozen more, retiring reluctantly at eighty-one and dying, also reluctantly, three years later. As the Admiralty's longtime senior civil servant it was he who actually made the place run; he who had launched the Royal Navy's aggressive program of global exploration that found employment for some of the ships and officers of the postwar navy.[31] While Chads' chief contact at the Admiralty was its short-service first secretary, Captain George Elliot (in this office just four years, later to become Admiral Sir George), Chads was careful to be responsive to the seemingly immortal Barrow, too.

Chads appears not to have communicated with Barrow while he was in France. All his letters to the second secretary were mailed when he was back home at Fareham, and once again unemployed. "In reply to yours . . . directing me to state what came under my observation as regards the conduct of the French Employees acting under the Revenue Laws on the occasion of the wreck of the Amphitrite," Chads wrote in an October 18 letter to Barrow,

I beg to acquaint my Lords Commissioners of the Admiralty that in my interview with Viscount Palmerston on the evening of my quitting for Boulogne [September 6] I named the subject to his lordship when it was expressly settled that it would be improper & indelicate [of] me to make enquiry into the conduct of these French authorities, as no reference had been made to that Government. I therefore cautiously avoided taking anything like evidence on the subject, as it would have been unjust to have heard one side of the Question without any power or means of procuring evidence in defense of the accused.

"From all that I heard in conversation," Chads continued,

I am led to the conclusion that the accusations against the French Employees are exaggerated, & made at a time of greatest excitement & horror at the events & the term of "inhuman" to them is not applicable. I believe myself the circumstances occurred nearly as follows. The French Authorities knew Boulogne not to be an exception to the general rule that there are always unhappily too many in all countries ready to take advantage of an unfortunate wreck to commit any crime for Plunder; therefore on this occasion it not being known there were Passengers but few persons were allowed to go to the beach to assist the Douaniers take the bodies as the females came ashore, when crowds rushed down and amongst them were creatures of this very worst description, and consequently there were instances of bodies being plundered and ill-treated, from which circumstances the Douaniers endeavoured to prevent others going and not being able to distinguish individuals, among those prevented were some with the very best intentions. The French Authorities I understood were personally on the spot. There can be no reason to doubt but that their motives & exertions were dictated by humanity, & I do not believe their actions in this instance were the cause of loss of life and if delay in saving anybody occurred it was from the cause I have before named, an endeavour to protect the bodies—and as the attention of the French Employees was not particularly given to this point a scene of plunder & robbing of the wreck to the greatest extent ensued.

The reports of the mutilations of the bodies I think originate, not from what took place on the beach, but from occurrences at the Hospital previous to internment.

On the subject of the Laws as respects shipwrecked persons I can only speak from opinions I heard the spot, never having read them myself. As I understand, it is the "lois sanitaires" that requires amendment, as they do not admit of a body thrown ashore being at once received (at least they are so acted on) without reference to the superior authority, by which delay life may become extinct, whilst it can be no preventive to the introduction of disease which I conclude to be the sole intention, leaving a feeling that inhumanity has been exercised towards the unfortunate sufferer.

Chads' judgment that the *douaniers* had acted in good faith very likely drew heavily on Hamilton's statement in his own defense of some four weeks earlier. In that description of his hours on the beach between 9:00 PM Saturday and 2:00 AM Sunday, Hamilton wrote,

It appeared to me that the authorities were taking the most active measures to save any of the crew that might be washed on shore. [?] that the Customs House Officers & Gendarmes were keeping the people off who wished to assist in saving any bodies that might reach the shore. I immediately inquired into the truth of the statements, but as far as my own observations & my own inquiries went I [?] find it to be well founded.

I walked about on the beach, contemplated the wreck, and closely watched that no impediment should be thrown in the way of saving the lives of the unfortunate individuals shipwrecked.

56

Hamilton's and Chads' conclusions aside, there is other evidence that *douaniers* viewed their role at shipwreck sites differently from what was described by their apologists, and that *L'Annotateur*'s critique was perhaps not harsh enough. The petition to Lord Palmerston from Boulogne's expatriate Britons reminded his lordship about the wreck of the English brig *William* near Boulogne five years ago, "when the ultimate recovery of a poor man of colour rescued alive was prevented by the Douaniers, who, hindering the approach of anyone towards him with needful succor, suffered him to die on the shore!!" (As *L'Annotateur* later confirmed to its readers, *William*'s sole survivor had been confined by the *douaniers* in an old lime kiln near Le Portel and allowed to die inside without medical attention.) The petition then referred his lordship to news that *Amphitrite* was not the only British registry ship wrecked on the coast of the Pas-de-Calais that night whose survivors might have run fatally afoul of the Douane.

The other was the Honorable East India Company Chartered Ship *Ann & Amelia*, just over five months out of Calcutta for London with a cargo worth £100,000 when landed on the company's docks. The latest in a 2,700-ship-long stream of East Indiamen that since the early seventeenth century had sucked the products and produce of East and South Asia around Africa to England.

Built in 1816 of Indian teak in Chittagong by James Macrae, a transplanted Scot, for the shipping magnate Joseph Somes, *Ann & Amelia* was rated at 587 tons, more than twice *Amphitrite*'s size. Her first decade at sea had been spent in local and Far East trade. Despite her seventeen years afloat generally in tropical waters, *Ann & Amelia* was almost certainly sound, well equipped, and ably manned when she sailed sixty miles down the Hooghly River in March to leave Calcutta, the capital and chief commercial city of British India, behind. Nine women and seven children sailed as passengers. In her hold the ship carried hundreds of bales of silk and boxes of indigo, and thousands of bags of saltpeter, presumably for the manufacture of gunpowder.

This was the ship's third charter since she was taken up for East India Company service in 1826.[32] The centuries-old company—for many decades a rapacious hybrid of colonial government and commercial enterprise—lost its monopoly of trade with India in 1813. But in 1833, the year before its China monopoly was also taken away, "John Company" could still afford to hire the best ships and crews. On occasion, the passage to London had been known to take eight months, but *Ann & Amelia*'s ocean voyage, with Captain William Compton in command for the first time, was a swift one. Out of Calcutta at the start of spring; around the Cape of Good Hope; a mandatory stop at St. Helena Island near the end of June; and into the English Channel by midsummer. (Under steam and through the Suez Canal forty years later the same passage would take only four weeks.)

According to First Officer Simpson's entries in the deck log, at noon Tuesday, August 27, *Ann & Amelia* was at 49° 01' north and 9° 13' west, sailing through fine weather. His navigational fix (logged as combining "observed latitude" and "longitude by chronometer") put *Ann & Amelia* some 150 miles west southwest of Lands End in the Atlantic approaches to the English Channel, and roughly 400 miles west of *Amphitrite*, then out of Margate Roads for the Downs and a planned overnight pause in her progress.[33]

That day and the next passed bright and clear with light airs, conditions good enough to permit repairs on deck to a torn mainsail. Thursday was pleasant also, with breezes blowing gently from the west through a summer sky. When a jolly boat came alongside *Ann & Amelia* that afternoon to put the pilot on board, everyone would have taken his arrival as proof that the long voyage was practically over. Since leaving Calcutta she had sailed roughly 12,000 nautical miles, and after many months at sea, *Ann & Amelia*'s crew and passengers must have been eager to arrive at the company's docks on the Isle of Dogs and finally to set foot on land. Friday's skies remained clear even while the morning's moderate westerlies gained strength during the day. Not far to the east, however, *Amphitrite* was already ensnared in rough weather.

For *Ann & Amelia* Saturday, August 31, began with changed sky conditions and ended in disaster. Simpson recorded that morning came with a "hard gale and thick weather," bringing winds out of the north-northwest. At 4:30 in the afternoon the Isle of Wight was visible off the port beam, meaning the ship had averaged only three knots since the noon fix on Tuesday. Soon thereafter, with the East Indiaman now more than halfway up Channel, what had been a hard gale blew into "a complete hurricane."

During her final seven hours afloat, *Ann & Amelia* was shoved by the storm nearly due east, some thirty miles across the Channel, to what the stranded crew would soon discover was Berck-sur-Mer on the French coast. "At 11:45 [PM] the ship struck the ground, surging dreadfully." Simpson wrote. His next log entry explained what followed the impact: "The topmasts went a few minutes after the ship struck. Sea breaking over her in every direction. Cut away the main and foremasts. Mr. Skelton, 2nd officer, Lt. Frazier 7th Bengal Cavalry (without orders) lowered the starboard quarter Boat at the same time calling for volunteers. . . . The boat had scarcely left the ship when she was dashed to pieces and all perished excepting Lt. Frazier (who reached the shore by swimming). Midnight the gale blowing with great violence seas breaking over the ship fore and aft."

The four who drowned when the boat broke up included a midshipman and two seamen. Hamilton reported in a September 4 letter forwarding to the Foreign Office dispatches recovered from both wrecks and the mail from India that Skelton and Frazier had taken "possession of the only boat on board *unknown* to the master" in their fatal attempt to reach shore. Minutes later the crew began to collect the spars to assemble a raft from them, but, Simpson continued, "at 1:30 the ship began to lay more quiet. Found the tide was leaving the ship fast. Lashed the mainmast to the [?] rail and ring bolts to act as a shore to keep the ship from falling over. At 3 found the water leave the ship so fast that at daylight we could walk on shore. Sent the dispatches, passengers and a great quantity of luggage on shore also a quantity of the ship's stores."

Beginning on Monday, September 2, and during the next two weeks when the tide permitted, *Ann & Amelia*'s cargo was hauled ashore by a gang of French laborers more than fifty strong. By the time the last of the company's cargo was discharged from the wreck on September 14, almost 600 bales of silk, nearly 700 boxes of indigo, and 3,700 bags of saltpeter had crossed the beach, joining salvaged chains, cables, guns, and anchors.

A week later, still stranded in Berck, Captain Compton described the night of the great gale in an emotional letter to Consul Hamilton.[34] "At about 2 o'clock on the Sunday morning . . . finding the water leaving the ship [as the tide ran out] I desired the 1st Officer and two men to see whether they could reach the shore, the water appearing shoal," he began. What followed after Compton attempted to land his passengers and crew suggests that the worst interpretations of the behavior of the *douaniers* at Boulogne may not have been wrong. Only four from *Ann & Amelia* drowned Saturday night, but many more might have died:

> In a short time they returned informing me they had succeeded, *but that we would not be allowed to land, for the Guard drove them into the sea again.* I answered never mind them as we must, instantly giving orders for the ladies to prepare. In half an hour I had the happiness of seeing them safe over the ship's side, the remainder of my crew & passengers following, remaining to the last myself. I had requested Mr. Robio a French gentleman passenger, to go and see what he could do with the Guard on shore for I must insist on landing. He returned twice to me, calling & begging to me to come on shore with the hope of my having more influence with the Guard, informing me at the same time,

they were threatening to drive the ladies back into the water, many both passengers and crew calling to me to the same effect. On my getting to them I found the ladies sitting in greatest misery scarcely out of the water surrounded by about a dozen soldiers with their muskets presented threatening if we did not return to the ship to fire at us. I called for their Head, and told them I had no one sick (my surgeon being present), explained our situation, all to no effect. Go back, go back was the answer. This being impossible I took the ladies and marched off to a small hut or Guard House. They attempted to stop me, once or twice on the way. On reaching it some little kindness was shown by those within by kindling a fire. Fortunately the hut had one separate apartment, about six feet square where the ladies took shelter. In this horrid place, we were kept until 12 of the day, when a health officer arrived from whose appearance I hoped something better. Alas I was again to be disappointed. I instantly on seeing him gave him my word, also my surgeon's that no disease existed amongst us, begging of him at once to allow the ladies to be removed to the village. . . . It was two hours before I could get the permission. He first kept mustering my crew over & over again, then wished the passengers to be called out in the same way, ladies also. I told him it was impossible. He then went where they were, 4 or 5 individuals following & stood gazing at them for some time with such a want of sympathy and delicacy towards them that it really was disgusting.

The humanity shown to the crew and passengers wading ashore through the surf from her beached hull had consisted, her captain reported sarcastically, "in the Douane refraining from firing upon people escaping from a watery grave." "I have given what I fear you will think a very long statement, but I wish to be as minute as I possibly could be," Compton concluded to Hamilton, relating his experience to *Amphitrite*'s, "so that you may be made acquainted with every particular, the better able to judge how far correct the reports at Boulogne are."

Spared drowning, Captain Compton could now mourn the loss of his fortune, his share in the ship and its cargo, and all his personal possessions on board, down to the perishables in his private cuddy stores. "The wreck of my ship has been to me a very severe loss (not being insured)," he later wrote to Palmerston. "How hard, my Lord, after getting a great part of my property safe on shore, to have it taken from me and destroyed. At least to the amount of £600 in nautical instruments and stores alone. The ship has become a total loss, entirely from the officer of the French Marine not allowing her to be secured in the first bed she made."

Beginning midmorning November 10 and for a few days following, what remained of *Ann & Amelia* was on put up for sale at auction on the beach at Berck and in a salvage store in the town. The ubiquitous Adamses, businessmen and politicians of Boulogne and neighboring towns, were the auctioneers. The list of what was on offer that had appeared in *L'Annotateur* earlier in the month included the ship's hull (allegedly still sound enough to be bailed out and refloated), her spars, the sails ("in very good condition"), chains, cordage, nearly new water casks, anchors, guns, many pulleys, four compasses, thousands of pounds of copper sheathing, and "countless miscellaneous objects too numerous to mention." Parted out and sold, *Ann & Amelia* disappeared from the record. All that was left behind after mid-November were her former master's complaints about the *douaniers*.

57

According to Richard Taylor, a Londoner visiting Calais during the weekend of the gale, French Customs officers had been heartless there, too. Writing to the Royal Humane Society in February 1834, Taylor reported that a survivor from a Dutch vessel homeward bound from Surinam was left to die at the water's edge September 1 because the *douaniers* on duty "sent into the town to inform the authorities, *without whose presence or orders they would not suffer any one to touch the body*. . . . It was a full half hour before any answer returned from the authorities, and in the mean time the man was quite dead."

Even discounting a certain amount of reflexive francophobic storytelling, the thrust of the accumulated evidence from Boulogne, Berck, and Calais is clear: Official French actions on the beaches of the Pas-de-Calais during the gale were directed first at the prevention of smuggling and the enforcement of quarantine, next at the suppression of looting and the salvage of ships' stores and cargo, and only last and with no sense of urgency toward the preservation of life—at the possible expense of some few of the unfortunates on board *Amphitrite*. The editor of the *L'Annotateur* recognized this, but Captain Chads did not, and because official London saw the wreck through his and Hamilton's eyes and not through the eyes of the press or petitioners, the Foreign Office (and the Admiralty) misunderstood what had happened and why.

"All was done to save and restore life" through that night, Captain Chads concluded, "medical aid was not wanting. . . . The convenience and comforts of the Marine Hotel were immediately thrown open by the open-hearted proprietor, Mr. Barry; and there were some of our own countrywomen, Mrs. Austin, Mrs. Curtis, Mrs. Jeffreys and Miss Hawes, with their servants, who, setting aside that which would have been false delicacy on such an occasion, and with firmness of mind, not-withstanding the horror and heart-rending scene that had so suddenly burst upon them, undertook all the offices of most kind and tender nurses." Chads was correct in this assessment, but—gently warned away from the subject by Palmerston—he missed or misunderstood the larger issue. The result was a British failure to press effectively for a change in relevant French law and organization. How that failure reflected itself in the outcome of later wrecks on the same coast can only be imagined.

Palmerston had the issue of French quarantine laws and shipwreck raised to the British ambassador in Paris, Lord Granville Leveson-Gower, several times. Lord Granville, reputedly "the handsomest man in Regency England" and a compulsive high-stakes gambler who was then approaching the end of his first decade of service in Paris, was a savvy diplomat. Granville's initial approach to Victor, Duc de Broglie, then in his first term as French foreign minister, produced in January 1834 only the bland assurance that officers of the Marine and Health Departments already had the authority to instruct customs house officers to act "with respect to persons who may escape from a wreck as circumstances may require."

There was also a promise from Prince Charles Maurice de Talleyrand, a supple politician reincarnated in 1830 as King Louis-Philippe's ambassador in London, that "he would lay the subject before the government, and he had no doubt that every attention would be paid to the present state of the custom and sanitary laws in France. " That's what Talleyrand told the captain of the steam packet *Ferret*, who took him to Calais from Dover in autumn 1833, he was going to do. It is unlikely that he did it. There is nothing in the correspondence between the Duc de Broglie and Talleyrand about *Amphitrite*, although the August 1833 gale is mentioned there, and de Broglie complains about how it interrupted mail service.[35]

Goaded by Clayton's and Hawes' threat to raise the subject on the floor of the House of Commons, the Foreign Office continued pinging on Lord Granville and he on the French for evidence of substantive progress in their review of relevant law. London's effort in February to elicit more explicit information from Paris produced only the news in June that the French Finance and Marine Departments were "at present engaged in an examination of regulations in force with regard to persons who may escape from vessels wrecked on the coasts of France with the view of ascertaining the possibility of modifying what may be objectionable in those regulations."[36] Despite the apparent high-level interest, nothing in the later record suggests that any meaningful amendment to existing practice emerged from *Amphitrite*'s suffering, not withstanding Lord Palmerston's expressed willingness to press for reform if that were indicated and some vague conversations about the subject at high levels in London and Paris.

A partial explanation for London's reluctance to push the French harder might be found in the fact that British shipwreck practices turned out to be not very different from those of the French, as *L'Annotateur* disclosed in a column. If survivors of a foreign wreck discovered on shore in Great Britain could not be isolated in a suitable empty building, the paper told its readers, they were to be sequestered on the beach inside of a kind of corral made from salvaged spars and rope from the wreck, tented over for protection from the weather by its sailcloth, and kept there until disposition instructions arrived from London.

From Woolwich bound to Botany Bay,

The Amphitrite o'er sea,

And perished in the dreadful gale,

One hundred and thirty-three.

CHAPTER 8

$\diamond$

His Majesty's Consul at Boulogne

58

Hundreds of people were eyewitnesses to *Amphitrite*'s destruction on the Boulogne sands the last day of August. By the end of the first week of September many thousands in the United Kingdom and France also knew of the catastrophe, thanks to conventions of nineteenth-century journalism, which permitted the unattributed, verbatim use by one newspaper of the reporting found in another. In this same, informal way news of the wreck and its great loss of life soon crossed the Atlantic and appeared in American papers that autumn.

By mid-September, with the publication of Captain Chads' several reports in newspapers, most of what was known about *Amphitrite*'s last voyage by the British government was also familiar to the public. All but the information on the lost transport's convict manifest: the names and ages, trial date and courts, and sentence of each. The Home Office resolutely refused to disclose these details. Despite polite but determined importuning by an unnamed reporter from the *Morning Post*, who twice in mid-September approached John Henry Capper, the longtime superintendent of convicts at the Home Office, for it, that information was never released. Capper's explanation for his negative response can serve as a sample script for any bureaucrat stiff-arming the press.

"The calamity was a most melancholy one," Capper told the reporter on September 12 (using the nineteenth century's favorite synonym for "tragic"), "and the feelings of the relatives and friends of the unhappy sufferers had already been most painfully harrowed up; and any further publication, particularly if it included names, would only tend to renew those feelings of grief which were beginning to subside." As for those persons described by the reporter as "in a state of anxious uncertainty" by their ignorance of who was listed in Amphitrite's "fearful catalogue of death," Capper averred that no such uncertainty existed, because "every one of the unfortunate convicts who had quitted this country in the Amphitrite had full and frequent opportunities, both before & after being put on board, of communicating with their friends both personally and by letter. Most of them were probably frequently visited by their friends and relatives up to the very time of the ship sailing."

Capper, who had been for many years "the Superintendent of Ships and Vessels Employed for the Confinement of Offenders under Sentence of Transportation," certainly knew better: Visits to or exchanges of letters with convicts in prison might have been possible for some, but once out of its walls and embarked, the women would have been in near complete isolation from family and friends. Among the likely reasons for Capper's resolute silence was the protection of the Home Office from embarrassment. No list of names available to Whitehall totaled the reported count of Amphitrite's victims. Owen's commonly quoted census of the drowned—108 women, 12 children, and 13 crewmembers—included six more convicts than did any official count. That discrepancy (and it might have been Owen's counting error, but it became the accepted number in most contemporary accounts of the wreck) was never explained. Moreover, official confirmation of the convicts' ages would have heightened convictions that most of those lost were young and naïve, vulnerable to reform and hardly hardened criminals beyond redemption.

Thanks, too, to the press, the idea that the British consul in Boulogne had done something wrong and many had drowned because of it had very long legs. Short squibs about the wreck of Amphitrite appeared as column filler in many European and North American newspapers throughout the autumn and winter of 1833. Most editors found it easy to sound indignant, even though they didn't necessarily have the all details in hand. Thus on December 3, the Charles Town, Virginia, Virginia Free Press & Farmer's Repository told its readers that great blame had been laid on the English consul in Boulogne, who if "he had performed his duty, the lives of all on board might easily have been saved." The Virginia Free Press identified the far-off miscreant as none other than the "once famous" Beau Brummel, "the chief of English exquisites, and for many years the arbiter of fashion and gentility in London."

To a weekly newspaper in Charles Town, Virginia (West Virginia was still thirty years away), Brummel and the elegantly furnished dandies of Regency England must have appeared to be an exotic foreign species, one probably capable of anything. Several decades later the fashion phenomenon had to be explained even to Britons. "Dandyism fifty years ago was an elaborate art," John McGilchrist wrote perhaps semiseriously in 1865, "which absorbed the services of many attendant and ancillary arts—tailorism, boot-manufacturing, perfumery, snuff-taking, and the art of wielding a cane. . . . Brummel, who by the common consent of many of the women and all of the men, bore the undisputed sway was of the meanest origin and utterly destitute of any known source of income."[1]

Those snips aside, in his glory days George Bryan Brummel (1778–1840) ran on a very fast track. The prince regent, later George IV, had vied with him for the status of chief dandy, heady stuff for a man whose start in life was being the son of Lord North's private secretary and the grandson of an innkeeper. Viscount Palmerston, "gay, half-polite, half-tantalizing, but wholly amusing," was also prominent among the ranks of the dandies into his thirties.

In May 1816, his £30,000 inheritance entirely dissipated, Beau Brummel fled from London to Calais, then, like Boulogne, reopened after the war as a continental sanctuary for English debtors. He lived there, unemployed and in increasingly mean conditions until King George IV (who now despised him) died in June 1830. Three months later, under the new king, Brummel was appointed consul in Caen, down coast on the Orne River, in residence among Englishmen "of small income and large laziness" with little to do. The stipend was four hundred pounds per year, exactly what Hamilton was paid for his duties not far away at the much busier port of Boulogne, but most of Brummel's annual salary was signed over to his banker as payment on a huge debt. Left with only eighty pounds per year, Brummel was soon desperate. Worse yet, the Caen consulate was closed in March 1832, casting him adrift again. (Ironically, he had suggested the closure as a government economy, expecting assignment to some other sinecure.) During the next eight years his life collapsed further into poverty, degradation, and sickness. In March 1840 Brummel, aged sixty-one, died miserably at the Asylum du Bon Sauveur in Caen of tertiary syphilis, killed by the disease before he could be poisoned by the treatments (mercury, arsenic, and iodide) for it.

59

The real subject of the *Virginia Free Press'* garbled story was not Beau Brummel but Consul William Hamilton, age forty-five when *Amphitrite* materialized unexpectedly in front of the Marine Hotel out of the weather and on the ebbing tide. He was to remain at his post in Boulogne for the next forty years.

Hamilton's adult life began when he joined the Royal Navy in 1803 and was from 1805 for nine years during the Napoleonic Wars a prisoner in Verdun.[2] Some 1,100 Britons were held under parole in this fortress city on the Garonne River, where a tenth of the population was British prisoners or internees. Far inland from the Channel coast, Verdun was a place from which escape would have been difficult, but confinement under parole (a promise not to attempt escape) might not have been too arduous, at least for some. "Ordinary prisoners . . . were allowed to take jobs. Officers were given parole and allowed limited freedom. . . . Senior officers and wealthy civilian internees and their families led comfortable lives," wrote Robert and Isabelle Tombs describing the scene. "Gambling, drinking, dueling, horse racing and sex provided something of a home from home."[3]

"According to a Boulogne tradition," the story goes, in 1814 and finally at liberty, Hamilton married nineteen-year-old Claudette Rebière, his jailor's daughter, who had helped him in a failed escape attempt.[4] After the long confinement in Verdun, he never recrossed the English Channel to stay. Release and freedom at war's end was followed by several years as vice consul in five different Low Country ports and then in April 1822 by an appointment as vice consul to Boulogne.

On June 28, 1826, the London Gazette announced his promotion: "The King has been graciously pleased to appoint William Hamilton, Esq. (sometime British vice consul at Boulogne), to be His Majesty's Consul at the place."[5] That achieved, Hamilton spent nearly half a century representing His Majesty's government's maritime and commercial interests in this busy port and along the adjacent thirty-five miles of the Pas-de-Calais coast. While he hung on in Boulogne, eleven foreign secretaries passed through the ministry on Downing Street, some several times.

Decades of service notwithstanding, Hamilton's was not the well-known name in London or elsewhere on the British Isles that it was among ship masters, tourists, and expatriates in Boulogne. Newspaper readers in the capital with good memories might have recollected the consul at Boulogne-sur-Mer as the author of an April 1831 letter to editors alerting Britons that graves in the city's cemeteries would soon be emptied of corpses and the associated monuments removed by local authorities unless the sites were leased "in perpetuity or for a term of years" by interested parties. Two years later, in the spring of 1833, his follow-on letter announced the deadline had arrived.

Through most of the nineteenth century but especially in its earlier years, British consuls were the Foreign Office's stepchildren, bereft of the glamour and status afforded to diplomats. The duties of a consul, Lord Palmerston

Fig. 21

"Sir William Hamilton, Late the British Counsel at Boulogne." After a photograph by John J. E. Mayall, 1873. Hamilton (1789–1877), the eldest of the eight children of a sometime Royal Navy surgeon, left "Monkland," the family estate in Lanarkshire, central Scotland, and went to sea at fourteen, several years after his father's death. What might have become a life in the navy was derailed by his capture and long captivity in France, and by the end of the Napoleonic Wars. This is Hamilton at eighty-four, forty years after *Amphitrite* broke up at Boulogne and several years before he died in that city. He was the British consul there for almost fifty years, from June 1826 until he retired in 1873. J. J. E. Mayall (1813–1901), British-born but American-trained, was a highly successful Victorian-era photographer. He owned several family-operated portrait studios in London and Brighton during the second half of the century. The portrait on which this image of Consul Hamilton is based was probably taken in the Mayall studio at 224 Regent Street, London, by Mayall's son, Edwin, when Hamilton visited the capital in 1873 to be "granted the dignity of a Knight." ILLUSTRATED LONDON NEWS, APRIL 19, 1873, 369. COURTESY JOHN WEEDY, WWW.ILN.ORG.UK.

instructed Benjamin Disraeli in the House of Commons March 1842—Disraeli
had just described the consular establishment as "a refuge for the destitute"
and then gone on to attack Palmerston's service as foreign secretary in the
guise of a proposal to merge the two services—"differed in every respect from
the duties of a diplomatist":

> A consul has to look after the vessels coming into the port where he
> resides. He has to settle the disputes between the masters of ships and
> their crew, and to listen to the complaints of British subjects against
> local authorities. He was also charged by law with the duty of reliev-
> ing distressed Englishmen, and of making advances to enable them
> to return home. These were not by their nature diplomatic duties.
> To diplomacy belonged the intercourse between nation and nation,
> and between the government of one country and the government of
> another. Consular duties related to the intercourse between the sub-
> jects of one country and the subjects of another. The two duties were
> essentially distinct.[6]

Harper's New Monthly Magazine, writing across the ocean in 1855, described
the same duties as "making out ship's papers and dealing in miniature diplo-
macy," not the real thing but a small-scale copy. Nothing nearly as grand as
managing the intercourse between nations.

In September, while continuing to address other claims on his time as
described to Disraeli by Viscount Palmerston, Hamilton turned to defend
himself from Wilks' threat to his livelihood and reputation. Typical of these
distractions was a tourist's anxiety to recover his "porte-manteau" (suitcase),
misplaced during the process of clearing French customs on arrival at Boulogne
from England. Not so typical was a request from Downing Street for his help to
find Mr. William Widgen's three small children, detained in Boulogne as hos-
tages by certain creditors of Widgen's wife, now adrift somewhere in Europe
without them. Their father, and the request's original author, was incapable of
participating in the search because he was confined as a debtor in Maidstone
Jail. If appropriate, Hamilton was told to apply to local authorities, "to cause
the children to be set at liberty forthwith," this (typically, as the Foreign Office
was miserly with its money) "without incurring any extraordinary expense
with respect to these children on the part of Her Majesty's government."

Wilks' accusations, first contained in his letter to Palmerston then col-
orized in his newspaper columns and finally presented to Captain Chads in
page after page of numbered paragraphs scribbled in white hot heat, when
Hamilton was barely into his second decade at Boulogne, powerfully threatened the consul. Chads' investigation had the potential swiftly to upend

Hamilton's comfortable, genteel life, to thrust him among Boulogne's hangers-on and *poseurs*, and onto a long slide down, beginning with a loss of status as a gentleman and potentially ending with the loss of most else besides. Hamilton had no security. He served in Boulogne entirely at the pleasure of the sitting foreign secretary, who could fire him for cause or for no cause at all, as Beau Brummel had found out to his misfortune eighteen months earlier. For a man with limited private means, the loss of the post, of the hundreds of pounds sterling each year in salary and fees that went with it, and of the expectation of a pension at the end, all these were suddenly at risk as September began.

Wilks' was not the only shrill voice calling for Consul Hamilton's head. Some local Pas-de-Calais newspapers, including *Le Propagateur* and *Le Nord*, found joining the hue and cry against the British consul irresistible. It fell to the more restrained *L'Annotateur* to remind French readers that Hamilton was, after all, "more subject to trial from his government than from the French press."[7]

60

Back in his office at 11:00 AM Saturday, after having satisfied himself that the London and Rotterdam Steam Packet Company's *Queen of the Netherlands*, probably helped by a favoring wind, had crossed safely overnight to England through heavy rain, Hamilton spent the hours until dinner doing paperwork. He returned to his desk just before 8:00 at night dutifully to read the Foreign Office mail just in by courier from Calais and to prepare his responses to it.

French practice had local authorities notify the consul concerned when a distressed foreign vessel appeared in a port's approaches. Neither "le commissaire de l'inscription maritime of Boulogne" (Monsieur Michelin, at home that afternoon *gravement malade*, "seriously ill") nor his subordinate, the "lieutenant du port" (Capitaine Jean Jacques Pollet, entirely hale but forgetful), did that on Saturday. Hamilton told Chads that when he ran across Pollet inside the Humane Society's shack later that night, he "publicly reproached [Pollet] for having omitted to apprise me, in any shape [?], of the event. He replied that it was no part of his duty to give me this information but had he thought of it, he would have done so as an act of courtesy. I replied that it might not be his duty but it was an act of courtesy which had never been withheld from me during the 11 years I have resided at this port."[8]

Hamilton did not learn that an English merchant ship was off Boulogne and in trouble from either French officials or from the Lloyd's agency in town— his usual sources for shipping intelligence. The first notice came instead in a letter carried by a breathless Jean-Baptiste Fusquel, Barry's manservant at the Marine Hotel, who had sped from there on foot the full length of the rue de Boston, then along any one of several streets paralleling the harbor's quays, and finally up the rue des Vieillards to its far end and Hamilton's house. A distance of about a mile, all uphill and likely hard going on wet streets through bad weather, but pushed for much of the way by a following wind. (Hamilton described his trip on foot in the opposite direction an hour later as struggling "against a gale of wind & sand which forced me to go a considerable distance backwards.")

Dated "Saturday evening," signed "John Wilks," and delivered at around 7:45 PM, the letter to Hamilton read,

> An English merchant ship is on the shore off the coast. Her crew will not come on shore—This may be the fault of the Captain. The crew are numerous and the vessel is a large one. All will be lost if some measures are not adopted.
>
> I apply to you as our English Consul to send off *coûte que coûte* [at all costs] an English sailor or crew or boat to the vessel calling on the Captain & crew to embark. I am known to you as the son of Mr. Wilks, the Member for *Boston*.

Wilks' dip into French made the point that he was educated, upper class, someone who merited the consul's attention. His self-identification was also meant to establish him as a substantial person (or at least the son of one), while dodging mention of his notorious past.

Wilks had arrived at the Marine Hotel on Tuesday from Paris, joining the town's usual summer crowd of citizens, resident foreigners, and vacationing tourists. He came "to spend a few days for the benefit of his health" and later would say that on arrival he knew no one in Boulogne, but that wasn't true. He knew Michael Barry and François Huret. Both men had occasionally helped him to send columns from Paris across the Channel to the *Standard*'s editor in London. In passing, he'd referred to Barry as his "agent."

Wilks wrote his shipwreck alert letter to Hamilton in the hotel's dining room amid a large group that included hotelier Barry, Sarah Austin, and a mixed bag of other agitated spectators of the scene, all now finished with their dinners (a limited menu served *prix fixe* for economy) and waiting for tea while staring out the room's windows and door at the three-masted vessel in trouble. Dinner had started early, at 5:00 PM (about the time when, not far off shore, Hunter had *Amphitrite*'s anchor let go, guaranteeing her destruction), because some guests planned a trip to the theater later that night. At 7:00 the meal was over and the theatergoers left by coach for rue Monsigny and the show, half a mile or so away toward the heart of the lower town. Not Wilks, however, who had been invited to join them but now, caught up in the excitement on the waterfront, declined. Minutes later he put pen to paper.

Boulogne's salts and landlubbers alike knew how this drama before them was going to end; they'd seen it before. "On Saturday, the 31st August," Sarah Jeffreys (another of the watchers out Barry's windows) later wrote to Captain Chads, "about 1/2 past 4 o'clock in the afternoon a large three masted vessel struck on the sands so near the shore that I could distinguish what the sailors were doing. It caused great excitement on account of her position. No vessel was ever known to get off the sands with such a heavy sea. There did not exist two opinions concerning her fate. All agreed that immediate assistance must be given to endeavour to save the crew it being low water and at the rising of the tide, she must immediately go to pieces." Just after 5:00, as dinner was put out, Barry also confidently predicted that the bark would be beaten to pieces as the tide came in, "but the crew may be saved," he added, assuming her captain was waiting for low tide an hour or so hence before sending his men through the surf to safety. High tide that night would be at 11:38. Long before then, her audience at Barry's believed, *Amphitrite* would be overwhelmed and dismembered.

Austin and Barry were among the chief witnesses Chads deposed and interrogated during his investigation. From them—and from Wilks, too—come the details of what was said and seen during the evening vigil at the dining room windows. Their accounts didn't agree. It's difficult to tell which of the three was telling the truth.

Almost certainly Sarah Austin was truthful, if only because she had no motive to lie. Her deposition is engagingly modest about her own role in events—no heroic standing in the surf pulling bodies ashore—one focused Saturday night and through the following week largely on protecting Rice and especially the injured Owen from interrogation, exploitation, and fatigue. (Fatigue probably deepened by the loss of blood drained several times from Owen by a French doctor, rebalancing his patient's four humors to restore health and vitality according to the day's best medical practice.) Towsey, adopted temporarily by one Lieutenant Colonel Maxwell, with whom

---

MAP 2 FOLLOWING SPREAD

Boulogne sur Mer in the Department of the Pas de Calais. From Clarke, *Bononia*, 1835. Boulogne as it was in the early 1830s, when the town's population was roughly 22,000, of whom several thousand were British expatriates. The sites marked are (1) the approximate place of the shipwreck, (2) the Humane Society's beach shack, (3) Barry's Marine Hotel, (4) Consul Hamilton's home and office at the top of the rue des Vieillards, (5) the hospital where *Amphitrite*'s dead were collected and prepared for burial, and (6) the churchyard where they were interred and where their memorial monument was erected twenty years later.

© THE BRITISH LIBRARY BOARD, SHELFMARK 576.A.31, PICTURE NO. 1023910.262.

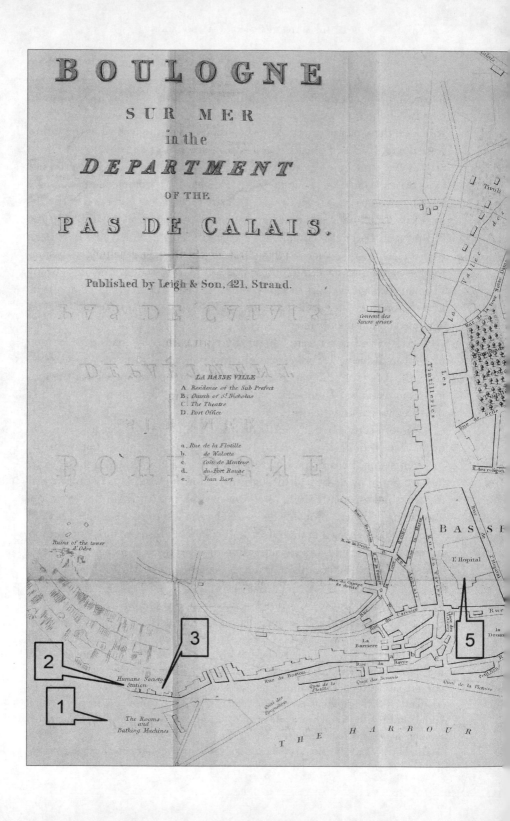

BOULOGNE

SUR MER
in the
DEPARTMENT
OF THE
PAS DE CALAIS.

Published by Leigh & Son, 421, Strand.

LA BASSE VILLE

A. *Residence of the Sub Prefect*
B. *Church of St Nicholas*
C. *The Theatre*
D. *Post Office*

a. *Rue de la Flotille*
b. *de Walotte*
c. *Coin de Menteur*
d. *du Fort Rouge*
e. *Jean Bart*

Convent des Sœurs grises

Ruins of the tower d'Odre

Humane Society Station

The Rooms and Bathing Machines

BASSI

l'Hopital

Tivoli

Les Tatilleries

R. des religieux

La Barriere

Rue de Boston

Quai de la Flotille

Quai des Demanis

Quai de la Victoire

THE HARBOUR

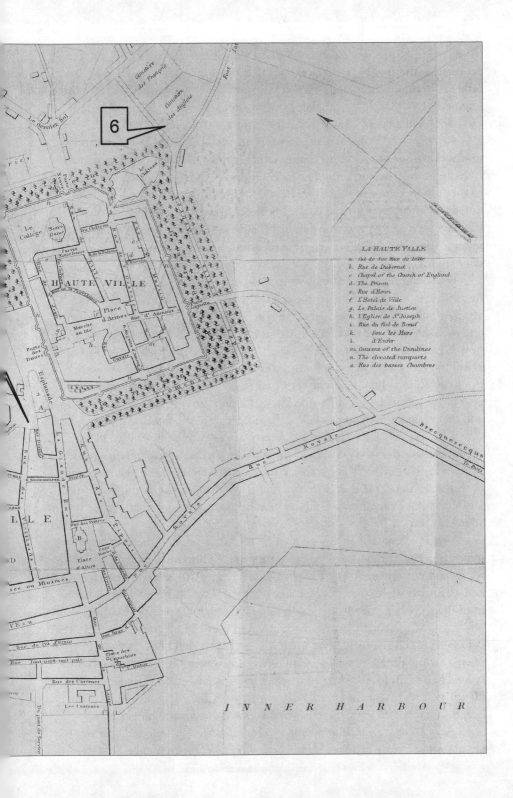

6

LA HAUTE VILLE

a. Cul de Sac Rue de Lille
b. Rue de Dubernet
c. Chapel of the Church of England
d. The Prison
e. Rue d'Henri
f. L'Hotel de Ville
g. Le Palais de Justice
h. L'Eglise de St Joseph
i. Rue du fiol de Boeuf
k.   Sous les Murs
l.   d'Enfer
m. Convent of the Ursulines
n. The elevated ramparts
o. Rue des basses Chambres

INNER HARBOUR

he stayed at 58 rue des Pipats for a month until his return to England, got no such mothering. In due course, in a nod to his prior service, Towsey was offered a second master's warrant in the Royal Navy, employment successfully engineered by Maxwell's name dropping at the Admiralty. He appears not to have accepted any assignment and left the navy at the end of 1838.

Austin's protection was not completely successful. Wilks, Clayton, and others easily managed to get access to the victims and to quiz them. Survivor quotations in the press supporting various lurid allegations prompted Chads to explain to the Admiralty "a vast deal has been said for the three poor seamen who were saved that they never uttered & their answers to questions tortured to answer the ideas & views of those who put them." Austin said she thought Wilks' alert letter to the consul left the hotel in Fusquel's hands close to 7:00 PM and that she later saw and spoke to the consul for the first time at about 11:00.

Wilks had no apparent motive to lie about Hamilton—he claimed that he neither heard the consul's name nor met him before Saturday night, hours after *Amphitrite* ran aground—but he was a charlatan and professional liar, and Wilks might have concluded that his route to regain respectability somehow began with being the champion of *Amphitrite*'s dead and the assassin of Hamilton's reputation. Nothing written about *Amphitrite* by anyone connected the John Wilks at Boulogne with the "Bubble Wilks" of the late 1820s, and it's possible that only Lord Palmerston knew the outraged reporter on the beach and the infamous joint stock company scammer were the same man.

Were he culpable, Hamilton's motive to lie was self-defense. If John Wilks' charges that the consul had been disgracefully slow to appear on the beach and had generally failed that weekend "to watch over the commercial & shipping interests of the greatest commercial nation in the world" were true and stuck, then Hamilton was almost certainly out of the job that defined his station in life.

Amphitrite's nationality was a mystery for hours because the ship flew no identifying flag. Perhaps hers had been stripped off Thursday or Friday by storm winds and not replaced. There was a fanciful report that she was first identified as British when two pigs of a characteristic English breed swam ashore from the ship, but that has to be some snarky French leg pulling. Nothing in any record suggests that barnyard animals were penned on the ship's deck at departure, and it's unlikely that any beasts on board could have survived the two preceding turbulent days at sea. Positive identification of the vessel came several hours before *Amphitrite* broke up, sometime after 6:00 PM, when Pierre Hénin returned from his failed mission to pass a line from the ship to the beach, and reported her nationality to the crowd outside the hotel.

"About 6 or 1/2 past I saw Hénin run past the window followed by a number of people," Barry deposed. "I ran out & after him. I with numbers of others were all enquiring what the vessel was, what she was laden with, how many hands on board, &c. He, Hénin, shook with cold and seemed terribly harassed, probably by his exertions & the numbers of questions. He answered me it is an English vessel. I went in and announced it at Table d'Hôte." After it was first revealed to Barry's guests, Hénin's stunning disclosure took more than an hour to reach Adam et Compagnie, the Lloyd's agency in Boulogne. Hénin, or perhaps Huret or one of his crew, was also the source of the news that a woman and three children had been seen on board the beached vessel. The natural assumption was that these four were members of the captain's family.

All that information absorbed, Wilks hastily wrote two letters and then read them to the group in the dining room. The first, to Consul Hamilton, was soon on its way. The second, addressed "to the Captain of the Ship on Shore off Boulogne," never went anywhere. Even more terse than the first, the second read, "Sir, I call on you & on your crew to abandon your vessel & save your lives. If you do not do so, I hold you responsible for all the lives of the crew. My father is the Member for Boston in England."

Wilks carried this letter a short distance to the beach, where, he later told Sarah Austin, he could find no sailor daring enough to take it to the ship, not even for ten guineas, nearly eleven pounds. "It was impossible," Wilks was told; no amount of money would be enough. Later, when he described the same event to Chads, the amount offered and declined swelled to hundreds of pounds sterling.

Not until Richard Rice, the first survivor, was carried to the hotel and had recovered enough to speak did anyone ashore know the complete truth about the ship. "Some one [he was Louis Bourgain] came in bringing a man in their arms," Sarah Austin wrote in her ten-page deposition, her crabbed handwriting deteriorating with every page, some lines furiously scratched out, others boldly underlined:

He was placed on a sofa in Mr. Barry's sitting room. I helped to rub him and to put hot water onto his feet and stomach. While I was holding his head, he looked at me & said: "I gave you a great deal of trouble." The next thing he said was ". . . a hundred women."

I said "Gracious God, what can he mean?" I thought he was delirious.

He said, "She was a convict ship bound to Sydney. We had 108 women & twelve children on board & 16 men!"

Several people began to question him! I said, "let him alone, he wants rest."

And then the bodies of the women began to be brought into the hotel. Perhaps two hours later the second survivor, Boatswain Owen, was carried into the hotel. The third, James Towsey, soon followed.

The hours of uncertain identity might account for the fact that not until 8:00 PM did Hercule Adam, a usually reliable source of shipping news for Hamilton, arrive at his house to alert the consul of the developing disaster. When Adam walked in the door, Hamilton was, he claimed, already changing into foul weather gear, having been informed fifteen minutes earlier of the emergency by the alert from John Wilks.

Just when Hamilton got Wilks' urgent summons and what he did in response to it were the central questions of Captain Chads' investigation. Wilks' answers to these questions were damning. Hamilton, he wrote, did not arrive on the beach until 10:30, "*dressed for a party or soirée,*" too late to do anything. Had he been there earlier, Hamilton might have ordered the captain to abandon his ship or, "by his presence, energy & zeal, as the representative of the greatest commercial country in the world, have encouraged the supine and have stimulated the flagging & timid" to aid in the rescue attempt. Instead, "nothing of this was done by the Consul" and 133 drowned.

61

Undersecretary of State Sir George Shee's Thursday, September 5, letter to Consul Hamilton was chilling.[9] Shee was the junior of Palmerston's two undersecretaries, and among his responsibilities was the supervision of the Foreign Office's consular service. In between the lines of his letter lay the unspoken threat that Hamilton's job was at risk. "The accounts which have been received in this country of the late melancholy shipwreck of the Transport 'Amphitrite' off Boulogne, with the loss of all aboard excepting 3 of the crew, appear to attach great blame to you, as HM's Consul, for not having been present to render that prompt & necessary assistance which it was your duty to afford, and which, if it had been rendered, would it is said have been the means of saving the lives of all the persons on board," he wrote. "I am therefore directed by Viscount Palmerston to desire that you will lose no time in forwarding to his lordship specifick answers to the following questions." (Hamilton's answers, sent to London the following Tuesday, are in italics.) The questions constituted Palmerston's own investigation of Wilks' accusations, paralleling the more formal Admiralty inquiry that he had provoked:

1st; Where your place of residence is situated.
My place of residence is at the top of the rue des Vieillards between the high and low towns.

Hamilton's choice of residence was an unusual one for a consul. Along the Atlantic and Mediterranean coasts most consuls lived where they had a view of the waterfront and easy access to its facilities, businesses, and sailors' haunts: the focal points of their largely maritime mission. Hamilton's home, however, was "in a distant and inconvenient part of town," almost as far from salt water as it was possible to be in Boulogne-sur-Mer. All its windows looked inland, the wrong way to see anything but city streets and neighboring buildings. Perhaps being close to local government centers was more important to him, or perhaps it was the attraction of the site, fronting the esplanade and across from the *sous-préfet*'s office, near the Promenade des Petits Arbres, the tree-sheltered walk that encircled the old city's wall.

Hamilton and his family lived there comfortably until not long before his death, sharing a building at the northeast end of the rue des Vieillards ("old men," called rue Félix Adam after 1923) with a school next door, just down slope from Sous-préfet Launay Le Prévost's office and the western gate into the old walled city. The *sous-préfeture* is still there today, but a municipal school of fine arts now stands on the ground where the Hamiltons lived.

By midcentury, and perhaps as early as 1833, the consulate operated a second floor, one room passport office down at the port, located in a shop building between a fish market and a carriage stand. The modest operation, manned by Hamilton's assistant, filled with the sounds and smells of the street and sparely furnished, was an easy target for *Punch*, the satirical humor magazine. "The demand for economy at our diplomatic establishments has been promptly met at Boulogne-sur-mer. . . . The locality chosen has an air of extreme cheapness," *Punch* cracked in 1851, before getting to its point: objecting "to the system of eking out the pay of a Consul by imposing a fee of 4s. 6d. on such a miserable mockery as obtaining a passport at Boulogne."

Whatever the reason for his choice of residence, the result was that through Saturday afternoon Hamilton was unaware of the great drama playing on the beach less than a mile and a half from his home. Others were ignorant of it, too. "It should be observed," Chads explained to Elliot later, "that although there are about 50 British naval and military officers residing in Boulogne, in all parts of the town, I have not been able to discover a single individual who knew of the circumstance [of the wreck] at the time it occurred."

Still, this particular observation made for a thin defense. Chads knew (and Elliot would have known, also) that none of these worthies in retirement had any duty to assist British shipping or responsibility to stay informed about marine traffic in and about the port of Boulogne, unlike Hamilton, who in exchange for four hundred pounds per year had both. (This annual salary put Boulogne at the middle of the ten British consular offices in France, halfway between Marseilles at six hundred pounds and Corsica at two hundred pounds.)

2ndly; Where you were when the Amphitrite stranded.

I was at the office of the Consulate and had not left it the whole day from 11 o'clock in the forenoon.

Saturdays were work days in Boulogne. Market days, too. Despite the weather, some shops and stalls on le place Dalton in the *basse ville* were open August 31, as would be the theater later that night. Hamilton's working day began early that morning, hours before *Amphitrite* appeared under storm canvas off Fort de l'Heurt's stone tower, south of the harbor's entrance.[10] After an early morning trip down to the port, Hamilton had dutifully returned to spend the rest of the day in his office. An image of dedication reinforced by his answer to Palmerston's next question and simultaneously a denial of reports in the press that he had been at a dinner party during the early hours of the calamity and later appeared on the beach incongruously dressed in formal attire. (His wife, Claudette, went to the soirée alone, as confirmed to Chads by Monsieur Adam and Rear Admiral Sidney Horton, apologizing to the hosts on arrival for her husband's absence.)

3dly; At what time and by what means you first heard of the wreck.

Being in my office at about 8 o'clock in the evening opening the usual packet from the Foreign Office and about to prepare the one for that department when a letter No. 1 was brought to me from Mr. Wilks conveying the first intimations I had of a vessel being in distress off the port. I desired the messenger, who had left, to be called back and requested him to say that I would immediately attend to it.

Some four hours had passed between *Amphitrite*'s appearance off shore and Hamilton's realization that an English merchant ship was in extremis in front of the port. Sworn statements by Fusquel (Wilks' messenger), Adelle Martel (the courier from Calais, who said he delivered the Foreign Office's dispatch case at 7:15 PM), Hamilton's servant, Racine, and his housekeeper, Mrs. Polhill, generally confirmed Hamilton's account of the arrival of Wilks' letter.

4thly; What steps you took in consequence.

Having hastily despatched the packet for the Foreign Office, I went instantly to prepare myself for the night, if necessary, on the beach; —when in the act of doing this Mr. H. Adam brought me a letter No. 2 confirming Mr. Wilks' report and verbally told me that it was then unnecessary to be in such a hurry as I would not now do anything for the ship. I replied that I should nevertheless hasten to the beach.

Hercule Adam (1796–1885), a local banker and merchant as well as a principal in Adam et Compagnie, was a native Boulonnais, one of a large family of businessmen that was prominent in the city and also in the nearby towns, where their banking company had branch offices. Adam spent only ten minutes with Hamilton, time enough to deliver his letter and to confirm that he, too, heard the ship's master had refused assistance. "I said to Mr. Adam," Hamilton later wrote in his statement to Chads, "what on earth could induce the captain to refuse assistance. He replied that he could not tell, and said positively that it was too late to do anything more for the vessel, adding that I had no occasion to hurry myself."

5thly; At what hour you came down to the beach.

As far as I can remember from the hurry & agitation; the time taken in dispatching the packet, in preparing myself, conversing with Mr. Adam, & struggling down to the beach against a gale of wind and sand, it might be somewhere about 9 o'clock.

Hamilton's servant said that right after Adam left, his master outfitted himself in "strong boots, a cap & shaggy cloak" and about 20 minutes after 8 o'clock headed down to the port, the lower half of his face swaddled in a large cravat for further protection. Exactly when Hamilton was seen on the beach became a focus of Chads' questioning of witnesses. No one said as early as nine and several claimed to have seen him there as late as eleven.

Sarah Jeffreys was one of these persons. "The Consul came to the hotel near 11 oclock," she wrote in her deposition. "I pointed to him the hour—and detailed to him the distressing scene I had been a witness to—Mothers clasping their infants to their bosoms in agony were washed ashore, a more distressing sight was never seen." Jeffreys was one source of reports that bodies found on the beach were still warm, suggesting that a very short time in the water had separated life from death.

"When you arrived on the beach," Chads asked Hamilton during his notably brief (six softball questions) formal interrogation, "had any of the bodies washed ashore?" "None," Hamilton responded, establishing with his answer a time of arrival around 9:00 PM, which Chads accepted.

6thly; What measures were take by you to save the crew and the passengers.

Upon arriving at the beach it appeared to me that the most active measures were employed by the Authorities, under the existing circumstances for the purpose of picking up and saving the wrecked crew, it not being then known that there were any passengers on board. I found a report current

upon the beach that the Gendarmes & Custom House officers prevented
the people from saving the crew, but which I could not ascertain as far as
my own observations & queries went, to be well founded.

It being out of the power of myself or any human being, after the time I
arrived on the beach, to have conversation with the ship I directed my efforts
to prevent any impediments being thrown in the way of picking up and as far
as possible saving the lives of the unfortunate individuals shipwrecked.

Hamilton closed his letter with the hope that "the investigation now going on by the Commissioner sent hither to inquire into this lamentable case will fully exculpate me from any blame on the occasion." His answers would have been delivered to Palmerston by week's end, but the foreign secretary waited until long after Chads' final report was in hand before having a reply sent.

62

"John Wilks of Paris" delivered his dual purpose statement, an outline history of the wreck of *Amphitrite* largely as experienced at Barry's hotel starring himself and a detailed indictment of Consul Hamilton, to Captain Chads on Wednesday, September 11.

After its second page Wilks referred to himself everywhere in the third person, as "Witness." His purpose in doing so went beyond establishing his membership in the group of people who had been, in Chads' words, "actually present on the Beach or near it" late on August 31. Wilks' additional point was to emphasize in legalese that he had seen more than a shipwreck— he'd observed crimes in a setting of catastrophe. Crimes of omission committed by Consul Hamilton that one after the other had resulted in dozens of deaths, notwithstanding "Witness'" own efforts to save *Amphitrite*'s crew and convicts. "Witness finally repeats," he concluded his indictment, "that he is convinced that if Consul had used his best efforts he might have been able to save the whole of the crew & convicts—or at any rate to rescue a great number of them."

While "extremely boisterous" weather tore at Boulogne Friday night and Saturday, Hamilton could not have been ignorant of the danger to British shipping, Wilks insisted, but he was indifferent to it. Reflecting this indifference, the consul failed to be present on the beach Saturday afternoon and early evening, when it was still possible to communicate with *Amphitrite* from shore and to command Hunter to abandon ship. Wilks, who said he interrogated Towsey, Owen, and Rice about it practically as they came ashore, told Chads that all three survivors believed Hunter would have "immediately" obeyed an abandon ship order, if received. "They could speak and understand what was going on," Wilks said of the three to lend credence to what they allegedly said to him, but the answer to what he asked them was unknowable.

Whether or not Hamilton actually had the authority to command Hunter to abandon ship, to contract and pay for emergency services on the beach-front, or to offer rewards to stimulate heroic rescue attempts—among the other things Wilks believed the consul should have done but did not—wasn't clear to anyone at the time. To anyone but Wilks, that is, who believed that the answer to all three questions was yes.

The first question, of course, was moot. By the time Hamilton arrived on the beach, around 9:00 PM if, what he swore to was true—later than that or even much later based on some witness' testimony—*Amphitrite* was no longer accessible and her time was just about up. At about 9:15, according to Sarah Jeffreys, "she went to pieces," forcing everyone who'd been on board into the water, most quickly to drown. Too late for Hamilton to command anything. It's an odd thought, anyway, the idea that a ship's master had to be ordered to act to save his own life and those of his crew and charges in a wreck is bizarre. ("In ordinary cases," the *Examiner* of London patiently explained to a letter writer confused about the same point, "it is not necessary to order seamen to save their lives.")

Hamilton was uncertain of his authority to compel the captain to land if he refused to do so, and nothing from the Foreign Office after the fact has clarified the issue for the record. The only detailed public commentary on the consul's authority on the beach, or lack of it, came in an *Examiner* article on the "Conduct of Consul Hamilton at Boulogne." Since 1828 the *Examiner*, a liberal daily, had been edited by the famously articulate Albany Fonblanque, and it's possible he was the author of this anonymous defense of Hamilton:

> It has been assumed that the Consul might have sent an ORDER to land the crew and passengers, and that the crew and passengers would have been saved if such an order had been transmitted in time. It will startle many of our readers to hear that British Consuls have no authority whatsoever over vessels of their country, whether afloat, in port, or stranded; and that they alone among such foreign agents are without the power of even demanding the inspection of a ship's papers under any circumstances. If it had occurred to the Consul, on the occasion of the Amphitrite's stranding, that the assertion of a feigned authority might have saved many lives, he would, perhaps, have practiced the pious fraud; but it neither follows that the French authorities would have suffered effect to be given such directions, nor that the master would have recognized in Mr. Hamilton's commission

a guarantee sufficient to release him from the heavy pecuniary responsibility that weighed upon him.

To enlighten Chads and to bolster his argument that the cause of Hamilton's
failure to act decisively in other matters was an absence of will rather than a
lack of authority or resources, Wilks included with his statement a copy of
the relevant chapter of the Consular Act of 1825—how he got the text of the
law in Boulogne is a mystery; he asked Chads for its return—addressing disbursements permitted to be made by consuls in the event of shipwreck.[11] The
eighteenth chapter of the act, Wilks noted helpfully, beginning on page 835,
was relevant. And maybe it was as written, but the act, intended by Foreign
Secretary George Canning to professionalize Great Britain's consular service,
was never fully implemented or funded and Hamilton's near-instinctive aver-
sion to spending public money was based on long experience.

Later this same lack of vigor, in Wilks' eyes, was the explanation for the
consul's failure to line the beach with men paid to carry torches to illuminate
the shore, permitting survivors to perish unseen in the dark on the beach.
Approaching sunset on the Boulogne waterfront the last Saturday in August,
horizontal visibility under layers of clouds and in the rain would have been
several hundred yards at most, down to a few dozen after a quarter past nine,
when the last minutes of twilight faded into darkness. Except when the moon
broke through the clouds a would-be rescuer had to stumble over a survivor or
a body to find her or him. In the 1830s, off the gas-lit high streets of major cities, there was little escaping the dark out of doors.

"But when the wreck took place, was everything done that might have
been to have saved the crew and the convicts?" Wilks had asked rhetorically
in *The Times* of September 5. "Decidedly not. . . The British Consul ought to
have ranged with lights at least 200 or 300 people along the cost to pick up the
bodies." Torchlight, Wilks argued, was the answer to this problem, and Consul
Hamilton's failure to arrange hundreds of beachwalkers wielding torches was
yet another of his crimes of omission that night. During his investigation of
the wreck, Captain Chads rightly dismissed this charge in a sentence: "All
agree it would have been impossible to have used torches from the state of the
weather, it blowing a tremendous gale of wind."

Wilks' implications that a better prepared beach party and more compas-
sionate French customs officers would have resulted in more lives saved are
probably false also. The time to have saved the people on board was before
their ship broke up, not after. It is possible that some few of *Amphitrite*'s unfortunates were thrown up on the beach still alive, and died exhausted in the surf,
but it is much more likely that once on shore the drowned vastly outnumbered
the near-drowned and there was very little life saving to be done.

That Hamilton had no authority to intervene in the management of the rescue effort was a matter of French law remembered by nobody until *L'Annotateur* drew attention to the fact days later in one of its columns. Although France had signed treaties with Portugal, Prussia, Sardinia, Spain, and Sweden that gave their consuls such a right in the event of shipwrecks of their countries' vessels, no agreement had been reached with Great Britain. Hamilton had no official status on the waterfront Saturday night, and no more influence on events than any curious private citizen had. The responsibility to take charge of and manage life-saving operations for a British wreck was by law exclusively French. Whatever special consideration was shown the British consul was a matter of courtesy, as Capitaine Pollet had reminded Hamilton, nothing else.

63

Before Chads could assess Consul William Hamilton's performance of duty he had to reconstruct the weekend of the storm at Boulogne, focusing on the eighteen hours or so between midafternoon Saturday (when Hunter deliberately drove *Amphitrite* intact onto the bar after looking, he supposedly told the mate, to "run her up as high as possible") and midmorning on Sunday (by which time any realistic hope that the sea would surrender further survivors was gone). Chads did this by interrogating volunteer witnesses. The only nonvolunteer Chads saw was the consul, directed by his masters in London to answer questions the Admiralty's commissioner put to him.

Chads believed there were fifty or sixty British naval and military officers living in Boulogne and he sought these out directly, evidently having special confidence in their perceptions. Chads recruited these men to testify by handwritten posters, probably exhibited in those hotels and boarding houses most popular with British expatriates and tourists. All other candidate witnesses were nominated to Chads by Wilks or Hamilton.

In a letter delivered two days before he formally presented his own charges, and sounding very much like the prosecutor he wanted to be, Wilks wrote to Chads on September 9 that he "proposed to call" four more witnesses in addition to the twenty-nine he'd named earlier. His finished roster was the obvious product of several days determined research to identify the players on the beach Saturday night. An outsider in Boulogne on a short visit, Wilks must have scurried about furiously to recruit quickly so many strangers to describe their experiences, dramatic stories he hoped would substantiate his critique of Hamilton's performance.

Most of his nominees were Frenchmen who worked on or near the water: François Huret and the ten crew members of his pilot boat, the three who had

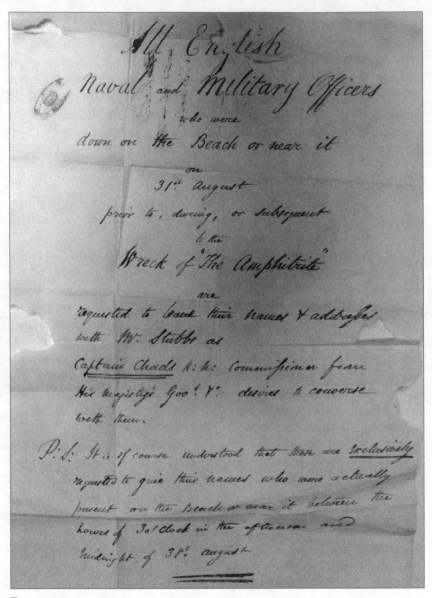

FIG. 22

Captain Chads' poster soliciting eyewitnesses to the wreck of *Amphitrite* from among British officers living in Boulogne. The announcement's postscript clarified that "it is of course understood that those are *exclusively* requested to give their names who were actually present on the Beach or near it between the hours of 3 o'clock in the afternoon and midnight of 31st August."

NATIONAL ARCHIVES OF THE UNITED KINGDOM, REF. ADM 1/1688.

carried the survivors ashore, and the four who'd staffed the Humane Society shack that night. Among the others, five were fellow guests at Barry's hotel. Two prospective witnesses nominated by Wilks declined to testify, although one of them, Sarah Jeffreys, did submit a deposition. In between her lines, it is possible to winkle out a mild critique of Hamilton.

If Wilks were smart and not merely cunning, he knew that his case against the consul was going to be difficult to prove even if his witnesses dutifully verified the details in his charge sheet. The merits of Wilks' case against the consul aside, Hamilton was playing on his home court with all the personal contacts and professional credits that more than ten years living and working on the rue des Vieillards gave him in any controversy with a transient foreigner. Moreover there was much that united Chads and Hamilton. It's not difficult to imagine a past in which Hamilton had been spared French capture and captivity, continued to serve in the Royal Navy, and turned out in middle age to be very much like the man investigating his performance of duty.

Against this all Wilks had to energize his suit was the public outrage he was working to foment. The emotional focus among expatriates in Boulogne, however, fixed not on Hamilton's performance but on prompting changes to French law, which they feared without amendment guaranteed human tragedies after every wreck. For their part the city's relatively few French citizens engaged in current events sought to rein in overbearing douaniers, not to discipline the British consul. Across the strait in England the popular focus was likewise less on what the consul had or had not done but either on purifying the flawed, and perhaps corrupt, mechanics of chartering convict transports or (for a small group of reformers philosophically opposed to transportation) on discrediting the entire system that exiled unfortunates. Excepting Wilks' shrill, solo voice, there developed in late summer 1833 no call in either country for Hamilton's head.

Still, given how England worked in the 1830s, Wilks didn't need a constituency to succeed. All he needed was Lord Palmerston to agree, but after his first letter to the foreign secretary, the way to Palmerston turned out to be through Captain Chads. It didn't help Wilks that Chads quickly discovered from several sources at least two of his specific accusations were false (that Saturday morning Hamilton had been disinterested in the fate of the Friday night packet and that Saturday evening, while *Amphitrite* was dying on the beach, the consul was at a party).

Hamilton countered Wilks' accusations with his written defense on September 14, identifying twenty-nine people by name as "proofs" of events as he described them in his chronology of Saturday night. Fluent in French and a familiar face in town and on the waterfront, Hamilton would have had no problem collecting people to speak to Chads under oath in his support.

The men and women he proposed came from across the spectrum of resident Britons and local citizens: former members of Parliament, retired officers, and civilians on one side; public officials in uniform and out, men from the professions, crafts, and trades, fishermen, members of his household staff, and even a few filling unskilled jobs on the margins of the economy on the other. Hamilton also identified eight serving or retired British officers to Chads among his prospective witnesses, a list of Royal Navy veterans led by Admiral Sir Willoughby Lake, KCB (a five-year resident of the city) that included three other flag officers, a captain, and several lieutenants.

Chads finished his assessment on Wednesday, September 18, and reported his conclusions in a letter to Elliot the same day.[12] Earlier he'd described his investigation of Captain Hunter as attentive to even small detail. This final report he characterized as "most diligent and patient." Chads extracted four specific charges against Hamilton from Wilks' public and private—they amounted to the same thing—accusations, and he quickly dismissed all four.

His key finding was that "the loss of a single life cannot be attributed to the want of conduct in the Consul." Hamilton, Chads concluded, had "quitted his house for the beach" at 8:15 PM, soon after learning about the calamity, was "on the beach before the ship went to pieces," and in good time to watch *Amphitrite*'s last hours in fading twilight. Not until bodies began to wash ashore, did the consul or anyone else realize that the ship had been carrying passengers. Hamilton then remained on the beach until past 2:00 AM Sunday, "rendering such assistance as he could on so distressing an occasion."

"From the foregoing established facts," Chads wrote Elliot, "I beg to state as my conscientious opinion, that William Hamilton, Esq., His Majesty's Consul, is most fully and entirely exonerated from all and every charge and imputation made against him, and I feel it my duty further to add, that the testimonials of his conduct as a public officer reflect great credit upon him." In a postscript that suggests Chads was a man of some natural grace, he added that "the Consul does not know of my opinion as now given, and I would remark that he is naturally under some anxiety."

Relieving the anxiety of others came to his mind, too:

> In conclusion of this most melancholy subject, I beg leave to add as some consolation to the relations and friends of the unfortunate sufferers that they may be assured all was done to save and restore life— that medical aid was not wanting, there having been to the credit of the gentlemen of that profession in this place not less than seven giving their assistance. The convenience and comforts of the Marine Hotel were immediately thrown open . . . and there were some of our own countrywomen, Mrs. Austin, Mrs. Curtis, Mrs. Jeffreys, Miss

Hawes, with their servants who . . . not withstanding the horror and heart rending scene that had suddenly burst upon them, undertook all the offices of most kind and tender nurses.

Consul Hamilton's absolution came in two parts, preliminarily from Chads in September and finally near the end of October via Undersecretary of State John Backhouse, the latter expressing to Hamilton Lord Palmerston's satisfaction with the results of the investigation. The consul's response to Backhouse was heartfelt, if a bit greasy:

I trust that I shall be pardoned for stating that the formal inquiry into the circumstances of that distressing event, by affording a public opportunity of vindicating my character from accusations, the utter injustice of which must have been well known to those who proffered them, has been to me the best consolation for the mental disquietude under which I necessarily laboured, and I beg to advise his Lordship that the present expression of his satisfaction will stimulate my exertions to deserve his future approbation.

Captain Chads' exoneration of Hamilton, *Amphitrite*'s senior officers, and French officials on the beach was not universally admired. "Junius Redivivus," in a letter to the *Examiner*'s editor three weeks later, on October 9, 1833, spoke anonymously for the captain's critics. "The public are not contented with the report of Captain Chads," Junius Redivivus wrote. "He is a man of Tory principles; and one of the axioms of Tory as well as Whig faith, is to screen all public servants from punishment due to misconduct":

A scene of hideous and unnecessary horror has been enacted, and, as usual, nobody is to blame. The French douaniers did their duty in pushing drowning people back into the waves; the Consul did his duty, in being absent from the spot; the Captain did his duty, in not suffering the prisoners to land; and the surgeon did his duty, in keeping them on board. . . . It is no light matter and no light imputation, when such a waste of human life has occurred. All may be straight forward, but the public would like to see the evidence, in order to use their own judgment upon it.

Whoever he was, Junius Redivivus' frustrated complaint, that horrible things had happened yet no one was responsible, would be echoed after every one of the transport shipwrecks to come.

64

The usual fate of bodies discovered on the beaches of the Pas-de-Calais after a shipwreck was a quick stripping by the first man to find the corpse and hasty concealment in the dunes. This customary practice offended the prefet of the department, who in mid-February 1843 wrote his subordinate at Boulogne that it was immoral and showed a lack of respect for the dead. He asked that such "disappearances" be stopped.[13] *Amphitrite*'s many dead were buried with more ceremony, but it's certain they had all been subjected to the same surreptitious frisking on the sand that was to attract the prefet's criticism ten years later.

The ship's anonymous dead first appeared in the burial register of the English Chapel in Boulogne on September 2, next to Reverend James Lindsey's handwritten notation that fifty-eight women, two men, and four children "drowned in the wreck of the Amphitrite—Augst 31," were interred that day. The sixty-four followed by nearly two months the most recent interment of an expatriate English resident of Boulogne, one Mary Dowling, John Dowling's wife, dead at sixty-one presumably from natural causes.

The last of *Amphitrite*'s convicts and crew to be found were buried in the English Cemetery nearly seven weeks later, October 17: two men, two women, and a child. Two days later Elizabeth Sarah Morgan, John and Sarah Morgan's nine-month-old daughter and among the least of Boulogne's British expatriates, went into the same ground. These two funerals, of Mary Dowling and tiny Elizabeth Morgan, spanned those of the shipwreck victims. In between several other residents came to the natural ends of their lives. Eliza Murray, fifty-one, wife of the Honorable Charles Murray, was buried on September 6. Florence, two, of no last name (she was the illegitimate daughter of someone whose name was obscured in the record) was buried September 20, as were Susan Bowles, forty-three, and Jane Seaton, thirty-six, on September 21 and October 15, respectively. Those from the ship interlaced with those from the city on Lindsey's register.

Nearly fifty of *Amphitrite*'s dead were never found. It's possible that some bodies washed up elsewhere on the French coast and either were not discovered or were never associated with the wreck at Boulogne. Eighty-five, including five children and two boys, lie in Boulogne. The last two mentioned were older children or perhaps the youngest members of the crew. These five, or seven, represent the only firm count there is of children on board the luckless vessel and it is almost certainly incomplete, perhaps by nearly half.

The adult bodies included those of eight men. Owen and Towsey identified four: Surgeon-Superintendent Forrester, the second mate, the cook, and a seaman. The four were laid in the cemetery on September 3, in one of the two trenches excavated for the common graves for those drowned in the storm.

FIG. 23

Monument to *Amphitrite*'s dead. Photograph by Susan Jampoler, August 2009. This obelisk stands in what was in 1833 the Cimetière des Anglais in Boulogne, just beyond the castle at the eastern corner of the city wall, a short walk via the Gayole Gate from the chapel of the Church of England. It's no longer surrounded by the graves of expatriates who died in Boulogne. The memorial monument was erected twenty years after *Amphitrite*'s dead were interred. Its incised text, now barely legible, reads in French, "Here lie the bodies of 82 unfortunate [victims] of the English ship Amphitrite, grounded on the Boulogne coast August 31, 1833." In the 1930s the monument was enclosed by a wrought-iron fence encompassing a plot much too small to contain the common graves of the dead. The fence has since been removed, but the surrounding open space is still very small.

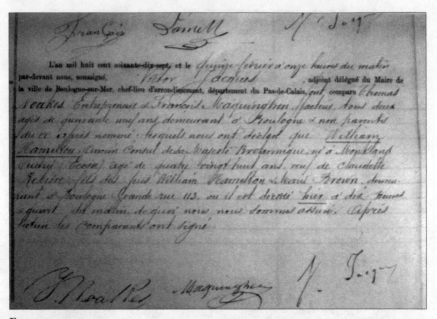

FIG. 24

Consul William Hamilton's death certificate. Photograph by Agnès Caboche, January 2010. After sixty-two years of marriage, Claudette Hamilton predeceased her husband by fewer than twelve months. She died in April 1876 in her early eighties, he the following February 14, at age eighty-eight. Both Hamiltons long survived Admiral Henry Ducie Chads, dead April 7, 1868, after two months ill with bronchitis, whose investigation had saved Hamilton's honor and also his livelihood. Hamilton died at 10:15 in the morning at 133 Grande rue, not far from the family's old home on the rue des Vieillards. (Once the Argentine consulate in Boulogne, 133 Grand rue is now a museum honoring General José de San Martin.) Hamilton's death certificate was witnessed by the mayor's deputy assistant and two local businessmen. It is possible that he was the last living British prisoner held by the French during the Napoleonic Wars. COURTESY VÉRONIQUE DELPIERRE, ARCHIVES DE BOULOGNE.

Forrester's wife, who if she could doubtless would have objected to eternity in the close company of female convicts, either didn't float to shore, or did but was not recognized.

In late November Hamilton sent a dispatch to the Foreign Office inquiring how the cost of the funeral in Boulogne (amounting to 1,553 francs and 35 centimes, roughly £62 or less than £1 per person) was to be booked. The reply said the amount should be included in the consulate's current account, after first being converted to pounds sterling at the average rate of exchange for the year as prescribed by the relevant Foreign Office circular dated March 18.

"A regulation," the letter's author at the Foreign Office sniffed, "which you have omitted to attend to in your correspondences on this occasion."

Hamilton finally retired as Her Majesty Queen Victoria's consul in Boulogne-sur-Mer in 1873 at age eighty-five. On February 21 the *London Gazette* reported the queen was "pleased to direct Letters Patent to be passed under the Great Seal granting the dignity of a Knight of the United Kingdom of Great Britain and Ireland" to William Hamilton, Esq. The knighthood— adding him to a list of several other nineteenth-century "Sir William Hamiltons," including the first, the British diplomat in Naples famously cuck-olded by Admiral Horatio Nelson—commemorated a life in government ser-vice a full seven years longer than her record-breaking reign. Whether his knighthood was granted for achievement or merely for endurance, for a pro-fessional expatriate he had done remarkably well.

65

News about *Amphitrite* arrived in Australia in January 1834. That's when the colony's free and convict residents became aware of this first wreck of a hired convict transport and its dreadful loss of lives. The fact that the names of the lost were unknown caused great distress. The discovery prompted a predict-ably outraged editorial in the *Sydney Gazette*'s issue of January 24, a text that Sarah Austin could have ghost written:

> It makes the blood run cold to read of such horrors. If ever there was
> a *multiplied* murder, it was in the case of those helpless beings, whose
> lives might have been saved, but for the obduracy of their tempo-
> rary gaolers. A woman too—a *woman* was found, who advised that
> they should be abandoned to their fate, at the very moment when
> preservation was offered to them! It will not be believed in after-
> times—it will not be credited, that men & women could deliber-
> ately consign nearly two hundred of their fellow creatures . . . on
> the cold-blooded plea that they had no orders to save them. British
> humanity has hitherto been a theme of story and song. Henceforth,
> the word will become a mockery. The name of "Amphitrite" and her
> immolated human cargo must ever raise a blush on the cheek of a
> true-hearted Englishman. The oppressor & the oppressed are now no
> more; but the frailties of the latter will in future days be counted as
> nought when contrasted with the barbarity of the former.

Eighteen thirty-three was the deadliest year in the transportation of British convicts to Australia and Tasmania since the atrocious passage of the

Second Fleet in 1790. But there was worse to come. In 1835, 139 drowned in the wreck of the transport *George the Third* on April 12, 127 of them male convicts. Nearly 230 others died on May 13 and during the days that followed, most of them women and children, from among the 241 sailing in the female convict transport *Neva*. Finally, when the transport *Waterloo* parted her anchor lines and blew aground near Capetown, South Africa, on August 28, 1842, 172 men (including 143 convicts), 4 women, and 14 children drowned in the storm-driven ranks of breakers that filled the sea between the ship and the beach. Four tragedies in less than ten years—more than 550 lives lost at sea, nearly half of them women and children.

A certain Mrs. Martin, wife of one of the soldiers of *George the Third*'s embarked army guard detachment, lived through the first wreck. Her survival was specially noted by an admiring press because, in the great tradition of such reporting, she was said to have clung resolutely to life atop the flotsam for two days with an infant at each breast (one of the babes was not hers but was born and soon orphaned during the crossing) and a third child clasped between her knees. No such uplifting story, true or false, emerged later from *Neva*'s extended agony or *Waterloo*'s sudden destruction.

The masters of *George the Third* and *Neva* had blundered tragically, running their commands up on rocks in good weather after months at sea and not far from their destinations. Although otherwise the two catastrophes were nothing alike, there was another common element in the wrecks: Captains William Moxey of *George the Third* and Benjamin Peck of *Neva* were apparently taking their sailing directions from James Horsburgh's *India Directory; or Directions for Sailing to and from the East Indies, China, New Holland, Cape of Good Hope, Brazil, and the Interjacent Ports.*[14] Neither ship was carrying the first edition of the Admiralty's encyclopedic local sailing directions, *The Australia Directory*, published in 1830. Moxey, during the investigation, conceded that he "was not aware that there was a book of sailing instructions for navigating the coast of the Australian colonies."

George the Third's passage to Van Diemen's Land with 308 on board—convicts, crew members, a detachment of guards from the Fiftieth Regiment of Foot (the Queen's Own) and 23 of their family members—was the first trip to the colony for the master and his ship, and a troubled one long before her wreck. Six weeks out, a fire in her after-hold near the magazine threatened, before it was swiftly doused, to blow up the ship. Later, when *George the Third* rounded South Africa, scurvy made its first appearance. Then, about the time she came abeam Australia from the west, victims of the disease started going over the side into the water.

Early April 12, passing Tasmania's southern cape with fifty or sixty ailing convicts on board for whom they could do nothing, Captain Moxey and

Surgeon-Superintendent David Wyse agreed that the fastest possible passage into Hobart Town was essential. Moxey opted to approach the port with caution. Sailing slowly under double-reefed topsails with the foresail braced up, frequently casting the lead line, and with anchors ready to let go, he elected to go north through the D'Entrecasteaux Channel, instead of via the usual, more easterly route through Storm Bay.[15] "One great inducement to proceed up the D'Entrecasteaux Channel," *The Times* quoted Moxey as testifying, "was to get to Hobart-town with the least possible delay, from the dreadful and increasing sickness on board and total want of every sort of nourishment. The mortality amongst the prisoners was dreadful; we buried five men in one day."

The destruction of *George the Third* just after 10:00 PM some fifty miles south of her destination on a submerged rock was the result of the officers' decision to take this short cut, combined with Moxey's reliance on an imperfect chart and upon Horsburgh's sailing directions, which said nothing about the obstruction. During the investigation that followed, it developed that the first volume of *The Australia Directory* did mention the rock, some dozens of square feet across and rising to within three feet of the surface. Soon after impact, "about the fifth shock," the mainmast went over the starboard side, carrying the mizzen topmast along with it; minutes later the main deck was completely under water.

There's a handsome oil painting of this wreck in the collection of the National Gallery of Australia done in 1850 by the Norwegian-born paroled convict Knut Bull: Several small, forlorn figures stand on a beach spotted with a few crates and barrels; behind them and just off shore a dismasted hulk lies aground on her port side, washed by huge waves as sinuous as sea snakes, all beneath a peaceful turquoise sky. Bull (1811–1889), sentenced to fourteen years for forgery and transported in 1846 in *John Calvin*, made a successful living as a painter in Tasmania during the 1850s. He apparently liked shipwreck paintings.

Bull painted two of the 1842 wreck of *Waterloo*. His source for their details would seem to have been impeccable. It was Dr. Henry Kelsall, surgeon in *John Calvin*, who had been in *Waterloo* when her voyage came to a sudden end. But evidently Bull had no such expert source to help with the details of the wreck of *George the Third*. The romantic scene he painted looks much more like the grounding of the transport *Hive* in Wreck Bay near Sydney than it does of *George the Third* atop a submerged rock approaching Hobart.

Thanks to her master's inept seamanship, the bark *Hive* grounded on December 10, 1835, a day or so out of port but so gently that only 1 of the more than 250 on board (most male convicts from Ireland) died during the subsequent evacuation of the ship. Later in the month gale winds finally finished off the beached ship, long after she'd been stripped of cargo, stores, and equipment.

Unlike *George the Third*, *Neva* had already once transported convicts to the colony, in 1833, and so had her master. *Neva*'s voyage was smoother than was *George the Third*'s; its end, however, was even more tragic. Out of Cork for Sydney on January 8, 1835, with 159 women and 55 children on board, *Neva* was on May 12 in the approaches to the western entrance of the Bass Strait, the obstruction-studded passage that connects the Indian Ocean to the Tasman Sea and separates Australia from Tasmania. Her slow and uneventful crossing had been marked by a few cases of scurvy, including one that, ironically, would soon contribute to the death of the surgeon-superintendent, the terminally unfortunate Dr. John Stephenson.

At approximately 5:00 AM on May 13, *Neva*, her master having ignored the cautions in Horsburgh's *Directory* about the dangers of proceeding at night, ran aground in clear weather and under a full moon upon one of the out-croppings of Harbinger's Reefs, inside the strait off the northern tip of King's Island. Bedlam followed as one after the other of *Neva*'s boats broke up dur-ing launch and their complement drowned. Her last moments, filled with nearly submerged women reaching with outstretched arms into the sea for the hands of their children, might have resembled those of *Amphitrite*. One hun-dred forty-five of the women in *Neva* drowned—one-quarter of all those lost between the sailing of the First Fleet and the arrival in 1853 of the last trans-port carrying women, *Duchess of Northumberland*.

The handful of survivors of the grounding, including at first Captain Peck, the first mate, twelve convicts, and eight sailors, camped out on the island for weeks subsisting on salvaged rum and fresh wallaby meat. Not until late June did news of *Neva*'s fate reach the colonies' chief settlements. A cascade of investigations and reports soon followed. Although no investigator then or since established exactly why and where off King Island *Neva* met her fate, all manner of contributing errors were uncovered, including failures to compen-sate adequately for the current and for compass error.

George the Third and *Neva* were the second and third ships to be lost in just over two years time, pounded apart while transporting convicts. Their quick destruction raised yet again accusations in London about the excessive age and poor condition of chartered transports passing through Deptford on their way to the convict colonies.

The dreadful news from the antipodes duly absorbed, on December 10 (coincidently the same day that *Hive* met her fate far away) *The Times* deliv-ered its diagnosis of error and call for an investigation as grandly as if the news-paper had viewed the two calamities from atop Mount Olympus. The losses of *George the Third* and *Neva*, *The Times* pronounced, had triggered "an almost universal demand for inquiry into the true case of these accidents, more strict and extended that any which could take place in a distant colony, where the truth, as everyone knows, might be easily suppressed, or the evidence warped so as to shift the responsibility on any parties but those to whom the real blame must belong."

Those dismissive slaps delivered, *The Times* went on to describe the transport contracting process as inherently corrupt:

The examinations should take place, not of the wretched survivors on these occasions, who are utterly unable in general to form a judgment of the sea-worthiness of any vessel, and who [have] not the courage to deliver their real opinion. If they have any, but of the whole system under which vessels are hired for this particular service. We have no doubt that the most culpable remissness does in this respect exist, and that vessels wholly unfit for the service are engaged. It is the general practice, we understand, to take the lowest tender, and though something like the form of a survey and report is gone through, there is not a practical man in the Captains' Room at Lloyd's who does not know that the whole proceeding is a farce.

And, *The Times* insisted, unsafe ships were being sent to sea:

In the brief report of an inquiry said to have been instituted on the spot, we are told that "no blame is attributable to the master, officers, crew, or indeed anybody else. The ship had been well found, and great kindness was shown to the poor creatures both before and after the wreck!" As if these circumstances had anything to do with the only important part of the inquiry, the sea worthiness of the Neva, which never seems to have presented itself to the minds of the parties. . . .When the present crazy class of ships run aground, scarcely a chance remains for the lives of those on board, though the shore may possibly be close at hand. . . .

The investigation at Hobart-town into the loss of George the Third showed that the ship was too old and frail to be chartered for so long a service; and in the last melancholy catastrophe there is more than ground for suspicion that the same defects existed.

"We trust," *The Times* concluded, "that no causes of a party nature will prevent the most strict enquiry into the present system of fitting out ships for the conveyance of convicts, now that so many dreadful disasters have apparently been produced by it."

Between May 1835 and the end of transportation in January 1868, a fifth convict transport was wrecked during her passage from Britain to the colonies.

She was the twenty-seven-year-old *Waterloo*, lost in Table Bay at the Cape of Good Hope in August 1842. Her wreck (in a crowded anchorage, simultaneously with that of a nearby troop transport, *Abercrombie Robinson*) and its horrific loss of life prompted the now-familiar outburst of editorial outrage, this time in the *South African Commercial Advertiser*, soon quoted in London.

Both vessels were driven to ground August 28 while at anchor at the mouth of the Salt River in weather that was described in apocalyptic terms: "It was raining in torrents, the forked lightning was blinding, the thunder was stunning. It was as dark as pitch." Some critics noted, however, that the weather had not been so bad as to drive any of the twenty or so other ships anchored in the bay onto the shore.

Abercrombie Robinson managed, remarkably, to get everyone to shore safely through the surf. Most of the survivors were soldiers of the reserve battalion of Her Majesty's Ninety-first Regiment of Foot, but four families of officers and eighty-four of the regiment's wives and children were also on board. Passengers' baggage and government stores were successfully offloaded during the next several days. All that was left for her master, John Young, to do was, as he wrote the owner, "put the ship for sale, as she now lies, for the general benefit" and to make his way to London.

The convict transport *Waterloo* went aground five hundred yards (a "double musket shot") away from *Abercrombie Robinson*. If the troopship's successful evacuation was a model of tight discipline and good order, *Waterloo*'s grounding was of hysteria and sheer bedlam, perhaps heightened because the captain was ashore. "She took the ground between eleven and twelve o'clock in the forenoon," the *Commercial Advertiser* described, "and in fifteen or twenty minutes became a mass of rubbish. And now ensued a most piteous massacre. In about two hours and a half, amidst the crumbling heaps of their perfidious prison—of men, women and children one hundred ninety four were crushed, disabled and drowned. There was no preparation for saving life made on board or ashore . . . [nothing] to show that the Government or people here had ever before heard of such a thing as a shipwreck."

"About 10 o'clock," an observer wrote, "the Waterloo gave a sudden lurch, and parted from all her anchors, and came broadside in amongst the breakers. . . . After two or three heavy rolls, her three masts went over the side with a dreadful crash. . . . About 11 o'clock, within half an hour after she struck, the Waterloo parted in two . . . within one hour and a half of the Waterloo striking, not a particle of her was to be seen. She had literally gone to pieces; and horrible to relate, out of 350 souls, 250 have met a watery grave."

Waterloo's convict dead were men, not women, but in most other respects this last catastrophe resembled *Amphitrite*'s. *Waterloo* also broke up in sight of hundreds, and her quick destruction in the surf immediately raised questions

about her seaworthiness, the contracting process that had selected her, and
the seamanship skills of her master, who had selected the anchorage.

66

In the end it was not corrupt contract practices sending a weary, runt transport to sea that were the root causes of *Amphitrite*'s destruction and the deaths
of almost all on board. Despite near automatic accusations of criminal behavior in the press, especially in *The Times*, substantially the same solicitation,
bid, and selection process, and the same ship surveys at the same Royal
Dockyard, had been (and would be through thirty-plus years into the future)
used to launch literally hundreds of other convict transports thousands of
miles to Australia and Tasmania. The record of success is extraordinary. Of all
those 779 voyages halfway around the world during more than eighty years,
you can count on the fingers of one hand the number of chartered ships that
were shipwrecked in transit. The 774 that did make it safely, both ways, suggest that there was no systemic problem. Although not "most perfectly safe,"
the convict transportation system, whatever its many other faults, was about
as safe as government and seamanship could make it in the eighteenth and
nineteenth centuries.

Chads and Le Cerf were correct. *Amphitrite*, Appledore-built and just over
thirty years old when Captain Hunter took her down the Thames for the last
time, was not at fault. Everyone on the beach at Boulogne that night was
also right. Up on the sand with her anchor down and the tide coming in,
Amphitrite was doomed, but not because she wasn't sound.

The public disbelief that met reports of ships swiftly destroyed when
aground reflected the ignorance of landlubbers about the magnitude of the
enormous forces at work and the inherent fragility of beached hulls. As successive waves collapsed around the ship, the energy that had propelled tons of
seawater toward the sands focused again and again on the boxy hull held fast in
the sand. No wooden vessel could survive long a beating by an immeasurable
quantity of seawater, every cubic foot of which weighed sixty-four pounds—
twice the weight of a round shot from the heaviest big gun.

Nor was the fault poor seamanship. William Moxey of *George the Third*,
Benjamin Peck of *Neva*, John Nutting of *Hive*, and Henry Ager of *Waterloo*—
especially Nutting and Ager, both of whom left their first mates in charge at
the crisis—were guilty of bad seamanship, and the latter two of criminally negligent leadership. John Hunter was not. Hunter's short cruise through an over-
powering storm might have, should have, ended much like Captain Young's of
Abercrombie Robinson did: with everyone safely ashore.

LOSS OF THE AMPHITRITE.

FIG. 25

"The Wreck of the Convict Transport Amphitrite, carrying women prisoners to Australia, at Boulogne Harbour in 1833." *Chronicles of the Sea* was a British weekly published on Saturdays beginning with issue 1 on January 6, 1838, and ending sometime in 1840 with No. 119. It sold for a penny. Each issue contained a half-dozen or so "faithful narratives of shipwrecks, fires, famines, and disasters incidental to a life of maritime enterprise," plus an occasional poem. "Shipwreck," wrote the editor in his preface to issue 1, is "a calamity against which there is the least resource, either to prevent its occurrence or lessen its effects; and where courage, skill, and patience are too often unavailing, except to protract a struggle with destiny, which at last proves to be irresistible." This half-page, entirely imaginary illustration of the wreck of *Amphitrite* appeared on the cover of issue 14, March 24, 1838.

What destroyed *Amphitrite* and drowned all but three on board was not any of these things. It was a lack of imagination.

Turner, together with the lesser artists who envisioned *Amphitrite*'s death in the Channel, and Bayly, and his fellow poets who described it in rhyme, had an advantage. Each of them was in his way describing the past. When first Huret and later Hénin came alongside *Amphitrite* during their bold attempts to warn Hunter of dreadful danger, they were dismissed by the captain, their messages ignored. And so Hunter, Forrester, and his fatally vain wife lost a chance to see clearly into their own future.

None of them could imagine their ship disintegrating under the pounding of the surf, her masts coming down, the poop torn off, and the deck awash with panic-stricken women clustered atop it in the instant before they and their children were swept into the water—exactly the vision that J. M. W. Turner had in his studio on Harley Street two years later, when he turned toward his easel and started to paint. They and 130 others died because of this failure.

ACKNOWLEDGMENTS

E leanor Finlay, of South Hobart, Tasmania, generously shared with me the research she did over many years on the women who rode *Amphitrite* to their deaths, and much else about this story. I'm indebted to her scholarship and her open-handed assistance.

Agnès Caboche of Boulogne-sur-Mer, France; Terry Lilley of Bromley, England; and John Stevenson of Edinburgh, Scotland, were also my partners in researching this story. Agnès diligently scoured her home city's municipal archives, its library (La Bibliothèque des Annonciades), and the records of Boulogne's Société Humaine des Naufrages to reveal the French perspective on what happened long ago. Terry helped yet again with the maritime and specifically naval aspects of the story. John unearthed court records and other sources in Scotland about his countrywomen who unwillingly played so prominent a part of *Amphitrite*'s last voyage. I am grateful to the three of them, as I am to Tracy Burk, of Burke, Virginia, who together with Agnès helped with translations from the French.

Dr. Joost Bierens (VU University Medical Center, Amsterdam), Jim Burk (Burke, Virginia), Michael Roe (Professor Emeritus, University of Tasmania, Hobart), and Virginia Wood (Humanities and Social Sciences Division, Library of Congress, Washington, D.C.) kindly read all or important parts of the manuscript in draft, as did Lea Finlay. Their comments have improved it. The errors and flaws that remain are mine.

My thanks are also due to the following people, each of whom contributed to telling *Amphitrite*'s story: Emilie Bremond-Poulle (University of Paris), Bill Edwards-Bodmer (Mariners' Museum Library, Newport News), Charles Brodine (Naval History and Heritage Command, Washington, D.C.), Robert Betteridge and Elaine Brown (National Library of Scotland, Edinburgh), Mary Buckingham (National Weather Service, NOAA), Patrick Claxton (Erie Maritime Museum and the brig *Niagara*), Alain Dannely (Société Humaine de Naufrages, Boulogne-sur-Mer), Véronique Delpierre (Archives Municipales de Boulogne-sur-Mer), Joan Dixon (Appledore Historical Society, Appledore, England), Alain Evrard (Le Portel, France), Bethan Gwonas (Dolgellau, Wales), Lona Jones (National Library of Wales, Aberystwyth), Robert Protheroe Jones (National Waterfront Museum, Swansea), Miriam Kelly (National Gallery of Australia), Otto Mayr (Lucketts, Virginia),

Iain MacKenzie (Admiralty Library, Portsmouth, England), Alain Montigny (Boulogne-sur-Mer), Jill Moore (Proudman Oceanographic Laboratory, Liverpool), Karen Pitts (National Library of Medicine, Bethesda, Maryland), Patrick Poison (Bibliothèque Municipale, Boulogne-sur-Mer), Cecilia Powell (Turner Society, London), Sheena Taylor (Carnegie Library, Ayr, Scotland), Daniel Tintillier (Boulogne-sur-Mer), Pat Widgett (North Devon Maritime Museum, Appledore, England), and Carol Young (Saltcoats, Scotland).

At the Library of Congress I was assisted by Mitsi Anders, Carol Armbruster, Jeffrey Bridgers, Georgia Higley, and Judith Robinson. Anita Barrett, Loudoun County Public Library's interlibrary loan associate, and the research librarians at the Rust Library in Leesburg, Karim Khan, Holly Peterson, Betsy Quin, and Oona Pilot, were generous with their help, too.

My wife, Suzy, passed up more amusing things to assist with research in archives and libraries in England, Scotland, and France. She also assembled the illustrations, maps, and charts.

The title and subtitle are from *Horrible Shipwreck!* a broadside published by Menzies of Lawnmarket, Edinburgh, the week after the wreck in 1833, and held in the collection of the National Library of Scotland, Shelfmark F.3.a.13 (126). The cover illustration, J. M. W. Turner's unfinished *Fire at Sea*, is reproduced with permission of the Tate, London. The extract from *The Fortune of War* by Patrick O'Brian, published by HarperCollins, Ltd., © 1979 by Patrick O'Brian, was reproduced by permission of Sheil Land Associates, Ltd. and of W. W. Norton and Company. The quotation from Steven Shapin in the *New Yorker* is used with his permission.

Andrew C. A. Jampoler
June 2010

NOTES

The chapter epigraphs are stanzas from "The Melancholy Loss of the *Amphitrite*," quoted in Hugh Anderson, *Farewell to Old England: A Broadside History of Early Australia* (Adelaide: Rigby, 1964), 151–53.

Chapter 1. Fire at Sea

1. Martin Butlin and Evelyn Joll, *The Paintings of J. M. W. Turner*, rev. ed. (New Haven: Yale University Press, 1984). Butlin's and Joll's two-volume, prize-winning, and pricey art history has been recognized since publication of the first edition in 1974 as the definitive catalogue of Turner's work in oil paint.
2. Although *Wreck of a Transport* suggests one, there was no timely rescue attempt from shore when *Minotaur* ran aground. The Dutch, at war with England in 1810, didn't appear until the morning after the disaster, too late to save anyone. The Haak Sands were a famous ship trap. At Christmas one year later, HMS *Hero*, another 74-gun ship, grounded in the same place, drowning all but eight of her crew, a toll even worse than *Minotaur*'s.
3. Simon Schama, "The Patriot," *New Yorker*, September 24, 2007.
4. *Descriptive and Historical Catalogue of the Pictures in the National Gallery* (London: Her Majesty's Stationery Office, 1889), 163.
5. Cecilia Powell, "Turner's Women: The Painted Veil," *Turner Society News* 63 (March 1993): 14.
6. Many in Great Britain continued to use "Botany Bay" as the generic name for the colony long after its relocation to Sydney.

Chapter 2. Crime and Punishment

1. Arthur Schrader, "'The World Turned Upside Down': A Yorktown March, or Music to Surrender by," *American Music* 16, no. 2 (Summer 1998): 180–216.
2. Charles Wilson Peale, more correctly his studio, painted a portrait of General Washington at Yorktown for the comte de Rochambeau, but this was a copy of Peale's painting of Washington after his triumph at Battle of Princeton with the details changed to relocate the scene from New Jersey to Virginia. David Hackett Fisher, *Washington's Crossing* (Oxford: Oxford University Press, 2004), 429.
3. War with France began in February 1778, with Spain in June 1779, and with Holland in November 1780. For shipping shortages and their effect on the ability of Great Britain to sustain the fighting, see Syrett, *Shipping and the American War*. "Thus," he concludes, "at the end of 1782 lack of shipping had brought the transport service to the edge of an abyss from which only peace could save it" (105).

4. In 1783 George III offered—threatened—to abdicate twice in favor of the Prince of Wales. Five years later he had his first bout with insanity, since the 1970s diagnosed as probably a symptom of porphyria, a rare, hereditary blood disease.

   In his review of *The Correspondence of King George the Third* that appeared in *New England Quarterly* 2, no. 1 (January 1929), historian S. E. Morison described the king as "a man of exemplary private life, limited intelligence, and tireless energy, who could never see more than one side of a question, and who regarded all who took the other side as bad men, ungrateful subjects, or even anarchists. George III meant well, but was prevented by his limitations and defects from doing well. He did his best for the country—including the colonies—according to his lights; but his best was not good and his lights were few and narrow" (161).

5. The long war against France strained the British economy to its limits. The first crisis came very early, in the spring of 1797, after a French-supported, American-led comic opera invasion of southwestern Wales near Fishguard Bay by 1,400 ruffians in captured uniforms triggered a panicky run on the Bank of England that forced the abandonment of the gold standard. After victory in 1815 the bank began edging warily back to gold by tightening interest and reducing the supply of bank notes. Its draconian measures worked, bolstering the pound sterling by eventually halving prices, but only at the expense of the elevated unemployment that accompanies deflation.

6. The German Hanover dynasty spanned nearly two hundred years of British history, 1714–1901, and encompassed the reigns of six monarchs: Georges I through IV, William IV, and George III's granddaughter, the long-service Queen Victoria.

7. West, *History of Tasmania* 2:109. West was a leader of the local movement opposing transportation, and his commentary was colored by this stance.

8. The text of the treaty is available on the Library of Congress Web site at http://mem ory.loc.gov/egi-bin/ampage?collid=1lsl&fileName=008/lis1008.db&recNum=93/.

9. 39 Eliz., cap. 4, passed in 1597, the thirty-ninth year of the queen's reign. All three usually defined in English Poor Law as able-bodied men who refused to work, as distinct from the unemployable (children, the aged, etc.) and the temporarily unemployed. Later laws relating to deportation or indentured servitude abroad included 18 Car. II, cap.3. and 12 Anne II, cap. 23, enacted in 1713. Four years later, in 4 Geo. I, cap. 2 and cap. 11, transportation was explicitly specified as a punishment.

10. After 1680 slave labor overwhelmed indentured servitude as a factor in the economy of the colonies. The more ready availability of African slaves in the 1700s, despite their relatively higher initial cost, was one factor in colonialists' easy rejection of continued drafts of former convicts from the British Isles. Between 1619, when the first twenty slaves were put ashore at Jamestown by the Dutch ship *White Lion*, and 1860, when the last decennial census was conducted before the Civil War, the population of slaves in the United States grew to 3.95 million men, women, and children, nearly 15 percent of the total population.

11. Even so, the number hanged, 7,000 of 35,000, was still large enough to put England far ahead of every other European state in the execution of its citizens. Of

those hanged in England and Wales between 1770 and 1830, two-thirds swung for committing crimes against property, not against persons. Only a fifth of the condemned were executed for murder or attempted murder. Gatrell, *Hanging Tree*, 7.

12. A small collection of malefactors' petitions from around 1730 held in the Corporation of London Records Office and discovered in 1988 by Kenneth Morgan suggests that many might have preferred whipping, branding, or any other punishment over expulsion to the colonies. Morgan, "Petitions against Convict Transportation," 110–13.

13. "An Act for the further preventing robbery, burglary, and other felonies, and for the more effectual transportation of felons . . . ," 1718, 4 Geo. 1, cap. 11. The act subsidized convict transportation for felons from London and seven neighboring counties at the rate of three pounds per convict.

14. "Freedom dues" were customarily paid by masters to their indentured servants at the end of contract terms. Masters and colonial legislatures often distinguished between servants who had volunteered to serve and those who had been transported, denying the latter dues that were paid to the former.

15. Morgan, *Benjamin Franklin*, 73–75. Franklin went through a cranky spell in 1751. In that same year he railed against the influx of Germans into Pennsylvania, fearing that his state "in a few years would become a German colony," filled with the "most stupid of their own nation."

16. A. Roger Ekirch, *Bound for America: The Transportation of British Convicts to the Colonies, 1718–1775* (Oxford: Clarendon Press, 1987).

17. From A. Roger Ekirch, "Great Britain's Secret Convict Trade to America, 1783–1784," *American Historical Review* 89, no. 5 (December 1984): 1285–91. Ekirch retells the story of the *George* and her human cargo in the epilogue to his *Bound for America*.

18. An attempt in late 1785 to import convicts into British Honduras by the same entrepreneurs, who had finally given up on Nova Scotia and the United States, failed in the face of settlers' resistance.

19. A short, mid-nineteenth-century description of the legislative and penitentiary histories of the hulks, from which this is drawn, is in "History of the Hulks," *Penny Cyclopædia of the Society for the Diffusion of Useful Knowledge* 25 (London: Charles Knight, 1844), 145–47.

20. Building on civil experience, hulks would later be used to hold French prisoners during the war with Napoleon. The Napoleonic Wars (1793–1815) produced a huge number of war prisoners. At the peak, the year before Waterloo, Great Britain held more than 80,000 former crew members from French navy ships and privateers. Until 1803, French captives were held in former Royal Navy hulks under navy control, but their growing numbers must have overwhelmed the number of surplus hulls available. After that year French sailors were confined in large camps in the interior and their officers were paroled to the countryside. N. A. M. Roger, *The Command of the Ocean* (New York: W. W. Norton, 2004), 501.

21. Edwin G. Burrows, *Forgotten Patriots: The Untold Story of American Prisoners During the Revolutionary War* (New York: Basic Books, 2008).

22. These and other statistics on the convict hulks are from Campbell, *Intolerable Hulks*.

23. Tasmania, then Van Diemen's Land, was first colonized in 1803. Roughly one-third of all convicts transported to Australia were sent there.

24. Andrew Tink, MP, before the NSW Assembly Australasian Study of Parliamentary Conference dinner, October 7, 2005.

25. Bewell, *Romanticism and Colonial Disease*, 11. See also Philip D. Curtin, "The End of the 'White Man's Grave'? Nineteenth Century Mortality in West Africa," *Journal of Interdisciplinary History* 21, no. 1 (Summer 1990): 63–70.

26. Banks inherited his father's estates and great wealth in 1761, after which he elected to use the money to support his fascination with natural history and science. In 1768, at twenty-five, he boarded *Endeavour* at the head of an eight-man team (and two pet greyhounds) determined to do science, for which privilege and accommodations he had paid some ten thousand pounds to the Admiralty. Only Banks and one other of the eight survived what was a fabulously successful collection expedition but dangerously lethal voyage.

27. Frank Lewis, "The Cost of Convict Transportation from Britain to Australia, 1796–1810," *Economic History Review*, 2nd ser., 41, no. 4 (1988): 507–24.

28. Henry Baynham, "Robinson, William (bap. 1787, d. in or after 1836)." *Oxford Dictionary of National Biography*, Oxford University Press, September 2004, http://www.oxforddnb.com/view/article/73929/ (accessed June 20, 2009).

29. [William Robinson], *Nautical Economy; or Forecastle Recollections of Events during the last War, Dedicated to the brave Tars of Old England by a Sailor, politely called by the Officers of the Navy Jack Nastyface* (Cheapside [London]: William Robinson, 1836), 56–60. Available as a Google book (http://books.google.com/).

30. Joseph Somes, later together with his sons, owned and operated the largest fleet of convict transports. Bateson, *Convict Ships*, 301.

31. Lang was also the author of *Transportation and Colonization*, from which this is drawn.

Chapter 3. His Majesty's Hired Transport *Amphitrite*

1. From Steven Shaplin's review of Stephen Johnson's *The Ghost Map: The Story of London's Most Terrifying Epidemic—and How It Changed Science, Cities, and the Modern World* (2006) in *New Yorker*, November 6, 2006.

2. Kerr, "1832 Cholera Epidemic in Ayr," 18.

3. Out of a population of 1.5 million. Creighton, *History of Epidemics in Britain* 2:821. New York City, with a population one-third as large as London's, saw 3,515 die of cholera in 1832. Seven other cholera pandemics arose between the 1830s and 1910. Not until 1854, thanks to the brilliant work of Dr. John Snow, was cholera recognized to be a water-borne disease.

4. Bateson, *Convict Ships*, 251–52.

5. Mawer, *Most Perfectly Safe*, 58.
6. The exhaustive two-volume study was written in 1891–94 by Dr. Charles Creighton (1847–1927), a Scottish physician and one-time lecturer at Cambridge. See especially vol. 2., chap. 9, "Asiatic Cholera," 793 et seq.
7. Kudlick, *Cholera in Post-revolutionary Paris*, 4.
8. Haines, *Life and Death in the Age of Sail*, 59–60.
9. By the mid-nineteenth century merchant ship owners in the United Kingdom were free to choose among three different measures of capacity for ship registration, those established by relevant parliamentary acts in 1773 ("builder's tonnage, old measure"), 1833, or 1854, all defining different units of tonnage.
10. ADM 37/8536.
11. Ration items included specific daily amounts of biscuit, fresh meat and vegetables, oatmeal, sugar, chocolate, and tea. When fresh food was not available, salt beef and pork, flour, and dried peas were substituted.
12. Oxley, *Convict Maids*, 125.
13. From "Facts Relating to the Condition and Treatment of Females Convicts on their Passage to Botany Bay," *The Times*, October 16, 1833, 5.
14. The British were not uniquely benighted in so far as the care of small children was concerned. Childhood everywhere in the late eighteenth and early nineteenth centuries was hard. Steven Mintz says that nine children age seven to twelve years old from Rhode Island comprised the entire labor force of the first textile mill in the United States. A few decades later, preteen door boys, driver boys, and breaker boys labored through long shifts in Pennsylvania coal mines in damp and near-complete darkness, while above ground young weavers put in fourteen-and-a-half-hour days. See Steven Mintz, *Huck's Raft: A History of American Childhood* (Cambridge: Belknap Press, 2004).
15. Young Frederick Engels put it in his first book, *The Condition of the Working Class in England in 1844*, published in 1845 in German and in 1887 in English.
16. The manifesto's translation first appeared in the *Red Republican*, a short-lived British socialist newspaper published by George Harney.
17. Although industrial child labor was investigated by Parliament in 1816 and again in 1819, the first real reform came years later in the 1833 Factory Act, passed after hearings chaired the year before by Michael Sadler, an MP from Leeds. His "Report of the Select Committee on Factory Children's Labour, 1831–1832" exposed horrific abuses of the very young on the factory floor. The 1833 act prohibited children under nine in textile factories and reduced the working week to forty-eight hours for children aged nine to thirteen. Thirteen to eighteen years olds were permitted to work twelve hours per day. See Clark Nardinelli, "Child Labor and the Factory Acts," *Journal of Economic History* 40, no. 4 (1980): 739–755.
18. The quoted phrases are from Rachel Vorspan, "Vagrancy and the New Poor Law in Late-Victorian and Edwardian England," *English Historical Review* 92, no. 362 (January 1977): 60.

19. From Appendix 2 to the *Instructions for Surgeons-Superintendent*, "Proportions of Particular Stores to be Provided for Convict Ships."

20. From Wilkes' *Narrative of the United States Exploring Expedition*, quoted by William Clark Russell in his *Betwixt the Forelands* (London: Sampson, Low, Marston, 1891), 152.

21. These scant details from the September 10, 1833, *Ayr Observer*, which published a paragraph reporting the wreck of *Amphitrite* and the death her master, native son John Hunter.

22. But even then scurvy was a consequence of careless inattention to diet, as the fate of many aboard the transport *George the Third* showed again in 1835.

23. The Lachlans were not done with the Hunters after *Amphitrite* sank. In 1834 Hunter's estate went into probate in Ayr, Scotland, the family's home. Joseph Lachlan the elder, a practicing solicitor in the west of Scotland and father of the London ship broker, served as the estate's lawyer.

24. ADM 101/68/9, December 2, 1831–June 8, 1832.

25. Burnett served until 1855 in the post, reporting directly to the Admiralty and retitled three times during the next twelve years, finally to "Director General of the Medical Department of the Navy." Burnett also served for a time as physician to King William IV.

26. ADM 6/186.

27. Many of these losses could be attributed to the pathologically wicked master of the *Neptune*, Donald Trail, whose ship alone counted for nearly two-thirds of the dead.

28. Mortality statistics from the appendices in Bateson, *Convict Ships*.

29. Richardson, *Pleasant Passage*, 65.

30. G. C. Cook, "Richard Dobson Kt MRCS (1773–1847) and the Inferior Status of Naval Medicine in the Early Nineteenth Century: End of the Fleet Physicians," *Notes and Records of the Royal Society* 59, no. 1 (2005): 35–43.

31. The authorized enlisted strength of the Royal Navy during the Napoleonic Wars topped out in 1810–12 at roughly 114,000 men. The navy's average authorized enlisted strength during the last year of the war was 72,500, down more than one-third from the peak years. The officer employment peak, 5,682, some 56 percent of which were lieutenants, came in the last year of the war. Masters (666), commanders (762), captains (824), and three grades of admirals (total 219) fleshed out the rest of the officer corps in 1815. In both cases maximum manpower levels came after the fleet had begun to dwindle in size. Royal Navy statistics from William Laird Clowes, *The Royal Navy: A History from the Earliest Times to the Present*, vols. 5 and 6 (London: Sampson Low, Marston, 1900 and 1901).

32. The long-lived New Monthly Magazine was published in London between 1814 and 1884 and edited during 1833 (when it was called the *New Monthly Magazine and Literary Journal*) by Samuel Carter Hall. Quotations about the wrecks of *Amphitrite* and of *Earl of Wemyss* from the magazine's "Commentaries" are from a digitized volume covering issues from the last third of 1833 available as a Google book.

33. That image and its accuracy, or inaccuracy, would open a rich vein of femi-
nist scholarship at the end of the twentieth century. See, for example, Damousi,
Depraved and Disorderly.

34. Average convict ages as calculated by Finlay in "Convict Women of the
Amphitrite," 123–24.

35. John Hunter Sr.'s will, among other items, is in the Glasgow Commissary
Court records, CC9/7/82, and Glasgow Sheriff' Court Inventories, SC 36/48/10,
and Janet Hunter's end-of-life documents are in Ayr Sheriff Court Inventory
Records, SC 6/44/20. All in National Archives of Scotland, Edinburgh.

36. Stephan Talty, *The Illustrious Dead: The Terrifying Story of How Typhus Killed
Napoleon's Greatest Army* (New York: Crown, 2009), 36.

37. Comte Philippe-Paul de Ségur, a French general on Napoleon's personal
staff, lived through and wrote about the debacle in a memoir that has become
the basis for all subsequent scholarship about the campaign. "On the sixth of
December, the day following the departure of the Emperor [Napoleon abandoned
the dregs of his army at Smorgorny, and his small party left for Paris in several carriages and sleighs]," he wrote,

> the sky became still more terrible. The air was filled with infinitesimal
> ice crystals; birds fell to the earth frozen stiff. The atmosphere was abso-
> lutely still. It seemed as if everything in nature having movement or life,
> down to the very wind, had been bound and congealed in a universal
> death. Now not a word, not a murmur broke the dismal silence, silence
> of despair and unshed tears.
>
> We drifted along in this empire of death like accursed phantoms.
> Only the monotonous beat of our steps, the crunch of the snow, and
> the feeble groans of the dying broke the vast mournful stillness. . . .
> The soldiers who had been most resolute until then lost heart com-
> pletely. At times the snow opened up under their feet. . . . It was as
> if this hostile earth refused to carry them any longer, laid snares for
> them in order to hamper them and retard their flight, and so deliver
> them up to the Russians, who were still on their trail, or to their terrible
> climate. (Count Philippe-Paul de Ségur, *Napoleon's Russian Campaign*
> [New York: Time-Life Books, 1965], 268)

38. Steven Englund, *Napoleon: A Political Life* (New York: Scribner, 2004), 417.

39. ADM 12/27F, Court Martial No. 1,280.

40. Forrester's letters about Byron are quoted at length in Medwin's odd *Angler
in Wales* 2:198–214, following this introduction of the surgeon: "Forrester, however, afterwards surgeon on board the Convict ship lost off Boulogne, poor fellow!
wrote two very interesting letters describing a visit to [Byron] at Missolonghi, a
few weeks before Byron's death." The letters are unsourced and there is no indication to whom they were written. Medwin's biographer credits the Forrester letters

as being "some of the best pages in Medwin's book." See also Bewell, *Romanticism and Colonial Disease*, 129.

41. James Forrester's examination status from a letter to Eleanor Finlay from the Royal College of Surgeons of England of October 19, 1989. The details of Forrester's subsequent navy career are from "Surgeons Vol. II Part II pp. 178–415," ADM 104/15, National Archives, Kew, England.

42. *Amphitrite* was smaller than every other transport vessel except the 146-ton brig *Experiment*, which carried her crew of twelve and sixty convicts from Cork to New South Wales via Rio de Janeiro in early 1809.

43. The June 28, 1895, issue of the *New York Times* reported that "the armored coast defense vessel" USS *Amphitrite*'s sea trials, conducted by Commodore Thomas Selfridge the day before, were highly successful, although "some disappointment was expressed by the [inspection] board that the ship showed only seven knots speed, although designed for ten knots."

44. For the second USS *Amphitrite*, see John D. Alden, *The American Steel Navy* (Annapolis: Naval Institute Press, 2004), 93–94.

45. The last named, George Lyall Sr. (1779–1853), was also the most distinguished. In addition to his private shipping interests, presidency of the Shipowners Society in the 1820s, and directorship of the New Zealand Company (a wool and flax promotion joint stock company), Lyall was also a director of the East India Company during the 1830s and 1840s, and the chairman of that company's board for several years in the 1840s. Off and on during the same two decades, Lyall held a seat in the House of Commons as a member from the City of London. His memory lives on in place names near Wellington, New Zealand.

46. Mawer, *Most Perfectly Safe*, 34.

47. *Select Committee on Causes of Shipwrecks*, Art. 12.

48. Mawer, *Most Perfectly Safe*, xiii.

Chapter 4. The Convicts

1. From *Orders and Regulations for the Army—1837*, quoted in Clem Sargent, "The British Garrison in Australia 1788–1841, Guard Detachments on Convict Transports," *Sabretache* 42 (September 2001): 33–38.

2. Bateson, *Convict Ships*, 134–39. The New South Wales Corps was commissioned expressly for service in Australia. Its soldiers, Robert Hughes explained, "were poor stuff even by the current low standards of the British Army. Most of them were scum, and they found service in New South Wales the best alternative to beggary or crime. Few of the officers were better than the men." Robert Hughes, *The Fatal Shore* (New York: Alfred A. Knopf, 1987), 105. That "scum" is an apt description has since been challenged, but the corps' officers were arguably a bigger leadership problem than the men. Awarded large land grants, assigned convict labor, and able to trade for their own account, New South Wales Corps officers became a powerful economic force in the colony, a sometime rival to its appointed political leadership.

3. From one of the collection of broadsides at the National Library of Scotland, Edinburgh. Shelf mark F.3.a.13(77).
4. Damousi, *Depraved and Disorderly*, 9–11.
5. West, *History of Tasmania* 2:116.
6. Beddoe, *Welsh Convict Women*, 16–20.
7. Kay Daniels, *Convict Women* (Sydney: Allen and Unwin, 1998), 43.
8. Damousi, *Depraved and Disorderly*, 35.
9. Finlay's excellent monograph, "Convict Women of the *Amphitrite*," 119–30, is the only scholarly study focused on the women lost when *Amphitrite* broke up.
10. Fry's flattering description is by Lady Jane Franklin, the second wife of the star-crossed Arctic explorer, who met Fry before the Franklins left for the convict colony on Van Diemen's Land, where he was to be governor. Lady Franklin's husband, Sir John, would later vanish mysteriously in Arctic Canada while commanding a two-ship expedition searching for the Northwest Passage. The disappearance of both vessels and their crews after August 1845 eventually triggered dozens of futile search and rescue expeditions.
11. "Opium-eating" was neither a crime nor a vice in early-nineteenth-century England, and Fry had a lot of company in her addiction. Laudanum, tincture of opium, was an ingredient in virtually all patent medicines of the era, from the "drowsy syrups" casually administered to colicky children to quiet them to the specifics for any number of adult diseases and conditions, including migraines, fevers, diarrhea, and cholera. So common was its use, and so powerful were its effects on the senses, that Martin Booth argues the European Romantic Revival, a European literary movement roughly between 1775 and 1835, was fueled by laudanum's warping of perception and the imagination. Samuel Taylor Coleridge was probably laudanum's most famous beneficiary and victim. The addiction finally killed him in 1834, after fourteen years of illuminating his poetry, about the time the idea that opiates were harmless began to be questioned. Martin Booth, *Opium: A History* (New York: St. Martin's Press, 1996).
12. Elizabeth Fry, *Observations on the Visiting, Superintendence, and Government of Female Prisoners* (London: John and Arthur Arch, 1827). Newgate Prison's Governor Wortner told the *Morning Post* that there were thirty-nine convicts from his prison on board *Amphitrite* when she broke up. *Morning Post*, September 13, 1833, p. 3.
13. AD 14/33/39 and JC 26/1833/53, National Archives of Scotland, Edinburgh.
14. Beddoe, *Welsh Convict Women*, 128. The other sixteen women from Wales convicted of transportable offenses during the course of 1833 who actually shipped out for Australia were parceled out into four other transports, *Edward, William Bryan, Numa,* and *Buffalo,* all of which made port safely.
15. The "act" is a reference to "An Act for the Better Regulating the Business of Pawnbroking," 39 & 40 Geo. III, cap. 99.

Chapter 5. Underway in Thick Weather

1. Merchant shipbuilding on the Thames, always a boom and bust business, also fell on hard times after the mid-1860s. Economic cycles aside, the Isle of Dog's great distance from sources of essential raw materials eventually became a handicap that even ingenuity and hard labor could not overcome. London's East End yards had dominated English shipbuilding for decades, but once iron ships replaced wooden ones, yards on the Thames quickly lost contracts to competitors on Scotland's Clyde River and on its northeast coast that had the good fortune to be located closer to iron and coal mines.

2. *Royal River*, 316.

3. The tide rose nearly six meters, nineteen feet, at Woolwich twice a day, some two hours later than high water at the mouth of the Thames. On August 25, 1833, low water was at 2:24 AM and 3:18 PM; high water came at 9:10 AM and 9:57 PM. Hunter would not have left his anchorage to set off downriver after dark, so an evening departure seems unlikely. Predicted hindcast tides from the Proudman Oceanographic Laboratory, Liverpool, England. In early 1833 the Admiralty published a tide prediction table for London and the naval dockyards at Sheerness, Portsmouth, and Plymouth. A comparison of predicted versus observed tides for that year is in Paul Hughes and Alan Wall, "The Admiralty Tidal Predictions of 1833: Their Comparison with Contemporary Observation and Modern Synthesis," *Journal of Navigation* 57 (2004): 203–14.

4. Thursfield, *Five Naval Journals*, 8.

5. Noire, *New British Channel Pilot*. The Port of London extended from London Bridge to the North Foreland at the mouth of the Thames. The port operated under the traffic management of Trinity House Corporation, since 1513 responsible for river navigation.

6. Information on time of day, sails aloft, wind direction, and ship position is from the survivors depositions and from "The Shipwreck," *United Service Journal and Naval and Military Magazine* 3 (1833): 149–59. "The whole of this paper," the unnamed author of the article says about his sources, "is the result of many inquiries, and in many places an actual copy of the written statement made by Mr. [James] Towsey, one of the three survivors. It has been read to him, and is confirmed by his testimony given to the British consul here."

7. *United Service Journal and Naval and Military Magazine*, 1833, pt. 3, 151.

8. Chambers didn't think much of Winstanley. He went on to describe the architect and builder of the lighthouse famous in song as amusing "himself with the curious but useless mechanical toys that preceded our modern machinery and engineering, as alchemy and astrology preceded chemistry and astronomy. . . . The lighthouse was just such a specimen of misapplied ingenuity as might have been expected from such an intellect."

9. Approaching a hundred years after a modest start in a London coffee house in the 1680s, seventy-nine Lloyd's underwriters had joined together in the Society of Lloyd's, becoming the world's largest and most successful marine insurance group. The society's leading position as a central marketplace for private insurance

underwriters remained unchallenged for the next two centuries, until five consecutive years of billion dollar–plus losses beginning in 1988 forced a fundamental restructuring.

10. "Nautical Magazine, &c.," *Nautical Magazine* 20, no. 20 (October 1833): 623. *Amphitrite* was first on the *Nautical Magazine*'s list of the "important particulars." The *Earl of Wemyss* wrongly identified as a steamer, was second, and then followed a long list of ships known to have foundered, capsized, run aground, been dismasted, or otherwise suffered in the great gale.

The *Nautical Magazine* began publication in 1832 under its editor, then Captain (later Rear Admiral) Alexander Bridport Becher, RN, who since 1823 had been employed in the Admiralty's hydrographic office, where he would serve for another thirty-two years. Becher was the magazine's editor for nearly forty years. At first the magazine was subsidized by the government in recognition of its utility to mariners. Among its articles was the first exposition of the Beaufort Scale. Becher was also the author of several books, most notably *Navigation of the Atlantic Ocean; With an Account of the Winds, Weather, and Currents Found Therein Throughout the Year*. The fourth edition, published in 1883, is available as a Google book.

11. *The True Causes of the Numerous Wrecks of Merchant Shipping Clearly Explained . . . by a Surveyor of Shipping* (Kirkcaldy: Reid & Son, 1832).

12. Mowat and the Forth Ports Authority, *Port of Leith*, 336.

13. In 1896 Rudyard Kipling set their sacrifice to rhyme and dialect in a stanza of "Soldier an' Sailor, Too," his tribute to the Royal Marines. The reference is something of a non sequitur in that only four marines were aboard *Birkenhead* when she sank.

The *Birkenhead*'s distant example might have shaped the response to catastrophe of some of the male passengers and crew sailing in RMS *Titanic* sixty years later. The gross survival rates of the women and children riding *Titanic* after she hit the iceberg (74 and 52 percent, respectively) were much higher than that of men (20 percent). Significantly, despite what James Cameron's blockbuster 1997 movie depicted, class had less to do with survival than did gender: women in third class survived in a higher percentage than did men in first class. Indeed, some of the world's wealthiest and most powerful men elected to die rather than to co-opt a seat in the lifeboats. Some others did not, and their craven actions survive as the basis of the legend that endures today.

14. Quoted in Bernard Phillips, "Shipwreck at Brancaster," http://www.northcoastal.co.uk/shipwreck.htm/.

15. From "Verses on the Loss of the Amphitrite Female Convict Ship, in Boulogne Harbour, September 1833," *Court Magazine and Belle Assemblée* 3:129. The *Court Magazine and Belle Assemblée* was published from 1832 to 1837 as the successor to *Bell's Court and Fashionable Magazine, Addressed Particularly to the Ladies*, published from 1806 until 1832 and a strong contender for the century's most awkwardly titled magazine. After 1837 the magazine was renamed the *Court Magazine and Monthly Critic*. Each of these popular ladies' magazines included fiction, verse, articles, reviews, and fashion news.

16. "La pluie était avidement demandée par les habitants de nos plaines, dont les mares sont depuis longtemps taries par la sécheresse," le *Mémorial dieppois*, September 2, 1833.

17. Alexander McKee, *Death Raft* (London: Souvenir Press, 1975). With that bit of wisdom, McKee launched into his story of the destruction of *Medusa*, a leading candidate to retire the title of "Most Horrific Shipwreck." The chief competitor to *Medusa* for this tragic distinction, skipping back two centuries and *Amphitrite* aside, was the loss of the Dutch East Indiaman *Batavia*, run aground in June 1629 onto Morning Reef, west of Australia, during a crossing from the Netherlands to Java. Shipwreck led swiftly to mutiny and to a complete collapse of social order among the survivors, ending in human degradation and hellish suffering otherwise imaginable only in a Hieronymus Bosch painting. See Mike Dash's *Batavia's Graveyard* (New York: Crown, 2002).

Chapter 6. Boulogne-sur-Mer

1. It's also possible that Caesar's second invasion of Britain was launched not from Boulogne but from Wissant, some fourteen miles north, toward Cap Gris Nez. Being able clearly to see your destination from the place must also have been the reason that in 1785 the French balloonist Pilâtre de Rozier selected Boulogne for his flight to Dover on June 15, in what was to be the first Channel crossing attempt from France to England. The hydrogen balloon at the top of his complicated, two-part rig caught fire almost immediately after lift-off. In the ensuing crash both riders died, de Rozier in sight of his horrified fiancée.

2. Exactly one hundred years later, Willem of Orange proved that a successful amphibious invasion of the British Isles was possible in modern times, at least if it were unopposed. (Although Willem, soon King William III, crossed the Channel fully prepared to fight, he didn't need to, much. James II's Catholic absolutism—copied from that of Louis XIV—was so unpopular that he was soon tipped from his throne in a not-altogether-bloodless revolt.) A Franco-Spanish attempt in the summer of 1779 to duplicate Willem's success collapsed under its own weight.

3. From Fernand Nicolay, *Napoleon at the Boulogne Camp*, trans. Georgina L. Davis (London: Cassell, 1907), 239.

4. Stanfield, *Stanfield's Coast Scenery*, 88. William Clarkson Stanfield (1793–1869) served in merchant ships and the Royal Navy during the wars with France as a young man and later went on to a successful career as a marine artist. He was elected to membership in the Royal Academy in 1835, at age forty-two.

5. Ten years later Boulogne's English community had moved upmarket. In a book for English sportsmen detailing "angling excursions in France and Belgium," the city was described as "a modern, fashionable watering-place, so crowded with English as to wear the appearance of an English town." Palmer Hackle, Esq., *Hints on Angling* (London: W. W. Robinson, 1846).

6. "Consuls and Vice Consuls, Return to an Address to his Majesty, dated 16 August 1833," House of Commons Parliamentary Papers, 1833 (756). In 1832, 660

British registry ships entered France, 276 of them at Boulogne-sur-Mer, representing 16,667 of 67,924 tons.

7. "Romeo" Coates inherited his planter father's fortune in 1807 at age thirty-five, and from then until he had dissipated it, he lived a spectacular life as a gilded London dandy and dreadful amateur actor. His appearances on stage were universally panned. Coates later retired—near bankrupt—to Boulogne, where he met and married his wife, the daughter of a Royal Navy lieutenant. The two returned to London, where he died in 1848 at seventy-six, the victim of a street carriage accident. From British History Online, http://www.british-history.ac.uk/report.aspx?compid=45185/.

8. A set of "Waterloo teeth" is illustrated on the Web site of the British Dental Association,http://new.bda.org/museum/collections/teeth-and-dentures/waterlooteeth.aspx/.

9. "An Account, by an Eye Witness, of the Wreck of 'Amphitrite' August 31st and September 1st, 1833, on the Coast of Boulogne," *Fraser's Magazine for Town and Country*, November 1833, 557–60. Established in 1830, *Fraser's* continued publication through a number of changes of editor until 1882. Among them, one of the magazine's founding editors, the Irish author William Maginn, was the most colorful; he wrote well-regarded features, fought a duel against a member of Parliament, spent time in debtors prison in 1842, and later that year died of tuberculosis at forty-eight. In the 1840s John Wilks Jr., living again in England after his extended French exile, joined the magazine's staff.

10. The *Idler* began publication as a weekly in May 1837. This quotation is from numbers 56–57, March 10, 1838. Sabertash was John Mitchell (1785–1859) in real life, beginning in 1833 a regular contributor to *Fraser's* of a feature on "manners, fashion, and things in general" and author in 1842 of *The Art of Conversation, with Remarks on Fashion and Address*. A career army officer, he wrote several books on military subjects and articles for the *United Service Journal*.

11. *The Sixtieth Annual Report of the Royal Humane Society, Instituted 1774, to collect and circulate the most approved and effectual method for recovering persons apparently drowned or dead; to suggest and provide suitable apparatus for, and bestow rewards on, those who assist in the preservation and restoration of life, 1834* (London: J. B. Nichols and Son, 1834), 19.

12. Russell, *Betwixt the Forelands*, 156.

13. As reported in Nahum Capen, *Annals of Phrenology*, vol. 1 (Boston: Marsh, Capen & Lyon, 1834) and quoted in the *United States Telegraph*, issue 261, November 1, 1834, p. 1484.

14. Gall's own exposition of his theories, *On the Origin of the Moral Qualities and Intellectual Faculties of Man, and the Conditions of their Manifestations*, was published in 1835 as the first six volumes of the Phrenological Library in a translation by Winslow Lewis (Boston: Marsh, Capen & Lyon).

Criminals' skulls were easy to acquire in the early 1800s; their bodies were often turned over to anatomists for scientific dissection. Not so those of the better classes. For a while craniologists' requirements for research materials truly representative of the whole society had the intelligentsia of Central Europe fearful about the postmortem fate of their heads.

15. Quoted from *Sixtieth Annual Report of the Royal Humane Society*, 19–20. The likely source of the description is Sarah Austin.

16. Heine's letter to Coste was added in 1958 to the Carl M. Loeb Heine Collection of the Harvard College Library, where it is held in Series II, Ms. Ger 108.3, "Letters to various correspondents." The letter is quoted in French and discussed in Stuart Atkins, "Heine and the Amphitrite," *Harvard Library Bulletin* 14, no. 3 (Autumn 1960): 395–99.

The enclosed note to which Heine's letter refers has been lost. Heine never wrote again about *Amphitrite*, passing on the opportunity to incorporate what he had seen that summer's evening in Boulogne into either his prose or poetry. The only other time the name appears in his work, in his poem "The North Sea," Amphitrite is not the ship but a "stout fishwoman" laughing at something the god Poseidon has said.

17. Lady Lucie Duff-Gordon (née Sutherland, 1863–1935) was a fashionista who, together with her husband, Cosmo, survived the sinking of RMS *Titanic* and the lawsuits that followed.

18. The Austins' summer in Boulogne-sur-Mer in 1833, when *Amphitrite* broke up, was the first of four family visits to the city. That initial visit was made possible by the generosity of John's father, Jonathan Austin, and separately by the sudden promise of lucrative employment for John in London in autumn. Those weeks in Boulogne were meant to be a rest cure for Sarah's husband, once again depressed to the point of near-immobility by the prospect of paid employment.

Father, mother, and daughter returned to Boulogne and to the Marine Hotel the next summer, in August 1834, and stayed into October. Their third visit, beginning in July 1835, was not a vacation but a flight from penury: John Austin had proved himself, yet again, unable to work productively, and the Austins, like many other English families in the city, went there to live on the cheap, this time in the furnished rooms of a boardinghouse on the Quai de la Flotille. Katherine Frank, the author of a biography of Lucie, described the family in this period as living in "impoverished purgatory." The Austins left a year later in something like sudden triumph—astonishingly, John had been offered a senior civil service post on this island of Malta. In 1843 the Austins, daughter Lucie now grown, married, and the mother of a one year old, were back in Boulogne for the summer, for what appears to have been the last time. The chronology and these details of the Austins' several visits to Boulogne come from Frank's *Lucie Duff Gordon*, 62–120.

19. Some details of the Austins' lives and their marriage, and of Sarah Austin's role in *Amphitrite*'s wreck and the rescue effort, come from her granddaughter Ross' carefully censored book, *Three Generations of English Women*. A century later, drawing on eighty-two letters from the Austin and Pückler-Muskau correspondence rediscovered in Jagiellonian University's library archives, in Cracow, Poland, Lotte Hamburger and Joseph Hamburger described Austin's "epistolary"

affair with Pückler-Muskau in *Contemplating Adultery, the Secret Life of A Victorian Woman* (New York: Fawcett Books, 1991). Their first book about the Austins, *Troubled Lives: John and Sarah Austin* (Toronto: Univ. of Toronto Press, 1985), was written without the benefit of this cache of revealing letters.

20. *John Stuart Mill Autobiography*, Harvard Classics, vol. 25 (New York: P. F. Collier & Son, 1909), 52–53.

21. Herman Graf von Pückler, a descendant determined on restoring the family property at Branitz, says he found the Pückler-Muskau diaries that were source materials for the book. See his "Recovering a Family Heritage: A Personal Experience in East Germany," in *Cultural Heritage and Post-war Recovery*, ed. Nicholas Stanley-Price (Rome: ICCROM, 2007).

22. John Sterling, the short-lived author of *Arthur Coningsby* and other neglected works, didn't think much of the book or the prince. July 9, 1832, he wrote Sarah to say, "I have been reading the travels of that Prince Prettyman, to whose book you have shown so much more favour than you would have bestowed on the author. . . . I do not deny that your *protégé*, the Prince, is rather lively, and perhaps as things go in Germany, a good deal of a gentleman, in spite of his bad waltzing; but his utter ignorance of the literature, morals, politics, and religion of England, is ill-compensated by some dashing sketches of scenery, and by his wearisome descriptions of the manners of a small knot of people who, so far as I ever saw, were despicable and ridiculous." Ross, *Three Generations of English Women*, 85–86.

23. Butler, *Tempestuous Prince*, 196–208. Eliza Butler is the author of the only general biography of the prince in English. Given that it was written in 1929, *The Tempestuous Prince* is a remarkably indulgent work, tolerant, even understanding, of the prince's lusty behavior. Butler's academic career included endowed professorships at Manchester and Cambridge.

24. Quoted in Hamburger and Hamburger, *Contemplating Adultery*, 67. The addressee of the letter is not identified. Sarah is claiming credit for the recovery of Owen and Rice.

25. Linnell's painting is No. NPG 672 in the National Portrait Gallery's primary collection, Lady Russell's is No. NPG 598.

26. Frank, *Lucie Duff Gordon*, 330.

27. The discussion of the physiology of drowning and the history of resuscitation techniques are drawn from Joseph J. L. M. Bierens' Ph.D. thesis, "Drowning in the Netherlands: Pathophysiology, Epidemiology, and Clinical Studies" (University of Utrecht, 2004)

Chapter 7. The Admiralty Investigation

1. ADM 1/5435. For its part, the Admiralty took away the correct lesson from recent history: After *Java* Royal Navy frigates were no longer permitted to engage American frigates in ship-to-ship duels. Attacking them was to be left to ships-of-the-line or squadrons.

2. John Wilson Croker, a Dublin-educated lawyer and sometime member of Parliament, was first secretary of the Admiralty for more than twenty years, from 1809 to 1830. For more on Croker, see Fergus Fleming, *Barrow's Boys: A Stirring Story of Daring, Fortitude, and Outright Lunacy* (New York: Grove Press, 1998).

3. HMS *Monarque* was Admiral Byng's own flagship. The story has the admiral himself bravely commanding the assembled firing squad to shoot him. Byng began his mission in squadron command with a defeatist attitude so apparent in London that his replacement had been dispatched to the Mediterranean even before the battle. The admiral's listless leadership during that engagement and the subsequent withdrawal of his intact squadron to Gibraltar permitted the French to seize Fort St. Philip and to take over the island, a British possession for the past forty-eight years.

    The George Henry Preble Collection in the U.S. Navy Department Library at the Washington Navy Yard contains three contemporary published reports on the Byng court-martial on board HMS *St. George* and a bound volume that includes four related pamphlets. Byng's career was not a complete failure; he lives on in history as a powerful cautionary tale. An effort by his descendants in Bedfordshire to obtain a pardon for the admiral on the 250th anniversary of his execution failed in 2007.

4. "[*Java's*] crew was exceptionally ill-suited to the voyage," reports Chads' entry in the *Encyclopedia of National Biography*, "an unusually large proportion had never been to sea before, and many had been drafted from prisons. She carried also sixty-eight supernumeraries, and when she sailed from Spithead on 12 November 1812 she had on board nearly 400 men all told. Owing to overcrowding, bad weather, and the rawness of the ship's company, drill was almost entirely neglected, and the guns were rarely, if ever, exercised" (833).

5. Chads told his court-martial that *Java* had lost 22 killed and 102 wounded, and that *Constitution's* losses were 10 killed and approximately 44 wounded. William James, *A Full and Correct Account of the Chief Naval Occurrences of the Late War between Britain and the United States of America* (London: T. Edgerton, 1817; reprint, Annapolis: Naval Institute Press, 2004).

6. Commodore Bainbridge's report of the action was dated January 3, 1813.

7. She was the eldest daughter of one James Pook, of the Hampshire County gentry. Coming from the home county of Portsmouth, England's great naval base on the Channel, Elizabeth Townshend would have known better than most what to expect as the wife of a navy officer. She died in 1861, predeceasing her husband, then Vice Admiral Chads, by seven years.

8. William Laird Clowes, *The Royal Navy: A History from the Earliest Times to the Present*, vol. 3 (London: Sampson Low, Marston, 1898). Beginning in 1882 Clowes (1856–1905) developed expertise in naval matters and history that was recognized twenty years later when he was knighted. His seven-volume history of the Royal Navy was published between 1897 and 1903 and included among its several coauthors "Col. Theodore Roosevelt, Governor of New York" (who was president when the sixth volume was released) and Captain A. T. Mahan, the

nineteenth-century U.S. Navy's best-known theorist and author of the seminal study *The Influence of Sea Power Upon History, 1660–1783.*

9. ADM 12/27F, Court Martial No. 422. Captain James Davies, RN, the surviving officers, and the enlisted crew of HMS *Guerrière* were court-martialed in October 1812 for the loss of their ship to USS *Constitution.* That court "honorably acquitted all the officers and company," finding "that the ship was in a very defective state which was more from accident than enemy's fire."

10. Clowes, *Royal Navy* 6:205.

11. Before his newspaper pieces and items in *Fraser's*, Wilks wrote several books while attempting to build a law practice: *A Christian Biographical Dictionary* (London: R. Clay, 1821), available as a Google book; a fawning biography, *Memoirs of Her Majesty Queen Caroline Amelia Elizabeth, Consort of George IV King of Great Britain* (London: Sherwood, Neely and Jones, 1822), also a Google book; and *Bianca; A Fragment* (London: R. Clay, 1823), his first foray into fiction. After he returned to England about 1840, Wilks wrote a second novel, *The Tory Baronet; or, Tories, Whigs and Radicals, by One who Knows Them* (London: Richard Bentley, 1841); vol. 3 is a Google book.

12. Richard Davenport-Hines, "Wilks, John (ca. 1793–1846)," *Oxford Dictionary of National Biography* (New York: Oxford University Press, 2004). My sketch also draws on the unsigned article in the 1900 edition of the dictionary.

13. *The Times*, September 26, 1862, p. 2.

14. Mike Munro, "Welsh Iron & Coal Mining Company," *Welsh Mines Society Newsletter* 41 (November 1999).

15. *Gentleman's Magazine and Historical Review* 42:629.

16. "Social and Political Life Five and Thirty Years Ago," *Fraser's Magazine for Town and Country* 42 (July–December 1860): 118. *Fraser's* claimed that Wilks was exposed as the *Morning Chronicle*'s radical correspondent by "an eccentric general officer" who traveled to Paris expressly to unmask the letter writer signing himself "O. P. Q." The other candidate author of these letters was Caleb Charles Colton, an English eccentric living in Paris as a result of indebtedness from gambling. He shot and killed himself in April 1832.

17. *Preston Chronicle*, issue 1,037, Saturday, September 7, 1833.

18. Feature articles in *The Times* did not show a reporter's byline until 1967. Wilks' authorship of these two letters is inferred by the reference to his note to Consul Hamilton. Letters to the editor were usually published anonymously until 1945.

19. The bathing machines—they resembled small enclosed wagons—served as mobile cabanas. Inside each of them one or two men or women, hidden entirely from view, could change into the modest swimsuits of the day and then ride to and from sex-segregated beaches and their concealing waters. These colorful carts hinted at Boulogne-sur-Mer's more usual late summer attraction, wading—most vacationers could not swim, and in the yards of fabric they wore would have been hard-pressed even to float—in the Channel's surf while the water was still warm enough to enjoy.

20. *Court Magazine and Belle Assembly*, issue 3, March 1, 1834, p. 128.

21. The wreckage was described for the record by Victor Le Cerf in a deposition he gave to Chads on September 20.

22. *The Times*, October 16, 1833.

23. Captain the Honorable George Elliot, RN (1784–1863) was in 1833 roughly midway through a life in the Royal Navy that had begun in 1794 on board HMS *St. George* and was to end in 1855 with his retirement. A Nelson protégée, Elliot's brilliant career lost luster after 1840, even as he rose to admiral in 1853. Elliot, John Barrow pointed out in his memoir, was the only Scot to hold the position of first secretary during the forty years Barrow served in the Admiralty. His son and namesake (1813–1901) also rose to flag rank in the Royal Navy.

24. His plan was to take statements from and question Wilks and witnesses nominated by him, with Hamilton present so that the latter "might know the extent of the charges." Wilks was to be permitted to sit in on these interrogations. Chads would then question Hamilton and, later, witnesses nominated by him. For his part Wilks wanted to interrogate witnesses anytime the consul was permitted to be present and threatened unsuccessfully to appeal to the Foreign Office if Chads refused him. This and subsequent quotations from Chads' investigation are from *Orders and Communications Relating to Inquiry of Loss of Amphitrite Convict Ship, 1834*, House of Commons Papers No. 427, vol. 47.

25. Hercule's oldest brother, Alexandre, was mayor of Boulogne for nearly fifty years, until 1857. The Adams of that generation were powerful men locally. Powerful and also durable: Achille (treasurer of the Humane Society in 1833) lived into his late seventies, Hercule to his late eighties, and Alexandre to ninety-six. Félix Adam (1866–1919), Boulogne's mayor during World War I until his death, was Achille's grandson and Hercule Adam's grandnephew. He welcomed the arrival of the British Expeditionary Force at Boulogne in 1914.

   The failure in November 1930 of Boulogne's Banque Adam, after 1911 no longer the family's financial flagship but public and perhaps the most important of France's regional banks, prompted the collapse of many other provincial banks and deepened the turmoil of the depression decade.

26. *Reliance*'s wreck was followed six weeks later with that of *Conqueror*, out of Calcutta laden with silk and general merchandise.

27. From "Mr. *James Jones Towsey's* further Examination, on Oath, 20 September 1833," No. 7, Enclosure (D) of *Orders and Communications Relating to Inquiry*.

28. *The True Causes of the Numerous Wrecks of Merchant Shipping Clearly Explained: and an Appeal to the Nation, in the Cause of Humanity, to Apply the Remedy* (Leith: Reid & Son, 1833), 40.

29. FO 27/477.

30. During the 1830s John Backhouse (1784–1845) was the senior of two undersecretaries in the foreign office, responsible for its administration and the office's correspondence with Great Britain's most important counterparts: France, Spain, Russia, Prussia, the United States, Denmark, and Sweden. Backhouse and his successors were the "permanent" undersecretaries, and his and their junior colleagues were styled "government" undersecretaries, whose tenure was affected by politics.

Charles R. Middleton, "John Backhouse and the Origins of the Permanent Undersecretaryship for Foreign Affairs, 1828–1842," *Journal of British Studies* 13, no. 2 (May 1974): 24–45. The same division existed in the Admiralty, but there the second secretary (John Barrow in 1833) was the permanent official and the first secretary (then Captain George Elliot, RN) the political appointee.

31. For more on this remarkable figure again see Fleming, *Barrow's Boys*, and Barrow's own memoir.

32. Her other two charters were between Whampoa, China, and Quebec in 1825–26 (Captain Henry Ford) and again in 1829–30 (Captain William Richards). Deck logs for all three voyages are held at the British Library, IOR/L/MAR/B/80B, 80C, and 80D.

33. Deck log quotations are from IOR/L/MAR/B/80D, 174–181.

34. Captain Compton's later letters detailed the stripping of his ship, her destruction due to French disinterest and incompetence, and his financial losses.

35. Archives du Ministère des Affaires Étrangères, *État des fonds de la correspondance politique: Angleterre*, Carton 642 (août–décembre 1833), Film no. 11469.

36. Backhouse to Clayton on June 19, 1834, quoted in *The Times*, June 15, 1834, p. 6.

Chapter 8. His Majesty's Consul at Boulogne

1. John McGilchrist, *Lord Palmerston: A Biography* (London: George Routledge and Sons, 1865), 49. There are at least eight book-length biographies of Brummel, of which the latest and possibly the best is Ian Kelly's *Beau Brummel: The Ultimate Man of Style* (2006). He was also the subject of two very loosely biographical films. The more recent one, from MGM and now more than fifty years old, was decorated with Elizabeth Taylor and starred Stewart Granger as Brummel, reprising the role first filled by John Barrymore in 1924. Both screenplays drew on an 1890 drama, his first hit, by playwright Clyde Fitch.

2. Hamilton was not the only former prisoner of war on the beach Saturday night. Sarah Austin said Pierre Vanheeckote, of the Boulogne Humane Society, had spent seventeen years as a prisoner in England. Even while *Amphitrite* was intact on the sand Vanheeckote went to the Humane Society shack and fired up the boiler. Knowing what was to come, he wanted to ensure there would be hot water available when the ship broke up and the bodies started washing in.

3. Tombs and Tombs, *Sweet Enemy*, 274.

4. Marrying the jailor's daughter comes from John Goldworth Alger, *Napoleon's British Visitors and Captives 1801–1815* (New York: James Pott, 1904), 216. Upon publication Alger's book was criticized in the *New York Times* as containing "a singular amount of chaff," and he for being an "incorrigible gossip," so perhaps this part of the story is an invention, but Hamilton's detention and marriage are not and it's possible that Hamilton was quartered with the Rebières.

5. *London Gazette*, issue 18624, June 28, 1826, p. 1648.

6. Thomas MacKnight, *The Right Honourable Benjamin Disraeli, M.P., a Literary and Political Biography* (London: Richard Bentley, 1854), 295–96.

7. "Naufrage de L'Amphitrite," *L'Annotateur*, September 5, 1833.

8. ADM 1/1688, No. 1, "Mr. Hamilton's Statement."

9. Sir George Shee, Bart. (1784–1870) was Palmerston's choice in 1830 for the junior position of government undersecretary, despite his reputation as a congenial lightweight. Excepting Hamilton's first report of the wreck, sent directly to Lord Palmerston, Foreign Office correspondence about *Amphitrite* was not addressed to or sent by Palmerston but came generally to or from Sir George, whose oversight encompassed consular affairs in France (and elsewhere) but not diplomatic relations with that country. In 1833 Shee, scion of an old Irish family with its seat in County Kilkenny, was in his last year in London. In 1834 he became minister to Prussia, and the next year he was posted to Stuttgart, where he remained for a decade.

10. Fort de L'Heurt, built in 1803–4 atop a prominent rocky rise, was an element of the defenses of Boulogne's southern anchorage during the Napoleonic Wars. The fort mounted howitzers and mortars on a semicircular gun deck some forty feet above the ground.

11. "An act to regulate the Payment of Salaries and Allowances to British Consuls at Foreign Ports and the Disbursements at such Ports for certain Purposes," 6 Geo. IV, cap. 87, passed in July 1825.

12. Enclosure No. 5 to *Orders and Communications Relating to Inquiry*.

13. M 1534, Departmental Archives du Pas-de-Calais.

14. *The India Directory*, first published in London in 1809, was one of the early, comprehensive guides to sailing in oriental waters. Reprinted in two volumes through midcentury in at least eight editions, it's likely that in 1835 Captains Moxey and Peck were both using the third, 1826, edition. The fourth edition of *The Directory* came out the next year.

   Horsburgh (1762–1836), a Scot from Fife, came by his interested in improving navigation naturally: In May 1786 he was first mate in the East India Company's *Atlas* when on a passage from Batavia to Ceylon she ran up on the island of Diego Garcia, in the Chagos Archipelago of the central Indian Ocean, and was destroyed, leaving her crew stranded for months on the uncharted tiny islet that is today best known as a British property and an American military airfield. *Atlas'* beached crew was eventually rescued by a surveying party, freeing Horsburgh to begin a fifty-year-long interest in marine charting, highlighted by his selection in May 1810 as the Honourable East India Company's second hydrographer.

15. The channel and Bruny Island are named after French rear admiral Antoine Raymond Joseph de Bruni d'Entrecasteaux (1739–1793) who for several years in the early 1790s led a two-ship expedition in the waters off New Holland, Van Diemen's Land, and New Guinea to find what had become of Jean-François de Galaup, comte de la Pérlouse, whose own two-ship, round-the-world expedition had not been heard from since March 1788. La Pérlouse was never heard from after he entered Botany Bay, and D'Entrecasteaux died at sea during his unsuccessful search.

BIBLIOGRAPHY

PRIMARY SOURCES

Government Documents

Instructions for Surgeons-Superintendent on Board Convict Ships Proceeding to New South Wales, or Van Diemen's Land; and for the Masters of Those Ships. London: William Clowes and Sons, 1838.

Regulations and Instructions for the Medical Officers of His Majesty's Fleet. By the Commissioners for Executing the Office of Lord High Admiral of the United Kingdom of Great Britain and Ireland, &c., October 1825.

ADM 1/1688. "Papers connected with the enquiry into the loss of the Amphitrite Convict Ship held by Captain Chads to be lodged in the Record Office." This voluminous boxed record (SE 30/1833) contains the original documents from Captain Henry Chads' three-week-long investigation, including Wilks' correspondence with Chads, and Chads' with John Barrow and Captain George Elliot, RN, at the Admiralty, and depositions and sworn testimony of persons named by Wilks and Hamilton. Much, unhappily, is in Captain Chads' near-illegible handwriting. The National Archives, Kew, England.

ADM 6/186. Candidates for Employment as Surgeons of Convict Ships. The National Archives, Kew, England.

ADM 12/27F. Index and Digest of Court Martial Verdicts, 1812–1855. The National Archives, Kew, England.

ADM 101/13/7. "Journal of His Majesty's Convict Ship 'Brothers.'" The National Archives, Kew, England.

ADM 101/68/9. "Journal of His Majesty's Convict Ship 'SOUTHworth.'" The National Archives, Kew, England.

ADM 106/3525. Papers relating to the charge of transports. The National Archives, Kew, England.

FO 27/470. Foreign Office General Correspondence before 1906, France. (Hamilton, Ashburnham, Scarlett, Consuls at Calais, St. Valéry, Boulogne, January to December 1833.) The National Archives, Kew, England.

FO 27/473. Foreign Office General Correspondence before 1906, France. 1833. The National Archives, Kew, England.

FO 27/477. Foreign Office General Correspondence before 1906, France. August–December 1833. The National Archives, Kew, England.

FO 27/478. Foreign Office General Correspondence before 1906, France. (To Earl Granville, January–June 1834.) The National Archives, Kew, England.

HO 11/9. "Transportation register of convicts bound for New South Wales on the convict ship Amphitrite (lost off Boulogne)." Pp. 215–22. The National Archives, Kew, England.

House of Commons Accounts and Papers

Orders and Communications Relating to Inquiry of Loss of Amphitrite Convict Ship, 1834. Accounts and Papers, 11th Parliament, Second Session, 1834. Paper No. 427. Vol. 47, p. 109.

Return of Hired Convict Ships, Transports, Packets and Warships that Foundered at Sea, since 1816. Session 1843. Paper No. 166. Vol. 52, p. 427. Chadwyck-Healey microfiche 47.360.

Select Committee on Causes of Shipwrecks, Report, Minutes of Evidence, Appendix, Index. Session 1836. Paper No. 567. Vol. 17, p. 373. Chadwyck-Healey microfiche 39 146-151.

Convict Trial Records

The legal records of *Amphitrite*'s convicts are held at the National Archives, Kew, England; at the National Archives of Scotland, West Register House, Edinburgh; and (for Ann Lewis only) at the Gwynedd Archives, Meirionnydd Record Office, Dolgellau, Wales. In general, these documents include precognition ("AD") records (papers prepared in advance of trial, for example), indictments and statements of witnesses, and justiciary records ("JC"), case papers, and summaries of trial court proceedings recorded in minute books.

Charts

Chart of the Coasts of Sand Banks of France, Belgium & the Netherlands from Boulogne to the Texel, Isaac Purdy. Published by R. H. Laurie. 1844. British Library. Shelfmark 14350 (2).

The Downs. The Coast of France Calais and Boulogne. The English Channel. 1828. British Library. Shelfmark 1086 (89).

The Entrance to the River Thames Exhibiting the Various Channels from the River Nore to the Downs. J. W. Norie, Hydrographer. 1817, corrected to 1832 & 7. British Library. Shelfmark 1240 (97) 13.

Entrance to River Thames. Inset Gravesend to London. 1817. British Library. Shelfmark 1240 (97).

Kent. Inset the Noire to Gravesend. 1817. British Library. Shelfmark 1240 (97).

Plan du Port de Boulogne et de Ses Environs. Levé en 1835 par les Ingénieurs Hydrographes de la Marine. Au Dépôt-Général de la Marine en 1840. Library of Congress, France, 192 (1840).

Steele's New and Accurate Chart of the Coast of France from Calais to Le Croizic. Environs of Boulogne. 1818. British Library. Shelfmark 14351 (8).

NINETEENTH-CENTURY SECONDARY SOURCES

Améro, Constant. Les Aventuriers de la Mer: Tempêtes-Naufrages-Révoltes-Hivernages. Paris: Société Française d'Imprimerie et de Librairie, 1899.

Anonymous. Ayrshire: Containing Map of the County, Ground Plan of the Town, Various Views. Together with Public Lists and Directory for Ayr and Environs, &c. Ayr, Scotland: William McCarter, 1832.

———. Beaux Traits de l'Histoire des Naufrages. Rouen, France: Mégard, 1834.

———. Brief Historical Reminiscences of the County and Town of Ayr . . . and Directory for Ayr, Newton, Wallacetown, &c. Ayr, Scotland: William McCarter, 1830.

———. [Burrows, Montague.] Memoir of Admiral Sir Henry Ducie Chads, G.C.B., by an Old Follower. Portsea, UK: Griffin, 1869. Originally published in United Service Magazine.

———. Perils of the Deep; or, Narratives of Dreadful shipwrecks and calamities of the sea: With an account of many narrow escapes from fire, famine, and a watery grave. Manchester: F. Johnson, 1844.

———. Rapport du Comité de Direction de la Société Humaine de Boulogne-sur-Mer a Messieurs les Membres de cette Société, sur les operations pendant la Saison de Bains de Mer en 1833. Boulogne: Imprimerie de Birlé-Morel, 1835.

———. The Royal River: The Thames from Source to Sea. London: Cassell, 1885.

———. The Sixtieth Annual Report of the Royal Humane Society, Instituted 1774, to collect and circulate the most approved and effectual method for recovering persons apparently drowned or dead; to suggest and provide suitable apparatus for, and bestow rewards on, those who assist in the preservation and restoration of life, 1834. London: J. B. Nicholas and Son, 1834.

Baker, Asher C., comp. H. O. 34, Sailing Directions for the English Channel. Part 1, South Coast of England. U.S. Hydrographic Office, Bureau of Navigation. Washington, D.C.: Government Printing Office, 1872.

Barrow, Sir John, Bart. An Auto-Biographical Memoir of Sir John Barrow, Bart., late of the Admiralty. London: John Murray, 1847.

Blakey, Robert. Angling; or, How to Angle, and Where to Go. London: Geo Routledge, 1854.

Brunet, J. *Almanach de Boulogne-sur-Mer, pour 1838*. Boulogne: Librairie Française et Étrangère de Watel, 1838.

———. *New Guide to Boulogne-sur-mer and Its Environs, Containing a Brief Historical Notice of the Town with a Description of Its Present Institutions, Curiosities, etc.* 1st ed. Boulogne: Watel, 1836.

———. *Noveau Guide dans Boulogne et ses Environs*. Boulogne: Librairie Française et Étrangère de Watel, 1864.

Clarke, Francis G. *The American Ship-master's Guide, and Commercial Assistant, being an enlargement of the Seaman's Manual, useful to Merchants, Ship-masters, Consuls, Supercargoes, Mariners and Merchants' Clerks*. Boston: Allen, 1838.

Clarke, James. *Bononia: or a Topographical and Historical Description of Boulogne and the Vicinity*. London: Leigh & Son, 1835.

Coghlan, Francis. *A Guide to France; or, Travellers their own commissioners; explaining every form and expense from London to Paris*. 4th ed. London: J. Onwhyn, 1829.

Creighton, Charles, M.A., M.D. *A History of Epidemics in Britain*. 2 vols. Cambridge: University Press, 1891–94.

de la Landelle, G. *Naufrages et Sauvetages*. Paris: Librairie de L. Hachette, 1867.

Deseille, Ernest. *Histoire de la Société Humaine de Boulogne-sur-Mer*. Boulogne: Imprimerie de ch. Aigre, 1876.

Hillary, Sir William, Bart. *An Appeal to the British Nation, on the Humanity and Policy of Forming a National Institution for the Preservation of Lives and Property from Shipwreck*. London: G. and B. Whittaker, 1823.

Lang, John Dunmore, D.D. *Transportation and Colonization; or; the Causes of the Comparative Failure of the Transportation System in the Australian Colonies*. London: A. J. Valfy, 1837.

Martel, M. E. *Catalogue Pratique de la Bibliothèque de la Ville de Boulogne-sur-Mer*. Boulogne: G. Hamain, 1899.

Medwin, Thomas, Esq. *The Angler in Wales or Days and Nights of Sportsmen*. 2 vols. London: Richard Bentley, 1834.

Murray, John. *A Handbook for Travellers in France: Being a Guide to Normandy, Brittany, the Rivers Seine, Loire, Rhône, and Garonne, the French Alps, Dauphiné, Province, and the Pyrénées, Their Railways and Roads*. London: John Murray, 1856.

Noire, J. W. *The New British Channel Pilot*. 11th ed. London: J. W. Noire, 1839.

O'Byrne, William R., Esq. *A Naval Biographical Dictionary . . .* London: John Murray, 1849.

Richardson, Henry. *A Pleasant Passage: The Journals of Henry Richardson, Surgeon Superintendent aboard the Convict Ship Sultana*. Fremantle, Australia: Arts Centre Press, 1990.

Ross, Janet. *Three Generations of English Women: Memoirs and Correspondence of Mrs. John Taylor, Mrs. Sarah Austin, and Lady Duff Gordon*. London: T. Fisher Unwin, 1888.

Smyth, W. H., Admiral. *The Sailor's Word-Book: an Alphabetical Digest of Nautical Terms*. Edited by Vice Admiral Sir E[dward] Belcher. London: Blackie and Son, 1867.

Stanfield, Clarkson. *Stanfield's Coast Scenery: A Series of Views in the British Channel*. London: Smith, Elder, 1836.

Taose, R. L. R. *What Are They Doing in Boulogne?* London: Hamilton, Adams, 1861.

West, John, [Rev.]. *The History of Tasmania*. 2 vols. Tasmania: Henry Dowling, 1852.

Zurcher et Margollé. *Les Naufrages Célèbres*. 3rd ed. Paris: Librairie Hachette, 1877.

MODERN SECONDARY SOURCES

Abell, Sir Westcott. *The Shipwright's Trade*. London: Conway Maritime Press, 1948.

Ackroyd, Peter. *Thames: The Biography*. New York: Doubleday. 2008.

Atkinson, Allan. "The Free-born Englishman Transported: Convict Rights as a Measure of Eighteenth-century Empire." *Past and Present* 144 (August 1994): 88–115.

Bateson, Charles. *The Convict Ships, 1787–1868*. Glasgow: Brown, Son & Ferguson, 1959.

Beattie, J. M. *Crime and the Courts in England, 1660–1800*. Princeton: Princeton University Press, 1986.

Beddoe, Dierdre. *Welsh Convict Women: A Study of Women Transported from Wales to Australia, 1778–1852*. Barry: Stuart Williams, 1979.

Bewell, Alan. *Romanticism and Colonial Disease*. Baltimore: John Hopkins University Press, 1999.

Bierens, Joost J. L. M., ed. *Handbook on Drowning Prevention, Rescue, Treatment*. Berlin: Springer-Verlag, 2006.

Brennan, Flora, trans. *Puckler's Progress: The Adventures of Prince Pückler-Muskau in England, Wales, and Ireland as Told in Letters to His Former Wife*. London: Collins, 1987.

Butler, E. M. *The Tempestuous Prince: Hermann Pückler-Muskau*. London: Longmans Green, 1929.

Butler, James Davie. "British Convicts Shipped to American Colonies," *American Historical Review* 2 (October 1896): 12–33. http://www.dinsdoc. com/butler-1.htm/.

Campbell, Charles. *The Intolerable Hulks: British Shipboard Confinement, 1776–1857.* Tucson, Ariz.: Fenestra Books, 2001.

Chambers, James. *Palmerston: "The People's Darling."* London: John Murray, 2004.

Chatelle, Albert. "Le Naufrage de l'Amphitrite, un centenaire tragique." *Revue de Boulogne* 87 (May 1933).

Courtney, Nicholas. *Gale Force 10: The Life and Legacy of Admiral Beaufort.* London: Review, 2002.

———. "Le Naufrage de l'Amphitrite." *Revue de Boulogne* 239 (July–August 1955).

Damousi, Joy. *Depraved and Disorderly: Female Convicts, Sexuality and Gender in Colonial Australia.* Cambridge: Cambridge University Press, 1997.

Desalle, Ernest. *Histoire de la Société Humaine et des Naufrages de Boulogne sur Mer, Souvenir du Centenaire, 1825–1925.* Boulogne: Société Typographique et Lithographique, 1925.

Des Rumeaux, Henry. "Le naufrage de 'l'Amphitrite.'" *Revue de Boulogne* 62 (April 1931).

Devereaux, Simon. "The Making of the Penitentiary Act." *Historical Journal* 42, no. 2 (1999): 405–33.

Dickie, John. *The British Consul: Heir to a Great Tradition.* New York: Columbia University Press, 2007.

Eckerson, Carolly. *The Girl from Botany Bay.* Hoboken, N.J.: John Wiley & Sons, 2005.

Ekirch, A. Roger. "Bound for America: A Profile of British Convicts Transported to the Colonies, 1718–1775." *William and Mary Quarterly*, 3rd ser., 42, no. 2 (April 1985): 184–200.

———. *Bound for America: The Transportation of British Convicts to the Colonies, 1718–1775.* Oxford: Clarendon Press, 1987.

———. "Great Britain's Secret Convict Trade to America, 1783–1784." *American Historical Review* 89, no. 5. (December 1984): 1285–91.

Finlay, E. M. "Convict Women of the *Amphitrite.*" *Papers and Proceedings of the Tasmanian Historical Research Association* 34 (December 1991): 119–30.

Foucault, Michel. *Discipline and Punish: The Birth of the Prison.* Translated by Alan Sheridan. New York: Vintage Books, 1979.

Frank, Katherine. *Lucie Duff Gordon: A Passage to Egypt.* London: Tauris Parke Paperbacks, 2007.

Freudenberger, Herman, Frances J. Mather, and Clark Nardinelli. "A New Look at the Early Factory Labor Force." *Journal of Economic History* 44, no. 4 (December 1984): 1085–90.

Gatrell, V. A. C. *The Hanging Tree: Execution and the English People, 1770–1868.* Oxford: Oxford University Press, 1994.

Gillen, Mollie. "The Botany Bay Decision, 1786: Convicts, Not Empire." *English Historical Review* 97, no. 385 (October 1982): 740–66.

Haines, Robin. *Life and Death in the Age of Sail: The Passage to Australia.* Greenwich: National Maritime Museum, 2006.

Hamilton, George, Lt. Col. *The House of Hamilton.* Edinburgh: J Skinner, 1933.

Harding, Christopher, Bill Hines, Richard Ireland, and Philip Rawlings. *Imprisonment in England and Wales: A Concise History.* London: Croom Helm, 1985.

Hibbert, Christopher. *George IV: The Rebel Who Would Be King.* New York: Palgrave Macmillan, 2007.

Hood, Jean. *Come Hell and High Water: Extraordinary Stories of Wreck, Terror and Triumph on the Sea.* Short Hills, N.J.: Burford Books, 2006.

Ignatieff, Michael. *A Just Measure of Pain: The Penitentiary in the Industrial Revolution, 1750–1850.* New York: Pantheon, 1987.

Jones, Raymond A. *The British Diplomatic Service, 1815–1914.* Waterloo, Ont.: Wilfrid Laurier University Press, 1983.

Kerr, Sarah. "The 1832 Cholera Epidemic in Ayr." *Ayrshire Notes* 34 (Autumn 2007): 4–21.

Kudlick, Catherine Jean. *Cholera in Post-revolutionary Paris: A Cultural History.* Berkeley and Los Angeles: University of California Press, 1996.

Lamb, Hubert. *Historic Storms of the North Sea: British Isles and Northwest Europe.* Cambridge: Cambridge University Press, 1991.

Martin, Tyrone G. *A Most Fortunate Ship.* Annapolis: Naval Institute Press, 1997.

Mawer, G. A. *Most Perfectly Safe: The Convict Shipwreck Disasters of 1833–42.* St. Leonard's, Australia: Allen & Unwin, 1997.

McDonald, John, and Ralph Shlomowitz. "Mortality on Convict Voyages to Australia, 1788–1868." *Social Science History* 13., no. 3 (Autumn 1989): 285–313.

McGowen, Randall. "A Powerful Sympathy: Terror, the Prison and Humanitarian Reform in Early Nineteenth Century Britain." *Journal of British Studies* 25 (1986): 312–34.

Morgan, Kenneth. "Petitions against Convict Transportation, 1725–1735." *English Historical Review* 104, no. 410 (January 1989): 110–13.

Morgan, Edmund S. *Benjamin Franklin*. New Haven: Yale University Press, 2003.

Morris, Norval, and David J. Rothman, eds. *The Oxford History of the Prison: The Practice of Punishment in Western Society*. New York: Oxford University Press, 1995.

Mowat, Sue, and the Forth Ports Authority. *The Port of Leith: Its History and Its People*. Edinburgh: John Donald Publishers, 1995.

Oxley, Deborah. *Convict Maids: The Force Migration of Women to Australia*. Cambridge: Cambridge University Press, 1997.

Priestly, Philip. *Victorian Prison Lives: English Prison Biography, 1830–1914*. London: Methuen, 1985.

Rees, Siân. *The Floating Brothel: The Extraordinary True Story of an Eighteenth-Century Ship and Its Cargo of Female Convicts*. New York: Hyperion, 2002.

Richardson, Henry. *A Pleasant Passage: The Journals of Henry Richardson, Surgeon Superintendent aboard the Convict Ship Sultana*. Fremantle, Australia: Fremantle Arts Centre Press, 1990.

Robson, L. L. *The Convict Settlers of Australia*. Carleton: Melbourne University Press, 1970.

Shapin, Steven. "Sick City, Maps and Mortality in the Time of Cholera." *New Yorker*, November 6, 2006.

Sharpe, J. A. *Judicial Punishment in England*. London: Faber and Faber, 1990.

Shaw, A. G. L. *Convict and the Colonies: A Study of Penal Transportation from Great Britain and Ireland to Australia and Other Parts of the British Empire*. London: Faber and Faber, 1966.

Spierenburg, Pieter. *The Prison Experience: Disciplinary Institutions and Their Inmates in Early Modern Europe*. New Brunswick: Rutgers University Press, 1991.

———. *The Spectacle of Suffering: Executions and the Evolution of Repression, from a Preindustrial Metropolis to the European Experience*. Cambridge: Cambridge University Press, 1984.

Syrett, David. *Shipping and the American War, 1775–83*. London: Athlone Press, 1970.

Taylor, James. *Creating Capitalism: Joint Stock Enterprise in British Politics and Culture, 1800–1870*. Suffolk, UK: Boydell Press, 2006.

Thursfield, Rear Admiral H. G., F.S.A., ed. *Five Naval Journals: 1789–1817*. London: Navy Records Society, 1951.

Tombs, Robert, and Isabelle Tombs. *That Sweet Enemy: Britain and France: The History of a Love-Hate Relationship*. New York: Vintage Books, 2006.

Visse. Jean-Paul. *La Presse du Nord et du Pas-de-Calais au temps de l'Echo du Nord, 1819–1944.* Villeneuve d'Ascq: Presses Universitaires du Septentrion, 2004.

Warrell, Ian. *J. M. W. Turner.* London: Tate Publishing, 2007.

INDEX

177–81; Hamilton and, 185, 220,
224, 226, 230–31, 232, 233, 235; on
investigation, 194; Lord Palmerston
and, 183; published account of
wreck, 184–86; role in investigation, 188
William (brig), 206
William Bryan (convict transport), 50
Williams, Malcolm, 34
Williams, Margaret, 34
Williams, Mary Ann, 34
Williams, Thomas, 68
wind force scale, 109–10
Winstanley, Henry, 110–11
women: age of consent for, 89; as emigrants to prison colonies, 28–31; as
reformers, 46, 85–87. *See also* female
convicts

Woolrich Royal Dockyard, 41, 101–2
Worcestershire Herald, 82
workhouses, 45–46
"World Turned Upside Down, The" (bal-
lad), 11
Wreck of a Transport Ship, The (Turner),
4, 7
Wreck of the Medusa (McKee), 124–25
Wreck of the Medusa (Miles), 4
Wright, Alexander, 95

yellow fever, 23
Young, Jane, 94–95
young offenders, 89–91

ABOUT THE AUTHOR

Andrew Jampoler lives in the Lost Corner of Loudoun County, Virginia, with his wife, Susan, a professional geographer, and their two golden retrievers. He is an alumnus of Columbia College and the School of International and Public Affairs, both of Columbia University, in New York City, and of the Foreign Service Institute's School of Language Study. Earlier in life Jampoler commanded a maritime patrol aircraft squadron and a naval air station while serving in the U.S. Navy. Later he was a senior sales and marketing executive in the international aerospace industry.

Horrible Shipwreck! is his fourth book from the Naval Institute Presss. He is now working on a history of the American Protective League, the quarter-million-man-strong amateur, civilian posse chartered by the Department of Justice during World War I to help it hunt "Kaiserite" spies and saboteurs and to preserve homeland security. This new book is scheduled to be published in 2013.

His first book, *Adak: The Rescue of Alfa Foxtrot 586*, was recognized by the publisher as its book of the year in 2003. *Adak* is the true story of a navy patrol aircraft ditching in the North Pacific Ocean in October 1978, at the height of the Cold War. Ten of the fifteen aboard survived. *Sailors in the Holy Land: The 1848 American Expedition to the Dead Sea and the Search for Sodom and Gomorrah* is a history of the U.S. Navy's curious expedition down the River Jordan and across the Dead Sea in two small boats. *The Last Lincoln Conspirator: John Surratt's Flight from the Gallows* tells the true story of Surratt's flight to Europe, capture in Egypt, and trial in Washington, D.C., for his part in John Wilkes Booth's plot to assassinate President Lincoln.